The Organ

from its Invention in the Hellenistic Period to the end of the Thirteenth Century

JEAN PERROT
Docteur ès Lettres

Adapted from the French

Translated by
NORMA DEANE

London

OXFORD UNIVERSITY PRESS

NEW YORK   TORONTO

1971

Oxford University Press, Ely House, London W. 1

GLASGOW NEW YORK TORONTO MELBOURNE WELLINGTON
CAPE TOWN SALISBURY IBADAN NAIROBI LUSAKA ADDIS ABABA
BOMBAY CALCUTTA MADRAS KARACHI LAHORE DACCA
KUALA LUMPUR SINGAPORE HONG KONG TOKYO

ISBN 0 19 318418 4

Originally published by A. & J. Picard & Cie, Paris 1965
This revised translation © Oxford University Press 1971
First published 1971

The Organ

Introduction

THE SCOPE OF THE BOOK

The origins of the noble instrument whose imperious or solemn sound is so familiar to the modern ear reach far back into antiquity. Indeed, the organ, in its essential elements, was already in existence several hundred years before the birth of Christ. In the course of this long career it exercised a strong influence both on the manufacture of instruments and on musical writing. The piano keyboard, for instance, derives directly from that of the Graeco-Roman organ, and the position of the hands on that primitive manual probably contributed in no small measure to the evolution of polyphonic music.

The history of the instrument reveals many surprising facts. Contrary to expectation, its invention was not the work of a musician, but of an engineer obsessed by a purely technical problem, namely how to replace the pipe player's limited supply of breath by a continuous, regular flow of air generated by a machine. Its subsequent fortunes are extraordinarily varied. It started life as a mechanical novelty, and as such aroused considerable admiration. In Rome it became the normal accompaniment to the games in the amphitheatre, and the favourite distraction of several music-loving emperors. In the capital of the Eastern Empire it was regarded more as a prestige symbol, and the Basileus liked to have it played in the presence of foreign envoys, to impress them with the splendour of his court. In the West, the organ was regarded with some suspicion by the early Church Fathers, who felt that it was too deeply implicated in the world of paganism; however, with the support of the faithful, it gradually succeeded in making its way into the sanctuaries during the Middle Ages. There, despite the violent opposition of some members of the clergy, it eventually prevailed, until in the fourteenth century it was the ultimate desire of every cathedral chapter in western Europe to possess a monumental instrument in keeping with the majesty of their church's soaring vaults. What had once been the supremely pagan instrument became in time almost exclusively the handmaiden of the Christian religion.

The invention of the organ was not a gradual process. The Alexandrian Greek Ktesibios, who discovered how to feed an enormous panpipe with an artificially contrived air stream at a constant pressure, and how to control each pipe by means of a keyboard with springs, was certainly the instrument's true creator. There is no evidence in any known text that even a crude form of such a machine existed before his time. The only attributes of the modern organ lacking in the machine invented by Ktesibios were the wind-chest and its separable stops, and these were added by some unknown inventor before the end of the first century B.C.

The fact that we possess detailed texts on the mechanism of the ancient organ is undoubtedly due far more to the originality of the wind mechanism than to the musical effects the instrument produced. The stream of air generated by pumps was compressed by a process so ingenious that it continued to intrigue men's minds throughout Antiquity, the Middle Ages, and the Renaissance. The very name *hydraulic instrument*, bestowed by its inventor, created an ambiguity which has given rise to a great number of errors, in both ancient and modern times. However, Hero of Alexandria and Vitruvius have each left a precise technical description, in Greek and Latin respectively, of the mechanism of the air supply and the wind-chest of this organ. Furthermore, throughout Antiquity poets, orators, grammarians, and historians all make passing references to the instrument, and even these brief observations can yield valuable scraps of information.

The majority of these texts have been known for some considerable time: but far-fetched interpretations or bad translations have infiltrated histories of music, and some of these are reproduced time and again without the slightest attempt at verification. In view of this I have made every effort not only to complete my inquiries but to verify my source material. In order to achieve this I have had to examine Greek, Latin, and Byzantine documents word by word, and to offer a translation of texts which until now have existed only in their original language. Parallel with this I have tried to study in detail works in French and other languages devoted to the history of the organ, some of which are of considerable value, despite their limitations.

Of equal importance was the study of ancient objects showing representations of the instrument—statuettes, bas-reliefs, mosaics, and graffiti. For a reasoned evaluation of such material I had to see it for myself and obtain good photographs of examples which had hitherto been known only through mediocre or faulty sketches. This work was greatly facilitated by the sympathetic attitude of most of the archaeological museums that I visited in France and elsewhere in Europe, and I take this opportunity to express my gratitude to their curators.

I have in addition tried to unearth new iconographical material—a truly thankless task, for, since the important archaeological finds are in most cases known and catalogued, I was obliged to sift through innumerable fragments of pottery and examine any recently uncovered mosaics. The fruits of all this labour were modest indeed; but the only new representation of the hydraulic organ which came to light, on a patterned fragment of vase in the Musée des Antiquités Nationales at St.-Germain-en-Laye, is sufficiently interesting to encourage further research. It is, moreover, entirely possible that certain metal components of the instrument—pnigeus, sliders, or pump levers—are still lying unidentified in the store-rooms of some museum in one country or another.

It seemed to me absolutely essential to examine *in situ* the small organ found among the ruins of Aquincum, near Budapest, a priceless example of how the instrument was made in the third century A.D. The great courtesy extended to me there enabled me to make a thorough study of the instrument and take all the necessary measurements.

Lastly, I felt that a work devoted to the history of the pipe organ, although based on the analysis of historical and archaeological evidence, ought to be rounded off by a serious experimental study. With this in mind I have attempted, despite various problems, to create as faithful a reproduction as possible of the hydraulis, by scrupulously following the description given by Vitruvius and referring to the iconographic evidence of the time. The work has brought its own rewards, for the reconstruction has taught me a great deal. I was able to weigh up the advantages and disadvantages of the mechanism, and at the same time gain some insight into the difficulties that confronted its inventor. I went on to take some interesting measurements of pressures, and was thus able to form my own conclusions on a number of controversial issues, such as the evenness of the sound, the manoeuvrability of the manual, and the amount of work involved in manipulating the pumps. The reader will therefore hardly find it surprising if numerous references to the results of these experiments are incorporated in my conclusions.

Research, study, the revision of ancient texts; measurements, comparisons, the discussion of iconographical documents; the actual reconstruction of a hydraulic organ based on Hero and Vitruvius: I should never have embarked on such an undertaking had it not been for the constant encouragement of my mentor, Jacques Chailley, Professor at the Sorbonne and Director of the Institut de Musicologie, who at all times supported the project and gave me the benefit of his extremely valuable advice. My thanks are also due to Professor Henri Marrou of the Sorbonne, who unhesitatingly agreed to supervise my complementary thesis, despite its unusual subject—it is devoted entirely to the technical details of my reconstruction of an ancient organ. I should also like to express my gratitude to my friend Norbert Dufourcq, Professor at the Conservatoire National de Musique, who has gone to considerable trouble to advise me on certain chapters of this work.

I should in addition like to acknowledge the valuable information supplied by Professors J. Fontaine and P. Lemerle of the Sorbonne in connection with the interpretation of several obscure texts: by my friends F. Braemer, in charge of research at the Centre National de la Recherche Scientifique, and G. Ville of the Faculty of Arts at Lille, formerly of the Ecole Française in Rome, for everything concerning the iconography; by M. and Mme Chrétienne, *agrégés* of the University, and by a learned Lebanese priest of the Scholasticate of the Holy Ghost at Kaslik, who examined a number of passages in Latin and Arabic on my behalf.

Finally, my thanks are due to the curators of a great number of libraries both in France and abroad, whose kindness was inexhaustible and who in many instances went to great trouble to facilitate my research.

PREVIOUS WORKS ON THE SUBJECT

It would seem appropriate and interesting to begin with a short review of the historical works which deal with the hydraulic organ of the ancients. We shall see how the imagination of musicologists was, until fairly recent times, sidetracked into false or fanciful conceptions. In fact, the principle upon which Ktesibios based his wind mechanism, which was at once very simple and very ingenious, was only properly understood when, instead of indulging in learned discourse of a rhetorical nature, investigators took the trouble of building a scale model of the machine they were trying to analyse.

Although the apparatus was clearly described in Roman times by the engineers Hero and Vitruvius, it was regarded by the circus-going crowds and by most of the eminent men of the day as something mysterious. Vitruvius informs his readers that any attempt to describe such a complex object, obscure in itself, is a difficult undertaking, and that if anyone wishes to fathom how the apparatus functions he would be better advised to go and see it for himself. In the days of the Antonines, even a learned encyclopedist like Athenaeus of Naucratis appears to be in some doubt as to the mechanism of the organ, and is content to reproduce a number of different opinions which are more or less contradictory. The construction of the wind-chest, pipes, and keyboard was generally understood: but the presence of the water inflamed the imagination, and few had any real idea of what it was supposed to do.

It is hardly surprising, then, that after the barbarian invasions western Europe lost sight of the organ altogether. It is not until the ninth century that the first signs appear of a move towards historical research, most probably stimulated by Charlemagne, and scholars applied themselves to studying or translating ancient manuscripts brought back from Constantinople and the Arab countries. It is thought that Eginhard saved the *De Architectura* of Vitruvius from oblivion:[1] at all events he embarked on a

[1] It is significant that the oldest known manuscript of Vitruvius dates from the ninth century (British Museum, Harleianus, no. 2767).

detailed analysis of the text, as we know from a letter he wrote to his son, in which he asks his advice concerning certain difficult passages.[2] As early as the reign of Louis the Pious the expression 'hydraulic organ' (organum hydraulicum) occurs in a few chronicles and poems: but it is unlikely that there was any move towards resuming the manufacture of these instruments. Despite the use of the adjective 'hydraulic', the instruments referred to were presumably bellows organs, which had been known since the late Roman Empire and were used at the Byzantine court.

As we shall see, statements of the most disarming absurdity were made by the monks engaged in the manufacture of organs when they felt obliged to express themselves on the subject of the hydraulic organ. Their errors undoubtedly spring from their ignorance of Hero of Alexandria's treatise, which so aptly complements that of Vitruvius. The oldest known manuscript of Hero's work dates back only as far as the thirteenth century. This is the Venice manuscript, no doubt brought to that city direct from Byzantium. But it was not until the Renaissance that Federico Commandini made Hero's work generally available by translating it into Latin, at that time the only language understood by the majority of scholars. In the course of the description of the ὄργανον ὑδραυλικόν, the role of the water is clearly explained, and Hero's exposition faithfully rendered.[3] A curious though more or less correct drawing accompanies this translation.[4] A few years earlier, in 1556, the Italian Barbaro had produced an Italian translation of Vitruvius. This was illustrated with a more fanciful sketch of the instrument, riddled with inaccuracies, from the placing of the counterweights on the valves to the organ case itself, which displays all the features of Italian Renaissance style in its purest form.[5] (Plate XIX, no. 1)

In 1636 Mersenne considered the question of the ancient organ in the chapter of his *Harmonie Universelle* entitled 'To discover whether the ancients possessed Organs, and to observe what is missing from this treatise.' 'It is not difficult to resolve this problem,' he says, 'since Vitruvius gives an account of this instrument in the thirteenth chapter of his tenth book.'[6] However, he does not pursue the matter, and seems not to have been greatly interested in this historical point.

In his *Traité des instruments de Musique*, dating from 1640, Pierre Trichet gives his own version of the problem of hydraulic organs: 'They are supplied with air from cisterns and small chests filled with water, or by means of certain stopcocks.'[7]

[2] See below, p. 216.
[3] F. Commandini, *Heronis Alexandrini Spiritalium Liber* (Urbini, 1575), pp. 78–9.
[4] p. 78. It is reproduced in Pl. XIX, no. 2.
[5] *I Dieci libri dell'architettura di M. Vitruvio* (Vinegia, 1556), p. 165.
[6] F. Marin Mersenne, *Harmonie Universelle* (Paris, 1636), pp. 387 ff.
[7] Ed. F. Lesure (Neuilly, 1957), p. 49.

This illustrates a misconception which occurs frequently in works written at this time, whereby the hydraulic wind mechanism of Ktesibios is confused with another system of Alexandrian origin which was taken up by Arab authors.[8] In this water ran into a closed container, and the air displaced by the water was used to operate a set of pipes. Another process, to which Trichet also refers, used the air carried by water flowing from a hard-running tap. It is true that an organ worked by the air produced by an apparatus of either of these types qualifies as 'hydraulic'; but clearly it has nothing in common with the Graeco-Roman instrument. During the Renaissance these 'hydraulic organs' became very fashionable. They played automatically, like musical boxes, and G. Schott gives a detailed account of them under the significant heading *De musica hydraulica Modernorum, sive de Organis automatis et autophonis, solius aquae auxilio sonantibus.*[9]

Another reference, this time in Father Kircher's *Musurgia Universalis*, which appeared in 1650, describes musical automata based on the Graeco-Arab principle under the heading 'organa hydraulica':[10] but the author confesses his inability to account for the presence of the water in Vitruvius's organ. He hazards a guess that the water was set in motion by the compressed air in the funnel, in such a way as to impart a special tremolo effect to the sound of the pipes. The charm of this tremolo was for him the distinguishing characteristic of the hydraulic organ.[11]

In his famous treatise *L'Art du Facteur d'Orgue*, Dom Bédos admits that he, too, is at a loss to explain the function of the water in Vitruvius's analysis, which he finds 'obscure and unintelligible'. He conjectures that the hydraulic organ derived its name from the waterfall that was used to activate the bellows:

The ancients are known to have divided organs into two main species, hydraulic and pneumatic. Neither will play except by air pressure, produced in hydraulic organs either by a falling stream of water, as in our great smiths' forges, or otherwise by a current of water which, by turning a paddle-wheel as in certain of our Factories, moved levers and pumps similar to those on our pneumatic machines. . .[12]

---

[8] See below, p. 203.

[9] Gaspar Schott, *Magiae Universalis Naturae et Artis* (Bamberg, 1654), ii, 1. See also Salomon de Caus, *Les Raisons des forces mouvantes* (Frankfurt, 1615), Problem XXVI: 'A hydraulic machine, by means of which organs will sound with water and without the aid of bellows.' The question of 'water organs' is admirably treated by Susi Jeans in 'Water Organs', *Music, Libraries and Instruments* (London, 1961).

[10] *Musurgia Universalis* (Rome, 1650), ii, p. 334.

[11] Schott's and Kircher's concepts of the hydraulic organ of the ancients may be seen in Pl. XIX, no. 3, and Pl. XX, no. 1.

[12] Dom Bédos des Celles, *L'Art du Facteur d'Orgue* (Paris, 1766–78), Preface, pp. vi and vii.

On the subject of the hydraulic organ constructed by the monk Gerbert at the end of the tenth century in Rheims Cathedral,[13] the author naïvely adds: 'It remains to be seen how it was possible to build a hydraulic Organ in Churches, where normally rivers or streams are not conveniently to hand to provide running water or waterfalls.'

Kircher's view, that the sole function of the water was to lend the music a characteristic tremolo, is categorically discounted by the English writer Isaac Voss in 1673, in a work entitled *De poematum cantu et viribus rhythmi*.[14] In it he discusses at some length the hydraulic organ, the principle of which he appears to have grasped: at all events he presents a drawing of the instrument which is quite accurate.[15] But it is the celebrated Claude Perrault, who is thought to have designed the Colonnade of the Louvre, who undoubtedly deserves the credit for having been the first to present a lucid and definitive explanation of the hydraulic organ. In his translation of Vitruvius, published in 1673, he defines the precise role of the water in the instrument,[16] and he sums it up in his *Abrégé des dix livres d'architecture de Vitruve*:[17]

The organs played by means of two Pistons which were raised and lowered within the body of the pumps. By violently thrusting air into a funnel inverted in a brass cistern half-filled with water, the Pistons exerted pressure on the water and forced it to rise all around, inside the cistern, with the result that the weight of this water, re-entering the funnel, forced the air into the pipes and made them play, producing the same effect as that achieved by bellows in our Organs.

The text of the translation is illustrated by an elaborate drawing of the hydraulic organ as Perrault imagined it to have been,[18] and from which it is obvious that the author had no knowledge of any iconographical evidence dating from Greek and Roman times.

Despite this excellent definition, confusion and error continued to mar the work of a number of musicologists writing about the instrument. Thus in the *Musical Dictionary* of James Grassineau, published in 1769, we read that the hydraulic organ is a musical machine operated by means of water, which may be heard in the vineyard grottos of Italy.[19] Here again the allusion is to Kircher's automatic organs.

Two years later the ancient organ is the subject of a monograph some

[13] See p. 226.
[14] Oxford, 1673, p. 99.
[15] p. 100.
[16] *Les dix livres d'architecture de Vitruve, corrigez et traduits nouvellement en François, avec notes et figures* (Paris, 1673), p. 297, note 3.
[17] Paris, 1674, pp. 216–17.
[18] p. 229. See Pl. XIX, no. 4.
[19] *A Musical Dictionary* (London, 1769), p. 171.

thirty pages long brought out in Göttingen in 1771 under the name of A. L. F. Meister and entitled *De Veterum Hydraulo*.[20] The author, a teacher of philosophy, had read Voss, Kircher, and Perrault, whom he quotes from time to time: but his work contributes nothing new to the question. In 1791, however, an interesting English translation of Vitruvius's *De Architectura* was published in London by William Newton, a relation of the celebrated scientist, which showed a perfect comprehension of the principle governing the wind mechanism. An original drawing illustra.es the working of the machine, but, like that of Perrault, it is not based at all on Roman iconography.[21]

In 1867 a doctoral thesis was devoted to the hydraulic organ. Its author, R. Gräbner, called it *De Organis Veterum Hydraulicis*, and submitted it to the University of Berlin in 1867. Here the function of the water is clearly stated:

Aqua igitur eo consilio adjecta est ut aer cum in pnigeo superabundet aquam deprimat, cum autem deficiat ab aqua, quae est in arca, aequilibrium cum illa aqua in pnigeo depressa efficere studente rursus suppeditetur, qua re et prohibetur quominus unquam aer fistulas deficiat, et efficitur ut spiritus arcae influens semper sit aequabilis. . . .[22]

Gräbner, who is extremely critical of Voss, records his amazement that so much nonsense is still being written about the instrument: 'De qua re tam perspicua quod in magnis erroribus homines docti versati sunt atque etiamnunc versantur non satis mirari possumus.'[23]

Though in 1865 Fétis[24] was apparently still ignorant of the principle underlying the hydraulic pump, Clément Loret took up the question once again in a brochure entitled *Recherches sur l'orgue hydraulique*, published in 1890. In it he gives a French translation of the texts of Hero and Vitruvius.[25] But it was not until 1905 that a German author, H. Degering, brought out the first important historical study devoted to the instrument.[26] This contained a serious review of the literary sources, a discussion of the texts, and a photographic iconography which, for its time, was of good quality.

In 1921 Gastoué produced a pamphlet giving a concise history of the organ in ancient times and in the Middle Ages:[27] and in 1931 H. G. Farmer published a most interesting work on the instrument's Oriental origins[28]—

[20] *Novi Commentarii Societatis Regiae Scientiarum Gottingensis,* vol. ii.
[21] *The Architecture of M. Vitruvius Pollio, translated from the original Latin* (London, 1791), pp. 249 ff. See Pl. XX, no. 2.
[22] p. 19.
[23] p. 20.
[24] *Histoire générale de la musique* (Paris, 1869), i, p. 518.
[25] pp. 8–19.
[26] *Die Orgel, ihre Erfindung und ihre Geschichte bis zur Karolingerzeit,* (Münster, 1905).
[27] A. Gastoué, *L'orgue en France de l'Antiquité au début de la période classique* (Paris, 1921).
[28] *The Organ of the Ancients from Eastern Sources* (London, 1931).

Arab, Syriac, and Jewish—including a number of unpublished Arabic texts. One final work of great musicological interest appeared in Budapest in 1934. It contains a detailed account of a small Roman organ dating from the beginning of the third century, discovered by chance in the ruins of Aquincum in Hungary.[29] There are in addition good encyclopedia articles by Tittel[30] and Charles Ruelle.[31]

I have deliberately made no mention of a great number of articles in periodicals, straightforward compilations which say nothing new and do not scruple to repeat incorrect or entirely fictitious data without any attempt at verification.

The actual reconstruction of a hydraulic organ of the Graeco-Roman type is a task which others have undertaken in the past.[32] Their motives, however, were different, since their sole object appears to have been to verify that Ktesibios's wind mechanism was in fact capable of making the pipes sound. With this in mind, the other authors who embarked on the experiment, as far as we know, built scale models, since these were quite adequate for the purpose. My model was fundamentally different. I wished not only to confirm the fact that the mechanism worked satisfactorily but in addition to measure pressures, calculate the loss of air, and assess the volume of the sounds produced. I was also curious to discover how difficult it was to construct an instrument of this type (for this reason I used only those tools which a simple artisan might have possessed), and what disadvantages or short-comings there were in its performance, in order to try to explain why it was discarded. It therefore seemed better to reconstruct a full-sized hydraulic organ such as is shown in the iconographic evidence, where the presence of human figures makes it possible to calculate the scale.

I have tried to find the names of those who have in the past attempted to reconstruct hydraulic organs—but they are few and far between. In the Middle Ages Gerbert of Aurillac, who became Pope under the name of Sylvester II, is believed to have installed an instrument of this type in Rheims Cathedral, before the year 980.[33] In the seventeenth century, according to the anonymous author of the *Historiae Musicae Gallus*, one Fr. Sebastian Carme also built a hydraulis,[34] and by his own account the architect Perrault followed suit in 1774:

[29] Lajos Nagy, *Az Aquincumi Orgona* (Budapest, 1934).

[30] Pauly-Wissowa, *Real Encyclopädie des klassischen Altertums* (Stuttgart, 1893–), art. 'Hydraulis'.

[31] Ch. Daremberg and E. Saglio, *Dictionnaire des antiquités grecques et romaines* (Paris, 1900), iii, art. 'Hydraulus'.

[32] I shall not deal with the various sketchy or fantastic reproductions which have been made, such as the instrument in the Deutsches Museum in Munich, no. 40037.

[33] See p. 226.

[34] Quoted by Gerbert, *De Cantu et Musica Sacra* (St. Blasien, 1774), ii, ch. III, p. 138.

I believed that in addition to the reasons I have given for the verisimilitude I find in the interpretations I have given of Vitruvius's texts, I might, like him, add the fruits of the experiments made when I was constructing the machine now in the Royal Library. . . . I had the machine built exactly as described in my translation and as shown here, with 16 degrees for the 16 sounds; there are four pipes for each degree, representing a hydraulic tetrachord, that is to say with four ranks. Three of these ranks are tuned to the three genera, being the Diatonic, Chromatic, and Enharmonic.[35]

Dom Bédos, however, specifically says that the instrument was a scale model: 'He [Perrault] even had a small copy of an Organ made, based on his own conception of Vitruvius's organ. This machine was placed in the Royal Library.'[36]

Later, in 1874, the English musicologist W. Chappell, author of a history of music in which the organ occupies a great deal of space,[37] constructed a scale model of a hydraulic organ:

Mr. Chappell . . . was not content to translate from the Greek . . . but he has actually made, with the assistance of a friend, a working model sufficient to test the principle of the hydraulic organ, according to Heron's directions. The model, he adds with modest simplicity, answers perfectly.[38]

It is noteworthy that the man responsible for this reconstruction makes no reference to it in his treatise. We know a little more about the small hydraulic organ built by F. W. Galpin around 1900. Inspired by the model uncovered in the ruins of Carthage and dating from the second century B.C., Galpin undertook to construct a half-size model of the instrument prior to publishing a short treatise on it: 'Mr. Galpin began to construct an exact facsimile of the hydraulic organ 4 ft. high—that is, half size.'[39]

From the photographs published by *The Reliquary*, he appears to have carried out the work with scrupulous care.[40] Unfortunately, his experiments were confined to a single measurement, the height to which the level of the water rose—8·75 cm. The instrument was mainly an object of curiosity, and in 1904 it was presented to the Musicians' Company's Exhibition, where, with the cithara, it was used to accompany the hymn to Nemesis and Calliope, 'to the enthusiastic appreciation of a large audience'.[41]

The most recent known reconstruction is that by J. W. Warman in 1902.

[35] op. cit., p. 300, note 7.
[36] op. cit., Preface, p. v.
[37] *The History of Music* (London, 1874), i, ch. XIII, pp. 325–79.
[38] *Chambers's Journal of Popular Literature, Science and Arts* (London, 1874), p. 739.
[39] J. W. Warman, 'The Hydraulic Organ of the Ancients', *Proceedings of the Musical Association* (19 January 1904), p. 54.
[40] F. W. Galpin, 'Notes on a Roman Hydraulus', *The Reliquary* (1904), pp. 152 ff.
[41] *Scientific American* (19 November 1904).

This time the model was built on a very small scale indeed, its total height being less than 50 cm., and it bore no outward resemblance to the iconographic evidence. If the drawing published in the *English Mechanic and World of Science* of 3 July 1903 (copied from that in the *Illustrated London News* of the previous 20 June) is anything to go by, the workmanship was crude. The instrument had been presented the day before to the Royal Society of London, and the author maintained that the sole purpose behind the reconstruction was to demonstrate the inferiority of the hydraulic organ to the bellows organ.[42]

My own work in reconstructing a hydraulic organ in its original dimensions, according to the description of Vitruvius and the iconography of the time, was not designed to illustrate any preconceived ideas, nor to indulge a taste for picturesque local colour. It was purely and simply a piece of experimental research.

DEFINITIONS

One of the commonest problems in exploring the history of the organ, both in ancient times and in the Middle Ages, derives from the ambiguity of the word used to describe the instrument. While in English the term 'organ' has a perfectly defined meaning, the Greek ὄργανον can signify more than one thing. Basically it designates something to work with, a tool,[43] and hence an instrument in the general sense. Aristotle's treatise on logic is entitled *Organon* because the Peripatetics considered logic to be the tool, the instrument, of science in general. But it is also commonly used in a more specialized sense to refer to any kind of musical instrument.[44] Never, except in Byzantine literature of a very late date, is it used to mean 'pipe organ'.[45] Thus the name given by Hero of Alexandria (first century A.D.) to Ktesibios's invention means 'a hydraulic musical instrument'.

The adjective 'hydraulic', though commonly applied nowadays to the motive effects of water, has in reality a more complex significance. It combines the two words ὕδωρ (water) and αὐλός (aulos). The aulos was an extremely common reed instrument in the ancient world. It is mentioned in a vast number of texts, and very often depicted in iconographic material. We know that its vibrating lamella was made from a special type of reed.[46] Ὄργανον

---

[42] J. W. Warman, op. cit.

[43] e.g. Plato, *Laws*, iii, 667 c; Aristotle, *Polit.*, i, iv, 4.

[44] e.g. Plato, *Republic*, iii, x; Clement of Alexandria, *Paedag*, Migne, *Patrologie grecque*, viii, col. 440.

[45] Theodoret of Cyrrhus (*De Providentis*, 589) apparently uses the word in this sense, but in fact he is employing an explanatory periphrasis: 'The instrument (ὄργανον) composed of bronze pipes . . .' (*P.G.*, LXXXIII, 589).

[46] Theophrastus, *Hist Plant.*, iv, 2, 4; Aristotle, *De Audibil.*, 801 b ff.; Pollux, *Onomasticon*, ii, 108; iv, 70; vii, 153. It is most discouraging to see all the translations—even the most recent—rendering αὐλός as flute, which is really σῦριγξ.

ὑδραυλικόν therefore properly signifies 'an auletic instrument operated by water', a reference to its particular kind of wind mechanism.

According to Philo of Byzantium (third century B.C.), Ktesibios's instrument was known simply as ὕδραυλις—water aulos—at the time of its invention. Certainly Athenaeus of Naucratis uses this term,[47] as does Dio Cassius.[48] A related form, and a more logical one, ὕδραυλος, is employed by Nicomachus of Gerasa and the author of a Delphic inscription. Bellermann's Anonymous gives ὕδραυλα, while ὑδραύλης, denoting 'one who plays upon a hydraulic organ', occurs in an inscription from Rhodes and in a manuscript from Oxyrhynchus. Thus the expression ὄργανον ὑδραυλικόν and the term ὕδραυλις always refer to an 'organ with pipes', and leave no room for ambiguity (despite the synecdoche, by which the whole instrument is described by the name of one of its essential components, the wind mechanism).

In Latin the situation is unfortunately quite different. Where the Greek expression ὄργανον ὑδραυλικόν is transposed in full into Latin as 'organum hydraulicum', there is, of course, no room for doubt, and this term is used by Pliny the Elder, Suetonius, Tertullian, Ammianus Marcellinus, and Sidonius Apollinarius. Another unambiguous word is 'hydraulus', the Latinized form of ὕδραυλος, which occurs in Cicero, Vitruvius, and Pliny the Elder. The variant 'hydraula' is used by Suetonius and Martianus Capella, and is also found in a third-century inscription. Petronius has 'hydraulis', and Servius 'hydraulia'. The shortened form 'hydra' appears on the dedicatory plaque of the Aquincum organ, dating from A.D. 228.

The picture becomes more confused when the expression 'organum hydraulicum' is abbreviated to the single word 'organum'.[49] In the time of Augustus, Vitruvius used a more rational abbreviation by writing *De Hydraulicis*, '*organis*' being understood.[50] But 'organum' on its own is ambiguous, for, like ὄργανον in Greek, it denotes a tool, any kind of instrument, or a machine.[51] Vitruvius, following Greek sources, draws a clear distinction between 'machinae' and 'organa'. The former took several men to work them, as in the case of ballistas or the shafts of a winepress; while the latter, as, for instance, the crossbow and the anisocyclus,[52] would be

---

[47] *Deipn.*, iv, 174.

[48] We shall come to these texts later.

[49] It is certainly not true that the adjective 'hydraulicum 'gradually disappeared because the hydraulic organ was superseded by the bellows organ, as Tittel says (Pauly-Wissowa, *Real Encycl.*, art. 'Hydraulis'). It was simply that the term was abbreviated, and in its shortened form gradually passed into everyday speech, just as today we say 'cinema' instead of 'cinematograph', though etymologically the contraction does not make sense.

[50] *De Architectura*, x, 8. Some manuscripts have the contracted form 'hydraulis'; but that in the British Museum, which is the oldest (Harl. 2767, fol. 150) gives 'hydraulicis'.

[51] e.g. Columella, *De Re Rust.*, iii, 13, 12; Pliny, *Nat. Hist.*, xix, 20.

[52] *De Arch.*, x, 1.

handled by a single man. This distinction, which might have some bearing on the history of the organ, was probably not absolute, for Vitruvius lists among the 'machinae' the Archimedean screw, and we know from Athenaeus that one man operating that particular device was capable of emptying the bilges of a ship.[53]

Like ὄργανον in Greek, 'organum' is the general term applied to all musical instruments.[54] But from the time of the late Empire and probably before that, it is frequently used on its own in place of 'organum hydraulicum' to describe the pipe organ. Boethius and Cassiodorus, Lampridus, Porfyrius Optatianus, and St. Augustine all use it in this sense. Augustine remarks:

'Organum' is the general term used of all musical instruments, although nowadays it is customary to apply the word 'organum' to those which operate by means of a bellows . . . 'Organum' is a Greek word, as I have said, and is generally applied to all musical instruments; but the one equipped with bellows has another name in Greek.[55]

It follows that where the term 'organum' occurs in less accurate texts great care must be exercised. The context may allow the word to be translated as 'organ' if, for instance, it forms part of a catalogue of musical instruments: 'instrumenta, tibiae et organa et chordae'. In other cases 'organum' is clearly contrasted with certain musical instruments, and here again it most probably refers to the pipe organ, as in this passage from Boethius: 'Citharoedi quique organo ceterisque musicae instrumentis artificium probant.'[56]

On the other hand, and especially if it is in the plural, the word 'organum' may signify a group of musical instruments listed in detail elsewhere: 'Surda sit ad organa. Tibia, lyra, cithara, cur facta sint nesciat.'[57] But while such examples leave little room for doubt, others are more difficult to interpret. Suetonius, describing Nero's preparations for his campaign against Vindex, says: 'Primam curam habuit deligendi vehicula portandis scaenicis organis.'[58] In most translations 'scaenicis organis' is rendered by 'theatre organs'. This may be correct, but there does not seem to be any evidence to prove it.

Two somewhat vague words derive from 'organum' in its sense of meaning any kind of musical instrument: the noun 'organicus', used by Lucretius[59]

[53] *Deipn.*, v, 10.
[54] e.g. Juvenal, *Sat.*, vi, 380; Quintilianus, *Inst. Orat.*, xi, 20; St. Jerome, *De. Inst. Filiae*, 874.
[55] *In Ps. CL*, 7. The Greek name to which he refers is probably 'hydraulis'.
[56] *Inst. Mus.*, i, 34.
[57] St. Jerome, *Patrologie Latine*, xxii, col. 874. G. Reese (*Music in the Middle Ages*, New York, 1940, p. 63) is mistaken in thinking that this refers to an organ.
[58] *Nero*, xliv.
[59] *De Natura Rerum*, ii, 412.

to indicate a musician who plays an instrument; and the more common noun 'organarius',[60] applied to one who makes musical instruments. 'Hydraulus' gives 'hydraularius', a nonce-word used in the third century A.D. to describe someone who played the hydraulic organ.[61]

The ambiguity in the meaning of ὄργανον and 'organum' has given rise to a historical misconception, still extant, according to which the Old Testament Jews knew and used the pipe organ under the name *ugab*. In fact, the Greek of the Septuagint employs the word ὄργανον twenty-seven times,[62] mostly in the sense of 'tool' or 'kind of instrument'. In the Hebrew text, on the other hand, *ugab* appears only four times, evidently with no very precise significance: the Greek translates it indifferently as ὄργανον (Psalm 150:4), ψαλτήριον (Genesis 4:21), and ψαλμός (Job 21:12 and 30:31). Ὄργανον is also used to translate the word *thoph*, a tabor (Ps. 136:17).[63] The *ugab* seems to have been a wind instrument. Precise details are lacking,[64] but the context precludes its use as a generic term.[65] Modern experts in Old Testament music tend to identify it with the vertical flute or pipe.[66] It is interesting to note in passing that the *mashrokitha* referred to by Daniel (3:5, 7, and 15) is none other than the syrinx.[67]

The Vulgate quite naturally translates ὄργανον as 'organum' in a number of instances (Ps. 136, 150, and 151); but it also uses 'organum' to translate *ugab*. Puzzled by this lack of clarity, St. Augustine, as early as the fourth century, commenting on Psalm 150, decides that although the word 'organum' may signify 'organ', he himself feels that here it does not: 'Quod genus significatum hic esse non arbitror.'[68] This confusion accounts for the naïve misinterpretation of Psalm 136 on the part of medieval illuminators. A thirteenth-century manuscript now[69] in the Bibliothèque Nationale shows a musician attempting to hang up a cumbersome organ on the branches of a willow tree, in order to illustrate the words of the Vulgate: 'In salicibus in medio ejus suspendimus organa nostra.'[70]

---

[60] Ammianus Marcellinus, xxviii, 1; Firmicus, iii, 12, 10, and iv, 14, 17; St. Augustine, *Sermo* CCCI, vi.

[61] *C.I.L.*, iii, 10501.

[62] E. Hatch and H. Redpath, *A Concordance to the Septuagint* (Oxford, 1897), art. 'ὄργανον', p. 1008.

[63] R. Kittel, *Biblia Hebraïca* (Stuttgart, 1950), p. 1093.

[64] F. Vigouroux, *Dictionnaire de la Bible* (Paris, 1928), p. 1353; Sol Baruch Finesinger, *Musical Instruments in the Old Testament* (Baltimore, 1926), pp. 40–1.

[65] *A Dictionary of the Bible* (Edinburgh, 1900), art., 'Music'.

[66] *The New Oxford History of Music* (London, 1957), i, p. 296.

[67] *Dictionnaire de la Bible*, loc. cit.

[68] *In Ps. CL.*

[69] Latin section, no. 11560, fol. 36.

[70] Pl. XXVIII, no. 4.

Following this semantic investigation of the word 'organ', it is necessary to give a precise definition of what it represents for the musicologist. Since the third century B.C. the organ has been a complex instrument of a distinct type, composed of

(1) one or more ranks of sounding pipes;
(2) a wind-chest to store air;
(3) a mechanical blower, either a pump or a bellows;
(4) a keyboard to direct the air into the various pipes.

This definition, equally applicable to the ancient hydraulis and to our cathedral organs, makes it possible to eliminate a number of wind instruments which bear some relationship to the principal object of this study.

The syrinx, or panpipe, has a set of pipes, but has neither bellows nor keyboard. It probably served as a model for the sounding part of the Alexandrian organ.

The bagpipe consists of a skin bag acting as a reservoir, and two or three pipes. The air is supplied by the player's own lungs. This instrument, whose origins are unknown, made a late entrance on the Roman scene, for there is no reference to it prior to Suetonius, who reports that it was Nero's great ambition to make his mark as a utricularius or bagpipe player.[71] Dio Chrysostomos[72] also mentions the instrument, while Martial makes no secret of his disdain for the man who plays it, the ascaules.[73] However, the bagpipe would appear to have been known in Virgil's day, for there is a clear allusion to it in the opening lines of the poem *Copa* describing a dancing-girl of ill repute who performs to the harsh sound of an instrument played with the elbow: 'Ad cubitum raucos excutiens sonos.'[74] The bagpipe has neither a keyboard nor a rank of pipes; but it is of some interest to the organ historian in that the air pressure is maintained between breaths by pressing the elbow against the skin bag. A compensatory system of this type, designed to prevent the sound from dying away, may well have suggested a similar apparatus to the first men engaged in constructing wind organs.

The *shêng* is a typical Chinese instrument which is, however, widely known throughout Asia by a variety of names (*khen* in Laos, *shô* in Japan, etc.). It has twenty or so bamboo pipes, of varying lengths, arranged not in a row but in a circular formation, making a kind of tower. Each pipe has its own reed. An air reservoir, shaped rather like a teapot, supports the pipes, and has an opening into which the player blows. There is no keyboard, and the instrument is played in a special way. Each pipe has a hole near its lower end through which air can escape. If the player covers the hole with a finger the air is forced up towards the reed and causes it to vibrate. The origins of this instrument are certainly very ancient. It is mentioned in a

---

[71] *Nero*, LIV.   [72] LXXI, 381.   [73] *Epigr.*, x, 3, 6.   [74] *Copa*, 1–4.

chapter of the *Chou-King*, written in the second century B.C. and relating events from the remote past.[75]

The accordion, the 'poor man's organ', is equipped with a mechanical air pump worked by a bellows, as well as a keyboard; but it has no pipes. It is a recent invention, dating from the nineteenth century.

Finally there is a very old instrument which remains shrouded in mystery, but may well have been in some way related to the organ. This is the Jewish *magrephah*. It does not belong to Biblical times, for its tradition is recorded only in the *Talmud*, which dates no further back than the first centuries of the Christian era, when the organ was already widely used in the Near East. There are in actual fact two *Talmuds*, the Palestinian and the Babylonian. Neither was written prior to the end of the fifth century A.D., and the oral traditions they relate go back perhaps three centuries before that time. Unfortunately, the style of the *Talmud* is nearly always obscure[76] and the text often doubtful. In the treatise entitled *Sukkah*, from the *Palestinian Talmud* we read: 'The *magrephah* [is described by] Rab and Shmuel. One says that it had ten holes, and each emitted one hundred different sounds. The other says that it had one hundred holes, and each emitted ten different sounds. Altogether it gave one thousand sounds.'[77] The *Babylonian Talmud* is more interesting, and the *Arakin* treatise contains this information:

R. Simeon b. Gamaliel is alleged to have said that there was no *birdolim*[78] in the Sanctuary. What is a *birdolim*? Abaye says: it is a musical instrument operated by water pressure. There was no such instrument in the Temple because its sonority was so great that it spoiled the music. Rabbah b. Shila, in the name of R. Mattenah, under the authority of Samuel, says: there was a magrephah in the sanctuary. This instrument had ten holes, each producing ten different kinds of note. This meant a total register of some hundred different notes. A Tanna taught that it was an ammah [54 cm.] long and an ammah in height. A kind of sleeve emerged from it, having ten holes, each giving a hundred kinds of different notes, so that in all there were a thousand notes. R. Nahman b. Isaac [says], to remind us of what was said: The Baraitha exaggerates.[79]

This passage is interesting in that it makes a clear distinction between the hydraulis, an instrument well known in the Near East in the days of the Roman Empire, and the *magrephah*, to which there are several further

---

[75] A. Schaeffner, *Origine des instruments de musique* (Paris, 1936), p. 300. The first reference to a *shêng* appears around the year 1100 B.C.: C. Sachs, *The History of Musical Instruments* (New York, 1940), p. 124. B. Ugolinus, *Thesaurus Antiquitatum Sacrarum . . .* (Venice, 1744–69).

[76] Vigouroux, op. cit., art. 'Talmud'.

[77] Farmer, op. cit., p. 27.

[78] Read 'hydraulis'.

[79] *The Babylonian Talmud* (London, 1948, v, 5).

references in the *Talmuds*, and which was smaller and quieter. This *magrep-hah* was clearly an easily movable wind instrument with about ten poly-phonic pipes but no keyboard. A similar instrument is described in an Arabic treatise which will be discussed later;[80] it is not an organ, but more like an improved type of bagpipe.

[80] See p. 196.

Contents

INTRODUCTION   v

The scope of the book   v
Previous works on the subject   viii
Definitions   xv

Part One: The Organ in the Ancient World

I   THE INVENTION OF THE ORGAN   3

The Alexandrian background   3
Who invented the organ?   5
Where and when Ktesibios lived   10
The character and reputation of Ktesibios   14
Philo of Byzantium and Hero of Alexandria   17

II   THE HYDRAULIC ORGAN (1)   23

Preliminary inventions   23
Hero's description   27
Vitruvius's description   34

III   THE GRAECO-ROMAN ORGAN: THE EVIDENCE
OF THE TEXTS   43

To the middle of the first century A.D.   43
The second century A.D.   50
The first appearance of the bellows organ   51
The third century A.D.   54
The fourth century A.D.   56
The fifth and sixth centuries A.D.   63

IV   THE GRAECO-ROMAN ORGAN: ICONO-
GRAPHICAL EVIDENCE   71

The organ with orchestra and human figures   73
The organ with human figures   80
The organ alone   99

V   THE GRAECO-ROMAN ORGAN:
ARCHAEOLOGICAL EVIDENCE   107

The 'organs' in the Museo Nazionale, Naples   107
The organ in the Aquincum Museum   109

VI   GRAECO-ROMAN MUSIC   117

Musical theory and notation   118
The status of music   124
Musical instruments   126

VII   THE GRAECO-ROMAN ORGAN: THE PIPES
        AND THEIR TUNING   132

VIII   THE HYDRAULIC ORGAN (2)   143
        Some theoretical considerations   143
        The hydraulis reconstructed   147

IX   THE GRAECO-ROMAN ORGAN: A SYNTHESIS   154
        The hydraulic organ   154
        The bellows organ   161
        The organ as a solo and orchestral instrument   163
        The organists   164

Part Two: The Organ in the Middle Ages

X   THE ORGAN AND THE EASTERN EMPIRE   169
        The historical background   169
        The Byzantine organ   170
        The ceremonial use of the organ   173
        Organs at the Palace: The Golden Tree   177
        Organists   180
        Appreciation of organ music   181

XI   THE ORGAN IN THE ARAB WORLD   184
        The historical background   184
        The organ presented to Shih Tsu   185
        Muristus and pseudo-Jerome   189
        Musical automata   202

XII   THE ORGAN IN WESTERN EUROPE FROM
        THE EIGHTH TO THE TENTH CENTURIES   205
        The return of the organ   206
        Georgius the organ-builder   210
        'Organum hydraulicum' in medieval texts   216
        The Church's attitude to the organ   218
        The organ in the ninth and tenth centuries   222

XIII   TECHNIQUES IN ORGAN-BUILDING IN THE
        TENTH AND ELEVENTH CENTURIES   229
        The organ at Winchester   229
        The treatises of Theophilus and the Anonymous of Berne   232
        Making the pipes   233
        The wind-chest and manual   238
        The bellows and collector   245
        Siting the organ   249
        Measuring and tuning the pipes   252
        Scales and tessitura   260

XIV THE ORGAN IN WESTERN EUROPE FROM
THE ELEVENTH TO THE THIRTEENTH
CENTURY   265

The organ in the eleventh and twelfth centuries   265
The organ in the thirteenth century   269
Aspects of performance   274
The cymbalum   275

XV SOME ILLUSTRATIONS OF THE MEDIEVAL
ORGAN   277

XVI THE ORGAN AND ORGANUM   287

XVII CONCLUSION   292

APPENDIX: Original Texts concerning the Hydraulis and
the Medieval Organ   295

(a) Hero of Alexandria   295
(b) Vitruvius   296
(c) Theophilus   297
(d) Anonymous of Berne   302
(e) Aribo   304

INDEX OF INSTRUMENTS AND THEIR COMPONENTS   307

GENERAL INDEX   311

List of Plates

(The plates are to be found between pages 116 and 117. For full details refer to the pages listed after each plate.)

I   The Nennig mosaic (see p. 73)

II   The Zliten mosaic (see p. 75)
1. The first orchestra
2. The second orchestra

III   1. The consular diptych of Verona (see p. 79)
2. The Via Appia graffito (see p. 78)

IV   The obelisk of Theodosius at Constantinople
1. Right-hand organ
2. Left-hand organ

V   The Alexandrian terracotta statuette (see p. 77)

VI   The uninscribed sarcophagus of Arles (see p. 83)

VII   1. The stele in Autun Museum (see p. 95)
2. The Rheims vase (see p. 81)
3. The Roman terracotta (see p. 81)
4. The Copenhagen vase (see p. 82)

VIII   1. Aphrodisis' organ (see p. 86)
2. The British Museum gem (see p. 84)
3. The Rheinzabern vase (see p. 85)
4. The Tatarevo organ (see p. 87)

IX   1. The Nero contorniate (see p. 90)
2. A second Nero contorniate (see p. 91)
3. The Valentinian III medallion (see p. 89)
4. The Caracalla contorniate (see p. 91)
5. A second Caracalla contorniate (see p. 92)
6. The Saint-Germain fragment (see p. 104)
7 and 8. Other Caracalla contorniates (see p. 92)

X   The Saint-Maximin sarcophagus (see p. 94)

XI   1. The Orange medallion (see p. 93)
2. The Grenoble medallion (see p. 92)
3. The organist of the Carthage lamp (see p. 96)
4 and 5. Terracotta fragments in the Lavigerie Museum at Carthage (see p. 98)
6. The Carthage lamp (see p. 96)

XII   The Carthage lamp (see p. 96)
1. Front view
2. Back view

XIII   The lamp in the Copenhagen museum (see p. 98)
1. Front view
2. Back view

XIV   The sarcophagus of Julia Tyrrania (see p. 100)

XV   The Rusticus organ (see p. 101)

XVI   1. The Tarsus terracotta (see p. 99)
       2. Gentilla's organ (see p. 102)

XVII   1. The Rheinzabern terracotta (see p. 105)
       2. The organ in the Winghe manuscript (see p. 103)
       3. One of the Pompeii 'organs' (see p. 107)
       4. The author's reconstruction of a hydraulis (see p. 147)

XVIII The glass vase in the Museo Nazionale, Naples
       (see p. 105)

XIX   Earlier reconstructions (see pp. ix–xi)
       1. By Barbaro (1556)
       2. By Commandini (1575)
       3. By Schott (1654)
       4. By Perrault (1673)

XX   Earlier reconstructions (see pp. x–xii)
       1. By Kircher (1650)
       2. By Newton (1791)
       The Aquincum organ (see p. 109)
       3. The tabula summa
       4. The slotted sliders

XXI   The Aquincum organ (see p. 109)
       1. Pipes
       2. The sliders in position
       3. The springs

XXII   1. The automaton of Archimedes (see p. 202)
       2. Illustration in the St. Blasien manuscript (see p. 202)
       3. The Grado wind-chest (see p. 243)

XXIII The illustration in the manuscript of Hero's
       Pneumatics (see p. 28)

XXIV   1. The illustration in the Utrecht Psalter (see p. 278)
       2. The illustration in the Psalter of Eadwin (p. 279)

XXV   1. The Harding Bible (see p. 280)
       2. The Pommersfelden Psalter (see p. 280)
       3. The Cambridge Manuscript (see p. 281)

XXVI   The Munich Manuscript (see p. 283)

XXVII 1. The Cividale del Friuli Manuscript (see p. 282)
       2. The Belvoir Castle Psalter (see p. 282)
       3. The St. Blasien Manuscript (see p. 179)

XXVIII 1. The British Museum Manuscript (see p. 269)
       2. The Solomon Glossary (see p. 284)
       3. The Arras Manuscript (see p. 272)
       4. The Bibliothèque Nationale Manuscript (see p. 284)

PART ONE

The Organ
in the Ancient World

CHAPTER ONE

༄ঐ৩

The Invention of the Organ

THE ALEXANDRIAN BACKGROUND

The invention of the organ is really one of the fruits of Greek science. It took place at Alexandria during the Hellenistic age, at a time and place famous for learning and research.

Alexandria had been founded in 332 B.C. by Alexander, but its great fame as a centre of learning is due to Ptolemy Philadelphus, who became King of Egypt in 283 B.C. It is not certain whether he or his father, Ptolemy Soter, founded the Museum and the Great Library; but he took it upon himself to endow both these establishments with the means to pursue their work effectively.

The Museum was situated not far from the Palace, in the Brucheion district overlooking the harbour. It was a state foundation, under royal patronage. Every discipline was represented there—those of the 'philologists', who were concerned with texts, their analysis, grammar, and history; and those of the 'philosophers', including mathematics, astronomy, physics, and medicine. Adjoining the Museum was the Great Library, soon to house the largest collection of books in the world. The kings of Egypt commissioned a vast number of works to be purchased, copied, or translated, and books flowed into the Library from far and wide until, in the time of Callimachus, almost 500,000 manuscripts were available to readers.

The Ptolemies also knew how to attract most of the great scholars of the age. A certain number of them were fed and housed at the expense of the State, and it is easy to imagine that, relieved of all material cares and having access to a library containing virtually the sum total of contemporary knowledge, they were able to do good work. But there were other scholars who, for reasons unknown to us, worked in the Library without drawing a state pension—Theophrastus, for instance, refused this honour. Among the many learned men who lived in Alexandria early in the third century B.C. were Demetrius of Phalerum and Strato of Lampsacus, the former an orator and historian, the latter a physicist and philosopher; Herophilus the doctor, a pioneer of anatomy; the astronomers Aristyllus and Timocharis; the geometer Euclid; and the architect Sostratus, who built the Pharos. It was during this period that a large team of learned scholars translated the Old Testament into Greek. Later in the century we find the names of Canon of Samos, the astronomer; Erasistratus, the doctor; the engineer Ktesibios and the architect Dinocrates; Eratosthenes, who created mathematical geography: and Apollonios of Perga, whose *Treatise on conic sections* achieved lasting fame. During the second and first centuries the astronomer Hipparchus and the philosopher-astronomer Sosigenes both lived in Alexandria; and subsequent centuries produced Diophantus, the inventor of algebra, the mathematicians Menelaus and Pappus, and Theon and his daughter Hypatia. Later the influence of Christianity diverted men's interests from scientific research in Alexandria, and Islam brought about its final ruin.[1]

Greek scientific thought underwent a fundamental development at the beginning of the Hellenistic era. For Plato, concepts were more interesting and important than phenomena. Aristotle and Theophrastus, on the other hand, devoted themselves heart and soul to the study of sciences based on observation. Soon, philosophical speculation gave way to physical experimentation. Euclid's *Division of the Canon* and Ptolemy's *Harmonics* established that the pitch of a note is a function of the number of oscillations made by the vibrating part. Ptolemy also established the laws of refraction. In addition to his work in the field of mathematics, Apollonios of Perga constructed musical automata operated by running water. Archimedes experimented with levers, discovered in his bath the famous Principle, and devised practical appliances, such as the endless screw, for raising water. Strato of Lampsacus, in his work on tubes immersed in a liquid, seems to have wished to disregard accepted ideas, and, not content with passively observing nature, to have conducted experiments in the modern sense.[2] Ktesibios the engineer, of whose numerous inventions we shall be reading, was motivated by this same spirit of adventure.

It is remarkable that experimental science, whose prospects were so bright, should have disappeared so quickly, and remained in abeyance for so long: and it is particularly surprising that the practically minded Romans did not take advantage of this new and positive aspect of scientific thought.[3] The responsibility almost certainly lies with the influence of the Platonists: under the Empire, cultivated men made no secret of their disdain for those engaged in physical experiments.[4] They applauded the results, however;

[1] P. Brunet, *Histoire de la science* (Paris, 1957), pp. 12–13.
[2] G. Rodier, *La Physique de Straton de Lampsaque* (Paris, 1890), p. 118. This tendency to compare observation and experimentation emerges clearly in the Hellenistic period. See V. P. Zubov, 'Beobachtung und Experiment in der antiken Wissenschaft', *Altertum*, v (1959), pp. 223 ff.
[3] A. Lejeune, 'La Science grecque a-t-elle atteint le stade expérimental?' *Revue des Questions Scientifiques*, cxxviii (1957), pp. 321–43.
[4] Seneca, *Ad. Lucil.*, LXXXVIII, 21 to 28.

and the organ in particular was the object of constant admiration throughout antiquity as much for the principle on which it was built as for its contribution to music.

WHO INVENTED THE ORGAN?

Great inventions are said never to be the work of one man, and for this reason people have refused to acknowledge that the organ might have been conceived and created by a single person. And yet the texts establish that this is indeed what happened. The phenomenon will perhaps come as less of a surprise when one realizes that in its original form the musical part of the instrument was very small in relation to the mechanical part. Nevertheless, the invention forms a whole: and not one piece of evidence, literary, historical, iconographical, or archaeological, points to the existence of the pipe organ prior to the Hellenistic period. And it seems unfair to minimize the inventor's achievement, as Curt Sachs has done,[5] by reducing it to the simple process of harnessing a panpipe to a wind mechanism. To do this is to lose sight of the fact that from the outset the instrument was also fitted with a wind-chest and a manual, a brilliant conception which has come down to posterity and on which the structure of the modern organ is still based.

Only one ancient text, in *The Learned Banquet* (*Deipnosophistes*), offers any information relating to the invention of the organ. The work is by the grammarian Athenaeus, another Greek, from Naucratis in Egypt, who lived during the second century A.D., probably in the reign of Commodus. In this voluminous book, which has not survived complete, he recounts a great many anecdotes and quotes innumerable authors, well known and otherwise. He dilates at extraordinary length on a wide range of subjects, quoting sources which he never fails to acknowledge. His information appears to be genuine, and probably is, for although he spent the latter part of his life in Rome, where he wrote this work, he had lived for many years in Alexandria. The resources of the Great Library had certainly enabled him to compile a vast commonplace book from his extensive reading, for the number of stories and quotations he reproduces is enormous.[6]

The *Banquet* covers a great diversity of topics. 'There is nothing of value', says the introduction, 'to which the author does not make some reference in the course of the book.' And among these 'things of value' musical instruments occupy an important position. Moreover, one of the guests at the *Banquet* is a musician, one Alcides of Alexandria. Book IV contains an interesting dialogue between Alcides and Ulpian of Tyre, the subject being the invention of the organ. After a lavish repast—the menu includes roast pigs,

[5] op. cit., p. 143.
[6] We know that at the time of Caesar's expedition in 48, only the library burned down; the annex, the Serapeion, was spared. Later Antony gave Cleopatra the library of the kings of Pergamum, which contained 200,000 books.

thrushes, garden-warblers, egg yolks, oysters, fried fish, and Cretan cakes—
the talk turns quite naturally to meals and banquets in general:

They were still engaged in this discussion when the sound of a hydraulis was
heard close by. So pleasant and charming was it that we all turned towards the
sound, fascinated by the harmony *(ὑπὸ τῆς ἐμμελείας)*. Then Ulpian looked at
the musician Alcides and said: 'You, who are the most musical of men, do you
hear that wondrous symphony *(καλῆς συμφωνίας)* which caused us to look
round in rapture? How different from the great monaulos so common among
you Alexandrians, which inspires in its listeners pain rather than any musical
pleasure.' Then said Alcides: 'And yet this instrument, the hydraulis, whether
you classify it as a stringed or wind instrument, was invented by a fellow
citizen of ours, a barber by trade, whose name is Ktesibios. Aristocles records
the fact in his work *De Choris* in words something like these: the question
arises as to whether the hydraulis should be counted among the wind or
stringed instruments. Aristoxenus does not know it.[7] It is said that Plato gave
some slight idea of the structure of the instrument by making a night clock
resembling a hydraulis—as it were a very large clepsydra [water-clock];
indeed the hydraulic organ is similar to a clepsydra. Thus it should not be
regarded as a stringed instrument or one played percussively, but perhaps as a
wind instrument, because the air is supplied by the action of the water. The
reed pipes *(αὐλοί)* are set low in the water, which is agitated by a young man;
pipes[8] running across the instrument feed the air into these auloi, which produce a pleasing sound. The instrument looks like a round altar, and is said to
have been invented by a barber Ktesibios, then residing in Aspendus, in the
time of the second Euergetes. He is reputed to have become very famous,
and to have given lessons to his wife Thaïs.[9]

'In the third book of his work *On names* (which is a treatise on auloi and
musical instruments) Tryphon tells us that Ktesibios the engineer wrote about
the hydraulis. For my part, I am not sure whether he has not mistaken the
name . . . And that, Ulpian, is all I had to tell you concerning the hydraulic
organ.'[10]

Despite its occasional obscureness and uncertainty, this text warrants a
closer analysis in view of its historical importance, for it is based on sources
otherwise unknown to us. It asserts that the hydraulic organ, or hydraulis
(Athenaeus uses both terms indiscriminately) was the invention of an

---

[7] The verb εἴδω means both 'I know' and 'I know of', so that this might also be translated as 'Aristoxenus does not know [whether it is a wind or a stringed instrument]'
which would imply that he had heard tell of the hydraulis. But there are two obstacles to such an interpretation. First, it is hardly likely that the celebrated theoretician would have been unaware of the nature of such an instrument if it had existed
in his day. Furthermore, Aristoxenus died about 300 B.C., half a century before
Ktesibios's invention.

[8] I think this should be ἀξονῶν and not ἀξινῶν, which makes no sense here.

[9] This is probably where the quotation from Aristocles ends.

[10] IV, 75.

inhabitant of Alexandria named Ktesibios. The author of the *Banquet* has, however, no clear-cut personal opinion on the matter, and simply reports what he has read and recorded in his notes. He also quotes from memory, and expressions such as 'it is said', 'somewhat in these words', or 'presumably', point to the use of brief or very condensed notes. The sources, though, are specified as works by Aristocles and Tryphon. We know nothing of the former, though his treatise *De Choris* must have been a classic work in the time of the Antonines, for it is mentioned several times in the *Banquet*. Twenty-four distinguished men of this name are known to have existed in ancient times. Perhaps he was the famous citharist, of whom both Athenaeus[11] and Diogenes Laertius[12] speak, though there is nothing to confirm this. Paul Tannery makes him a contemporary of Apollodorus of Athens; but his reasons for assuming this are extremely tenuous.[13] We may, however, be sure that this Aristocles had never seen a hydraulis, for he is not even certain that it is a wind instrument.[14]

Tryphon is a slightly more familiar name. Athenaeus quotes him on a number of occasions, and he is mentioned in Suidas (tenth century), where the following details are given: 'Tryphon of Alexandria, son of Ammonius, grammarian and poet. Lived during and prior to the reign of Augustus.'[15] There follows a list of his works, including the περὶ ὀνομασιῶν, the treatise on the aulos and other musical instruments used by Athenaeus. Presumably this treatise was a form of dictionary, in which the word 'Hydraulis' was accompanied by a few lines describing the instrument and its inventor.[16]

Thus, among his notes Athenaeus preserved the texts by Aristocles and Tryphon—in a more or less condensed form—relating to the hydraulic organ: and in both the name of Ktesibios is linked with the instrument's creation. But surely there is some discrepancy? One speaks of Ktesibios the barber, the other of Ktesibios the mechanic. Athenaeus, clearly not too well informed, hesitates—are there perhaps two different men involved, or has Tryphon mistaken the name?[17] The uncertainty has been interpreted by

---

[11] XIII, 80.

[12] Ed. Gobet (Paris, 1850), vii, p. 162.

[13] P. Tannery, *Revue des Etudes Grecques* ix (1896), basing his argument on a reply made by Apollodorus to Aristocles (*Deipn.*, xiv, 40), concludes that the two men lived at the same period. But Athenaeus gives no indication that this is Apollodorus of Athens (*fl.* 150 B.C.).

[14] In another passage from the *Banquet*, a certain Emilianus wonders seriously whether the *magadis* is related to the aulos or the cithara (xiv, 35).

[15] *Suidas*, art. 'Τρύφων'.

[16] Athenaeus also says that Aristoxenus was the author of a work likewise entitled Περὶ αὐλῶν καὶ ὀργανῶν.

[17] Like a true grammarian, Athenaeus is prone to ponder on the names of people and things; for instance, in connection with the words describing the various meals taken in the course of the day he makes one of the guests say: 'It is moreover possible that the words have been confused' (i, 19).

some[18] as a qualified affirmation; according to them, there were probably two men, both named Ktesibios, both living in Alexandria, and both interested in the hydraulic organ. The unlikelihood of such a hypothesis is self-evident, and has already been pointed out.[19] Even Athenaeus's hesitant account does not justify a belief in the existence of two Ktesibioses, of whom one invented the organ and the other improved it. And although the author, represented by Alcides, displays some uncertainty, this only applies to Tryphon's assertion, and not to that of Aristocles. The real point of the dual hypothesis is to try to resolve another problem, namely the date of the organ's invention.

The mystery of Ktesibios's identity becomes much less puzzling if we refer to the technical writings of antiquity. Pliny the Elder, writing on the most illustrious engineers and scholars of past centuries, knows of only one Ktesibios whom he believes to have invented appliances based on hydraulic and pneumatic phenomena: 'Praise is due to Chersiphron of Gnossus for his Temple of Diana at Ephesus, a wonderful piece of architecture: to Philo of Athens, whose arsenal was built to hold four hundred ships: to Ktesibios for his theories on pneumatics and his invention of hydraulic machines (hydraulicis organis).'[20]

Vitruvius, too, singles out only one Ktesibios, the son of an Alexandrian hairdresser,[21] who from infancy showed an uncanny aptitude for engineering.[22] Vitruvius's evidence carries more weight than that of Athenaeus, for the former had access to the writings of Ktesibios himself, as we shall see, whereas the latter had no other source but the grammarians. Philo of Byzantium, who appears to have lived a generation later than Ktesibios, also attributes the invention of the hydraulis to him, albeit by implication. After all this, Athenaeus's hesitation, whether real or imaginary, seems unimportant. There was only one Ktesibios, son of an Alexandrian hairdresser, whose unusually keen intellect and mental perception helped him to become a first-class engineer.

But Athenaeus's remarks invite further comment. Aristocles recalls a tradition whereby Plato is credited with having in some measure anticipated Ktesibios's invention of the organ by constructing a night clepsydra, outwardly resembling the hydraulis and operated on the same principle. In

---

[18] Especially Susemihl, quoted by Tittel (in Pauly-Wissowa, op. cit., art. 'Ktesibios') and Degering, op. cit., pp. 6 ff.

[19] A. G. Drachmann, *Ktesibios, Philon and Heron* (Bibliotheca Universitatis Hauniensis, iv) (Copenhagen, 1948) and K. Orinsky (Pauly-Wissowa, art. 'Ktesibios')

[20] *Nat. Hist.*, vii, 125. It is tempting to translate 'organis hydraulicis' by 'hydraulic organs'; but elsewhere Pliny uses the word 'hydraulus' in this sense (ix, 8).

[21] But not himself a hairdresser, as Aristocles says.

[22] Vitruvius's text will be studied later.

reality it seems most unlikely that Plato ever knew of the pipe organ,[23] and some confusion has doubtless arisen from the fact that his works contain many references to music. Indeed, if Plutarch is to be believed, Plato had made a serious study of music in his youth,[24] and is said to have left an essay on the subject.[25] Whatever the truth may be, absolutely nothing is known of this night clock whose working principle has been the subject of some conjecture[26] and which has been related to a piece of apparatus attributed by the Arabs to Archimedes.[27] All this is purely hypothetical and without any real foundation. It would in any case be very strange if the ancient technical writers who dealt with machines—Philo, Vitruvius, Hero, and Pliny,—had omitted Plato's name from the list of those who were interested in engineering. Besides this, it is worth noting that Plato himself roundly condemns anyone who 'tinkers',[28] especially if he happens to be a philosopher. The clepsydra of which Aristocles had heard tell must have had a sound mechanism designed to mark the passing hours of darkness. Vitruvius describes an instrument of this type,[29] and unequivocally acknowledges its inventor to be—Ktesibios. As for the so-called resemblance between the hydraulis and a clepsydra of this kind, this could be based on the outward appearance of the water cistern, or on the presence of water in both pieces of apparatus.

Another interesting point about Athenaeus's narrative is the place where Ktesibios is supposed to have constructed his organ. The text says 'then living at Aspendus', which suggests a temporary sojourn. Aspendus was an important town in Pamphylia, in the southern part of Asia Minor,[30] the birthplace, according to Athenaeus, of the 'wise Diodorus'.[31] It has been suggested that the Aspendus meant here was a district of Alexandria. While this is possible, there is no actual basis, either historical or archaeological, for such a hypothesis. One might just as well accept that Ktesibios the Alexandrian spent several years of his life in Pamphylia, and that while he was there he constructed or conceived the principle of his hydraulis.

Athenaeus is not alone in attributing the instrument's invention to Ktesibios. Vitruvius appears to consider it an accepted fact in his day. In Book X of his *De Architectura* there occurs a description of the 'Machine

[23] I think that the passage from the *Republic* (iii, 399 d) 'Is not the aulos the instrument with the most sounds, and are not those instruments which give all the harmonies imitations of the aulos?' refers simply to the improved form of the aulos used by Pronomius (see below, p. 127).

[24] *De Musica*, ed. H. Weil and T. Reinach (Paris, 1900), 162, pp. 69–71.

[25] According to an Arab author (Farmer, op. cit., p. 11, note 14).

[26] H. Diels, *Antike Technik* (Leipzig, 1914), pp. 198 ff.

[27] See below, Chap. XI.

[28] *Laws*, viii, 846 b.

[29] *De Architectura*, ix, 8.

[30] Strabo, xiv, 667; Ptolemaius, v, 5, 7.

[31] P. Tannery, op. cit.

of Ktesibios which raises water to a great height' (De Ctesibica Machina quae in altitudinem aquam educit). At the end of his analysis, the author adds:

But this machine is not the only one Ktesibios[32] invented; there are many others, of divers kinds . . . Of the latter, I have selected those which are extremely useful or indispensable; in the preceding book I discussed clocks, and in the present one, appliances operated by water pressure. A description of the rest, that is to say those which serve no useful purpose and are designed for pleasure, is given in the *Commentaries* of this Ktesibios; to which those desirous of acquiring some knowledge of his ingenuity are referred.

Then Vitruvius continues: 'However, I shall not omit to explain . . . the theory of the hydraulis.'[33]

Without attempting to read too much into what Vitruvius says, it would seem that the conjunction 'however' (autem) here suggests a slight opposition to the preceding phrase. It is almost as though the author is trying to say: 'I have no intention of giving a description of all the machines invented by Ktesibios, especially those created purely for amusement, for which one need only consult his own book. On the other hand, I should not like to fail to give a broad outline of the principle on which the hydraulic machines are based.' There can be no doubt that in Vitruvius's mind this rated as one of Ktesibios's inventions.

There is also the testimony of Philo of Byzantium, who lived in Alexandria a short time after Ktesibios. After commenting upon his invention of the piston pump, he points out that this system was not only a theoretical concept but that it really worked. As an example, he quotes the hydraulis, whose pump was constructed in the same way and was used by Ktesibios to demonstrate once again the properties of air under pressure.[34]

Thus the writings of the technical experts of Antiquity agree in attributing the invention of the new musical instrument to a real historical person, Ktesibios.

WHERE AND WHEN KTESIBIOS LIVED

The name borne by the inventor of the organ was evidently not a common one in the Hellenic world. However, in Athenaeus's *Banquet* we find a reference to another Ktesibios, a philosopher from Chalcis on the island of Euboea, who was a ball game champion.[35] This Ktesibios, a disciple of Menedemus, seems to have been a contemporary of Timon (320–230). Demosthenes also mentions a Ktesibios, a nephew of Amytheon and a son of

---

[32] Latin authors latinize Ktesibios to Ctesibius. For clarity's sake, he is always referred to in this study as Ktesibios.

[33] X, 7.

[34] R. Schöne, *Philonis Mechanicae Syntaxis* (Berlin, 1893), iv, 77, 61, 41 ff.

[35] i, 26, and iv, 55.

Diodorus of Halensia:[36] while a fourth is mentioned by Lucian. This Ktesibios was a historian, whose sole claim to fame appears to have been that he lived to a ripe old age.[37] Two more Ktesibioses appear in Diogenes Laertius: one a poor man, old and sick, who is secretly aided by Arcesilas (died 229 B.C.);[38] and the other an unfortunate youth put to death by Epimenides (end of seventh century B.C.) in order to check an outbreak of plague in Athens.[39]

None of these men can be identified with the engineer, though for all we know he may have been related to or descended from one of them. His origins are in truth extremely obscure, the one certain fact being that he was a native of Alexandria. Athenaeus makes Alcides say this, quoting Aristocles, and it is confirmed by Philo and Vitruvius. It is a mystery why two authors, one presumably copying from the other, should believe him to be from Ascra, a town situated at the foot of Helicon and the birthplace of Hesiod.[40] Athenaeus the Engineer (not to be confused with the grammarian who wrote the *Banquet*) makes no reference to the source of his information,[41] which is later reproduced without comment by a compiler named Hero of Byzantium (sixth century A.D.).[42] At the very most it might be assumed that the Alexandrians bearing the name Ktesibios originated from Boeotia, unless, as Tittel has suggested, Athenaeus misread the word Ἀσπένδιος and transcribed it as Ἀσκρηνός.[43]

The period at which Ktesibios lived sets a much greater problem, though at first sight there appears to be no problem at all: Athenaeus of Naucratis, quoting Aristocles, places the engineer in the reign of Ptolemy VIII Euergetes, who ruled intermittently from 170 until 116 B.C. But there are complications. In an epigram retailed by Athenaeus,[44] an Alexandrian poet named Hedylus praises an invention of the engineer Ktesibios which has attracted considerable attention. This is a musical automaton in the form of a rhyton, installed in the temple of Arsinoë-Zephyritis. The rhyton, a type of drinking vessel whose curved shape was modelled on the horn of Amalthea, was conceived, again according to Athenaeus,[45] by Ptolemy Philadelphus (285–47) as an ornament to decorate the statues of his deified wife:[46] previously it had

---

[36] Πρὸς Εὐβουλίδην, ed. Teubner, iii, p. 259.
[37] Μακρόβιοι, 22.
[38] Arcesilas, *Diogenes Laertius*, ed. Gobet (Paris, 1850), Book iv, p. 102.
[39] Epimenides, ibid., i, p. 29.
[40] Pausanias, ix, 29; Strabo, iv, 409.
[41] C. Wescher, *Poliorcétique des Grecs* (Paris, 1867), p. 29.
[42] ibid., p. 263.
[43] Pauly-Wissowa, art. 'Hydraulis'.
[44] xi, 97.
[45] xi, 97.
[46] There are coins in existence bearing the effigy of Arsinoë, on which the rhyton is featured.

been known simply as a horn.[47] One might fairly deduce from this that at the very earliest Ktesibios was a well-known figure some little time before the queen died in 270, a hundred years before Ptolemy VIII Euergetes. A closer look at Hedylus's epigram sheds a little light on this important problem:

In his epigrams, Hedylus mentions the rhyton contrived by the engineer Ktesibios:[48]

All lovers of pure wine should go and see this rhyton in the temple of serene Arsinoë, lover of the West Wind. It is like the Egyptian dancer Besas, who gives forth a clear trumpet-like sound; such a sound is produced by the rhyton when its mouth is opened for pouring. It is not a summons to war. On the contrary, its golden trumpet is an invitation to mirth and revelry. The divine waters of the sovereign Nile have created a pleasant and ritual sound like this for the initiates who conduct the sacred ceremonies. If therefore there be young men who admire this clever invention of Ktesibios, let them hasten here to this temple of Arsinoë.[49]

Clearly, this passage is concerned not with an organ[50] but with a purely mechanical musical automaton,[51] which probably produced an unvarying melody, repeated like the tunes played by musical boxes. The quality of the sound resembles that of the trumpet ($\sigma\alpha\lambda\pi\acute{\iota}\zeta\epsilon\iota$)—the rhyton must have been fitted with a reed. The air stream is produced by the flow of some unnamed liquid, presumably water. This kind of perpetual wind mechanism is known to us through Arabic texts translated from the Greek, and is attributed to Apollonios of Perga. It will be discussed later.

Ktesibios's musical rhyton[52] was therefore installed in a temple dedicated to Arsinoë. A great many sanctuaries were built in honour of this queen; but Hedylus specifically tells us that this particular temple stood on the Zephyrion promontory,[53] east of Alexandria and not far from the mouth of the Nile.[54] The queen was of course Arsinoë II, sister and wife of Ptolemy Philadelphus, a woman who had played an important part in governing the

---

[47] Athenaeus, xi, 97.
[48] This is how Athenaeus presents the poem to his readers.
[49] Athenaeus, xi, 97. Text V.
[50] It is difficult to see why K. Orinsky considers this musical rhyton to be the ancestor of the hydraulis (Pauly-Wissowa, art. 'Ktesibios').
[51] It is by no means certain that the huge statue of Memnon at Thebes (Pausanias, i, xlii, 3; Tacitus, *Hist.*, ii, 61) had a musical mechanism which worked by the heat from the rays of the rising sun, as Susi Jeans believes (op. cit., pp. 189 ff.).
[52] Hero of Alexandria also describes trick rhytons, but they are non-musical (*Pneum.* xiii, xviii, xxviii).
[53] Strabo, xvii, 1, 16; *Stephen of Byzantium*, ed. Meineke (Berlin, 1849), pp. 295–6.
[54] It was still possible to see the ruins of this temple in 1869. The foundations measured 10·92 m. by 7·30 m.; each long side had four columns, and each short side had two (G. C. Ceccaldi, *Revue archéologique*, 1869, i, pp. 268 ff.).

country. During the last ten years of her life she had been the object of a private cult,[55] and on her death her royal consort built this little temple where the late queen, deified, was worshipped and assimilated to Aphrodite.[56]

From this it would appear that the inventor and creator of the musical rhyton was in all probability a contemporary of the poet Hedylus. Of the latter, unfortunately, very little is known. A native of Samos or Athens, son of a poetess, known and admired by Meleager, he seems to have excelled as a writer of satirical or erotic epigrams,[57] several of which are reproduced by Athenaeus.[58] It seems reasonable to assume *a priori* that the excerpt quoted above was written not long after the temple was erected, for it is unlikely that the queen's cult survived her death by more than twenty years.

Two other poets, Callimachus (310–235 B.C.) and his contemporary Posidippus, have left glowing accounts of this temple, no doubt hoping that their eulogies might serve to ingratiate them with the widowed king. Callimachus in one of his epigrams invests a shell with the power of speech, and makes it address 'the goddess of the Zephyrion':[59]

I was stranded on the banks of Ioulis in order that I, a pretty trinket, might become an ornament in thy temple, O Arsinoë . . .

Two short poems by Posidippus on the same theme have survived. Here is the first:

. . . And you must also propitiate the temple of Cypris-Arsinoë, both on land and sea; it was consecrated by the admiral Callicratus, the first to institute this name on the Zephyrion promontory. She will grant you a safe voyage, even in the midst of the storm, for she calms the waves for those who invoke her aid.[60]

And the second:

. . . Callicratus dedicated me in this spot, and proclaimed me a sanctuary of the Queen Arsinoë-Cypris. Pay homage to her as the Aphrodite of the Zephyrion. Come, chaste daughters of the Hellenes, and you, toilers of the sea, for the admiral has set up this sanctuary where it is sheltered from every wave.[61]

A comparison of these epigrams by Hedylus, Callimachus, and Posidippus strongly suggests that they were written at approximately the same time, and they could hardly have been composed in the reign of Ptolemy VIII

---

[55] P. G. Elgood, *Les Ptolémées d'Egypte* (Paris, 1943), p. 86.

[56] Catullus, *Carmina*, LXVI. The poem is said to be a translation from Callimachus (C. J. Fordyce, *Catullus*, Oxford, 1961, p. 328).

[57] See Radinger, Pauly-Wissowa, op. cit., art. 'Hedylos'.

[58] iv, 78; viii, 34; xi, 54, 71, 97.

[59] *Epigr.*, tr. E. Cohen (Paris, 1953), V, p. 112.

[60] From Athenaeus, vii, 106.

[61] *Monuments Grecs de l'Association pour l'encouragement des études grecques en France*, no. 8 (1879), pp. 29–30.

Euergetes more than a hundred years after Arsinoë's death. Moreover, unlike his predecessors, Euergetes was not well disposed towards Alexandrian intellectual circles, and during the bloody revolts and civil wars which sullied his reign he banished many scholars from the Museum, while others voluntarily gave up working there.[62] The times were unpropitious for scientific research.

Finally, in his *Garland*, Meleager links Hedylus with Posidippus and Asclepiades,[63] whom modern scholars place in the reign of Ptolemy Philadelphus.[64] Asclepiades is given the same nickname by both Theocritus and Hedylus,[65] and the same people are mentioned by all three poets. Thus Hedylus's epigram was in all likelihood written only a short time after the death of Arsinoë.

The question of Ktesibios's identity and the time when he was alive may thus be summed up as follows. There was only one engineer of that name, famous throughout antiquity and mentioned by all the great technical writers from Philo to Pappus. One of his inventions, which attracted considerable interest among the population of Alexandria, is extolled by a poet living at the time of Ptolemy Philadelphus and his successor, Ptolemy III Euergetes. Therefore the inventor of the organ must already have reached manhood in 270 B.C. Some people may well find it odd that the author of *The Learned Banquet*, a remarkably well-documented work, should mistakenly assert that Ktesibios lived in the reign of the second Ptolemy Euergetes. But it should be borne in mind that the text which has come down to us is only a résumé of the original, and that very possibly an error has crept in. Paul Tannery[66] suggests an ingenious explanation for this mistake, according to which the original text probably gave 'ἐπὶ τοῦ B[ασιλέως] Εὐεργέτου', which the copyist read and transcribed as 'ἐπὶ τοῦ δευτέρου Εὐεργέτου'.

THE CHARACTER AND REPUTATION OF KTESIBIOS

It is to Vitruvius that we owe the only information available relating to Ktesibios's early years:

These same authors [Aristarchus of Samos, Parmenion, Patroclus, etc.] also inquired into the methods of making clocks operated by water; the first was Ktesibios of Alexandria, who in addition discovered the power inherent in the air around us, and the pneumatic phenomena. It is interesting to note how he came to these discoveries. Ktesibios was born in Alexandria, his father being

[62] E. Bevan, op. cit., p. 346.
[63] H. Ouvré, *Méléagre de Gadara* (Paris, 1894), pp. 87 ff.
[64] P. Waltz, *Anthologie grecque* (Paris, 1928), ii, p. 143.
[65] Radinger, op. cit.
[66] *Athénée sur Ctésibios et l'hydraulis*, op. cit.; *L'invention de l'hydraulis*, *Mémoires Scientifiques*, III, no. 86, p. 282.

a barber. The boy, being endowed with a keen mind and great diligence, was by all accounts particularly interested in mechanical matters. One day, when trying to hang a mirror in his father's shop so that it might easily be raised or lowered by means of a weight attached to a concealed cord, he devised the following method. On the underside of a beam he fixed a wooden conduit fitted with pulleys. He then ran the cord along the conduit into a corner, and there constructed vertical tubes designed to take a sliding lead weight let down by the cord. When the weight slid down into these narrow tubes,[67] and compressed the air by the violence of its movement down through the mouth of the tube, it forced the quantity of compressed air into contact with the air outside the tube. The shock of the impact produced a clear, sharp sound. Whereupon Ktesibios, observing that the air being drawn along and released caused wind-pressure and sounds, exploited this principle, and was the first to construct hydraulic machines (*hydraulicas machinas*) and automata operated by water pressure, numerous devices designed to amuse, and in particular clocks which were worked by water.[68]

This account, though only an anecdote, conjures up a clear picture of the intelligent young handyman who preferred making outlandish machines in his father's shop to shaving the customers. It is possible that the father, noting his son's exceptional gifts, and perhaps on the advice of his friends, sent the youth to enrol in the classes in engineering and physics held at the Museum, though there is no proof that he did so. What we do know is that the practical character of the work carried out by Ktesibios is in line with the teaching of Apollonios of Perga, Strato of Lampsacus, and even Archimedes, whose experiments would certainly have been known in Alexandria at that time. But the most astonishing thing about this barber's son is the fertility of his mind and the bewildering diversity of his inventions. Vitruvius is lost in admiration: 'But this machine (for raising the level of water) is not the only remarkable invention of Ktesibios: he made many others, of different kinds.'[69]

As far as we know, however, these discoveries were all based on the elasticity of air and on hydraulic phenomena. They had been set out by the inventor himself in a book entitled *Commentaries*,[70] which, though now lost, must have been fairly easy to come by in Vitruvius's day, since he advises his readers to consult it.[71] The book was perhaps not as condensed as is implied by the later compiler Hero of Byzantium, according to whom Ktesibios did no more than give an outline of each of his machines, without elaborating on

[67] That is to say, when the mirror was raised. The weight served as a counterpoise.
[68] *De Architectura*, ix, 8.
[69] x, 7.
[70] Ὑπομνήματα (Athenaeus the Engineer, Wescher, p. 29; Hero of Byzantium, ibid., p. 262–3); *Commentaria* (Vitruvius, x, 7).
[71] x, 7. It is surprising that Athenaeus of Naucratis did not think of consulting this work, though it was perhaps too technical for a grammarian.

the details of their construction.[72] It is clear that anyone reading the commentaries needed a certain scientific background: 'Those desirous of reading the works of Ktesibios, Archimedes, and others who have written on this subject [engineering] will not be able to understand them without first having been instructed by philosophers.'[73]

Note that Vitruvius does not hesitate to couple the name of Ktesibios with that of Archimedes, an indication of the prestige still enjoyed in Roman times by the Alexandrian engineer. Elsewhere he again mentions them in the same breath when referring to scholars who have written books on machines, and follows this up with a list of names, including Diadus, Archytas, Archimedes, Ktesibios, Nymphodorus, Philo of Byzantium, Diphilus, Democles, Charias, Polyeidus, Pyrrhus, and Agesistratus.[74] Pliny the Elder likewise ranks Ktesibios among the most illustrious of all scholars,[75] while Philo of Byzantium, as we have seen, pays homage to him and had seen his creations in Alexandria. Athenaeus the Engineer also knows the work done by the inventor of the organ: 'Ktesibios of Ascra, who worked as an engineer in Alexandria, describes in his Commentaries how to storm ramparts without ladders, by using a machine of this sort.'[76]

This Athenaeus, who is probably referring to some kind of hoisting apparatus, may well have worked in Alexandria with Biton, Apollodorus, and Hero,[77] and it is possible, though by no means certain, that he lived around 200 B.C. His *Treatise on War Machines* is dedicated to Marcellus, perhaps the conqueror of Syracuse.[78] At all events, the memory of Ktesibios remained green for a very long time in Alexandria, since seven hundred years after his death the great mathematician Proclus (412–85) was still quite familiar with his work. In his *Commentary on Euclid* he, too, rates the inventor of the organ on a par with Archimedes.

There is also the science known as Engineering, which comprises part of the study of tangible and material things. From it derives the science devoted to the making of war machines, such as the defensive weapons that Archimedes built for the defenders of Syracuse: and also the science dealing with the construction of marvellous appliances. Some, like those elaborated by Ktesibios and Hero, function by means of blasts of air, while others operate by the use of weights.[79]

[72] Wescher, p. 264.
[73] That is to say, professors of the mechanical and physical sciences. Vitruvius, i, Preface.
[74] vii, Preface.
[75] *Nat. Hist.*, vii, 125.
[76] Wescher, op. cit., p. 29.
[77] These authors have been translated into Latin by Thévenot (*Veterum Mathematicorum Opera*, Paris, 1693).
[78] E. Miller, *Journal des Savants* (April, 1868), pp. 244 ff.
[79] Ed. Friedlein (Leipzig, 1873). Prologue I, p. 41.

The compiler Hero of Byzantium, not to be confused with Hero of Alexandria, also makes reference to Ktesibios, and reproduces almost verbatim the text of Athenaeus the Engineer.[80] The name crops up again in the scholia of Tzetzes, a Byzantine scholar of the twelfth century A.D., where the inventor of the organ is listed among the great men of classical technology: 'Such is the advice of those who have written on machines: Philo and Philaterios, Isoes, Archimedes, Hero and Dionysius, Sostratus and Pappus, Palladas the Athenian, Apollodorus, Ktesibios, Anthemios, and Patroclus. From them we have come to know many machines.'[81]

Farmer,[82] astonished by the fact that Ktesibios was apparently unknown to the Arabs at the time of the Caliphates, when the sciences were held in high regard, has suggested identifying the learned Greek Muristos, author of a treatise which has survived only in Arabic, with the Alexandrian engineer, on the grounds that the Arabic form of the word Ktesibios, *Qatasibiyus*, is graphically not unlike Muristos. However, as we shall see later, this interpretation comes up against several formidable stumbling-blocks.

PHILO OF BYZANTIUM AND HERO OF ALEXANDRIA

Before moving on to examine the work of Ktesibios, it is useful to consider that of the other two engineers who directly contributed towards handing down his legacy to posterity.

Philo of Byzantium, whose name has already cropped up several times, should not be confused with that Philo of Athens, who built naval installations in the days of Demetrius of Phalerum,[83] or with Philo of Tyana, a mathematician living in the second century A.D., or, of course, with Philo Judaeus. By his own account[84] he studied two different sciences, architecture in Rhodes and engineering in Alexandria, under the guidance of reputable masters. This explains how he was able to observe, in the latter city, the most interesting machines. Nothing more is known of him, though his name certainly derives from his native town: but was he actually a pupil of Ktesibios while in Alexandria? Some have maintained that he was, though they cannot prove it.[85] Certainly it would not have been impossible, for Philo seems to have lived a few years later than Ktesibios—perhaps in the succeeding generation.[86] When describing the technical achievements of

---

[80] Wescher, p. 256.
[81] 'Scholia ad Tzestzes Allegor', J. Cramer, *Anecdota graeca* (Oxford, 1836), iii, p. 381.
[82] *The Organ of the Ancients*, p. 19.
[83] Vitruvius knows and distinguishes between these two Philos (Preface to book vii).
[84] R. Schöne, op. cit., iv, 50, 16 ff.; 15, 19 ff.
[85] In particular Th.-Henri Martin, *Recherche sur la vie et les ouvrages d'Héron d'Alexandrie* (Paris, 1854), pp. 15 ff., and K. Orinsky, op. cit., art. 'Ktésibios'.
[86] According to A. de Rochas (*Traité des Fortifications de Philon*, Besançon, 1872) he lived in the second half of the second century.

Ktesibios he invariably uses the past tense.[87] Still, it is likely that in Alexandria he was able to see for himself the hydraulis whose principle struck him with its originality, and he defines the new instrument in a telling image—'a syrinx that is played with the hands' (ἐπὶ τῆς σύριγγος τῆς κρουομένης ταῖς χερσίν). It is while recording his astonishment that the air pump devised by Ktesibios functions perfectly well in practice that he relates the circumstances in which it was invented.[88] He also says that if her scholars have made Alexandria the world's foremost city, this is because her kings loved both glory and the arts.[89]

Philo's writings consisted in the main of a vast encyclopedic work entitled *Treatise on Engineering* (Μηχανικὴ Σύνταξις). Of this only three volumes have survived: the *Treatise on Artillery Machines* (Βελοποιϊκά) has come down to us in the original Greek, while both the *Treatise on Pneumatics* and the *Treatise on Fortifications* exist only in the Arabic version. The work also included a *Treatise on Mathematics*, another on *The Construction of Harbours*,[90] and a *Treatise on Automata* which Hero of Alexandria knew well.[91]

It is in the *Treatise on Artillery Machines* that the name of Ktesibios occurs several times. Occasionally he is subjected to criticism,[92] but more often he is warmly praised for having discovered the properties of compressed air and invented different appliances, in particular the pneumatic catapult, the cylinder pump, and the hydraulis. Like the *Treatise on Pneumatics*, the book is dedicated to one Ariston.[93] Now MS. no. 2755 in the Library of Hagia Sofia in Constantinople contains two *Treatises on Organs*, written in Arabic and likewise dedicated to Ariston. This is somewhat puzzling, and Carra de Vaux has concluded—perhaps a trifle hastily—that they, too, are the work of Philo.[94] It is certainly not inconceivable that he should have written something on the hydraulic organ. Hero could have been familiar with such a work and referred to it: but we have no proof that his was so.

In dealing with physical problems, Philo's ideas are in advance of his time. In his *Pneumatics*, for instance, he demonstrates the existence of air as a material substance, a bold concept for his day. To prove his theory, he takes a small Egyptian amphora, pierces the base, and plugs the resulting hole with

[87] For instance, when speaking of the invention of the hydraulis: ἡ φῦσα . . . ἦν χαλκῆ . . . ἐπεδείκνυτο δὲ ἡμῖν ὁ Κτησίβιος . . .
[88] Schöne, iv, 77, 15 ff.
[89] ibid., iv, 50, 37 ff.
[90] A. de Rochas, op. cit., p. 197.
[91] Pneum., Περὶ στατῶν αὐτομάτων, xx.
[92] Schöne, iv, 68, 40 ff. Philo claims that Ktesibios made a mistake in a theorem relating to the addition of a number of forces.
[93] 'Φίλων Ἀρίστωνι χαίρειν.' A. de Rochas assumes that he is the natural son of the last king of Pergamum, though there is no evidence that this is so.
[94] Carra de Vaux, *Le Livre des appareils pneumatiques et des machines hydrauliques, par Philon de Byzance* (Paris, 1902), p. 14.

wax; then he plunges it upside down into a tank of water. When the wax plug is removed, the water enters the amphora, expelling the air and filling the space it has occupied.[95] To the modern mind Philo's greatest achievement is that he devised the experiment which enabled Lavoisier, two thousand years later, to define combustion and analyse the composition of air: 'Fire destroys air', he writes; 'the water level rises in the vessel after the flame has died'.[96]

Philo of Byzantium had a great reputation. We have said that Vitruvius speaks of him in the same terms as Archimedes, Ktesibios, and Archytas. For various reasons, he is considered nowadays one of the principal representatives of the school of Ktesibios.[97]

Hero of Alexandria is another important link in the chain, since he has left a voluminous quantity of work containing almost all the elements which, according to Vitruvius, made up the substance of the *Commentaries*. It is here that we find a detailed description of the hydraulic organ.

A number of Hero's treatises survive: on *Pneumatics*—a text of capital importance in the history of engineering—on *Metrics, Dioptrics, Stereometrics,* and *Geometric Definitions*, all in Greek. There is also a fragment from the *Mechanics*, entitled Βαρουλκός, which has survived in the Arabic version.

The appliances described in Hero's *Pneumatics* are more sophisticated than those discussed by Philo. The influence of the ideas of Strato of Lampsacus, which had already left their mark on the young Ktesibios, is clearly discernible. Not only air but water and even steam are harnessed to operate the mechanisms outlined here. A great many devices are introduced in the *Pneumatics*, apparently designed to amuse, but also to surprise and even mystify, for the actual mechanical movement is generally concealed.[98] Sometimes they are grouped together in a marionette theatre.[99] In discussing these, Hero simply reproduces the mechanisms previously analysed by Philo, and indeed freely acknowledges his debt: 'As regards the automata fixed in one place, which I should also like to discuss, nothing is more novel, or more technically advanced, or at the same time more instructive, than the system outlined by Philo of Byzantium.'[100]

By and large, the machines described in the *Pneumatics* are built on a very small scale, and it is interesting to note that there does not seem to have been a use for big machines in the Roman Empire, where manual labour was

---

[95] P. Brunet and A. Miéli, *Histoire des Sciences* (Paris, 1935), Antiquité, pp. 488–9.
[96] Carra de Vaux, op. cit., pp. 103–4.
[97] W. Kroll, in Pauly-Wissowa, art. 'Philon von Byzanz'.
[98] Lynn Thorndike, *A History of Magic and Experimental Science* (New York, 1929), i, p. 190.
[99] See V. Prou, *Les théâtres d'automates en Grèce* (Paris, 1881).
[100] *Pneum.*, Περὶ στατῶν αὐτομάτων, xx.

plentiful and cheap.[101] However, the *Pneumatics* do deal with such things as pulley blocks, levers, capstans, complicated sets of gear-wheels, and endless screws. They also contain a description of an improved version of the fire pump and two versions of the hydraulic organ, one pumped by hand and the other operated by the movement of the wind. There is even an account of a small steam-driven jet engine.[102]

Hero of Alexandria was undoubtedly famous. St. Gregory of Nazianzus mentions him in the company of Hippocrates, Euclid, Ptolemy, and Plato.[103] Tzetzes and Theon are both familiar with his name, and in a letter to the doctor Lespiotus, an anonymous Byzantine scribe makes what may well be a reference to him: 'You are the most learned and philosophical of doctors! You know the works of Soranus and Hippocrates, of Galen, Herophilus, and Herodian, of Tryphon, Herodotus, and Hero . . .'[104]

Hero, like Ktesibios, seems to have been self-taught. Theon, rhetor of Alexandria in the second century A.D., says that before he became a philosopher, Hero had been a shoemaker.[105] Whether or not this is true, he displayed an early interest in the properties of air, as he says himself in the preface to his *Pneumatics*. He denied the concept of the void, so dear to the hearts of many philosophers: 'Vessels thought to be empty are not so. Anyone who has any acquaintance with physics is aware that in fact air is composed of tiny molecules, light and generally invisible . . . It is an established fact that air is a substance; and wind is nothing more or less than moving air.'[106]

His account of the hydraulic organ makes Hero of Alexandria a most interesting figure for the musicologist, and it is therefore important to establish exactly when he was alive. Unfortunately the range of possible dates is still very wide. Though he quotes Archimedes (who died in 212 B.C.) and Menelaus of Alexandria (who made observations at Rome in A.D. 98), he himself is not mentioned by any author before Pappus (end of third century). Neither Pliny nor Vitruvius, who list the names of all the learned men whose works were studied in their day, appear to have any knowledge of him, an omission which would be most easily explained by placing him in a later era. However, it is possible that both Pliny and Vitruvius, thinking of him as a pupil of Ktesibios, consider it unnecessary to record the name of the disciple, since they discuss the master. It has therefore been suggested that Hero lived in the reign of Ptolemy VIII Euergetes (170–116).[107] There are, however,

---

[101] F. Klemm, *A History of Western Technology* (New York, 1959), p. 35.
[102] *Pneum.*, ii, 11.
[103] Migne, *Patrologie Grecque*, xxxv, 781.
[104] J. Cramer, op. cit., iii, p. 189.
[105] A. de Rochas, *La Science des Philosophes* (Paris, 1882), p. 711.
[106] *Pneum.*, i.
[107] M. Letronne, *Recherches sur les fragments d'Héron d'Alexandrie* (Paris, 1851), p. 26.

certain obstacles to the acceptance of this hypothesis. Hero is the author of genuinely original mathematical treatises which earn him a place of honour in the history of science, and it is astonishing that Vitruvius makes no mention of them. The Latinisms he sometimes uses prove that he knew Latin: $\mu i \lambda \iota a$[108] (milia), $\pi \acute{a}(\sigma) \sigma \omega \nu$[109] (passum), $\mu \iota \lambda \iota \acute{a} \rho \iota o \nu$[110] (milliarium), are examples of this. Occasionally he apologizes for borrowing a word, as when, writing $\dot{a} \sigma \sigma \acute{a} \rho \iota o \nu$, he adds 'in Latin'.[111] It has been argued from this that he must have lived after Caesar's conquest of Egypt. Attempts have also been made to discover any chronological indications in his technical descriptions, even in the date of an eclipse of the moon which allegedly took place in A.D. 62: but the value of all this is dubious, especially in the case of the eclipse, where Hero merely outlines a method of working out the distance from Alexandria to Rome[112] by astronomy, and nowhere states that he himself has carried out such an experiment. A certain passage in the *Mechanics* has been thought to contain a definition by the Stoic Posidonius (died 49 B.C.), but the text is highly questionable.[113] Taking all the various arguments into account, it seems reasonable to situate Hero in the first century A.D., immediately following Vitruvius and Pliny. This is the most widely accepted view today.[114]

A perusal of the works of Hero of Alexandria reveals something truly remarkable. Not once does he mention the name of Ktesibios. True, he makes practically no references to anyone. He pays tribute to Archimedes, but alludes only casually to Philo and Menelaus. The only possible explanation for this strange omission is that the reader is supposed to take it for granted that the *Pneumatics* are a detailed and exhaustive account of the work done by Ktesibios. Such an interpretation is confirmed in four ways:

1. A late writer of the same name, Hero of Byzantium, to whom reference has already been made, names Ktesibios as the 'master' ($\kappa a \theta \eta \gamma \eta \tau \acute{\eta} s$) of Hero of Alexandria.[115] We do not know his evidence for this assertion, but probably it comes from his usual source, Athenaeus the Engineer. The implication in this case seems to be that Ktesibios was Hero's 'spiritual master', his inspiration, and not, as has been said, his actual teacher.[116]

2. A more disconcerting argument is the heading on some of the best of

---

[108] *Diopt.*, xxxviii, ed. Teubner, p. 314.
[109] ibid.
[110] *Pneum.*, 304, 10.
[111] '$\Pi a \rho \dot{a}$ '$P \omega \mu a i o \iota s$ $\dot{a} \sigma \sigma \acute{a} \rho \iota o \nu$' (*Pneum.*, 74, 5).
[112] *Diopt.*, xxxv, p. 302.
[113] Carra de Vaux, *Les Mécaniques d'Héron d'Alexandrie* (Paris, 1894), p. 29.
[114] P. Tannery, *L'invention de l'hydraulis*, op. cit.; T. Heath, *A History of Greek Mathematics* (Oxford, 1921), ii, p. 306.
[115] Wescher, pp. 262–3.
[116] As both Carra de Vaux (*Journal des Savants*, 1868) and A. de Rochas (*La Science des Philosophes*, op. cit.) believed.

Hero of Byzantium's manuscripts,[117] reproducing the treatise of Athenaeus the Engineer: ʽΗρωνος Κτησιβίου Βελοποιϊκά, which may be translated as 'Artillery Machines, by Hero, [disciple] of Ktesibios'. This is a logical interpretation, and corresponds to the much-quoted example Εὐσέβιος ὁ Παμφίλου, 'Eusebius, disciple of Pamphilus'. Here again there is no implication of a direct pupil-teacher relationship. A better interpretation, in my opinion, would be 'The Artillery Machines of Ktesibios, revised edition by Hero', the Hero in question being Hero of Alexandria, as a number of manuscripts state.[118]

3. A third indication is given in the work of Vitruvius, who states that Ktesibios invented and described certain specific appliances, among them a machine for raising the level of water and the hydraulic organ, as well as automata designed for entertainment. These same machines and automata reappear in the *Pneumatics*.

4. One final clue is provided by Proclus the mathematician. In his *Commentary on Euclid*, the name of Hero is associated with that of Ktesibios in the invention of pneumatic machines.[119]

From these facts we may assume that the essence of Ktesibios's knowledge and skill is present in the work of Hero of Alexandria, at least as far as the *Pneumatics* and *Mechanics* are concerned. Furthermore, it is possible to trace the evolution of Ktesibios's creative thought-processes from Hero's text, starting with relatively simple toys and ending with that amazing machine, the hydraulic organ.

[117] Vatican MS. Cod. Graec. 1164; Minas MS. Cod. Par. Suppl. Graec. 607; Paris MS. Cod. Par. Graec., 2442.
[118] Wescher, pp. 69 ff.
[119] See p. 16.

CHAPTER TWO

༄ഔ

The Hydraulic Organ (1)

PRELIMINARY INVENTIONS

If, as the evidence suggests, the organ was the personal invention of the engineer Ktesibios, it is likely that he did not achieve his object at the first attempt, and he must have built a number of simple prototypes. One might wonder what inspired a technician who specialized to such an extent in machines and automata to invent, of all things, a new musical instrument. However, we know that he amused himself by devising a clepsydra with sounding trumpets,[1] and by placing a musical rhyton in the temple of Arsinoë-Zephyritis. Music was much practised at Alexandria, and he may well have had the opportunity of seeing that other musical automaton, attributed in an Arabic treatise to Archimedes,[2] which consisted of a box surmounted by a statuette of a musician playing the aulos. Water entering the cistern forced out the air, which was then led to the aulos through a pipe concealed in the body of the figurine.[3] Ktesibios apparently based the automata he designed 'to produce intermittent bird-song'[4] on this very simple principle. Water flows into a small vessel mounted on a horizontal axle, the vessel being so balanced as to remain upright while it is filling and tip over as soon as the water reaches the top. The water then falls into a funnel, the tube of which leads into the bottom of a hermetically sealed cistern. At the top of this cistern is a pipe ending in a whistle concealed in the body of a bird, which is thus induced to sing at regular intervals. Another toy of the same type has several birds. The pipes leading to their whistles are fixed at different levels, so that they take it in turn to twitter. It is virtually certain that these singing birds were invented by Ktesibios. Philo of Byzantium was familiar with them, and he, too, has left a description.[5]

However, this system of blowing had at least two disadvantages. Everything stopped when the water had filled the cistern, and in addition only a very low air pressure was obtained. Ktesibios probably decided to tackle the

---

[1] *De Archit.*, ix, 8.
[2] Farmer, op. cit., p. 80.
[3] Pl. XXII, No. 1.
[4] Hero, *Pneum.*, ii, 5.
[5] Carra de Vaux, op. cit., p. 173.

problem afresh after devising his cylinder pump, for otherwise he could have worked his hydraulis with blacksmiths' bellows. This type of bellows had been known for a long time; and Homer tells us that their action could be extremely powerful.[6] Herodotus,[7] Theophrastus,[8] and other writers speak of the bellows that were used in metal-working; and in the first century A.D. Hero of Alexandria was still employing bellows consisting of air-filled bags which were squeezed to produce a stream of air.[9] It seems clear, however, that Ktesibios was intent on making use of the pump he had invented, and was not at all averse to demonstrating its effectiveness. Apropos the pneumatic catapult—another of Ktesibios's achievements—Philo of Byzantium gives this account of how the cylinder pump was conceived:

This appliance, invented by Ktesibios, was a purely mechanical arrangement, which made use of the laws of nature.

He [Ktesibios] had proved, in the pneumatic theorems discussed above (and referred to again below), that air is resistant, elastic, and extremely mobile; and that furthermore when it is trapped in a strong cylindrical vessel it can be compressed and subsequently expands rapidly, taking up the total volume of the cylinder. With his vast experience in engineering, Ktesibios quickly realized that this movement [of decompression] could, with the aid of articulated connecting-rods, produce a very strong tension and a powerful impetus.[10]

With this in mind he constructed cylinders,[11] in shape resembling doctors' medicine boxes, lidless, made of thin bronze so as to be resistant and strong, worked in its soft state, like wax,[12] and cast to give it strength. The inside of the cylinders was turned on a lathe and the surface polished until it was flat, even, and very smooth.

Next he inserted a bronze piston disc ($\tau\upsilon\mu\pi\acute{\alpha}\nu\iota o\nu$) able to travel the whole height of the cylinder while pressing hard against its circumference, and likewise treated so as to be smooth and polished. They both fit together so well that, though the air takes the full force [of the piston], there is no leakage.[13]

Be not amazed, therefore, or doubt that such an apparatus can actually be built, for in the syrinx which is played with the hands and is known as the hydraulis, the wind mechanism[14] which forced the air into a pnigeus placed in the water, was of brass, and wrought in the same fashion as the cylindrical vessels I have just described. Ktesibios proved this to us when he demonstrated

[6] *Iliad*, xviii, 468 ff.

[7] *Hist.*, i, 68.

[8] *De Igne*, 37.

[9] *Pneum.*, i, 39.

[10] These were, in fact, used in the compressed air catapult.

[11] $\Pi\upsilon\xi\acute{\iota}\varsigma$ is from $\pi\acute{\upsilon}\xi o\varsigma$, boxwood, hence a small boxwood box for ointments, or any kind of cylindrical box (Daremberg and Saglio, op. cit., art. 'Pyxis').

[12] i.e. when the heat of the forge has rendered it malleable.

[13] This serves to hold the piston perpendicular to the axis of the cylinder.

[14] i.e. the pump.

that air naturally has a powerful, rapid movement, and instructed us at the same time in the use of piston cylinders. . . .[15]

Apart from adding a set of valves to this apparatus, all he had to do was crank the piston shaft with a lever in order to have a pump. Drawing up and forcing back any type of liquid became a simple matter—this was the practical application of the Aristotelian principle that 'inhaling is traction, exhaling is thrust'.[16] On this basis Ktesibios constructed his double-barrelled fire pump, described by Vitruvius as being capable of raising water to a great height (*De Ctesibica machina, quae in altitudinem aquam educit*).[17] It was a suction and thrust pump, made entirely of bronze. In the cylinders pistons polished on the lathe and lubricated with oil slid up and down, operated by rods and levers, sucking up the water and forcing it into a closed cistern where the air was compressed. This pressure caused the water to rise to a great height, through a fork-joint shaped like an inverted funnel ('paenula ut infundibulum inversum'). Valves opened and closed with the movement of the water.[18]

It is interesting to note that Vitruvius apparently judges this pump to be ideal for raising the water level in an ornamental basin so as to make a playing fountain—here he is speaking as an architect. By contrast, Hero of Alexandria, giving details of an identical pump, describes it as a fire pump. Like the other, it has two bronze cylinders whose internal surface has been turned on the lathe, 'like the cylinders of the hydraulic organs' (καθάπερ αἱ τῶυ ὑδραύλεων πυξίδες).[19]

Both accounts clearly derive from a common source, which must be Ktesibios's book of *Commentaries*. Before this, the only pumps were probably of the type described by Apollodorus of Damascus, made of skin bladders filled with water. When pressure was applied to them, the liquid rose through lengths of hose-pipe made of ox-gut.[20] In Ktesibios's day it was still common to find pumps shaped rather like a lantern of supple leather, referred to by Philo of Byzantium as 'appliances for raising water from a well by an elegant process'.[21]

Ktesibios's cylinder pump appears to have been quite widely used in the Roman Empire, for one was discovered at Silchester in England and another at Castronovo in Italy.[22] In addition there is the letter written by Pliny the

[15] iv, 77, 15 ff.
[16] *Physics*, vii, 243 b.
[17] x, 7.
[18] Philo, who also describes this pump (Carra de Vaux, op. cit., p. 193), insists that each of these valves has its separate role.
[19] *Pneum.*, i, 28.
[20] Sorlin-Dorigny: Daremberg-Saglio, op. cit., art. 'Sipho'.
[21] Carra de Vaux, op. cit., p. 193.
[22] Sorlin-Dorigny, op. cit.

Younger to Trajan requesting delivery of a fire pump for the town of Nicomedia, which had none.[23] An interesting technical point about this pump designed by Ktesibios is that the water forced out by the pistons did not pass directly into the hose-pipe. Instead it was injected into a closed container, from which it was then forcibly expelled by the compressed air. This is the system still used today both in fire pumps and in domestic water supplies in countries where wells are the only source of water. This device for controlling water by pressure was evidently much admired in the Roman world. Seneca records his amazement at these fountains of liquid leaping up from the centre of the arena to the level of the topmost tiers of spectators in the amphitheatre under the pressure of air.[24] Hero tells of a toy based on the same principle: 'When air is blown into certain vessels, the liquid spurts up under the pressure of the air.'[25]

I have dwelt at some length on the fire pump because it represents a practical application of the piston cylinder invented by Ktesibios, as does the hydraulic organ to which we now turn. It should be fully realized that it was the concept of the machine as such, rather than any preoccupation with music, which inspired Ktesibios to create the hydraulis. Instead of moving the water by means of compressed air, he had the idea of compressing the air by the weight of the water. His cylinder pump was capable of compressing air, and thus was well able to feed a musical instrument of the aulos type. But to do this two conditions had to be met. Ktesibios had first to build up sufficient pressure to create a supply of air; but in addition he had to maintain that pressure at a more or less constant level, or the sounds produced would be uneven and unpleasant. He probably bore in mind that he had already made a toy automaton, so that all he had to do was to revive the same principle. Hero gives the following account of this contrivance:

A statuette on a pedestal base, holding a trumpet to its lips,
which it will play if air is blown into it.

Let there be a pedestal *ABΓΔ*,[26] supporting a standing figurine. Inside the pedestal let there be a hollow hemisphere *EZH* notched along its free rim.

From this hemisphere leads a pipe *ΘZ*, through which the air is led up through the statuette to the trumpet, which should be fitted with a reeded mouthpiece *(γλωσσίς)*. Then let water be poured into the pedestal through an aperture which should be hermetically sealed with a stopper when the pedestal is filled.

---

[23] x, 33, 2.
[24] *Quest. Nat.*, ii, De Fulminibus, ix, 2.
[25] *Pneum.*, ii, 2. This toy came back into fashion in the eighteenth century; J.-J. Rousseau was delighted by it: 'The Abbot of Gouvon made me a present some weeks ago of a little hero's fountain [*sic*] which I thought adorable . . . Could there be anything stranger in the world than a hero's fountain?' (*Confessions*, Book III).
[26] These letters refer to the drawings illustrating Hero's text.

Thus when we blow into the bell of the trumpet, the air from our lips will force the water in the hemisphere through the notches and cause it to rise into the pedestal. But if we suddenly stop blowing, the water will return to the hemisphere and compress the air (therein); this air, issuing through the mouthpiece of the trumpet, will produce a sound.[27]

With this marvellously ingenious contraption he thus succeeded in compressing the air by the weight of a mass of displaced water. Simply by attaching the pipe of the air pump to the neck of the hemisphere he could obtain air under pressure. At each stroke of the pump the water, expelled from the hemisphere by the incoming air, found its way into the pedestal-shaped cistern, and its level rose, so that the weight of the displaced liquid compressed the air. Between strokes of the pump, the level of the water in the cistern fell, that of the water in the hemisphere rose, and the pressure was maintained. Ktesibios was thus equipped with a powerful and entirely original type of wind-mechanism with which to feed a musical instrument whose sound potential might be practically unlimited.

He had still to discover how to distribute the air to a series of reed pipes. But here, by another stroke of genius, he conceived the idea of having a wind-chest, with draw-stops and a manual—an entirely new and revolutionary feature which was to have a tremendous influence on the design of instruments right up to the present day.

It seems very likely that in his great encyclopedia of engineering, Philo of Byzantium devoted a section to the hydraulic organ. The allusion he makes to the new instrument in his Βελοποιϊκά appears to suggest that in his day the hydraulis existed only as a prototype and was perhaps not yet beyond the stage of being a mechanical curiosity; a laboratory machine put on show for visitors to the Museum. Athenaeus, however, says that Ktesibios's wife took up organ-playing during her husband's lifetime.

But it was in the Roman world that the organ was destined to come into its own and win the acclaim of which we shall read. Indeed, it is from the Roman era that the two detailed analyses of the mechanism have survived. The first is the work of Hero of Alexandria, and dates at the earliest from the first century A.D. The second is by Vitruvius, and clearly refers to a much more sophisticated instrument.

HERO'S DESCRIPTION

Hero discusses the organ in chapter 42 of his *Pneumatics*. His text is clear and precise, and it is apparent that the author is an experienced engineer. Unfortunately there can be little doubt that his description has been modified by a copyist—the last paragraph records a detail omitted from the first

[27] *Pneum.*, ii, 10.

section. There is one omission which is technically surprising, and for which Hero is certainly not to blame: the machine lacks a valve, without which no air would reach the pipes. As we shall see, this part is not left out in Vitruvius's text.

The oldest manuscript copy of Hero dates only from 1250. This is the Venice manuscript. The text is accompanied by diagrams in three colours—yellow, green, and red (Plate XXIII). These diagrams certainly existed in the original, since the letters correspond. Moreover, it is highly unlikely that any transcriber would have been capable of inventing them.

So that Hero's reasoning may be easier to follow, it seems preferable to separate the account of the blowing mechanism from that of the wind-chest.[28]

Construction of a Hydraulic Organ

[The blowing mechanism]

Let *ABΓΔ* be a small 'altar' *(βωμίσκος)*[29] made of bronze and containing water, and let there be in the water a hollow hemisphere called a pnigeus *(πνιγεύς) EZHΘ*, inverted, and with an outlet for the water at the bottom.[30] Attached to the upper part of the pnigeus are two conduits *(σωλῆνες)* rising above the top of the 'altar'. [At the lower extremity,] these conduits open into the pnigeus. One of them, *HKΛM*, curves round to the outside of the altar, and communicates with a cylinder *NΞOΠ*. This cylinder *(πυξίς)* is open at its lower end, and its internal surface has been made perfectly smooth to fit a piston *(ἐμβολεύς)*. Let the piston *PΣ* be fitted into it so that no air may escape at the side,[31] and a strong rod *TY* be firmly attached to the piston. Let another rod *YΦ*, moving round a pin *Y*, be fitted to the first, and operate as a lever connected to an upright shaft *ΨX* solidly attached to the ground.

At the upper end of the cylinder *NΞOΠ* let another small cylinder *Ω* be placed, communicating with *NΞOΠ* and closed at its upper end, with an aperture through which air may pass into the large cylinder. Under this aperture place a thin metal plate which seals it and is prevented from falling by headed nails which pass through holes in the plate. This metal plate is known as the platysmation.

From *Z* let another conduit *ϛZ* extend into a transverse chamber *G⟩* on which the pipes *(αὐλοί)* rest, *,A*, which also open into the chamber.

. . . If therefore the lever is manipulated like a pump-handle, by lowering the end marked *Φ*, the piston *PΣ*, rising up, will compress the air contained in

---

[28] The letters are from the original diagrams. See that from the Venice manuscript, Pl. XXIV, and my version, fig. 1.

[29] This is a literal translation. The βωμίσκος is, in fact, a geometrical solid shaped like the frustrum of a prism. Elsewhere Hero himself gives the mathematical definition *(Stereometrics,* ii, 68).

[30] i.e. notched round its lower rim.

[31] And probably greased, like that of the fire pump.

the cylinder *NΞΟΠ*. This air will (1) close the aperture in the small cylinder *Ω* by pressing on the platysmation mentioned above; and (2) proceed towards the pnigeus through the conduit *MΛKH*. From the pnigeus it will rise through the conduit *ϛZ* into the transverse chamber G⟩ and finally reach the organ pipes. . . . The water is poured into the 'altar' so that the excessive amount of air in the pnigeus (by which I mean the air pushed out of the cylinder) may cause the water to rise, and the water compress the air so that each pipe should

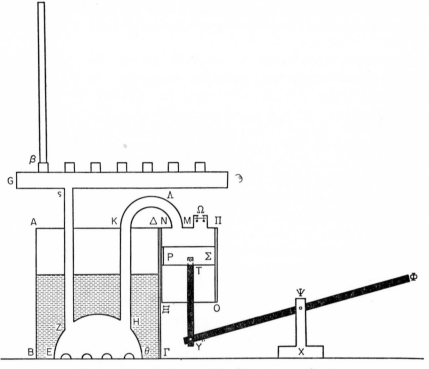

Fig. 1a. Hero's Organ. The blowing mechanism

always have sufficient supply to produce a note. By making the piston *PΣ* rise as we have described, the air from the cylinder is forced into the pnigeus, and by lowering it again, the metal plate in the small cylinder *Ω* is free to open, whereupon the large cylinder fills with air from the exterior. Then the piston, when pushed up again, forces the air once more into the pnigeus.

It is moreover preferable that the rod *TY* should move on a pin, which should be fitted to the base of the piston with a double stud *T*, through which the pin must pass so that the piston is not twisted, but moves up and down in a straight line.[32]

The description would be lucid were it not for the repetitions and omissions for which Hero is probably not responsible. It is easy to see how

[32] In other words, on the same axis as the cylinder.

the wind mechanism works, for the various component parts are accurately analysed. The cistern, made of copper or bronze, is shaped like a small altar and acts as a stand for the wind-chest and the musical part of the instrument. From the iconography its dimensions could be about 1 m. in height on a base 80 cm. in diameter. This base is incidentally nearly always hexagonal, a traditional shape which seems to have been retained for a very long time. It is certain that the water did not fill the cistern to the brim, or it would have overflowed when the pnigeus was filled by the air from the pump. This pnigeus sat on the bottom of the cistern, and indeed was probably fixed to it. It was a hemisphere, presumably made of metal, and though its exact measurements are not known, it is reasonable to assume that for a medium-sized instrument of the type illustrated in iconographical sources, this hemisphere might have had a diameter of approximately 60 cm. The lower edge had openings, perhaps notches, to enable the water to circulate between the cistern and the pnigeus, unless the latter simply stood on lugs. On this point, which is of secondary importance, Hero is not very explicit.

The word 'pnigeus' (πνιγεύς) already existed. Aristotle,[33] Aristophanes,[34] Theophrastus,[35] and Pollux[36] all use it in two senses: 'oven', or 'damper' (a cover to smother the flames of a fire). The Suidas lexicon gives it the same meanings. There can scarcely be any doubt that it was Ktesibios himself who chose the word to describe the hemisphere, perhaps basing his selection on the similarity between its shape and that of a piece of kitchen equipment, or on the fact that the air was highly pressurized and condensed in a narrow space. Philo lists this πνιγεύς as one of the component parts of the hydraulis, and Hero uses the word to describe similar hemispheres fulfilling the same function in two of the automata discussed in the *Pneumatics*.[37]

The air pump of the ὄργανον ὑδραυλικόν applies the principle of the piston pump as analysed by Philo. At the top of the cylinder an inlet valve is added, made simply of a thin metal plaque facing the corresponding aperture. The heads of two nails limit the extent of its downward movement. On the up-stroke of the lever this valve falls down, leaving the opening free; but when the piston rises in the cylinder the valve is forced hard against the roof of the cylinder, which it seals hermetically. The outlet valve is not described, but whether this is due to an oversight on the part of the copyist or to Hero's negligence is not known. All the evidence points to its existence, for without it the air forced by the piston into the pnigeus would return to the cylinder on the next upstroke. This second valve was probably located at the bottom of the conduit sZ, with the nails facing the opposite way to those fastening

[33] *De Part. Animal.*, ii, 8.
[34] *Clouds*, 96.
[35] *De Igne*, ii, 19.
[36] *Onom.*, vii, 110, and x, 54.
[37] i, 17; ii, 32.

the inlet valve. The function of the outlet valve was to shut off this conduit when the piston moved down the cylinder, and open it when the piston rose again.

The top of the cylinder has an additional part, described by Hero as a 'small cylinder', placed off-centre. The two would certainly have been soldered together. Philo and Hero stress that both cylinder and piston must be carefully smoothed on a lathe, so that they fit together without leaving the smallest gap through which air might escape. Such a pump is obviously well adapted to drawing up and compressing water, and Hero makes the point that the cylinders of the fire pump are absolutely identical to those of hydraulic organs. Note that the piston is not covered in leather, and comes in direct contact with the inner surface of the cylinder. These parts must have worn out very quickly, and it cannot have been easy to keep them air-tight.

The piston mounting is simple, and corresponds roughly to that used on farm pumps today. However, in view of the short stroke of the piston, it had to be fixed exactly on the axis of the cylinder to prevent it from jamming. For this reason Hero advocates joining shaft and piston with a pivot.

The air generated by the pump is forced into the pnigeus, where it presses on the water already there. This water escapes below and causes the level of the water in the cistern to rise; and it is the weight of the water displaced in this way which gives pressure to the air used in the wind-chest. According to the representations which we know of ancient organs, the height of the cylinder is often approximately half that of the cistern, that is to say about 50 cm. Its diameter varies considerably, but is rarely less than 30 cm.

Here now is that part of Hero's account which deals with the wind-chest and the manual:

[The wind-chest]

The pipes (αὐλοί), are placed in the transverse chamber, in ͺA, and open into it. At the lower ends of these pipes are fixed [devices shaped like] drawers (γλωσσόκομα), provided with apertures, ͺB. Let sliders (πώματα, literally 'shutters') be inserted into their slots, and these, too, should be perforated so that when they are pushed, their holes are exactly underneath the lower end of the pipes, and when they are pulled back, they no longer correspond, and the pipes are thus blocked.

Hence [the air] will pass into the pipes when the hole at the foot of the pipe corresponds to the hole in the slider, that is to say when the sliders are manipulated, either separately or all together; so that if the player should desire to make one of the pipes sound, he will open the hole corresponding to that pipe, and to cut off the sound at will, he has only to proceed as follows so that the holes no longer coincide.

Imagine one of these drawers, marked ‚*Γ* ‚*Δ*. Let its aperture be ‚*Δ*, and ‚E the corresponding pipe. Further, let there be the slider ₅*Z* corresponding to it, and ‚H ᵗhe hole in the slider not coinciding with the organ pipe, ‚E.

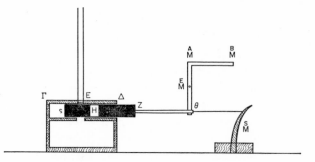

Fig. 1b. The wind-chest and manual

[The manual]

Suppose moreover a small, three-armed crank ‚*Z*, Θ$\overset{A}{M}\overset{B}{M}$ (ἀγκωνίσκος τρίκωλος) of which the arm, ‚*Z*, Θ is attached to the slider ₅*Z*. The arm Θ*M* moves about a median axis $\overset{z}{M}$. [pin] Now if, using the hand we depress the extremity $\overset{B}{M}$ of the crank towards the orifice Δ of the drawer, we shall push the slider inwards, so that when it is in the hole in, the slider will exactly coincide with the foot of the pipe.

Here now is the procedure by which, when the hand is withdrawn, the slider may be automatically pulled back out of alignment with the foot of the pipe. Beneath the drawers a rod $\overset{A}{M}\overset{B}{M}$ is placed, equal in length to the transverse chamber G⦚ and parallel to it. To this are fixed horn spatulas (σπαθία κεράτινα), springy and curving. Suppose that one of these spatulas $\overset{s}{M}$ corresponds to the drawer ‚*Γ* ‚*Δ*. A gut string is secured to the tip of this spatula and carried round to the extremity, ‚Θ, so that when the slider is pushed, the string becomes taut. If therefore the extremity $\overset{B}{M}$ of the crank is depressed, and the slider is pushed inwards, the string will pull on the spatula, straightening its curve by force. If [the hand] is withdrawn, the spatula, reverting to its original position, will pull the slider from the orifice so that the holes no longer coincide. All the drawers are fitted with this device.

And so, when the player wishes to draw sound from any pipes, he presses the keys corresponding to these pipes with his fingers; and to shut off the sound, he merely lifts his fingers, when the sliders will be drawn out and the pipes will cease to sing.[38]

We have here, then, the original wind-chest of Ktesibios's organ—or, at

[38] *Pneum.*, i, 42.

least, so it would seem. In design it is very simple, for the instrument has only one rank of pipes. The subsequent addition of several 'stops' complicated the mechanics of the instrument, but this problem had been satisfactorily solved—though it is not known by whom—by the end of the first century B.C. Here, however, each key, shaped like a double knee-joint, operates a perforated slider similar to our present-day draw-stops. When the key is depressed the hole in the slider moves to a position exactly beneath the foot of the corresponding pipe and the lower aperture of the drawer, whereupon the pressurized air rushes into the pipe and makes it sound. When the key is released a strong horn spring pulls the slider back to its normal position, the holes no longer coincide, and the air supply is immediately cut off.

Mechanically, this system is perfectly viable because of the small number of pipes that must have been used. But air leaks would certainly have presented a problem, and we may be sure that measures were taken to minimize these, perhaps by the application of some kind of grease between the slider and the drawer, or by a layer of thin leather—but this is pure conjecture. It must have been difficult to ensure any evenness of tension along the strings pulling back the keys: but it was essential that the keys should spring back to their normal positions immediately the finger was removed.

The term used to describe the pipes is αὐλοί (auloi), the αὐλός being a reed instrument, a type of oboe producing rather a penetrating tone. Several of the automata outlined by Hero also make use of a sounding reed;[39] the musical rhyton in the temple of Arsinoë-Zephyritis was fitted with a kind of trumpet. This was probably because these instruments were not designed to pass unnoticed. Ktesibios's hydraulic organ, with its abundant supply of highly compressed air, was certainly capable of producing quite a thunderous volume of sound. However, flue-pipes, either open or closed, also came into favour at a later date.

As far as the pipes are concerned, it is strange that Hero's account, so clear and thorough in dealing with the mechanical aspect of the instrument, should deliberately neglect the musical part. What was its compass—was it one octave or two? What were the lips of the pipes like? How were the pipes tuned, and to what notes? How were they held in their sockets? All of these, and many other questions, are left unanswered. The reason for Hero's silence is quite simply that he was an engineer and not a musician, and problems of acoustics were clearly of no interest to him. He gives instructions for building an organ, and, apart from the actual measurements, all the necessary data is there. But for information relating to the musical character of the instrument, it seems plain that we must apply to the pipe-makers and the musicians.

[39] *Pneum.*, i, 17; ii, 11 and 35.

In the *Pneumatics* the account of the hydraulic organ is followed by that of a curious machine described as an 'organ that sings when the wind blows'.[40] Here a small windmill directly operates the shaft of the cylinder. The air produced is channelled into the wind-chest and activates the pipes. But there is neither a hydraulic regulator nor a manual. Furthermore, this instrument would demand a very steady supply of air in order to work at all, and indeed it seems more like an engineer's fancy than a machine of practical use. Its inventor is not named: but Ktesibios was surely too experienced a technician to have put forward such a sketchy piece of work.

VITRUVIUS'S DESCRIPTION

The second detailed analysis of the ancient organ is once again the work of a technical writer, this time the architect Vitruvius. He, however, has some slight knowledge of the theory of music, and this emerges even in the first chapter of his Book I, where it is stated that the architect should be familiar with more than one science, including music. It takes a good musician, for example, to know where best to place the bronze vessels which act as resonators in theatres. Further, 'it would be impossible for anyone to construct hydraulic machines (hydraulicas machinas) and their like[41] without some knowledge of music.'[42] And, again in connection with vase resonators, Vitruvius does not hesitate to devote a whole chapter to the theory of Greek music.[43]

His description of the hydraulic organ is long and sometimes obscure. However, the reader is duly warned how difficult it is for a Roman to cope with scientific terminology: 'Technical terms which have to be used in these unaccustomed contexts greatly obscure the overall meaning.'[44]

A close reading of the text relating to the organ reveals an instrument decidedly more sophisticated than that of Hero, with two pumps in place of one, more efficient valves, and above all an improved type of wind-chest capable of feeding up to eight sets of pipes, separately or together.

All of this supports the belief that Vitruvius's organ post-dates that of Hero. In the *Pneumatics*, what is described seems in effect to be the actual prototype of Ktesibios's own organ, almost an experimental model; while Vitruvius's organ is a real musical instrument, producing, the text says, 'reverberating sounds with multiple musical effects'. It thus becomes as important for musicologists as for historians of architecture to estimate as nearly as possible when the *De Architectura* was written. Here, however, as in the case of Hero, the issue is complicated by a number of chronological uncertainties.

[40] i, 43. [41] An allusion to the hydraulic organ.
[42] i, 1. [43] v, 4. [44] Book v, Preface.

It has long been held that Marcus Vitruvius Pollio, author of the *De Architectura*, lived in the time of Augustus, and died at an advanced age in A.D. 26. Various writers have attempted to find historical arguments to justify this belief, of which the following are two. In the third chapter of Book III, Vitruvius refers to 'the' stone-built theatre—i.e. Pompey's theatre —as though it were a unique building in Rome. We know that the theatre of Marcellus and Balbus was not consecrated until A.D. 12, so that the *De Architectura* must have been written prior to that date. Elsewhere in the work he mentions the town of Mazaca in Cappadocia: but according to Eutropius, Suidas, and St. Jerome, the name of this town was altered by Tiberius to Caesarea.[45]

As against this, other evidence has been suggested which would place Vitruvius several centuries later. Ussing felt that the book is too badly written to be a product of the Augustan age, and that both the style and the language reflect a certain decadence. To his mind the treatise was not written by the architect, but by another Vitruvius who lived under the Antonines, perhaps even in the third century.[46] Similarly V. Mortet[47] argues that the *De Architectura* is the work of a grammarian who had compiled Varro, at some undetermined date, probably in the reign of Titus. Today none of these arguments seems very convincing. It is risky and always debatable to try to date a writer from his style, especially when the writer happens to be a scientist. What we can say is that Vitruvius is cited three times by Pliny the Elder (died A.D. 79),[48] and that in his work on the Roman aqueducts, written in 98, Frontinus refers to Vitruvius 'the architect'.[49] Although there were other prominent men who bore the same name,[50] it is highly unlikely that this 'Vitruvius architectus' was not the author of the *De Architectura*. Servius notes only one Vitruvius, 'who wrote on architecture'.[51] Furthermore, a recent book seems to prove that he did, in fact, live in the Augustan age,[52] and two eminent specialists in this field, Professor P. Ruffel and Professor J. Soubiran, have just published an important restatement of the problem in which they establish—apparently definitively—that Vitruvius was beyond all doubt a member of Augustus's entourage.[53]

---

[45] *Vitruve*, ed. Maufras, Paris, 1847, Preface. See also A. Terquem, *La science romaine à l'époque d'Auguste* (Paris, 1885), pp. 6 ff.

[46] J. L. Ussing, *Betragtninger over 'Vitruvii de architectura libri decem'* (Copenhagen, 1896).

[47] *Revue archéologique* (1902), 41, pp. 39 ff.; (1904), pp. 222 ff.

[48] Sources of Books xvi, xxxv, and xxxvi. 'In his voluminibus', writes Pliny, 'auctorum nomina praetexui' (*Nat. Hist.*, i, Preface).

[49] *De aquis urbis Romae*, xxv, 1 and 2.

[50] P. Thielscher, in Pauly-Wissowa, art. 'Vitruvius', col. 420 ff.

[51] *Aen.*, vi, 43.

[52] F. Pellati, *La basilica di Fano e la formazione del trattato di Vitruvio*, Rendiconti della Pont. Accad. di Archeol. (Rome, 1947–9), xxiii–iv.

[53] 'Vitruve ou Mamurra?' *Pallas*, xi (Toulouse, 1962), part 2, pp. 143–50.

It will be remembered that Vitruvius, who is careful to mention by name all those who have written works devoted to machines, makes no reference to Hero of Alexandria, who probably lived after his time. It is therefore surprising that the organ described by Vitruvius is so much more advanced than that of Hero. However, as we shall see, the paradox is only apparent. Vitruvius is working from a copy of Ktesibios's *Commentaries*[54]—and so is Hero. But Hero is primarily a mechanic, whose preoccupation is with the principle of the machine. And indeed he may simply be reproducing the relevant chapter in the *Commentaries*. Vitruvius, on the other hand, is obviously describing in detail an instrument he has seen with his own eyes, and whose external appearance has impressed him. The vagueness of his text is partly due to the fact that he dwells on minor details—leaping dolphins, cylinder brackets shaped like ladders, and so on.[55] At the end of his description he declares that in order to understand how the organ really works it is better to see it for oneself—this is probably just what he had done. Here is the chapter in which he deals with the instrument.

I shall not fail to give a textual explanation, as brief and explicit as possible, of the theory of the hydraulis.

A bronze vessel shaped like an altar is fixed to a base of solid wood. Rising from this base, to right and left, are iron bars, put together like ladders. Between these bars are set bronze cylinders carefully turned on a lathe so as to fit exactly [the diameter] of the pistons.[56] To the centre point of these pistons iron shafts are attached, linked to other bars by pivots;[57] the pistons are sheathed in soft leather.[58] In addition, apertures some three fingers wide are provided in the flat upper surface [of the cylinder]. Just beside these apertures, bronze dolphins, mounted on pivots, are set, and suspended on chains from the snouts of these dolphins are valves, or cymbals (cymbala) which hang beneath the cylinder apertures.

Inside the 'altar', where the water is stored, is the air-vessel [pnigeus],

---

[54] He strongly implies this in the preface to book vii.

[55] The treatise, like that of Hero, was certainly accompanied by explanatory diagrams: 'Item ejus rei erit subscripta forma' (Preface to book ix).

[56] Literally: moving bases. See fig. 2.

[57] These shafts and bars are the cranking apparatus of the pump.

[58] The majority of translators write 'skins with their wool still on', which makes nonsense here. He is probably referring to soft, white leather. Pliny says that certain fish are described as 'lanati' because of the whiteness of their flesh (*Nat. Hist.*, ix, 17). The phrase has nearly always been misunderstood. In his translation of Vitruvius, Perrault admits that 'it is difficult to unravel this passage, for we can only guess at his purpose in wrapping the pistons in woolly skins . . .' The problem arises from the fact that the oldest manuscript (Brit. Mus, Harl. 2767) has 'involutos', which can only refer to 'ancones', and it is certainly hard to see what purpose there would have been in sheathing the pump handles in leather. Like Degering and Tittel, I think that the word must be 'involutis', referring to 'fundis'. This belief is also shared by F. Krohl, *Vitruvii de Architectura* (Leipzig, 1912), p. 240.

shaped like an inverted funnel. Its rim rests on lugs three fingers high, which maintain a small gap between the funnel and the base of the 'altar'. Furthermore, above the neck of the funnel is a small chest which supports the top part of the machine, called in Greek the 'musical canon'. All along this chest are channels, four in number if the instrument is tetrachordal, six if it is hexachordal, and eight if it is octochordal.[59] Each channel is fitted with a stopcock, having an iron handle.

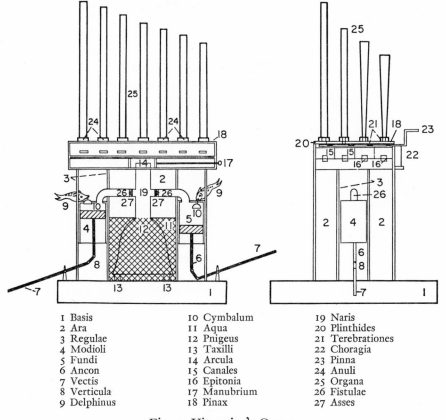

1 Basis	10 Cymbalum	19 Naris
2 Ara	11 Aqua	20 Plinthides
3 Regulae	12 Pnigeus	21 Terebrationes
4 Modioli	13 Taxilli	22 Choragia
5 Fundi	14 Arcula	23 Pinna
6 Ancon	15 Canales	24 Anuli
7 Vectis	16 Epitonia	25 Organa
8 Verticula	17 Manubrium	26 Fistulae
9 Delphinus	18 Pinax	27 Asses

Fig. 2. Vitruvius's Organ

When these handles are turned they make an opening from the chest directly into the channels. Also, for each of these channels the 'canon' has holes running crosswise, coinciding with apertures in the top board [of the chest], known in Greek as the 'pinax'.

Between this board and the canon, sliders are inserted, which are perforated with corresponding holes, and coated with oil to make them slide back and forth freely. [When closed] these sliders block the holes [in the

[59] These terms are borrowed from Greek musical theory, where they usually refer to the number of strings that go to make up the conjunct and disjunct systems (Bacchius Geron; *Introduction to the Art of Music*, 63).

board]; and they are called 'plinthides'.[60] Their back-and-forward movement shuts and opens communications.[61] These sliders are fitted with strong iron springs attached to the keys and any pressure on the keys immediately causes the sliders to move.

Above the board are holes through which the air coming from the channels can escape. Rings are soldered to these holes, into which the foot of each organ-pipe is set.

From the cylinders, unbroken tubes lead to the lateral apertures in the pnigeus, and from there to the apertures in the small chest. Well-turned valves are fitted to these orifices at the point where the tubes communicate with the cylinders.[62] The role of these valves is to prevent the air from returning once it has entered the small chest;[63] they cut off its retreat.

Thus when the levers are raised, the crank-rods draw the piston to the bottom of the cylinders; the dolphins on their pivots lower their cymbals, filling the empty cylinders with air. Then, when the crank-rods force the pistons up the cylinders, the impulsive force which causes the cymbals to seal off the upper exit, pushes the air trapped in the cylinders, causing it to move under pressure into the tubes, which lead it into the air-vessel [pnigeus] and, through the neck of the funnel, into the [small] chest.

A more vigorous movement of the levers sends a further supply of compressed air into the open stopcocks, filling the [corresponding] channels. And when the keys, operated by hand, continually cause the slides to move back and forth, alternately closing and opening the holes, loud sounds are produced, with an infinite variety of musical effects obtained by varying the rhythms.

I have done my utmost in this text to give a clear analysis of an obscure subject, but it is not easy to illustrate. This machine will readily be understood only by those who have some previous practical experience in this branch of knowledge. And any who find my description puzzling would certainly realize on seeing the instrument that it is constructed in a most curious and ingenious fashion.[64]

For all its obscurity, Vitruvius's exposition leaves out none of the important details. His style is somewhat stilted, as the author himself is well aware since he craves the reader's indulgence at the outset and again at the end.[65] But for those already familiar with the ὄργανον ὑδραυλικόν of

---

[60] 'Plinthid' is another term borrowed from geometry, where it is applied to a rectangular parallelopiped on a square base (Hero, *Stereometrica*, Theorem 9).

[61] Between the small chest and the pipes.

[62] Vitruvius expresses himself badly here. Are the valves situated exactly where the tubes enter the small chest or at the junction of the tubes and the lateral apertures in the pnigeus? Although this is mechanically unimportant, it is not made clear.

[63] These escape valves were omitted from Hero's account.

[64] *De Architectura*, x, 8.

[65] He adopts the same attitude at the beginning of ch. 4 of book v: 'I shall do my utmost (*ut potero*) to explain as clearly as possible what Aristoxenus has written.'

Hero, the mechanics of the instrument are easy to grasp. For the sake of greater clarity, the blowing mechanism and the wind-chest will be analysed separately.

1. *The Blowing Mechanism.* The principle here is the same as in Hero's text, and from the evidence it would seem that Aristocles, Philo, Hero, and Vitruvius all derived their information from the same source, the *Commentaries* of Ktesibios. Here, however, the practice is rather different. Two cylinders operate alternately, as in the fire pump. Hero's organ has only one, as has the instrument described by Aristocles—Athenaeus tells us that only one man was involved in pumping the air. These cylinders are placed to right and left of the cistern, each attached to a double metal frame shaped like a ladder, and fixed to a strong wooden base. The cylinders are of bronze, and according to Frontinus tubes of this metal are rigid and are not easily bent.[66] They are carefully turned on a lathe, and their internal surface is certainly oiled, like the cylinders on Ktesibios's pump. The pistons which slide up and down are rendered airtight by their leather sheath, easily replaceable when worn. This represents a definite improvement on Hero's instrument. The crankshafts, briefly described, are perfectly straightforward. The cylinders would appear to be cast in one piece, and their base is not soldered.

The upper openings in the cylinders have a wider diameter—three fingers or approximately 5 cm. Taking into account the proportions implied in the iconography, I am convinced that each cylinder had only one aperture, capable of admitting a more than adequate volume of air, as experiments have shown. The reason for Vitruvius's use of the plural 'foramina' is that he has just described more than one cylinder. The apertures are closed by valves whose diameter is perforce greater. Because of the cupped shape of these valves they are here referred to as cymbals. They are certainly more effective than Hero's platysmatia, having greater mobility. They are held in place by a short chain running from the centre of their cup to the dolphins' snouts, and the dolphins themselves, made of bronze, pivot on an axis perpendicular to their length. This axis is obviously placed nearer to the head than the tail, so that the centre of gravity is further back. In fact, these figurines act as counterpoise weights, holding back the cymbal at the lowest point of its course, and the weight of the animal's tail causes the valve to rise again when the piston's sucking action has stopped. The result is that these dolphins appear to plunge and leap while the organ is playing, an effect which doubtless amused or intrigued the audience. Nevertheless, it is surprising that Vitruvius makes so much of what is purely a minor detail. And why should a dolphin be chosen as an ornamental counterweight for the valve? There are two possible reasons, the first being that for the ancients

[66] *De aquis*, xxxvi.

the dolphin was the symbol of the watery element, and appears on the coins of a number of maritime cities.[67] Its presence on the hydraulic organ, where water played a key role, was thus perfectly logical. The second reason is that the animal, which was greatly prized in antiquity, was thought to possess not only feelings of maternal love and philanthropy, but in addition a pronounced taste for music—as illustrated by the legend of Arion—and especially, it was said, for the sound of the hydraulic organ, or so we are told by Pliny the Elder.[68] Hero describes a theatre automaton on which dolphins are shown sporting round a ship.[69] Undoubtedly, Vitruvius refers to an instrument he has just seen, though it would be wrong to infer from what he says that dolphins were always used to ornament the valves on hydraulic organs.

In the upper end of the cylinder, near the air inlet, there was another opening of which Vitruvius makes no mention, and the tube that brought the air to the neck of the pnigeus led into this. The escape valves, whose position is not specified, are certainly different from the inlet valves, and are not shaped like cymbals, but tapered like cones. Indeed, the instructions specify that they should be perfectly rounded on a lathe. It is not known exactly where these valves were located. Perhaps they worked vertically; if they did, their own weight would have eliminated the need for any return spring.

It would seem that Vitruvius's pnigeus is also hemispherical and funnel-shaped.[70] Its free edge is not notched, as in Hero's organ, and it rests simply on cubical lugs. Nothing is said as to how the pnigeus was fixed within the cistern, but it must have been attached in some way or it would have risen under the pressure of the air.

What happened, then, when the organ-blowers plied their levers alternately, was that one cylinder emptied while the other filled. If the pumping was carried out to a regular rhythm, the water level in the cistern did not vary a great deal. The pressure remained more or less constant, and the sounds coming from the pipes could be even.

2. *The Wind-Chest and Manual.* Vitruvius's wind-chest is particularly intriguing in that it reveals a remarkable technical improvement which would enable the performer to make use of one or more ranks of pipes at will. It would be interesting to know the name of the man behind this innovation.

[67] J. Cotte, *Poissons et animaux aquatiques au temps de Pline* (Paris, 1944), pp. 19–20.

[68] *Nat. Hist.*, ix, 8.

[69] Περὶ στατῶν αὐτομάτων, xxviii.

[70] In the store-rooms of the Museo Nazionale in Naples I was able to examine a bronze infundibulum (Cat. no. 73838) rounded in shape, whose diameter at its widest point is 22 cm. Four small funnels of similar shape are preserved in the Antiquarium of Pompeii. Vitruvius's pnigeus was probably much the same as these domestic implements.

Ktesibios can have had nothing to do with it, for Hero, always fascinated by new mechanical devices, would not have missed the opportunity to describe one so ingenious. However, the technical terms transcribed by Vitruvius—κανὼν μουσικός, πίναξ, τετράχορδος—suggest that this invention was once again the work of a Greek engineer. Organists must quickly have felt the need for different and strongly contrasting shades of sound; but it is not known precisely when the new type of wind-chest made its appearance.

This apparatus allowed the player to sound, separately or together, various sets of timbres and pitch-levels: reeds, open or closed flues, principal, octave, and fifth. From this point the instrument had at its disposal a potentially rich sound palette, and moved towards a new and highly individual aesthetic character.

Vitruvius's wind-chest is of a certain complexity. The air from the pnigeus does not, as in Hero's organ, come in contact with the small regulators operated by the keys. Instead it enters separate compartments running lengthwise along the wind-chest, one for each rank of pipes—four, six, or eight, according to the size of the instrument. Each compartment communicates with the 'small chest' by means of a valve with an iron handle, so that the air enters only those which are open. When the organist wishes to bring a particular set of pipes into use he opens the corresponding valve instead of pulling out draw-stops as in the modern instrument.

These compartments, which Vitruvius calls longitudinal channels, are surmounted by their respective ranks of pipes. Between the upper board, or pinax, which supports the pipes, and the top of the channels, are movable sliders similar to those of Hero. But instead of one hole, these have four, six, or eight, exactly corresponding to the lower ends of all the pipes sounding the same note of the scale. These sliders, or plinthides, are greased to reduce friction and help to make them airtight. Here the return strings and horn spatulas are replaced by iron springs which fulfil the same function—clearly a simplification in the regulating mechanism. The text contains no description of the manual with keys.

This wind-chest, though perfectly workable mechanically, is arranged the opposite way to today's equivalent, in which the air reaches the grooves after the player has depressed the keys which open the valves; only then is it directed to the various ranks of pipes by means of the registers, small regulators identical with those used in antiquity, but running cross-wise. Here, on the contrary, the air is first of all channelled towards the required set of pipes, and the action of the keys affects only the foot of the pipes. The reason for abandoning this system in the course of the Middle Ages was undoubtedly that as more and more pipes were added, the sliders became inordinately long, and consequently too hard to move. Probably another reason was that the keys, which had to remain on the same axis as the slides, could not be set closely enough together to allow for any real virtuosity in finger technique.

Vitruvius does not go into any detail on the subject of the organ pipes, stating simply that the foot of each fitted into a ring soldered to the roof of the chest. The iconography shows that a double transverse bar, slightly oblique, held the pipes upright: but Vitruvius gives no indication as to their nature. He describes them neither as 'tibiae' nor as 'fistulae', but simply as 'organa', that is to say 'any musical instrument', reeds or flues. Both types were doubtless used conjointly.

As we shall see, the organist always played upright, propped on a kind of high stool not described here, and placed behind the water cistern. His head and shoulders were seen above the tops of the pipes. From the positions shown in the illustrations, it is absolutely certain that he played with both hands, and was thus able to execute relatively quick passages with a wide variety of rhythms.

CHAPTER THREE

꒰ⱳ꒱

The Graeco-Roman Organ: the Evidence of the Texts

TO THE MIDDLE OF THE FIRST CENTURY A.D.

It is mainly from literary and historical sources, and from inscriptions, that we know in outline how the organ spread through the Western Roman Empire[1]—this is why it is important to study and interpret the relevant texts. But only the technical accounts of Hero and Vitruvius deal specifically with the organ. Otherwise, references to the organ are generally quite incidental: it may be a comparison inserted in the interests of rhetoric; or a piquant detail designed to add a picturesque touch to a dull occasion; or a grammatical point which some pedagogue is attempting to elucidate. Thus it is not uncommon, as we shall see, for a poet or historian to let fall a few words which shed valuable light on technical details of the pipe organ, its external appearance, or its use.

It was during the second half of the third century B.C., as I have endeavoured to prove, that Ktesibios conceived and built his hydraulic organ. The inventor's own wife, whose name was Thaïs, learned how to play it, and thus became the first organist in history. A few decades later—a generation or two at the most—the engineer Philo of Byzantium briefly recalls the principle of the hydraulis in his great encyclopedia of engineering. This much we know. But did Thaïs train any pupils? Was the instrument cultivated thereafter, and did it spread rapidly through the Greek world? Or did it remain a museum piece, a mechanical curiosity in a show-case to be exhibited to scholars passing through Alexandria? No definite information is available, and indeed there is here a considerable gap in the history of the organ. It is likely, however, that the instrument was played, that soon more players mastered it, and that gradually a circle of enthusiasts and informed listeners was formed. For the first reference to the organ, a hundred and fifty years after Ktesibios, is not just a quotation from some poet or encyclopedist, but a long inscription discovered at Delphi, recording the

---

[1] The organ in the Eastern Empire is the subject of Chapter X.

achievements of a player of the hydraulic organ named Antipatros. The text is worth quoting in full, since it is interesting for more reasons than one:

In the archonship of Cleandros, son of Timon; Polites, son of Asandros, Euclid, son of Heraclides, Dio, son of Callias, and Theoxenos, son of Polyon being members of the Boule, the following was agreed by the citizens of Delphi in full assembly.

Given that an embassy had been despatched by the city to Antipatros, son of Breucos and a citizen of Eleuthernes, a player upon the hydraulic organ (ὕδραυλος), and that this man arrived in Delphi at the invitation of the archons of the city; and given that he competed for a space of two days, covering himself with glory in a remarkable manner worthy of the god[2] and of both the city of Eleuthernes and our own city, by virtue of which he was crowned victor in the contest [and was rewarded with] a bronze statue, together with all the other tokens of honour, for his overwhelming performance in honour of the god. . . .

For these reasons, a decree was passed, in the name of Good Fortune, to sing the praises of Antipatros, son of Breucos, of Eleuthernes, performer on the hydraulic organ, for his reverence and devotion to the god, for the resolution he manifests towards fulfilling his art, and for his goodwill towards our city.

All honour, too, to his brother Cryton, son of Breucos, of Eleuthernes, and may the city grant to them and to their descendants special status (proxenia) and priority in consulting the oracle and approaching the tribunal, the right of asylum, exemption from all financial burdens, the right to the best seats at all the contests organized by the city, the right to acquire land and houses in Delphi, and any further privileges enjoyed by foreigners of special status and benefactors of the city. Let the archons send them the finest gifts, and invite them and their companions to the prytaneum for the city's common banquet. And lastly, let the archons see to it that the text of this decree be inscribed in the most conspicuous place in the Temple of Apollo, and let them send a delegation to the city of Eleuthernes to inform them of this.[3]

The name of the archon dates this inscription to the year 90 B.C. It provides a most important piece of information: the hydraulic organ was one of the instruments eligible to compete in the musical festival at Delphi, at least at that period. This means that the instrument was already widely known, and it must be assumed that the spectators appreciated its sound and its musical potential, since the competition lasted two whole days. At the beginning of the first century B.C. there must therefore have been a certain number of virtuoso organists in existence, and the fact that an artist quite foreign to the city—Eleuthernes was a town in Crete—should have made the journey in order to take part in the contest at the request of the

---

[2] Apollo.
[3] W. Dittenberger, *Sylloge Inscriptionum Graecarum*, 3rd ed. (Leipzig, 1917), ii, pp. 737–8.

municipality of Delphi, proves that his reputation was already established. We are told nothing of the other entrants, but we may assume that if they ventured to challenge the Cretan virtuoso they must have possessed a good technique and a comprehensive repertoire. A further significant point emerges from this text. Here we have Greeks, experienced and critical, connoisseurs in the full sense of the word[4] even in those decadent times, who were prepared to spend two days listening to the sound of the hydraulic organ, and whose enthusiasm permeates the words of their decree. These people, who were familiar with the subtleties of performances on the aulos and the cithara, clearly appreciated the new instrument with its fixed notes, which exercised an entirely different kind of charm. Was it perhaps the grandeur and authority of its sounds and the vigour of its rhythms which won the hearts of the citizens of Delphi? Were they susceptible, as we are today, to the magic power of the many pipes? At all events they were not niggardly with their rewards. The successful organist had his bronze statue, and the text of the decree was inscribed on the Temple of Apollo—a signal honour. Thus the Delphic inscription shows clearly that a hundred years before the birth of Christ the organ was already known and admired by Greek audiences, and was even eligible to participate in the musical festivals held in the town of Delphi.

These facts help to explain an outburst of Cicero's made less than fifty years later in his *Tusculan Orations*. In the third oration he sets out to show that the wise man is not accessible to grief, and to support his thesis he rejects the ideas of Epicurus, who held that to avoid grief all one had to do was use the imagination or memory to conjure up thoughts of the *res voluptariae*—love, gluttony, or music. Cicero, deriding this facile hedonism, condemns such a philosophy:

If you see someone dear to you prostrated by grief, would you offer him a sturgeon[5] rather than a treatise of Socrates? Would you urge him to listen to the voice of the hydraulic organ (hydrauli voces) rather than that of Plato? Would you have him feast his eyes on flower-beds? Or thrust a bouquet of flowers under his nose? Or burn perfume for him? . . . Such are the remedies advocated by Epicurus; [his book] is a manual of Dissipation.[6]

The sense of the argument is clear:[7] the music of the hydraulic organ is

---

4 The keenness of a Greek audience's ears, which detected even the slightest inaccuracies in intonation or rhythm, is discussed by I. Düring in *Ptolemaios und Porphyrios über die Musik* (Göteborg, 1934), pp. 143 ff.

5 The ancients normally considered the sturgeon to be a most expensive dish: Martial, *Epig.*, xiii, 91; Athenaeus, vii, 12; Horace, *Sat.*, ii, 4, 46-7; Macrobius, *Saturn.*, iii, xiv, 1-9; Pliny, *Nat. Hist.*, ix, 27.

6 *Tusculanes*, iii, xviii, 43-4.

7 Though A. Cellier and H. Bachelin appear to have misunderstood it in their work *L'Orgue* (Paris, 1932), p. 62.

listed among the most subtle of pleasures. Thus the appreciative comments of the guests at *The Learned Banquet* would seem to be entirely justified. Moreover, if we remember that Cicero lived in Greece from 79 to 77 B.C., it is permissible to assume that he may have heard the new instrument there, though it was still almost unknown in Rome, or at least that he was aware of the popularity of organ concerts with the public. In any case, this passage from the *Tusculan Orations* is extremely valuable in that it is the first piece of Latin evidence for the existence of Ktesibios's instrument.

It is not known exactly when the hydraulic organ made its appearance in Rome. Could it perhaps be the new invention to which Lucretius alludes in an enigmatic line from the *De Natura Rerum*? The poet observes that, in his day, there are marked advances in several of the arts, and adds: 'Recently, the makers of musical instruments (organici) have succeeded in producing delightful music (melicos sonores).'[8] It is not improbable that the reference is to the sound of the organ, and indeed it would be very surprising if someone as receptive as Lucretius were not interested in Ktesibios's invention.

If Virgil is indeed the author of the *Aetna* poem,[9] then the first Latin document containing an undoubted reference to the actual working of the hydraulis's wind machine dates from only a few years after the composition of the *De Natura Rerum*. In this work the grumblings of the volcano are explained as follows: enormous masses of water, resulting from infiltration, compress the air which is trapped in the earth's crevices, and this air, moving along its narrow subterranean channels, produces powerful and sustained noises. This same phenomenon, says the author, is responsible for the music of the organ and the howl of hydraulic sirens:

In great theatres, a dome-shaped instrument (cortina)[10] creates the music by means of water. Melodious with its variety of notes, it sings regulated by the performer's art, as a stream of air is propelled by water pressed up from below, as though with an oar.[11]

In these few lines there is a valuable reference to the presence of the organ in 'great theatres'. It would be intriguing to know exactly what part it played in the musical side of the performance. Did it provide a prelude? Was it played in the intervals, or used to accompany songs? Such questions are as yet unanswered. The actual principle of the hydraulic wind mechanism is explained very briefly indeed: however, the adjective 'irriguo' suggests the movement of the water, stirred up by the air coming from the cylinders;

---

[8] v, 334.

[9] See J. Vessereau, *L'Etna* (Paris, 1923), Introduction, pp. xiii ff.

[10] The cistern of the hydraulic organ. R. Hildebrandt (*Rhetorische Hydraulik*, Philologus, lxiv, 1906, p. 428) interprets this as Apollo's tripod, used in a wider sense.

[11] *Aetna*, 295–7.

and the verb 'subremigat', as Hildebrandt rightly points out,[12] seems to imply that the pumping is done by the organist himself, perhaps using his feet. We shall return to this problem of how the wind mechanism was operated.

The author of the *Aetna* poem is a little more specific when describing how the siren works:

For just as the shore re-echoes long to the sound of the tuneful Triton; the instrument functions by the pressure of the mass of water [collected within it], and of the air which is forcibly agitated, and trumpet-like (bucina) it emits long, booming notes. . . .[13]

This 'Triton Canorus' is probably based on the same principle as the trumpet toy described by Hero of Alexandria, where a mass of water compressed a quantity of air sealed in a tank. At a given moment the air, escaping under pressure, caused the reed of the apparatus to vibrate strongly. It was probably a similar instrument which was heard in the course of the sea fight given by Claudius in 53, a 'trumpet blown by a silver Triton which had been made to rise up from the midst of the lake by a mechanical device'.[14] This type of siren, of which a complete account has survived in Arabic, must clearly have had a pump made on the same pattern as that of the hydraulis.

The process of compressing air by a mass of water, invented by Ktesibios, was a constant source of wonder. Seneca refers to it in his *Naturales quaestiones*: 'For what sound is there without the compressing of air? Horns, trumpets, and those instruments which by means of water pressure (aquarum pressura) produce a more powerful sound than any that our mouths might utter—are not their effects explained by compressed air?'[15] Clearly Seneca knew of the hydraulic organ, though this is hardly surprising in view of the fact that, as we shall see, his pupil Nero was passionately fond of it. A further reference to the instrument occurs in a passage from the *De beneficiis*: '[God] has invented [countless sounds] that will provide melody, some produced by our own breath, others by outside means.'[16]

On the other hand, it is curious that the great encyclopedia of Pliny the Elder contains not even the briefest account of the organ, though Ktesibios is included as having invented pneumatic science and the science of hydraulic instruments. As far as the organ is concerned, Pliny merely repeats a popular

---

[12] op. cit., p. 433.

[13] *Aetna*, 292–4.

[14] Suetonius, *Claudius*, xxi. We know from Macrobius (*Saturnales*,i, viii, 4) that there were tritons blowing buccines on the roof of the Temple of Saturn in Rome: but perhaps they were simply decorative motifs.

[15] *Quaest. Nat.*, ii, vi, 5.

[16] *De Beneficiis*, iv, 6. It was A. Machabey who first drew attention to these two passages from Seneca ('Etudes de musicologie pré-médiévale', *Revue de Musicologie*, no. 56, November 1935, p. 232).

belief: 'Dolphins are susceptible to music and its harmonious sounds, but they take especial delight in the sound of the hydraulic organ (hydrauli sono).'[17] This tradition doubtless originated as a result of concerts given on board ship. Suetonius[18] tells us that Caligula often embarked a complete orchestra on one of the big galleys, where there was dancing and feasting, and it is quite likely that the organ featured in this type of gala.[19]

As we have seen, Vitruvius devotes an entire chapter of his *De Architectura* to a technical description of the organ, which he obviously admires. And Hero of Alexandria, who probably lived a generation or two after Vitruvius, is responsible for a less graphic but very accurate account, the text of which also has been translated above.

★   ★   ★

From the middle of the first century A.D., therefore, the hydraulic organ was a familiar instrument in the Roman world, and had passed the stage of being merely a novelty from overseas, since it could be seen and heard in Rome it-self. It was popular with theatre audiences and Imperial high society had already taken it up, Nero himself being, as we know, a particularly keen amateur. Nero was a real devotee of music, and it would be wrong to see him as nothing more than a third-rate dilettante greedy for applause. Since his youth he had made a serious study of the art under the best teachers, one of whom was the celebrated citharist Terpnos. He submitted daily to the most strenuous exercises in an attempt to improve his voice;[20] and he could perform on the lyre, often accompanying his own singing. In addition he wrote music,[21] and his melodies were sung in the suburban taverns of Rome.[22] Suetonius tells us that politics, and even his personal safety, took second place to all this, and when Vindex gave the signal for the revolt in Gaul, the Emperor was more put out by being described as a 'bad cithara player' than by the attack on his throne. Even at times of crisis he was engrossed in his organ studies, and when the situation deteriorated, 'he summoned a number of leading citizens to his house, and after consulting them briefly spent the remainder of the day showing them his hydraulic organs, of a new and hitherto unknown type which he demonstrated in detail, explaining the principle and complexity of each one and assuring them that he would shortly exhibit them all in the theatre, "if Vindex allowed it".'[23]

[17] *Nat. Hist.*, ix, 8.
[18] *Caligula*, xxxvii.
[19] Elsewhere Pliny claims (viii, 50) that stags can be caught by playing the fistula pastoralis, while Plutarch says stags and horses may be enticed by the sound of the syrinx and the aulos (*De Sol. Anim.*, iii).
[20] Suetonius, *Nero*, xx.
[21] Suetonius, xliii; Tacitus, *Annales*, xiv, 15.
[22] Philostratus, *Life of Apollonius of Tyana*, iv, 39.   [23] Suetonius, *Nero*, xli.

This passage contains an important chronological clue for organ historians. Since Vindex's revolt took place in 68, we may assume that the new type of instrument had not yet been revealed to the public at that date. And if we recall that Nero's journey to Greece had taken place the previous year, it is reasonable to suppose that this organ, still unknown in Rome, had been brought back there in the Emperor's baggage, and that he must have seen and heard it while abroad. Moreover, Suetonius's account would appear to imply that Nero's favourite instrument was also popular with the theatre-going public, thus corroborating the excerpt from the *Aetna* poem quoted above.

The scene described by Suetonius is also related in Cassius Dio. 'One night he issued a hasty summons to the most prominent among the senators and knights, as though to communicate to them some information relating to the current situation. "I have discovered", he said to them—and here I quote his very words—"how to make the hydraulic organ (ἡ ὕδραυλις) play louder and more melodiously".'[24]

If this narrative were authentic, we should have to conclude that Nero had a detailed knowledge of the secrets of organ-building. However, Cassius Dio's report seems suspect. The very fact that he situates this strange incident in the middle of the night inevitably recalls how Caligula sent an urgent summons to three of the most important consulars—again during the night—only to display himself to them in an actor's tunic, perform a dance to the sound of the tibia, and disappear without further explanation.[25] It seems obvious that we have a case of duplication here.[26] Be that as it may, the organ Nero was playing at that moment was a new type of instrument, capable of producing a more powerful tone and a more varied range of timbres. We may wonder whether the new machine was perhaps an improved version of the multi-channelled wind-chest described by Vitruvius; but it is difficult to see how the Emperor could have passed himself off as the inventor of this new apparatus, since it was beneath any musician to evince any interest in mechanical matters. Nero's real passion was for playing on the organ. 'Towards the end of his life,' says Suetonius,[27] 'he declared publicly that if his condition of life did not change, he would participate in the games to mark his victory . . . as a performer on the hydraulic organ (hydraula), the tibia, and the bagpipe.'[28]

The organ was not, however, solely a theatre instrument. If we accept

[24] *Hist. Rom.*, lxiii, 26.
[25] Suetonius, *Caligula*, liv.
[26] We do not have Tacitus's account of Nero's later years, since the *Annales* do not go beyond the year 66. The rest of the text is lost.
[27] *Nero*, liv.
[28] The *scaenica organa* he proposes to take with him on his expedition against Vindex are probably not organs, but theatre machines (*Nero*, xliv).

that the poet Petronius lived at this time,[29] then it must already have been an established custom for the music of the pipe organ to fill the amphitheatre during the gladiatorial combats. This emerges from a scene in the *Satyricon* describing Trimalchio's dinner, during which a servant carves the meat in time to the music:[30] 'The carver appeared instantly, moving in time to the music, thrusting with his knife at the victuals like an essedarius fighting to the accompaniment of a water-organ.'[31]

It seems to me that this text gives a clear indication that the role of the organ in the amphitheatre was not so much to please the unexacting crowd as to accentuate the rhythm of the various movements of the combatants at given moments. Indeed, the passage states specifically that the gladiator on the chariot, the essedarius,[32] must, like Trimalchio's major-domo, time his movements carefully to suit the rhythm of the music: 'ad symphoniam gesticulatus'. If the essedarius manipulated his weapons in time to the cadences of the organ, this implies that the instrument must have been loud enough to be heard above the noise of a chariot going at full speed, for we know that in this type of combat the gladiator never left his vehicle.[33] Furthermore, iconographical evidence confirms this very special function carried out by the hydraulic organ in the amphitheatre, whatever the category of gladiator involved.

THE SECOND CENTURY A.D.

By the second century A.D. the pipe organ had become a part of city life in the Roman world. It was an object of luxury, clearly much less common than the aulos and the cithara, but familiar to the musical theorists. 'Naturally,' writes Nicomachus of Gerasa, 'the stringed instruments . . . contrast with the wind: auloi, trumpets, syrinxes, hydraules . . .'[34]

By this time these hydraules have numerous sets of pipes, varied timbres and multiple notes, at least so Tertullian (160–225) tells us; and the following passage suggests what seems to be a very large instrument:

[29] This has been questioned (E. V. Marmorale, *La questione Petroniana*, Bari, 1948), but it appears to be an established fact (A. Ernout, *Pétrone*, Paris, 1950, pp. vii ff.; P. Veyne, 'Trimalchio Maecenatianus', *Hommages à Albert Grenier* (coll. Latomus, vol. lviii), 1962, p. 1624).

[30] Rich citizens employed major-domos who were also dancers ('structores saltantes': Juvenal, *Sat.*, v, 120–5) and at Trimalchio's house the banqueting tables were wiped to the sound of music (*Satyr.*, xlvii) and cleared by dancers leaping about while an orchestra played (xxxvi). Athenaeus tells us that the Tyrhennians kneaded their bread and whipped their slaves to the rhythm of the aulos (xii, 14).

[31] *Satyricon*, xxxvi, trans. W. Arrowsmith.

[32] On the essedarius, see the well-documented article of G. Lafaye in Daremberg-Saglio, 'Essedarius'.

[33] Seneca, *Ad. Lucil.*, iii, 29, 6.

[34] *Handbook of Harmonics*, iv, 20.

Consider the stupendous achievement of Archimedes: I mean the hydraulic organ. All these bits and pieces, joints, conduits for the sounds, stops for the notes, all its changing timbres and ranks of reed pipes—and all forming a single whole.[35]

Unless Tertullian is exaggerating—and his eloquence should be treated with caution—the organ thus described is of large proportions and has many pipes. By bringing together the terms 'tot commercia modorum' and 'tot acies tibiarum', Bellermann suggested that each set of pipes was tuned to a specific mode[36]—Lydian, Phrygian, Dorian, etc. It seems to me that this interpretation is indefensible, for if such a system had been used, many pipes would have been needlessly duplicated in view of the number of notes common to the various modes. In any case, there is no serious evidence to support this theory, which is based solely on the fanciful translation of the word 'modi' by 'modes', in the modern sense. A more rational rendering of 'tot commercia modorum' would be 'exchange of notes', implying sets of pipes corresponding at the octave and the double octave; an interpretation which seems to be borne out by the iconography.

Another striking feature of this text, which is otherwise strictly doctrinal in tone, is the sincere admiration of a layman for this ingenious, complex piece of machinery which had already aroused the enthusiasm of an expert such as Vitruvius. We can readily forgive Tertullian the confusion which makes him credit the illustrious Archimedes with the invention of the instrument. However, one important aspect of the text is that the Christian orator gives the impression that he is speaking of something he has seen with his own eyes. Perhaps this happened on his visit to Rome, probably in 204, during which he witnessed the games held by Septimius Severus. Tertullian's near contemporary Origen (185–253) was evidently also familiar with the organ. Comparing different instruments with spiritual things he says: 'The organ is the Church of God, comprising the contemplative and the active souls.'[37] Conceivably he is referring to the contrast between the flue pipes, with their sweet, veiled sound, and the more vibrant tones of the reed pipes.

THE FIRST APPEARANCE OF THE BELLOWS ORGAN

At this point it is necessary to go back a little in order to examine an event of capital importance in the history of the instrument. This is the appearance of the bellows organ, known somewhat confusingly today as the pneumatic organ. Up to now we have looked exclusively at the hydraulic organ, a remarkable but complicated machine, heavy and difficult to transport. Who

[35] *De Anima*, xiv (Migne, *P.L.*, ii, 669).
[36] Bellermann, quoted by Gastoué in *L'Orgue en France*, p. 17.
[37] *PG*, xii, *In Psalm CL*, 1684.

had the idea of replacing the pistons and the water cistern by a simple bellows—and when was this first done? It would be gratifying to know the answers to these questions, which are particularly vital in view of the fact that the new system gradually came to supersede the older apparatus. It has been stated, without any supporting evidence, that the pneumatic organ probably antedated the hydraulic organ;[38] but in fact there is no known text or monument to prove that this small instrument existed before the second century A.D.

As we have seen, the wind mechanism of the organum hydraulicum is in two distinct parts—a machine to produce the air, made up of pumps and tubes, and a pressure regulator comprising the cistern and pnigeus. Obviously there would have been nothing in this instrument's structure to prevent anyone from replacing the pumps by bellows of adequate strength, though the organ would still have been a water organ. Such a machine did exist, at least later on, for an Arabic text, translated from the Greek, analyses an instrument of this type, especially designed to give out powerful and sonorous signals in time of war.[39] But it seems that from an early date attempts were made to eliminate the liquid element also, and construct a new instrument having neither pumps nor water cistern, and conceived on a smaller scale so as to be more easily moved from one place to another. And so the small pneumatic organ came quietly into being, with its more modest volume adapted not to the amphitheatre but to private houses.

Though the pneumatic organ was probably already in existence during the first years of the Empire, it is hardly surprising that it should have occasioned such sparse and belated comment. The interest stirred up by the hydraulis was largely due to the complexity of its mechanism and the mysterious role of the water, which aroused the admiration of scholars and baffled everyone else. But there was no magic about the pneumatic organ. The bellows fit directly into the wind-chest and the workings of the instrument are as simple to understand as those of a set of bagpipes. A little organ of this type has survived to this day—the Aquincum organ, whose archaeological remains will be examined in detail in another chapter.

Although it seems highly probable, if not certain, that the pneumatic organ must from the outset have had a compensatory device to control the air pressure, it was not until several centuries later, with the development of an improved regulating system, that bellows were capable of feeding large-scale instruments. For this reason the pneumatic organ was always on a rather modest scale in ancient times. Julius Pollux, a grammarian of the second century A.D., makes a clear distinction between the hydraulic and the bellows instruments.

[38] Farmer, op. cit., p. 21.
[39] The Muristos organ will be dealt with in Chapter XI.

In contrast, the Tyrrhenian aulos[40] looks like an inverted syrinx. Its pipes are of bronze, and receive their air supply from below.[41] The smaller of these instruments is fed by bellows; while in the larger instrument, a current of air is produced by water forced upwards. The second instrument has the capacity to produce multiple notes *(πολύφωνός)*, and the voice of its bronze pipes is bolder *(ἰταμώτερον)*.[42]

The first point here is the curious title he gives to the organ—Tyrrhenian aulos. Pollus has just listed various types of aulos, without, however, actually describing them: Theban, Thracian, Syrian, Lydian, Egyptian.[43] But why should the organ, whether hydraulic or pneumatic, be qualified in this instance as a Tyrrhenian aulos? It is probable that the warlike character of the Etruscan trumpet, so often attested, is here equated with the cruel and martial role played by the hydraulis in gladiatorial combats.[44] In any case, Pollux's distinction is a real one. The smaller organ is the bellows organ; the sound issuing from its pipes is weak and it produces only a limited number of notes. The larger organ is the hydraulic organ, with its water compressor and its multiple pipes which give out a peal of sound. Pollux was, of course, an expert on contemporary terminology, and he is employing what was no doubt established usage.

The bellows of the pneumatic organ were most likely smaller versions of those used by blacksmiths, and may well have looked like those still used with open fires. Three lines from Ausonius, which are frequently quoted, give a good description of this familiar object whose valve alternately traps and releases the air accumulated between two beechwood boards.[45] It is a type of bellows often represented in ancient pictures.[46] This kind of wind mechanism offered decided advantages. Apart from being lighter and less expensive, it meant fewer worries about such things as leaks, rust, or frost in winter. It is a great pity that as yet no Roman iconographic material

[40] He is referring to the organ, as the rest of the passage shows.

[41] The syrinx is played with the lips of the pipes uppermost, while those of the organ point downwards. Hence the expression 'upside-down syrinx' *(ἀντεστραμμένη σύριγγι)*.

[42] *Onomasticon*, iv, 69–70.

[43] The phrase 'Tyrrhenus tubae clangor' is in Virgil *(Aen.,* viii, 526): The invention of the vertical trumpet was frequently attributed to the Etruscans. Silius Italicus also refers to the 'tuba tyrrhenea' *(Pun.,* ii, 19). This 'Tyrrhenian trumpet' *(τυρρηνῆς σάλπιγγος)* was essentially a military instrument *(Anth. Pal.,* vi, 350); the 'Tyrrhenian aulos' to which Antipater of Sidon refers (ibid., vi, 151) is only a war trumpet.

[44] See below, pp. 75 ff.

[45] *Mosella*, 267–9: Sic ubi fabriles exercet spiritus ignes
Accipit alterno cohibetque foramine ventos
Lanea fagineis alludens parma cavernis.

[46] F. Liceti, *De lucernis antiquorum* (Venice, 1652), pp. 739–42, figs. 1 and 2. See also Fr. Kretzschmer, *Bilddokumente Römischer Technik* (Düsseldorf, 1958), p. 13, fig. 13.

showing the pneumatic organ with its bellows has come to light. The drawing picked out by Mersenne[47] and thought to depict such an instrument, complete with organist and blower, in fact refers to a goldsmith's work-shop.[48]

Experiments reveal that, taking into account the substantial leaks inherent in a wind-chest with sliders, sets of ordinary bellows are incapable of supplying even an organ of the most modest dimensions with an adequate supply of air, for it is wellnigh impossible to avoid a complete failure of pressure inside the wind-chest during the return action of the bellows. The reconstruction of the Aquincum organ, based on the remains of the original instrument and now in the Aquincum museum, has two bellows which are manifestly inadequate. The sounds produced are unstable and lacking in musical character, despite the diminutive size of the wind-chest, whose capacity is not more than 2·5 cubic decimetres. I am therefore convinced that the Roman pneumatic organ must have had some kind of regulating device in lieu of the water element of Ktesibios's system. It could have taken the form of a simple reservoir made of some flexible material, such as a small leather bladder whose own weight would have been sufficient to force the air into the wind-chest between each stroke of the bellows. How-ever, since bladders and bellows were made of highly perishable materials, it would be too much to hope that archaeologists might one day unearth some more precise evidence of their construction.

It should be said, at this point, that the pipe instrument housed in the Museo Nazionale in Naples is probably not an organ in the sense in which we have defined it.[49]

THE THIRD CENTURY A.D.

From the end of the second and the first half of the third century A.D. we have three texts bearing on the history of the organ, each important in its own way. These texts testify to the instrument's popularity and to its wide distribution at a time when the Empire, having failed to maintain its former power, had passed to the defensive. While its thinly manned frontiers had already been breached by the first invaders, the organ was more in evidence and more popular than ever, to judge from the lively passage from *The Learned Banquet* quoted earlier. Its author, Athenaeus of Naucratis, who may still be admired for the wide range of his documentation, gives a number of details of capital importance for the musicologist. He tells us that even at that time the inhabitants of Alexandria were proud of the fact that their

[47] *Harmonie Universelle*, p. 387.
[48] I have been quite unable to trace this monument at the Villa Albani in Rome, where Mersenne claims he saw it.
[49] See Chapter V.

city had been the birthplace of the organ. The vivid scene recorded in the text proves that the hydraulis produced a sufficient volume of sound for the revellers, having reached their dessert, to hear it being played in a house near by, above the noise of their own discussions. But it was far from being a raucous cacophony, for they all turned towards the sound of the music, and each one praised its harmoniousness. The words ἡδύς, τερπνός, ἐμμέλεια, are a clear enough indication of their appreciation of this unexpected concert, a reaction which is all the more significant since the group includes several connoisseurs, among them the musician Alcides of Alexandria, to whom the instrument represents an exceptionally interesting means of expression: 'Do you not agree, most wise Ulpian, that the hydraulic organ is infinitely superior to the flute called Nabla?'[50]

The short but valuable text by Porphyry of Tyre (233–303) was written only a few years after Athenaeus. In his commentaries on Ptolemy he recalls the general principles of acoustics as applied to the aulos, on which the octave, fifth, fourth, and the other intervals are obtained by using half the length of the pipe—two-thirds, three-quarters, and so on through the other relevant fractions. He adds: 'A similar result was obtained from the *hydra*, where the sounds were produced by pipes attached to the instrument, and of unequal length.'[51]

Note the use of the term 'hydra', a somewhat unusual name for an organ, but one which recurs on the dedicatory plaque of the small Aquincum instrument, dating from 228. This, however, is not a hydraulis, but a pneumatic organ. Evidently it must have been customary to use 'hydra', a diminutive of hydraulis, of any kind of organ, water or bellows. Or is this perhaps a piece of word-play, with some underlying symbolic significance? Is he comparing the hydra, the tentacled monster with its hundred heads, to the machine with its banks of hissing pipes?[52] At all events, this passage from Porphyry proves that the name given to the Aquincum organ by either its maker or its donor is not entirely original.[53]

Another third-century text is of special value in that it imputes a liturgical role to the hydraulic organ—something quite exceptional in Antiquity. In addition, it seems to be connected with a purely local custom. Even so, its participation in a religious cult foreshadows in a remarkable way its later role in Christian ceremonies. The text comes from a Greek inscription,

[50] iv, 77.

[51] I. Düring, *Porphyrios Kommentar zur Harmonielehre des Ptolemaios* (Göteborg, 1932), p. 119.

[52] Writing of the auletes Midas of Agrigentum, Pindar (*Pyth.* xii) says: 'The goddess (Athene) made the aulos, an instrument endowed with all manner of sounds . . . and gave it to mortals under the name of "many-headed music" (κεφαλᾶν πολλᾶν νόμον).'

[53] As V. Sugar believed—*L'Orgue*, xxxvii (March, 1939), p. 2.

discovered in 1903 on the island of Rhodes by S. Saridakis.[54] The stone on which it is engraved measured 76 cm. by 70 cm., and served as a paving-stone in a ruined church at the time. In 1904 T. Reinach was able to re-examine the stone in a public garden.[55] The text records the liberality of one Marcus Aurelius Cyrus on his accession to the priesthood of Dionysus:

The people of Rhodes and the Council have honoured Marcus Aurelius Cyrus, son of Euplous the Pontorean,[56] priest of Bacchus-Dionysus, who has just been honourably invested with the priesthood in succession to his brother Marcus Aurelius Heliodorus, son of Euplous the Pontorean, and who has from his own privy purse offered a handsome present to the most worthy Council, amounting to 20,000 deniers, on condition that the revenue from 10,000 deniers shall be divided among the summer members of the Boule on his birthday, which falls on the first day of the month of Delios. The revenue from the remaining 10,000 deniers shall likewise be divided up by the winter Council, on the natal day of his brother Marcus Aurelius Hermes, son of Euplous the Pontorean . . . [Marcus Aurelius Cyrus] has made a further lavish gift on the occasion of the sacerdotal ceremonies: 10 [deniers] to each member of the Boule and 5 (deniers) to every citizen . . . and for the Dionysia and the Baccheia . . . Moreover, he has given 360 deniers to the player of the water organ charged with awakening the God[57] *(τῷ ὑδραύλῃ τῷ ἐπεγείροντι[τό]ν θεόν)* and 100 [deniers] to those who sang the God's praise. . . .

Out of his own fortune, therefore, this young priest of Dionysus maintains a choir and an organist; the latter, who has a hydraulic organ, has to play at all the festivals of the god. Reinach thinks that originally an auletes would have held this position,[58] but that here at least the organ eventually took over. This is the first known instance where the emotive power of the organ is applied to the field of religion, and thus this text is of considerable significance.

From the style of engraving characters used in the inscription, experts calculate that it must date from the third century, after Caracalla's edict (212) by which all the inhabitants of the Empire were granted the title of citizen.

THE FOURTH CENTURY A.D.

A strange work, written by one Porfyrius Optatianus, a contemporary of Constantine and not to be confused with the commentator of Ptolemy previously mentioned, dates from the beginning of the fourth century. This

[54] *Jahreshefte der oest. archäol. Inst. in Wien* (1904), pp. 92 ff.
[55] *Revue des Etudes Grecques* (1904), pp. 203–10.
[56] Pontoreius was one of the demes of the town of Ialysus, on the west coast of the island.
[57] Dionysos Liknites, apparently dead, was brought back to life by the singing of women named Thyades. See P. Perdrizet, in Daremberg-Saglio, op. cit., art. 'Thyades'.
[58] Op. cit., p. 210.

is a *Panegyric* addressed to the Emperor, who, for reasons unknown to us, had banished him in 324. It contains curious pieces of poetry deliberately constructed to represent in turn a Pythian altar, a syrinx, and an organ. The organ-shaped poem is written in gradually lengthening lines, imitating the regular progression of the pipes, while the manual is formed by a dedication, and more lines—very short—make up the wind-chest.[59] Porfyrius's piece describing the organ is significant for two reasons. Its title, Ὄργανον, is a shortened version of the term ὄργανον ὑδραυλικόν; this is the first time that the word appears in the precise and limited sense of 'organ'. Secondly, the poem describes a hydraulic organ of the standard type, but the shape outlined by the verses is incontrovertibly that of a bellows organ of the type found at Aquincum, whose dedicatory plaque referred to it as a 'hydra'. This indicates the growing confusion in the names applied to the two forms of organ: from the fourth century on it is usually impossible to know whether the organum is a pneumatic or hydraulic instrument. This ambiguity, which still obtained during the Middle Ages, gives rise to a number of unfortunate misapprehensions.

The translation of the 'pipes' part of the poem, the only section relevant to our study, is as follows:

O, if Clio would grant favour to this poet, as he ventures to measure out, on a half line's length, words flowing from one and the same Aonian spring, according to the Muse's one, unaltered law, keeping the rights of heroic verse intact: may she grant successful craftsmanship for my verse, allowing that the first part grow up to a longer finale by small steps, increasing with tiny advances until at last she concludes the final stage after complete ascent of the hill, on a full-scale line; counting out twice in a single space the elements of the line before, forcing equality on those too short and those too long by maintaining her laws; and making equal those lines most different to the eye, by a like timing and the same vertical rule, making equal in rhythm what is half in size. This will be a creation most apt for a variety of tunes and will rise richly melodious by steps of sound in the hollow rounded bronze, increasing with lengthening pipes. Placed beneath these comes a line of square-shaped keys whereby the musician's hand opens and shuts in time the openings for the air, showing off sounds that blend with pleasant rhythms; further below, water lies hid, agitated by swift blasts of air puffed from this side and that by the concerted movements of hard-working youths, turn and turn about, and fanned to greater volume by an answering blast. Hence arises a symphony of sound, rhythmical and apt for songs, able to follow the opened keys, which ever tremble to the slightest touch, or to conclude agreeable harmonies. And now shall the whole world be dazzled by its metre and rhythms.

[59] We know that this whimsical type of versification had previously attracted Theocritus, one of whose short poems, entitled *Syrinx*, forms the silhouette of Pan's favourite instrument. ΘΕΟΚΡΙΤΟΥ ΣΥΡΙΓΞ: Fr. Dübner, *Scholia in Theocritum* (Paris, 1849), p. 109.

Here, then, is Porfyrius Optatianus's poem. Note that each line is longer than the preceding line by one letter.

```
OSIDIVISOMETIRILIMITECLIO
UNALEGESUIUNOMANIANTIAFONTE
AONIOVERSUSHEROIIUREMANENTE
AUSURODONETMETRIFELICIATEXTA
AUGERILONGOPATIENSEXORDIAFINE
EXIGUOCURSUPARVOCRESCENTIAMOTU
ULTIMAPOSTREMODONECFASTIGIATOTA
ASCENSUIIUGICUMULATOLIMITECLAUDAT
UNOBISSPATIOVERSUSELEMENTAPRIORIS
DINUMERANSCOGENSAEQUARILEGERETENTA
PARVANIMISLONGISETVISUDISSONAMULTUM
TEMPORESUBPARILIMETRIRATIONIBUSISDEM
DIMIDIUMNUMERORYTHMOTAMENAEQUIPERANDO
HAECERITINVARIOSSPECIESAPTISSIMACANTUS
PERQUEMODOSGRADIBUSSURGATFECUNDASONORIS
AERECAVOETTERETICALAMISCRESCENTIBUSAUCTA
QUISBENESUBPOSITISQUADRATISORDINEPLECTRIS
ARTIFICISMANUSINNUMEROSCLAUDITQUEAPERITQUE
SPIRAMENTAPROBANSPLACITISBENECONSONARYTHMIS
SUBQUIBUSUNDALATENSPROPERANTIBUSINCITAVENTIS
QUOSVICIBUSCREBRISIUVENUMLABORHAUDSIBIDISCORS
HINCATQUEHINCANIMATQUEAGITANSAUGETQUERELUCTANS
COMPOSITUMADNUMEROSPROPRIUMQUEADCARMINAPRAESTAT
QUODQUEQUEATMINIMUMADMOTUMINTREMEFACTAFREQUENTER
PLECTRAADAPERTASEQUIAUTPLACITOSBENECLAUDERECANTUS
IAMQUEMETROETRYTHMISPRAESTRINGEREQUICQUIDUBIQUEEST

AUGUSTOVICTOREIUVATRATAREDDEREVOTA

POSTMARTIOSLABORES
ETCAESARUMPERENNES
VIRTUTIBUSPERORBEM
TOTLAUREASVIRENTES
ETPRINCIPISTROPAEA
FELICIBUSTRIUMPHIS
AUGUSTARITESAECLIS
EXSULTATOMNISAETAS
URBESQUEFLOREGRATO
ETFRONDIBUSDECORIS
TOTISVIRENTPLATEIS
HINCORDOVESTECLARA
CUMPURPURISHONORUM
FAUSTOPRECANTURORE
FERUNTQUEDONALAETI
JAMROMACULMENORBIS
DATMUNERAETCORONAS
AUROFERENSCORUSCAS
VICTORIASTRIUMPHIS
VOTAQUEIAMTHEATRIS
REDDUNTURETCHOREIS
MESORSINIQUALAETIS
SOLLEMNIBUSREMOTUM
VIXHAECSONARESIVIT
TOTVOTAFONTEPHOEBI
VERSUQUECOMPTASOLO
```

If the style of this curious piece of work is often lacking in clarity, this is explained by the considerable demands made on the poet by the genre—the last line has to have exactly twice as many letters as the first, while the metre must be adhered to.[60] The technical description of the organ is contained in the unequal phrases which represent the graduated series of pipes, beginning at line 14. These pipes are hollow bronze cylinders (aere cavo et tereto), but their exact number is not given.[61] The manual is made up of square, or at least rectangular keys, set a little lower than the mouthpieces of the pipes. These keys regulate the flow of air by sliders, as in Vitruvius's instrument. The water is under the wind-chest, out of sight in the cistern and activated by the thrust of the air from the pistons—not a single piston in this case, for Porfyrius uses the plural to describe the youths[62] operating them. These youths must pump with a very steady stroke, so that the air is properly compressed and the organist can make his pipes sound by the slightest pressure on the keys.

This unusual piece of verse gives us another interesting piece of information, albeit indirectly. It assumes that Constantine is familiar with matters relating to the organ—otherwise he would be hard put to it to understand and appreciate this example of literary virtuosity. Constantine's reply to the exiled poet shows that the offering met with his approval: 'Gratum igitur hoc mihi dicationis tuae munus fuit. Exercitatio mentis et naturae felicitas comprobatast . . .'[63]

Porfyrius Optatianus describes an instrument with a water-activated wind mechanism, that is to say a hydraulis. But what he sees is obviously a pneumatic organ, for his lines trace out its shape. The explanation is that the pneumatic organ slowly gained ground as its bellows improved. The instrument poetically evoked by the Emperor Julian the Apostate (332–63) is incontestably a new type of organ:

I see [here] a different kind of reed (δονάκων); no doubt sprung from soil of bronze. Not by airy breezes are they shaken. Instead a breath of wind rushing from a bag of bull-hide below finds its way to the lower end of cunningly perforated reeds. And a proud man with nimble fingers stands there manipulating the keys which give voice to the pipes. And they, quivering in response, squeeze out a delicate note.[64]

No mention here of either water or a pnigeus: this is a pneumatic organ,

---

[60] Hexameters. The lines representing the wind-chest are iambic dimeters.

[61] The fact that there are twenty-six lines is no reason to suppose that there are twenty-six notes. Theocritus's *Syrinx* has twenty lines: but the instrument probably never had twenty reeds.

[62] In Athenaeus's account, this operation was entrusted to a single youth (νεανίσκος).

[63] Hildebrandt, op. cit., pp. 455–6.

[64] *Anth. Pal.*, ix, 365.

though it is no longer the small-scale, portable instrument described by Pollux, for its dimensions are considerable. The organist plays in a standing position as for the hydraulis, and his proud bearing does not pass unnoticed. Apparently the air stream which activates the pipes does not come directly from a bellows, but accumulates in a pliable reservoir made of hide and probably compressed by a weight. Organs fitted with bellows of this type are depicted on the Obelisk of Theodosius in Constantinople.[65] The instrument mentioned by Julian is capable of producing pretty sounds, and of permitting virtuosity, since the artist is complimented on his nimble fingers; clearly the keys on the manual responded instantly to any pressure. Those of the hydraulic organ described by the poet Claudian (*c.* 400) have similar possibilities, but control very powerful sounds. Claudian mentions the organ in connection with the accession of Mallius Theodorus to the consulate in 399. Lavish celebrations were to be arranged for the people. The poet feels that these should be memorable entertainments, with impressive games in the amphitheatre, clowns, mimes, musicians playing on the tibia and cithara, and dancers of all kinds. But Claudian wants something more to create the true atmosphere of a great occasion: an organ recital is quite indispensable.

Let him whose light touch draws forth mighty sounds, controlling the countless voices of a field of bronze pipes let his fingers, wandering [about the manual of the instrument] make a sound of thunder, while within he stirs up violently, with a strong lever, the water from whose torment sweet music is born.[66]

Here the poet contrasts the powerful sounds produced by the organ with the lightness of the player's touch. This easy action of the hydraulis's manual is not merely poetic licence, for it is borne out by experiment. Where the keys have sliders they are no more difficult to play than the valved keys on an eighteenth-century organ. The many pipes, all packed together like the ears in a field of wheat, produce innumerable notes: Claudian's enthusiasm recalls that of Tertullian. How many pipes was an instrument of the type described here likely to have had? Fifty at the very most, if the iconography is any guide—a modest number by modern standards. But the juxtaposition on the tabula summa of the wind-chest of so many trumpets and flues, that sprang to brilliant life at the organist's slightest touch, made a tremendous impression on the Roman public. Certainly Claudian considered the organ to be a very special attraction, rating far above the antics of clowns or the playing of tibicines.

The last two lines of the passage raise a most interesting question.

---

[65] See p. 80.
[66] Claudian, *In F. Mallii Theodori consulatum*, 316–20.

Apparently it was the organist himself who operated the bellows handle, presumably with his feet: 'concitet' has the same subject as 'intonet'. This technical point will be discussed later.

The indispensable presence of the organ at scenes of great public rejoicing is further vouched for by a poet whose name is unknown but who was a contemporary of Claudian. This time the subject is a great wedding. For the ceremony to be conducted with due pomp, the house, says the writer, must be decked with ivy and laurel leaves, illuminated by thanksgiving fires and twinkling lights, and, most important of all, it should be filled with the sound of music, 'the sound of drums and stringed instruments, the tibia, the box-wood flute, cymbals, Pamphylian [?] horns and flute, the sistrum, and that instrument whose sounds issue from a bronze mouth, the wet organ—let it roar out notes engendered by its bellows'.[67]

The most surprising word here is the adjective 'wet' (humidum). It indicates that the organ in question is equipped with a hydraulic pumping device, though the poet specifically says that the air is produced by bellows (folligenas voces). Either there is some confusion, which would be excusable in a man of letters, or what is meant here is a hybrid instrument fitted with a hydraulic compressor but fed by bellows. This second hypothesis is probably the right one, for we know from an Arabic text which will be examined later that organs of this type actually existed.

Why did certain jaundiced observers choose this moment to deplore the progress that was being made in the manufacture of organs and blame the instrument for the general decline in culture and morals? The truth is that many people still regarded instrumental music as something rather degrading. The historian Ammianus Marcellinus, for instance, despises it, or at least affects to do so. While bewailing the decadence of the time of Constantius II and the Caesar Gallus, that is to say between 351 and 354, the author, who lived through this sorry period, says bitterly that everywhere he looks debauchery reigns supreme. The wealthy Romans lead lives of the most shameful extravagance, banquets are sinks of iniquity and women adopt a wild mode of life:

As things stand today, the few houses that once were centres for the cultivation of serious study are overflowing with the wanton playthings of sluggish idleness, re-echoing with the sound of voices and the jangle of musical instruments wafting through. The singer has ousted the philosopher. Where before the teacher of oratory was summoned, now it is the master of the revels whose services are in demand. The libraries are sealed forever, like tombs; and men make water organs and huge lyres (organa hydraulica et lyrae ingentes)

---

[67] *Epithalamium Laurentii*, 60–5; *Poetae Latini Minores*, ed. Teubner, (Leipzig, 1881), iii, pp. 298–9.

looking like chariots, as well as flutes and heavy instruments for play-actors . . .[68]

From these disillusioned words we may conclude that in the middle of the fourth century, though this was a time of great misfortune, hydraulic organs were being built on a larger scale than before. This development is confirmed by iconographical evidence.[69] What we do not know, however, is whether this growth in the size of the instrument represents an increase in the number of pipes or the use of longer pipes with a lower pitch. The second of these is more likely to have happened.[70] It is remarkable that the history of the organ, starting from the high-pitched syrinx, has seen a steady extension of sounds towards the lower register until, by the end of the Middle Ages, the compass reached four octaves below middle C on the 32 ft. pipes.

We have already seen that the word 'organum' on its own could mean 'organ' from the time of Porfyrius Optatianus. St. Augustine, in a text noted earlier,[71] explained the ambiguous nature of the term, and elsewhere he returns to the same theme: 'All musical instruments bear the generic name "organum"; and this word does not apply solely to the very large instrument (quod grande est)[72] fed by bellows.'[73]

In the following texts, which must date from the time of the great invasions, there can be no doubt that the instrument in question is the organ. A scholium of Juvenal, dating from the end of the fourth century, refers in connection with line 207 of the 8th Satire to the graduated pipes of the instrument, comparing them with the slanting purple stripes worn by the priests of Cybele on their ceremonial robes.[74] Lampridus, writing at the same time, says that the Emperor Elagabalus (218–22) tried to emulate Nero, and lists his musical talents: 'He could sing, dance, blow the tibia, sound the trumpet, play the pandora and handle an organ (organo modulatus est).'[75] According to this same author, Elagabalus's successor, Alexander Severus (222–35), a scholarly man who applied himself to the study of geometry and astrology, was also interested in music: 'He played the lyre, the tibia, the organ, and the trumpet.'[76]

---

[68] *Historia*, i, xiv, 18. In another chapter there is a reference to a certain Sericus, an instrument-maker (organarius) or perhaps an organist (xxviii, 8).

[69] See p. 90.

[70] It is difficult to see why R. Latouche speaks of a musical cacophony in connection with this passage (*Les Grandes Invasions*, Paris, 1946, p. 62).

[71] p. xvii.

[72] Which confirms what Ammianus Marcellinus says.

[73] *In Ps. LVI.*

[74] *Scholia in Juven. vetust.* (Leipzig, 1931), p. 148.

[75] *Heliogabalus*, 32.

[76] *Alex. Severus*, 27.

Another author of the *Historia Augusta*, Tribellius Pollio, records that the Emperor Gallienus (260–8), though not himself a performer, enjoyed listening to the music of the organ: 'It often happened that he went out to the strains of the tibia and returned to those of the organ, for he had commanded that his exits and entrances were to be made to the sound of music.'[77]

It is not known whether or not these imperial organs were operated by bellows. But the instrument mentioned in a strange document dating from the middle of the fourth century certainly has a hydraulic wind mechanism. This is a papyrus, discovered in Egypt, at Oxyrhynchus, by Grenfell and Hunt,[78] who place it between 324 and 355:

From Eutrygios to his assistant Dioscorus: greetings. Give to Gorgonios, who plays the hydraulic organ, according to the agreement, two *artaba* of wheat . . .[79]

Unfortunately the text does not say anything about this Gorgonios. But the settlement of his wages in kind is a curious anticipation of the custom established at the end of the Middle Ages by which church organists were paid at least part of their stipend with a fixed quantity of wine or firewood.

THE FIFTH AND SIXTH CENTURIES A.D.

In general, the Church Fathers mention the organ solely in order to draw edifying symbols from it. But at least one passage is of interest. Bishop Theodoret of Cyrrhus (387–450) proposes a bold symbolism linking the organ with the tongue:

In effect, this organ resembles the instrument with the brazen pipes which, using the air produced by bellows, produces, under the fingers of the artist, those harmonious sounds we all know . . . Art has learned from nature the ingenious process of creating this delightful music . . . See how the lung functions in the same way as the bellows, compressed and dilated, not by man's feet, but by the muscles round the thorax . . . Then the brain . . . forces the breath on to the teeth, as the air is forced into the brazen pipes . . . and thus the lyre, the cithara and the instrument of the brazen pipes are able to give forth, by the use of air or the touch of the fingers, a pleasant and rhythmic air. But the inflected voice can be produced only by the organ which we have just been discussing.[80]

Two items of information emerge from this curious comparison. We learn first that at Antioch, where this discourse was written between 431 and 437, the bellows organ seems to have completely supplanted the hydraulis. In

[77] *Gallienus*, xvii.
[78] *Egypt Exploration Fund* (London, 1898), i, no. 93.
[79] The Egyptian *artaba* was equivalent to approximately 30 litres.
[80] *P.G.*, lxxxiii, 589–92.

addition—and this is even more significant—Theodoret implies that the bellows are worked with the feet. A superficial reading of the passage might appear to suggest that the author is alluding to a forge; but the object in question is still the organ, since the parallel is maintained in the succeeding lines. The organist must therefore have played this new type of organ sitting down, his feet pumping the bellows alternately, while his hands ranged over the manual, exactly like a harmonium player.[81]

A poem written in Syriac by Isaac of Antioch, in the mid-fifth century, makes frequent reference to the hydraulis, but at this date the term may well mean the bellows organ:[82]

A wave of meditation rushed in upon me, and threw me from place to place, even now to that island of dry land which is set in a sea of sand, yea, even to the lovely city of the Greeks that looks out to sea, in the month of January last, when the music deprived the inhabitants of sleep. Every night, I would hear the sound of the citharas, hydraules, and harps, playing before the palaces of the princes. At an hour when it is sweet to sleep, the music was clearly to be heard. The merry note of the horns banished sleep, even though the passers-by slowed their steps, and the sound of their feet died away. The noise ceased, silence reigned, and it became possible to enjoy the sound of the cithara. . . . Every night the instruments were set out, the hydraulis in every way resembling a man, and only rational speech distinguishes man from the cithara. The musical instruments were like men without speech or reason trying to speak by compressing their strings. Men touched them and enfolded them in their movements; The instruments seemed eager to tell some common tale, but their tongues could utter nothing, their voices were like the voice of a man striving to deliver a well-prepared speech, and finding himself deprived of his lips and tongue. Before daybreak, the destitute assemble, crowding before the gates of the rich, and watching late into the night to ingratiate themselves with them. The flute was joined with the tongue, and the lips with the hydraulis, to make the looked-for sound as from a single mouth. By its loudness, the hydraulis dominated the other delicate sounds, but it united with them so that the music reached the top of the palaces; devoid of judgement and speech, the instrument joined forces with the men to make their voice heard far and wide. The sweet concord I then heard was wonderful. On a certain day I was asleep, and snoring, when the hydraulis sounded loudly, so that I awoke with a start, and rose up with my brothers to perform our religious duties. And we came to the psalm which was to be recited at that hour. . . . 'It is right to praise the Lord and magnify Thy name, O Most High.' But the music of the delightful hydraulis seduced my mind, as

---

[81] There is nothing in the text which proves that the organist himself is pedalling; perhaps this was done by an assistant.

[82] I am deeply indebted for this translation to a Lebanese scholar. The Syriac text has been published, together with a Latin adaptation which is not always very accurate, by G. Bickell, *Isaac of Antioch* (Giessen, 1873–7), pp. 294 ff.

though the strings of the lyre of my soul had been released: this music pleased me. In that moment the psalm returned to my mind, and tightened my weak strings . . . Let us ask the living God to let us sit on His right hand on the day of His coming, and may I be filled with His grace through His friends, Amen.

The events recorded in this poem are probably authentic. Upon reaching his monastery in Antioch, Isaac is unable to sleep for the noise in the city during the night;[83] citharas, horns, harps, and organs play incessantly before the gates of the rich men's houses, which are besieged by the poor in the hope of receiving alms. He notes that the strident sound of the hydraulis is clearly heard above the music of the other instruments, and is audible even on the palace roofs, rousing Isaac from a deep sleep. Disturbed by this 'delightful' music, the man of religion, having certainly read the works of St. Augustine, convinces himself that the singing of psalms, more suited to the monastic life, ought to occasion him greater pleasure.

An important point is suggested by this piece. The 'hydraulis' is here a mobile instrument.[84] Manhandled on shafts or pushed on wheels, it is brought each night to the gates of the princes' residences.

The last years of the ancient world still preserved the memory of the water organ. The grammarian Servius (*c.* 400), in his commentaries on Virgil, makes two references to it. Annotating the seventh *Eclogue* he writes:

The Muses are also themselves Nymphs. They are said to inhabit springs of water, and those who dedicated a fountain to the Camenae held this belief, for it is customary to offer them a sacrifice, not of wine, but of water and milk. And it is right that this should be so, for the movement of water produces music, as demonstrated by the hydraulic organ (hydraulia).[85]

Elsewhere, commenting on a line in the *Aeneid* (VII, 23):

Neptunus ventis implevit vela secundis

Servius gives the following interpretation: 'This is a physical expression, for wind is born of the movement of water, as witness the sound of organs (organorum).'[86] Note that 'hydraulia' and 'organum' are used indiscriminately to denote the hydraulic organ, yet another example of the vagueness discussed earlier. Contrary to what St. Augustine says, 'organum' signifies 'organ' regardless of its pumping system, and this usage carries more weight by the fact that it is found in the writings of a grammarian. A further grammatical note is contained in the third *Vatican Mythography*,[87] which was

---

83 Towns in the Near East had always been noisy because of the great multitude of musicians playing in the streets. Philostratus, iv, 2.

84 Unless it is simply a bellows organ.

85 *Bucolics*, vii, 21.

86 *Aen.*, vii, 24.

87 A. Mai, *Myth. Vatic. tres* (Rome, 1831), iii, p. 236.

certainly written at a later date: 'For in Greek water is ὕδωρ; hence *hydropicus*, one who dies from having drunk too much water; and *hydraulia* and *hydraula*, nouns coined to describe water organs (aquatica organa).'

There are very few other written sources of any importance dating from the fifth and sixth centuries. This dearth of material is related to the great invasions and the destruction that followed in their wake. The conquerors themselves were apparently not always musically inclined, at least if the tastes of Theodoric II, King of the Visigoths (453–66), are any criterion. In a letter written in 454, Sidonius Apollinaris, Bishop of Auvergne, observes that the King is a man of simple tastes, and that his meals are those of an ordinary private citizen, scarcely ever accompanied by music. No lyre, no cithara, no flute or drum is ever heard: 'The rooms never echo to the sound of hydraulic organs.[88] The prelate does not quote these facts in any spirit of reproach, for he clearly regards such habits as virtues which stand to the King's credit. But Theodoric the Great, half a century later, seems to have shown some interest in the organ, which he classes as one of those wonders that one admires without really understanding how they work. Speaking of his minister, Boethius, he writes:

He makes waters surge up from the depths and cascade down again; flames run evenly around;[89] organs thunder forth strange sounds; and fills the pipes with exotic blasts of air, which makes them utter a melodious sound . . .[90]

In a proclamation to the people Theodoric returns to the theme:

It is our desire that the entertainments arranged on festive occasions should bring joy to the people . . . It is our dearest wish that you should remain faithful to the teaching of your ancestors, so that under our laws you may continue to improve upon the wonderful heritage you have possessed since ancient times. It is customary among you to fill the very air with marvellous sounds . . . Your voices are sweeter even than that of the organ (organo), and by your art the hollow theatre echoes to the music of the cithara . . .[91]

Boethius himself is well versed in musical science and knows the pipe organ. In his treatise on music he lists, among the artists, 'the citharists and those who display their prowess on the organ and other musical instruments'. He is certainly familiar with the hydraulic organ, and even mentions, in a catalogue of different instruments, 'those which operate by means of water'.[92]

The principle of the hydraulic wind mechanism, where the water pressurizes the air, continued to fascinate men with inquiring minds, such as the

[88] Epist. II, *Ad Agricolam.*
[89] See Claudian, *Paneg. on Mal. Theod.*, 326–7; 'let us see flames flying in a circle, balls of fire . . .' He is writing of a circus programme.
[90] *Boethio Patricio Theodoricus Rex*, anno 507.
[91] *Populo Romano Theodoricus Rex*, anno 507–11.
[92] *De Musica.*, i, 34, and i, 2.

philosopher Simplicius of Cilicia, whose writings contain an observation of some interest: 'In fact, when water is poured into hydraulic organs filled with air, the small strips of reed (γλῶσσαι) in the trumpets or auloi, placed opposite the holes through which the air passes, demonstrate that air is really issuing from the holes by producing a sound.'[93]

Martianus Capella in the fifth century is the last Roman writer to mention the hydraulic organ. In a kind of encyclopedia of the seven liberal arts, with the curious title *De Nuptiis Philologiae et Mercurii*, the music of the daughters of Jupiter is described as follows:

And lo! before the gate there arose a sweet melody of great charm, sung by the choir of the Muses who had foregathered in honour of the nuptial vows, and set to a subtle rhythm. There was also the music of the tibias, and the sound of lyres, and the sonorous harmonies of hydraulic organs (hydraularum harmonica plenitudo).[94]

Elsewhere the author recounts what he has seen in his travels both real and imaginary:

I have conceded that the Egyptians have a fondness for the pandora, and have not challenged their ability to imitate birdsong on their shepherds' flutes, or the cracking of trees, or the purling of brooks. Everywhere I went I found citharists, kordax dancers and players of the sambuca and the hydraulic organs for the convenience and use of mankind.[95]

A further reference to the organ, 'organum', occurs in a chapter of the *History of Apollonius, King of Tyre*, in connection with marriage festivities:

The citizens are filled with joy, as are the strangers and travellers. A general feeling of great gladness is expressed by the citharas, lyres, songs and the sound of the organs accompanying the voices of the singers.[96]

To end this series of references to the organ dating from ancient times we have the interesting account given by the Senator Cassiodorus towards the middle of the sixth century:

The organ, then, is a kind of tower (quasi turris) composed of divers pipes (fistulis) into which sounds of great richness are introjected by air from bellows. To obtain this sound by means of seemly rhythmic action (modulatio decora) it is constructed with wooden keys (linguis ligneis) underneath; these, properly manipulated by the fingers of the initiated, produce a cantilena of great resonance and sweetness.[97]

Cassiodorus's organ has a touch of individuality in that its pipes are

---

[93] *In Phys.*, iv, 8.
[94] *De Nuptiis Philologiae et Mercurii*, ii, 117.
[95] Ibid., ix, 924.
[96] *Historia Apollonii Regis Tyri*, ch. 23.
[97] *Exp. in Ps. CL.*

arranged in the shape of a tower, as in the Chinese *Shêng*. The same arrangement recurs on a certain number of small medieval instruments. This organ,
which is fed by the air from several sets of bellows (flatu follium), obviously
has registers, since it is able if need be to produce very loud sounds as well
as soft, sweet ones: Cassiodorus makes a point of juxtaposing the adjectives
'grandiosonam' and 'suavissimam'. The dexterity of the player's fingers
(digiti) on a manual composed of wooden keys achieves a variety of musical
effects.

This author also mentions the organ in a catalogue of musical instruments:
'There are in existence three kinds of musical instruments: percussion
instruments, stringed instruments, and wind instruments . . . Wind
instruments produce sound by using the air that fills them, as with the tibias,
flutes, and organs.'

Apart from the two very valuable inscriptions analysed earlier, the field of
epigraphy yields two further references to the pipe organ. The following text
is engraved on a sarcophagus found at Aquincum, near Budapest:

Here lies, entombed in stone, a dutiful wife, the beloved Sabina. Well grounded
in the arts, she alone outshone her husband. Her voice was a delight and her
fingers plucked skilfully upon the stringed instruments; but now, untimely
snatched from life, she is dumb. Her years numbered three times ten, all but
five, alas! plus three months and twice seven days. In her lifetime she took
part in public concerts on the hydraulic organ, thereby giving great pleasure.
Be happy, you who read these lines; may the Gods preserve you. Lift up your
voice in solemn farewell to Aelia Sabina.

T. Aelius Justus, stipendiary organist to the 2nd Legion Adjutrix, her
husband, erected this monument at his own cost.[98]

It is impossible not to feel moved by this ultimate farewell of an organist
to his wife, who was likewise dedicated to the art of music.[99] But apart from
this the inscription is of considerable historical interest. It tells us that certain
legions had a paid organist attached to their strength. Perhaps he took part
in the drill exercises, though this is mere conjecture, and in no other document is there the slightest allusion to this unusual army appointment.[100]
I should like to offer another hypothesis. It is not inconceivable that the 2nd
tiegion Adjutrix had its own gladiators to entertain the troops in their free
Lme. After all, the 30th Legion, encamped on the banks of the Rhine, had
them at this same period, as we know from the inscription on a vase preserved

---

[98] *C.I.L.*, iii, 10501; Lajos Nagy, *Az Aquincumi orgona*, op. cit., p. 9.

[99] This husband-and-wife devotion to the organ is reminiscent of Ktesibios and his
wife Thaïs.

[100] All we know is that every legion had its trumpeters, horn-players, and buccinatores,
whose role was specifically defined. Vegetius, *De re militari*, ii, 22.

at Colchester.[101] Aelius Julius would in that case have been one of the 'contracted' personnel attached to the military amphitheatre.

The sarcophagus was discovered in 1881 in an ancient Roman cemetery at Aquincum, and the text, thought by experts to be from the end of the fourth century, confirms that even in small garrison towns a long way from Rome recitals on the hydraulic organ were a regular occurrence.

In another inscription—this time in Greek—engraved on a stele from Asia Minor[102] now in the Louvre, we have a very concise description of the pipe organ. Without actually mentioning the instrument by name, the text, representing the epitaph of a gladiator, Melanippos, makes an obvious allusion to it:

You who pass by, you see me dead, me, Melanippos, a retiarius of the second class, a valiant fighter in the amphitheatres. No more I hear the sound of the bronze trumpet, nor, in my combats, do I rouse the clamour of the unequal pipes (ἀνίσων αὐλῶν). They say that Hercules was victorious in twelve contests; and, having brought a like number to a successful issue, I met my death in the thirteenth.

At their own cost Thallos and Zoë have raised this monument to the memory of Melanippos.[103]

The 'unequal pipes' are those of the hydraulic organ, which with the trumpet and horns, frequently accompanied gladiatorial combats. This is proved by several iconographical sources which will be examined in due course. The expression 'ἀνίσων αὐλῶν' has its Latin equivalent in Prudentius's 'disparibus calamis';[104] and should not be confused with the terms 'tibiis imparibus' and 'tibiis paribus' which occur in certain manuscripts of Terence, and refer to the pipes of the accompanying aulos.[105] In Melanippos's epitaph, the context leaves no room for ambiguity.

A further three inscriptions have been related to the organ, but without any degree of certainty, and they are reproduced here purely in the interests of completeness. The first is from Arles, and commemorates one Q. Candidus Benignus:[106]

> . . . NEMO . ORGANA . QUI . NOSSE
> T . FACERE . AQUARUM . AUT . DUCE
> RE . CURSUM . . .

[101] This vase is illustrated in J. Toynbee, *Art in Roman Britain* (London, 1962), pp. 176–7. It shows two venatores and two gladiators, with the names of the combatants and the inscription 'Legionis XXX'.
[102] I am indebted to P. Dewambez, who allowed me to examine and photograph this stone.
[103] L. Robert, *Les Gladiateurs dans l'Orient Grec* (Paris, 1940), pp. 234–5, no. 298.
[104] *Apotheosis*, 389.
[105] J. Marouzeau, *Térence* (Paris, 1942), i, p. 25.
[106] *C.I.L.*, xii, no. 722.

The editor of the *Corpus* sees in this an allusion to the hydraulic organ, but to my mind there is nothing to justify such an assumption. More probably the reference is to an architect engaged in building aqueducts—in Cicero[107] 'ductus aquarum' is the term for an irrigation canal and in Frontinus[108] it means the canalization of the aqueduct, while Juvenal describes a man who built canals as 'conductus aquarius'.[109]

However, the subject of an inscription from Beneventum is certainly a maker of instruments:[110]

> M . LUCILIO . M . L
> DIOCLI . TIBICIN
> ARTIFIC . ORGAN
> LIBERTIS . ET . LIBERTAB
> EIUS . ARBIT . . .
> M . OFILLI . TERTI .

This might perhaps be interpreted as 'M. Lucilio . . . tibicin[i] artific[i] organ[ario]' (M. Lucilius . . . a player of the tibia and a gifted organist), but such a reading is purely hypothetical.

The final text is too mutilated to allow of any interpretation. In the *Corpus* it is quoted as referring to the organ, but while this is possible, there is no supporting evidence.[111]

> TUSSI
> ORGAN
> AETOMA

This was inscribed on a marble plaque discovered at Metz and subsequently lost.

Such, then, are the various written sources, either describing the pipe organ or alluding to it, which date from Greek and Roman times up to the disintegration of the Western Roman Empire. From these texts it has been possible to trace the birth of the instrument, its development, its heyday, and its metamorphoses. In the following chapter we shall look at the pictorial representations of the organ that have come down to us from the past.

[107] *De legibus,* ii, 1.
[108] *De aquis,* xiii, 1; xcviii, 2.
[109] *Sat.,* vi, 332.
[110] *C.I.L.,* ix, no. 1719.
[111] *C.I.L.,* xiii, no. 5949.

CHAPTER FOUR

The Graeco-Roman Organ: Iconographical Evidence

Besides the literary evidence, the history of the organ in antiquity may be traced through the graphic images which have survived, engraved or sculpted in stone, or patterned in mosaics. Such pictorial representations, whose number is still, let us hope, not completely known, are of the utmost importance, for while the texts explain how the instrument worked or discuss the sounds it made, they practically never offer any information concerning its outward appearance. Fortunately, this gap is filled by the iconography, which is relatively abundant—to date we know of almost forty illustrations of organs. Almost all of these show the hydraulic organ as described by Vitruvius, with a structure virtually unchanged from the time of its invention up to the eve or the disintegration of the Western Empire. Even its measurements, which are easy to calculate when a human figure is represented beside it, are nearly always identical for the base and wind-chest. The explanation is that, firstly, there could scarcely have been more than three or four sets of pipes without increasing the air leaks and making the manual too difficult to manipulate. Secondly, it was impossible greatly to reduce the volume of the water cistern or the cylinders, since the output of the air would then have been insufficient and the pressure too irregular. A somewhat similar phenomenon exists in modern times, where, for essentially technical reasons, the external appearance of the large-scale church organ has remained virtually unchanged for six hundred years.

The bellows organ appears much less frequently in the iconography. No doubt it made a smaller impact on the public and remained for a long time a 'drawing-room' instrument, of modest proportions. The bellows themselves are seldom depicted—no doubt these were detachable, and were only fitted on when the instrument was actually in use. However, the external appearance of the pneumatic organ was presumably not very different from that of the small positive of the Middle Ages in the West.

The organ is portrayed in several different media. Bas-reliefs are frequent, on sarcophagi, funeral steles, and the ivory of a diptych. Statuettes and terracottas, though their exact function is often not clear, allow us to study the instrument in three dimensions. Mosaics have the added advantage of colour. The instrument is also depicted on an engraved gem-stone and on a number of contorniate medallions.

It is important to try to date this evidence, though not always easy, even with the help of inscriptions. It is just as important to know where the object originated; unfortunately in a great many instances the exact provenance is unknown, since collections were too frequently assembled in a totally un-scientific way. The representation itself must be subjected to a methodical scrutiny and interpreted, though with due reservations. Sometimes, for example, the design is defaced or roughly executed, or else the perspective is bad. Again, the sculptor or mosaic worker may have relied on his memory, which could account for a number of errors: for instance, the low pipes are sometimes placed to the right of the player, whereas in more careful repre-sentations they are to his left, as they are today. (Even Raphael, in his famous picture of St. Cecilia, pictured her with an organ whose pipes are the wrong way round.)[1]

To simplify their task, artists quite often left out pumps, levers, and organ-blowers, and on several illustrations the absence of these men raises the problem of how the wind mechanism was operated. I am convinced, for reasons which will be set out in due course, that some organs were played without the aid of organ-blowers: the organist, like the present-day harmo-nium player, used his feet to pump the air as the music and the pipes required. As we shall see when analysing the iconographic material, the instrument is most frequently shown in the setting of the amphitheatre, sometimes accompanied by trumpets and horns.

Besides the pictorial evidence, a very few archaeological relics have been unearthed—the small 'organs' of Pompeii, of which only the frame and a few pipes remain, and the pneumatic organ of Aquincum, which is much more complete. The latter deserves separate study, and will, in fact, be the subject of a detailed analysis, for it represents a valuable example of organ manu-facture in the third century A.D. Let us hope that some day—and this is still possible—chance will bring to light the complete mechanism of a hydraulic organ. Such a discovery would yield musicologists and technological historians much detailed information, relating not so much to how the instrument worked—for nowadays this is well understood—but to how the various component parts were actually designed. For instance, we know very little about the manual, since it is nearly always out of sight in the iconography. The public saw the other side of the organ, and consequently this is the side which is illustrated. In this we have an analogy with the

---

[1] Like those on the elegant positive depicted on a sixteenth-century Flemish tapestry in the great hall of the Château de Loches.

church organ as illustrated since medieval times, where the manuals, located between the positive and the great organ, never appear.

It should be said at this point, in connection with the iconographic material, that a number of very dubious pictures have been published, more especially in the last century, which have been falsely interpreted as representing organs. In some cases the instruments involved are large syrinxes; in others, the objects described have no association with music;[2] and, as we have seen, the bas-relief cited by Mersenne shows a goldsmith's workshop and not an organ.[3] Such documents are not treated here, since they do not merit discussion.[4]

It is difficult to classify the various images of ancient organs. As a rule their dates are too vague to make any chronological catalogue possible. It seems more logical to group them together according to the scene they illustrate. I shall therefore describe in turn representations of:

The organ with orchestra and human figures.

The organ with human figures.

The organ alone.

THE ORGAN WITH ORCHESTRA AND HUMAN FIGURES

1. *The Nennig mosaic* (Pl. I). Nennig is a small village in the Saar some 40 km. from Trier, not far from the right bank of the Moselle. There, in 1852, were discovered the remains of an elegant Roman villa dating roughly from the time of Hadrian.[5] The floor of one of the rooms is adorned with a magnificent mosaic in an excellent state of preservation, measuring 16 m. by 12, picked out in fresh, bright colours. It consists of nine medallions, seven of them octagonal and two square, separated by geometric motifs and depicting various scenes from the amphitheatre: gladiatorial combats and venatio. One of the medallions, which lies at the actual entrance to the room, shows the orchestra, consisting of a hydraulic organ and a horn. This section of the mosaic was damaged by bombardment during the last war, but by 1960 it had been skilfully restored.

The organ fits the description given by Vitruvius, and is equipped with two lateral pumps. The hexagonal plinth is set on a small platform—likewise hexagonal—whose perspective is very well conveyed by the design. The six-sided water cistern is decorated with rectangular panels surrounded by mouldings. To the upper part of the cistern on each side a strong cylinder is

---

[2] As, for instance, the object mentioned by O. Jahn in *Denkmäler und Forschungen, Archäol. Zeitung*, Jahrgang XXV (September, 1867), pl. ccxxv, no. 1.

[3] This is used as a frontispiece for Vol. ii of J. N. Forkel's *Allgemeine Geschichte der Musik* (Leipzig, 1801).

[4] Degering has dealt very thoroughly with these alleged organs (*Die Orgel*, pp. 85–6).

[5] K. Parlasca, *Die römischen Mosaiken in Deutschland* (Berlin, 1959), p. 35, back-dates it to the third century.

attached, supported by an oblique bracket. There is no sign of either crank-shafts, levers or organ-blowers, perhaps a conscious omission on the part of the artist, anxious not to overcomplicate his design. However, it is possible that the wind mechanism was operated by the organist himself, who could have worked a pedal. If this were so, however, the piston-rods ought to be visible.

Resting on the cistern is a kind of table, again hexagonal and decorated with mouldings. This is the wind-chest, in which the pipes are implanted. These pipes, twenty-seven or twenty-eight in number, appear to be packed very closely together, and to have a very small bore. Their variation in height is slight, the shortest being about three-quarters the height of the longest. Flue pipes cut to these specifications would sound a fourth apart, which would suggest very small intervals indeed. However, there is no evidence that these are flue pipes rather than reeds, or even that the artist took a really close look at his model: he has placed the bass pipes to the organist's right and the trebles to his left.[6] It is very likely that the pipe section of the instrument is here represented in a purely conventional way. A supporting bar is visible, running slantwise across the pipes, but there is no sign of lateral supports.

The organist is shown behind his instrument, his head and shoulders rising above the pipes. He is a pleasant-looking man whose clean-shaven face is young, relaxed, and healthy. He has a good head of hair, with a lock or two falling over his brow. His fine black eyes are turned attentively to his left. His broad shoulders are draped in a loose garment fitting closely round his neck. Judging by the design, his hands should come somewhere half-way up the tallest pipe, but the manual is hardly likely to have been located so high unless the keys had a vertical part at least 25 cm. deep, which would seem mechanically improbable. A more rational explanation would be that whoever drew the sketch for this mosaic reproduced the instrument from memory, with no regard for detail.

On the organist's left stands the cornicen, dressed in a loose, light-coloured mantle and wearing sandals. The expression on his bearded face is more serious, and across his forehead he wears a bandeau to hold his hair in place.[7] His face and eyes also are turned towards the left, and in his hands he holds the cornu, an enormous horn whose mouthpiece is close to his lips. It is clear that both he and his companion are following the course of the fight, and are ready to strike up the moment the signal is given. The colours, whose role here is probably more decorative than descriptive, are for the

---

[6] Cl. Loret, having failed to appreciate this anomaly, has reproduced the mosaic the wrong way round (*Recherches sur l'orgue hydraulique*, Paris, 1890, p. 27).

[7] Juvenal implies that the cornicines who played in the amphitheatre were particularly looked down upon (*Sat.*, iii, 34–6).

most part blue and ochre. The wind-chest and the slanting bar on the pipes are light blue; the cylinders and the mouldings on the cistern, and also the pipes, are pale yellow; while the cistern is a light sepia.

From the stature of the two men it is easy to estimate the size of the organ, which lies in approximately the same plane as the cornicen. The over-all height of the instrument, from its base to the tip of the tallest pipe, is slightly more than 2 m. The water cistern, 85 cm. across, is 1 m. in depth, including the base. The cylinders are about 30 cm. high, with a diameter of 20 cm. The longest pipe measures almost 80 cm., and the smallest 60 cm. All the pipes have the same diameter, about 3 cm., and the width of the whole rank is 85 cm.

Despite the artist's carelessness, it is fairly obvious that this is a fine instrument, elegantly decorated. It is impossible to tell whether it had more than one rank of pipes. Perhaps the designer of the mosaic had seen his model in the amphitheatre at Trier, which the owner of the property would certainly have frequented.

One advantage of this scene is that it shows that the hydraulic organ was not only a solo instrument but blended quite happily with the horn. Prob-ably the combination of their two distinctive timbres produced impressive, martial-sounding music well suited to the violence of gladiatorial combat.

2 and 3. *The Zliten mosaic.* Shortly before the First World War the Italian army of occupation in Tripolitania brought to light one of the most import-ant pieces of evidence we have relating to the history of the organ. This is a large mosaic, its colours still very bright, decorating one of the rooms of a vast Roman villa built by the sea at Dar Buk Ammera, not far from the Zliten oasis.[8] The central part of this mosaic is ornamented with fish and geometric designs; and running all along its edge a narrow band shows in detail a great munus enlivened by the presence of two orchestras, each consisting of a trumpet, organ, and two horns.

In the first (Plate II, no. 1), beside the traditional hermes, we see on the left the tubicen, elegantly clad, and blowing into a long trumpet which he holds with both hands. The instrument, measuring about 1·50 cm. judging from the player's height, ends in a small conical bell. To the right and on the same plane are the figures of the horn-players, likewise smartly dressed and seated on stools. They appear to be in the middle of a piece, for both have their lips to the mouthpieces of their instruments. Note that the horns, like the one in the first mosaic, are identical with those found at Pompeii.

[8] The mosaic is now in Tripoli Museum. A good description of this mosaic is given by S. Aurigemma, in 'Mosaico con scene d'anfiteatro in una villa romana a Zliten in Tripolitania, *Dedalo*, iv (1923), pp. 333–61, and vii (1923), pp. 397–414. A résumé of this text is included in the *Journal des Savants* (May 1924), by R. Cagnat.

Between the tubicen and the cornicines, but slightly to the rear, stands a hydraulic organ with its organist. The organ is similar to the Nennig instrument, but its water cistern is rectangular, whereas the other was hexagonal. The panel facing us is decorated with mouldings in a geometric pattern. This cistern, which stands on quite a narrow plinth, is dark yellow in colour, shaded in black and red. Flanking it are the pumps, though neither crankshafts nor levers are shown. The absence of organ-blowers in this extremely detailed scene leads to the assumption that the organist himself operated the pumping mechanism with his feet.

The wind-chest, a little wider than the cistern, supports ten pipes arranged in the modern order, trebles on the player's right. The height of the smallest and largest pipes are in a ratio of about 1:2 which, in the case of flue pipes, implies a compass of approximately an octave. But perhaps the artist was attempting to depict a set of reed pipes, for though their upper orifices are perfectly visible, they have no lips. The manual, hidden by the pipes, is located a few centimetres above the wind-chest, judging by the position of the organist's right elbow. This time the organist is a slender young woman with a sensitive, resolute expression. Her very dark eyes closely follow the course of the fight, and her short hair lends her a surprisingly modern air. Her long-sleeved robe is dark green, banded with blue.

From the organist's height it is possible to gauge the dimensions of the instrument. Its overall height would seem to be not more than 1·80 m. The wind-chest is 65 cm. across and 12 cm. deep: the cistern is 75 cm. deep, the longest pipe measures 60 cm., and the shortest 30 cm.

The scene pictured here, reminiscent of the Nennig design, is full of life, and it looks very much as though the musicians are actually playing. One of the gladiators has just been struck down, and the victor is preparing to cut his throat as soon as the 'summa rudis' releases his arm.

The second orchestra (Plate II, no. 2) depicted at the opposite end of the mosaic, is very like the first, and has the same instruments. The tubicen, dressed in a white tunic and with a large red cloak thrown over his right arm, holds a long trumpet to his lips. The organ appears between the two cornicines, but appreciably behind them. The base and water cistern are clearly visible, but the pumps seem to be missing. To Aurigemma[9] this suggested that the instrument is a bellows organ; but in fact it has all the characteristics of the hydraulis. However, the wind-chest is rather unusual in that it appears to be made in two distinct parts separated by a narrower intermediate section. From the player's position, the manual would seem to be located very high.

The organ has eight pipes, and here again the trebles are to the right of

[9] op. cit., p. 352.

the player. No supporting bar is visible, nor is there any sign of lateral uprights. The largest pipe is slightly more than twice the length of the smallest, and if these are not reed pipes the tessitura thus exceeds the octave. The organist's head and shoulders appear above the pipes, and again the player is a woman—perhaps it was the custom in this particular province. She has a round face, with her hair drawn up into a chignon on the crown of her head, and her expression is rather disagreeable. All the musicians are looking to the left, where two gladiators, a retiarius and a secutor, are locked in combat. The concentration of the musicians leads to the assumption that they had to strike up at precisely determined moments in the course of the struggle.

The hair style of the first organist would date the mosaic to the time of the Flavians: but Georges Ville, who has carefully examined the mosaic *in situ*, has concluded that parts of it at least cannot date from before the reign of Trajan.[10] I cannot agree with Aurigemma's suggestion that the combats shown here were to commemorate the games given by the legate Valerius Festus. Even though the latter was in the vicinity of Zliten in 69[11] and settled there the disputes which had arisen among the native peoples, there is nowhere any suggestion that on this occasion he gave a great *munus* which might have been the subject of this mosaic.

4. *Alexandrian terracotta* (Plate V). This terracotta statuette is probably the oldest representation of an organ known to us, and it comes from Alexandria, the very birthplace of Ktesibios. Formerly part of the Gréau collection, it is now in the Louvre.[12] In his catalogue Fröhner described it as follows:

Alexandrian dwarf playing the trumpet (salpinx) beside an organ. He is ithyphallic and dressed in a brief, short-sleeved tunic. From behind the organ appears the head of a woman, wearing a diadem. On the reverse side, the piece is engraved with triangles and curved lines. Pale yellow clay. Height: 13 cm.[13]

Most experts calculate that the piece dates from pre-Christian times, probably from around the end of the Hellenistic era. Although it is rather a rough piece of work, it gives some idea of what the ὄργανον ὑδραυλικόν may have been like at this time. The instrument is not appreciably different from those we have just seen, and fits the descriptions of Hero and Vitruvius. A wide water cistern is mounted on quite a deep base. To the right a pump is shown, though without its handle. It is impossible to tell if there is a corresponding pump on the left-hand side, since the place where it would be

---

[10] *Les jeux de l'amphithéâtre, des origines au règne de Trajan*, thesis, in preparation.
[11] Tacitus, *Hist.*, iv, 50.
[12] Cat. no. C A 426.
[13] Gréau Collection, *Catalogue* (Paris, 1891), no. 1214.

is masked by the trumpet player. The wind-chest, which appears to be roughly as wide as the cistern is deep, is decorated with grooves running across it. Fourteen pipes are visible, trebles to the right of the organist: but there are neither bar nor uprights to hold them steady. The pipes are not evenly graduated, but remain roughly the same height from the seventh onward. Clearly the modeller was anxious to leave a space for the head of the organist, who is once again a woman. Her face is stern and lacking in charm, and a diadem crowns the thick mass of hair covering part of her forehead. Neither her shoulders nor her breasts are visible.

The trumpeter, a misshapen dwarf,[14] obscures the whole of one side of the organ. He is blowing carelessly into his instrument, whose bell is almost trailing on the ground. Everything suggests that the statuette is a caricature, or a scene from a comic play, if the players' costumes are any guide. It seems ridiculous to suggest that this is a portrait of Ktesibios, whose prestige was always so high, and his wife Thaïs,[15] or to interpret it as a representation of Queen Arsinoë.[16]

5. *The Via Appia graffito* (Plate III, no. 2). This graffito, again featuring a scene from the amphitheatre, is traced on one of the walls of a Roman villa discovered under the basilica of S. Sebastian in Rome.[17] It is a simple sketch, the work of a child or at least some non-professional artist.

It shows two pairs of gladiators fighting to the music of a hydraulic organ, a trumpet, and a horn. On the left, the tubicen is blowing into his trumpet, which he holds pointed downwards: on the right stands the cornicen. Between these two musicians, and slightly behind them, is the organ. Its deepish base supports a water cistern taller than it is wide, and on each side are the pumps, whose piston-rods are also shown. The pump handles are worked by two short-robed figures who grip them in both hands. The top part of the cylinders seems to be incorporated with the wind-chest, which is very shallow. To either side of this we see the silhouettes of two youths whose role is not clear. The organ has approximately twelve pipes, held steady by a slanting transverse bar fixed to uprights. The treble pipes are to the left of the organist, whose head is barely distinguishable.

14 The Louvre has a number of these 'grotesques' from the Hellenistic era, several of them afflicted with a variety of pathological deformities. See the article by D. and M. Gourevitch, 'Terres-cuites hellénistiques d'inspiration médicale au Musée du Louvre', *La Presse Médicale*, 71, no. 55 (25 December 1963), pp. 2751-2.

15 This is suggested by Tittel in Pauly-Wissowa, op. cit., art. 'Hydraulis'.

16 Degering, op. cit., p. 72.

17 Published by C. Mercurelli, 'Hydraulus graffito su epigrafe sepolcrale del cimeterio di Commodilla', *Rivista di Archaeologia cristiana* (Città del Vaticano, 1938), p. 95. See my sketch, fig. 3.

The hydraulic organ drawn here is about 2 m. high, judging by the stature of the figures. The graffito probably dates from the end of the second century or the beginning of the third century.

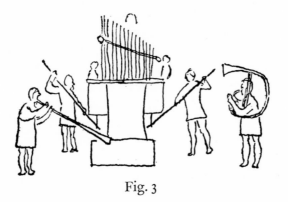

Fig. 3

6. *Consular diptych of Verona* (Plate III, no. 1). This fine Byzantine diptych, preserved in the Capitulary Museum in Verona, dates from 517. It shows the Emperor Anastasius I seated on a magnificent throne, dressed in his robes of triumph. Underneath are representations of circus scenes. The upper section features two racehorses with their drivers, and the lower a group of ten people, five of them children. In the foreground a juggler is demonstrating his skill with five balls, to the left a musician is blowing into a large syrinx with seven reeds, and to the right another is seen playing on a hydraulic organ.[18]

This instrument, seen rather from one side, consists of a water cistern of the usual type, mounted on a narrow base and flanked by two tall air pumps. The left-hand pump is worked by a child, who is vigorously cranking the lever, and the right-hand pump is evidently being cranked by someone else who is out of sight. Very little of the wind-chest is visible: the pipes, six in number, are open at the top, and held in place by two slanting bars. The treble pipes are to the organist's right, and part of his body is shown. He is young, with a great deal of curly hair. His right hand is on the manual, resting on the treble notes, while his left hand, obscured by the pipes, may well be playing in the bass, judging by the angle of his body. His head is turned towards the juggler, as though he were timing his music to the latter's movements. The height of the instrument seems to be not more than 1·80 m.

It is a gay scene, lacking the tragic shadow cast by the gladiatorial combats on the other mosaics we have studied. It no doubt represents celebrations organized by the Emperor.

[18] R. Delbrück, *Die Consulardiptychen* (Berlin/Leipzig, 1926), iii, no. 19.

7 and 8. *The organs on the Obelisk at Constantinople*. On the base of the obelisk erected by Theodosius the Great in 390 in the centre of the hippodrome at Byzantium, various circus scenes are carved. One of these shows an orchestra composed of several instruments—syrinx, aulos, and two organs. The Emperor is seen standing on the *pulvinar* (platform) surrounded by his dignitaries. In his right hand he holds a crown, to be awarded to the victor. Below him, before an audience of forty or so spectators, the dancing-girls move in time with the music. At either end of the orchestra there is an organ.

However, these are not hydraulic organs, for they look quite different, and are actually fed by great bellows. The right-hand organ (Plate IV, no. 1) consists of a wind-chest serving as a base, connected by a long tube to a capacious bellows, on which two children are standing. There are eleven pipes supported by a slanting bar. The treble pipes are to the left of the organist, whose head appears at this side, as though he were following the course of the spectacle in order to fit his music to it.

The left-hand organ (Plate IV, no. 2) is almost identical, though it has only eight pipes, their lips plainly visible.[19] The supporting bar is horizontal, but this time the treble pipes are to the right of the organist, and it seems as though the sculptor's main consideration was the symmetry of his design rather than its accuracy. In fact, the organist's head appears on the same side as the treble pipes, and it is also on this side that the bellows is shown, again with two children perched on it.

The wind-mechanism of these two organs presents an embarrassing problem. It hardly seems likely that the bellows represented here actually generated air, for it is difficult to imagine the young organ-blowers raising the upper board to fill the bellows with air and then scrambling up on them to empty them again. In any case, the organ could have been played for only a brief moment using this system. A more reasonable explanation seems to be that there were other bellows, manually operated by experts and producing air which was piped into the bellows shown on the bas-relief. These large bellows would then have functioned as regulator-compressors, with the weight of the children fulfilling the function of the stones placed on the bellows of present-day organs.

This piece of evidence illustrates perfectly the place of the organ in the secular ceremonial of the Byzantine court, as described in the texts analysed in chapter X.

THE ORGAN WITH HUMAN FIGURES

Illustrations showing the organ with a variety of human figures, but without other musical instruments, form the largest group. The people involved,

[19] Because the lips are not shown on the right-hand organ, G. Bruns concludes, a trifle hastily, that it has reed pipes (*Der Obelisk und seine Basis*, Istanbul, 1935, p. 67).

whether performing or merely listening, always contribute something of interest to each example.

9. *The Roman terracotta* (Plate VII, no. 3). This small pottery fragment, now in the Museum of the German Cemetery in the Vatican, just beside St. Peter's, is said to come from the Villa Ludovisi and to have been found in the closing years of the last century.[20]

In the foreground is a man with a thick head of hair. His right arm is extended in a gesture of declamation or greeting, while his left rests on the stole of a costly *toga picta*. Behind him is a great decorated double door, possibly belonging to a temple or a theatre. To his right, but clearly somewhat behind him, is an organ—a hydraulic organ, whose water cistern is embellished with volutes. There must have been a pump to the right of it, but unfortunately the clay is broken at this level. The organ-blower, a child, is, however, plainly visible. Leaning his left elbow on the wind-chest, he is apparently pumping with his right hand. The wind-chest looks as though it is made in two parallel sections, with the lower of the two containing the mechanism, and the upper corresponding to the tabula summa which supports the pipes. There are seven of these, supported by a transverse bar, the trebles being to the left of the organist, whose head and shoulders appear above the instrument. He, too, has thick hair, and as he plays he attentively watches the movements of the principal figure.

Most writers see the latter as a singer. While this is possible, it is significant that his mouth is closed. Is he not more likely to be an actor acknowledging the acclaim of the crowd outside the doors of a theatre?

This piece of terracotta dates at the earliest from the end of the third century.

10. *The Rheims vase* (Plate VII, no. 2). A hydraulic organ decorates a small bronze vase now in the Petit Palais in Paris, and said to have been discovered at Rheims in 1852. It was formerly part of the Gréau collection.[21] Ovoid, 8·5 cm. high, and with a diameter of 4·5 cm. at its widest point, the vase is covered with motifs arranged in two bands. On the lower frieze are various animals, a lion, a boar, a panther, an antelope—all part of a venatio. The upper frieze depicts a munus, showing two pairs of gladiators in action, their names inscribed above the scene. Near the usual Hermes, Datius, the secutor, is seen attacking the retiarius Attiolus, and further along the

[20] Le Blant, *Comptes rendus de l'Académie des Inscriptions et Belles-Lettres* (1887), p. 114; G. Wilpert, 'Un Capitolo di storia del vestario', *L'Arte* (1898), p. 112.

[21] Fröhner, op. cit., p. 79, no. 373; A. Chabouillet, *Revue Archéologique* (1851), viii, p. 419. My thanks are due to Mme Cotté, curator of the Petit-Palais Museum, for allowing me to examine and photograph this vase.

Thracian Heros lies where he has been struck down, in a good position for having his throat cut by Audax. The summa rudis, who is controlling the fight, is touching Audax with his stick to halt the struggle until first the editor and then the crowd have decided whether or not the defeated man is to be spared. Two slaves hold up a notice on which the word 'Perseverate' is written—probably the verdict that was passed.[22]

The organ stands between the two groups of combatants, its main features clearly recognizable. The base, in two distinct parts, is itself mounted on a shallow decorated dais. The almost square outline of the water cistern is ornamented with three small circles placed to form a triangle. On either side are the pumps, whose levers are not shown: but on the right is an organ-blower who seems to be working in a kneeling position. Possibly the handle he is cranking is behind the organ and operates both pumps at once. The wind-chest, topped by the tabula summa, which is clearly visible, supports eight pipes describing a steep downward slant—the largest pipe is about five times the length of the smallest. The treble pipes are to the right of the organist, of whom nothing can be seen but his head.

On the vase, the organ is 19 mm. high and the wind-chest 10 mm. across. In relation to the figures of the gladiators, who are on roughly the same plane, the instrument is not quite 2 m. high, and the wind-chest approximately 1 m. across: the tallest pipe measures 50 cm., and the smallest 10 cm. The pumps average 50 cm. in height.

Note that here again the hydraulic organ appears in a scene illustrating that stage in the combat immediately preceding the dispatch of the vanquished gladiator. Presumably the instrument was always heard at this sombre moment.

From its shape, it is generally thought that the Rheims vase dates from the second half of the second century or early in the third century.

11. *The Copenhagen vase* (Plate VII, no. 4). The same type of scene is represented on the clay vase found in 1870 at Thorslunde, in the neighbourhood of Roskilde, and now in the Nationalmuseet in Copenhagen. Unfortunately it was broken when found, and a number of pieces are still missing. It is 7 cm. in height and decorated with a polychrome design, roughly drawn, showing a gladiatorial combat. We can make out three men involved in the struggle, as well as a hydraulic organ with its organist. The instrument has a broad base on which the water cistern is mounted. This cistern, wider than it is deep, displays on its front panel the design of a vase patterned in squares, whose significance is not clear. There are two lateral pumps fixed between the base and the wind-chest. A little below the middle point of each run

---

[22] Héron de Villerosse and Thédenat (*Les Trésors de vaiselle d'argent*, Paris, 1885, p. 89) were mistaken in thinking that this scene represented a school for gladiators.

two parallel horizontal lines, perhaps marking the division between piston and cylinder. The wind-chest is wide and quite deep, and, unlike the base, it is not horizontal, but slightly slanting, probably to convey some idea of the perspective. It is decorated with a criss-cross pattern of lines. Fourteen pipes are visible, all with the same wide diameter, supported by a narrow oblique bar. The graduation in height is slight, the largest pipe being about 1·7 times the size of the smallest. A vague suggestion of the organist's head appears above the pipes, but there are no organ-blowers.[23]

The colours are here purely decorative. Base, cistern, pumps, and pipes are tinted ochre, and the wind-chest is green.

The archaeologists of the Copenhagen Museum place this vase in the third century: but other experts[24] calculate that it belongs at the earliest to the fourth century, perhaps even the fifth.

This decorated vase was found, together with other funeral objects, beside a skeleton. Probably it was intended to propitiate the Gods in the name of some gladiator killed in combat or of a patron of the *munus*.

12. *The uninscribed sarcophagus of Arles* (Plate VI). This great uninscribed sarcophagus was discovered at Arles, at the Alyscamps, near the entrance to the Clos des Capucins. At the present time it is housed in the Musée Lapidaire. It is 2·22 m. in length, 86 cm. high, 80 cm. across, and is in a bad state of preservation, the motifs decorating its front having become worn and defaced. Unfortunately its original inscription has disappeared, chiselled off to make room for a new text engraved on a marble plaque which has in turn been lost.[25] This inscription took up the central space. To the left we see a temple and a figure apparently in the act of sacrificing; on the right there is a hydraulic organ with an organist and two organ-blowers.

This instrument, which has nine pipes, is of a somewhat special type, and indeed the cistern, wind-chest and pumps have rather unusual features. Could it be an example of the local style of manufacture? Its hexagonal cistern is tall and narrow, sits on a broad, sturdy base and supports the central section of the wind-chest. Two horizontal pipes, one above and one below, connect it on either side to the cylinders. The function of the upper pipe is clearly to bring the air from the pump to the neck of the pnigeus; but the lower pipe seems to be there simply to hold the cylinder firmly parallel to the cistern.

A special feature of the pumps is that their height is more than four times their diameter, though that is not to say that the piston ran all the way up

[23] Engelhardt gives a concise description of the scene in 'Statuettes romaines et autres objets d'art . . .', *Mémoires de la Société des Antiquaires du Nord* (1872), pp. 59 ff.
[24] Engelhardt in particular.
[25] E. Espérandieu, *Recueil général des bas-reliefs de la Gaule romaine*, Paris (1907), I, no. 180.

and down the cylinder. Actually, if we look closely at the pump levers, we find that their pivot, which seems to be supported by the base, is marked by a slight curve, clearly seen on the right-hand lever. This point is some four-fifths of the way down, and it is easy to see that the movement of the piston-rod was quite restricted. Note, too, that here again the task of working the levers is entrusted to adolescents. One is reminded of Athenaeus's account, in which it is an urchin, νεανίσκος, who carries out this work; in Porfyrius Optatianus it is done by youths. The attitude of the two organ-blowers represented on this piece suggests that no great effort can have been involved.

The wind-chest, considerably wider than the cistern, is flat, and supports nine pipes set rather wide apart and held in place by a slanting crossbar supported in turn by two lateral uprights.[26] Only one set of pipes is visible, though others may be concealed behind it. The treble pipes are to the organist's right, and the lowest pipe of all is scarcely more than a third as long again as the highest pitched. No lips are visible, so that this may be a set of reed pipes. Above them appear the head and shoulders of the organist, whose arms, slightly extended, indicate beyond all doubt that he is playing with both hands. Though his features have been obliterated, his attitude reflects a degree of nobility, recalling the 'proud man' described by the Emperor Julian. The approximate dimensions, calculated from the height of the organist, of the instrument are as follows: overall height, a little more than 2 m.; cistern, 1 m. deep by 60 cm. across; cylinders, 75 cm. by 15 cm.; largest pipe, 52 cm.; smallest pipe 40 cm.; diameter, less than 5 cm.

This is presumably not an amphitheatre scene. At a guess, the deceased, whose identity is unknown, is both the organist of the right-hand scene and the figure in the temple on the left. Perhaps it is the sepulchre of a priest who also played the organ.

This sarcophagus is generally dated to the third or fourth century.

13. *The British Museum gem* (Plate VIII, n. 2). The origin of this very fine stone, a piece of reddish sardonyx, now in the British Museum, is unknown.[27] All we know is that it was once part of the Hertz collection.[28] Oval in shape, it measures 13 by 9 mm. and shows a hydraulic organ, delicately engraved, together with its organist and two organ-blowers hard at work. The design has been executed with meticulous care.[29]

The instrument is a large one, of the normal type. It has a base, on which

---

[26] Degering counts these as pipes, making his total eleven; probably he had never actually seen the sarcophagus, and was working from an indifferent sketch.

[27] H. B. Walters, *Catalogue of the engraved gems and cameos* (London, 1926).

[28] 122, no. 1051.

[29] Our photograph shows the positive cast.

stands the water cistern, cylindrical, adorned above and below with a circular band perhaps designed to strengthen it. A vertical bar in front probably serves the same purpose.

On either side of the cistern is a pump, composed of a cylinder and a plainly visible piston. A pipe runs from the top of the cylinder to the wind-chest, implying that in this case the air is led directly into the κανών μουσικός which itself communicates with the funnel of the pnigeus. Mechanically this arrangement is perfectly workable. To the piston is attached a piston-rod joined to a lever. Each lever is operated by a boy, the one on the left holding his almost at the top of its upward swing, the one on the right almost at its lowest point. This suggests that the pumps function alternately, so that the water level in the cistern does not fall, and the air pressure within the wind-chest remains constant.

The wind-chest is wide, and appears to be slightly concave. There are roughly thirteen pipes, the smallest to the organist's right. They are held by the customary slanting bar; but there is no sign of any lateral uprights. The highest pitched pipe is approximately three times smaller than the lowest, and would therefore sound a twelfth above it. If there are indeed thirteen pipes, the manual would give more or less the Pythagorean diatonic scale, with the added B flats. The lips of the pipes are not shown: but these are unlikely to be reed pipes. It is obvious, however, that the engraving is very detailed, suggesting that the craftsman was reproducing a model that was there for him to consult.

Above the pipes we see the head and part of the body of the organist, and by comparing the respective heights of the man and his instrument we can gauge that the overall height of the organ is 2·30 m., the length of the largest pipe 90 cm. and the smallest 30 cm., and the width of the wind-chest 1·15 m.

Along the top right-hand curve of the gem runs the inscription WΛΛ, which a number of epigraphists interpret as follows:

AM[ICUM] V[OTUM] V[OVIT]
He has fulfilled a vow of friendship.

Degering hazards the guess that the gem was presented to some famous organist by an admirer, and this is probably not too far from the truth.

Experts at the British Museum date this gem to the third century A.D.

14. *The Rheinzabern vase* (Plate VIII, no. 3). This graceful vase, with its egg-shaped belly and tapering neck, is 13 cm. high and 6·5 cm. across at its widest point. At present it is on show at the Speyer Museum, and originally comes from Rheinzabern.

On its sides we see a gladiatorial combat, with two men fighting. A retiarius, armed with the regulation net and trident, swoops down on his opponent, a secutor, who waits with his dagger drawn. Beside them is a third figure, playing the organ and closely watching the fight.

The instrument, though highly stylized, is still recognizable as a hydraulic organ. The water cistern is represented by a kind of square tank decorated with simple geometric motifs. On either side are the pumps, symbolized by small oval shapes. No wind-chest is shown, and the pipes seem to rise straight out of the water cistern. They appear to number ten, with the treble pipes to the right of the organist, and there is no visible supporting bar.

Above them rise the head and shoulders of the player, whom we see in profile, for his gaze is fixed on the gladiators on his right. The hair is long and curling, and there is a necklace round the neck. The face is probably that of a woman.

This little vase, probably nothing more than a trinket or keepsake, is thought to be from the third century.

15. *Aphrodisis' organ* (Plate VIII, no. 1). An interesting illustration of a hydraulic organ was published in 1904 by Carl Patsch.[30] This piece of evidence, relatively unknown, is a funeral stele measuring 0·85 m. by 0·50 m., found in the Kostat house in Sop, in 1900.[31] It shows two figures standing full-face. On the right is a woman, apparently about forty years old, wearing a long robe falling in folds about her feet, and what looks like a knee-length cape. Her left hand grasps an indeterminate object—possibly a mirror—which she presses to her breast, while her right hand rests affectionately on the shoulder of a younger and smaller woman. The girl is bareheaded and dressed in a short, full garment. There can be little doubt that they are, in fact, mother and daughter.

On the girl's right stands a hydraulic organ. The customary plinth is square and is rather deep, and supports a squat hexagonal water cistern decorated with mouldings at its base and upper edge. The wind-chest, ornamented with a simple trellis pattern, carries nine pipes held in place by a slanting crossbar, though there are no lateral uprights. As far as may be judged from the design, the pipes appear to have lips. The smallest is more than half as long as the largest pipe, and the trebles are to the right of the organist. The manual side of the instrument is not shown, but the girl's right hand is undoubtedly resting on the keys.

The hydraulic organ shown here seems extremely small—barely as tall as the organist herself. However, it is probably represented in a purely

---

[30] *Schriften der Balkankommission*, iii: 'Das Sandschak Berat in Albanien' (Vienna, 1904), p. 166, fig. 138.

[31] Thought to be no longer in Albania. No photograph is available and for the moment we have to make do with Patsch's sketch.

conventional way, to symbolize the fact that it was the dead girl's favourite instrument. Her name is commemorated in the following inscription:

ΑΦΡΟΔΙΣΙΣ ΕΤΩΝ Κ ΧΑΙΡΕ ΛΥΚΑΗΜΗΤΗΡ ΕΠΟΙΕΙΖΩΣ

('To the memory of Aphrodisis, aged twenty years. [This monument] was erected by Lucas, her mother, in her lifetime.'[32])

This stele, which the lettering of the inscription and the sculptor's technique date to the end of the second century or the beginning of the third century, is interesting in that it testifies to the presence of the hydraulic organ even in such an outlying province.

16. *The Tatarevo organ* (Plate VIII, no. 4). This appears on a small funeral monument discovered in Bulgaria in 1936.[33] Excavations in the vicinity of Tatarevo, a small village in the Borissovgrad district approximately 40 km. south-east of Philippopoli, revealed this white marble stele consisting of a rectangular base and a prism-shaped column, reaching an overall height of 1·05 m. On the front of the base are three figures. On the left stands a gladiator, wearing an iron mask and protected by a huge rectangular shield. On the right his vanquished opponent, seated on the ground, raises his right hand in a plea for mercy. Between the two appears a curly-haired summa rudis. He wields a heavy sabre in place of the customary baton, and his gesture indicates clearly that he is ordering the winner to refrain from delivering the *coup de grâce* to the wounded man. We recognize this as the phase of the struggle most frequently depicted in gladiatorial scenes.

Half-way up the column, above the figures, the sculptor has carved the amphitheatre organ, on a greatly reduced scale. Again it is a hydraulic organ, with a tall, slender water cistern, two pumps, a wind-chest, and a rank of nine pipes.

The cistern, mounted on its plinth, appears to be hexagonal, widening towards the top, under the wind-chest, which is made in two parts, one superimposed on the other and both of approximately the same depth.

On either side of the wind-chest and extending slightly below it are two rounded objects representing the pumps. Two figures, which look like children, are seated on these, with their backs towards us, though their faces are turned in the direction of the audience. They are undoubtedly engaged in pumping the handles of the wind mechanism, despite the

[32] I am most grateful to F. Braemer and H. Pflaum, who were good enough to examine and date this evidence for me.

[33] A description is given in the *Bulletin of the Bulgarian Archaeological Institute*, xiv (1940–2), pp. 217–18. Professor Alföldi drew my attention to this monument in 1952, when he sent me a manuscript monograph by Zlaska Morfova of the National Library in Sofia.

peculiar position of the arms on the left-hand figure.[34] The overall height of the instrument sculpted in the marble is 24·5 cm., but the execution is too roughly done for us to make any sense of the various anomalies present in the design. An organ constructed as shown here would be incapable of even standing by itself.

Beneath the figures, the monument carries the following inscription:

ΕΠΙΠΤΑΣ ΠΟΥΛΣΑΤΩΡ

(Epiptas pulsator)

Epiptas is a Thracian name, unknown elsewhere. In Latin, the word 'pulsator' usually means 'he who strikes'; but from the end of the first century A.D. it could sometimes have the additional meaning of 'he who plays upon a stringed instrument'.[35] It has been suggested that in this instance the sculptor is referring to a certain type of gladiator who specializes in a particular method of attack:[36] but it is not impossible that Epiptas is the name of the man shown between the two combatants, and that he is perhaps their fencing-master (*doctor*), their trainer, who takes his turn at playing on the hydraulic organ in order to co-ordinate and infuse rhythm into his pupils' movements.[37] Zlaska Morfova rightly draws attention to the fact that, contrary to what J. Colin says, the amphitheatre orchestra was not necessarily composed of professional musicians. A well-known graffito from Pompeii actually shows an armed gladiator sounding the cornu during the parade.[38] The fact remains that the hydraulis shown on this stele appears in a decorative, purely secondary role, and I feel, in the last analysis, that it is there simply to conjure up the special atmosphere surrounding the combats in the arena.[39] When they wished to pay homage to an organist Roman sculptors did not hesitate to place the instrument in the forefront of the monument concerned, as, for instance, on the sarcophagus of Julia Tyrannia, the Aphrodisis stele or the Rusticus marble.

Zlaska Morfova dates the Tatarevo monument to the second century or

---

[34] Z. Morfova ('Image of a classical organ in the Museum of Archaeology, Sofia', *Acta Archaeologica*, Budapest, 1962, xiv, 3–4, pp. 398–9), assumes that the levers are placed very high. But the mysterious presence of similar small figures on the Via Appia graffito, where the organ-blowers are shown in the foreground has already been noted. See p. 78.

[35] Valerius Flaccus, *Argon.*, v, 693; epitaph of Aelia Sabina; Corripus, *Iohann.*, iv, 577.

[36] Louis Robert, *Hellenica* (Paris, 1949), vii, p. 135–40; Jean Colin, 'Secutor et Iaculator-pulsator, vocables techniques de l'arène', *Mnémosyne* (1954), pp. 50–6.

[37] B. Gerov, quoted by Louis Robert.

[38] Daremberg-Saglio, fig. 3577, p. 1585. The authenticity of this evidence is unfortunately not completely certain.

[39] Despite the very strong arguments put forward by Georges Ville (*Recherches sur l'armement, l'équipement et la technique des gladiateurs romains*. Unpublished dissertation presented to the Ecole française in Rome, 1960).

the beginning of the third. Professor Lemerle, who was consulted on this point, opts for the third century on the evidence of the inscription.

17–24. *Contorniate medallions.* The whole question of contorniate medallions bears on the history of the organ because a number of them bear the image of the instrument on one of their surfaces. Thus it becomes necessary to know their significance and to be able to date them approximately.

The term contorniate is applied to a bronze medal, of considerable size, each face of which has a circular furrow traced near the outer rim. The front face of the medal usually bears the head of an emperor, while the reverse depicts a scene which is nearly always connected with the amphitheatre. However, it does not necessarily follow that the contorniates are contemporaneous with the prince shown on the face. Basing their assertions on styles of writing, incorrect titles, and actual errors, experts have definitely established that they did not exist until the late Empire, and that most of them are no earlier than the second half of the fourth century.

It is interesting to note how often Nero and Caracalla, who were both great circus patrons, figure on these medals. These contorniate medallions were struck to commemorate games or contests in the amphitheatre. They are not coins, and today it is generally agreed that they were probably good-luck tokens offered to the various favourites by their admirers.[40] Those of particular interest to us here may have been struck for musical festivals, a hypothesis which is strengthened by the fact that the favourite's name is always accompanied by some good-luck formula: 'Nika', 'Vincas', or 'Placeas', with the organ on the reverse face.

To date we know of the existence of twelve contorniates showing an organ—in each case a hydraulic organ. This is hardly surprising, for in the West the bellows organ was at that time incapable of producing a sufficient volume of sound to make it useful in the amphitheatre.

17. *The Valentinian III medallion* (Plate IX, no. 3). This is a very large medallion, 53 mm. in diameter. It comes from the collection of Queen Christina of Sweden, but its origins are unknown.

On the face is a bust, in profile, of the Emperor Valentinian III,[41] who reigned from 424 until 455, with the inscription: D N PLAVALEN-TIANUS PF AUG.

The reverse, which bears the words 'Placeas Petri', shows a hydraulic organ with two organ-blowers and an organist. Although roughly executed, the scene is an interesting one, for the organ is of an unusual type, probably very advanced. The water cistern, mounted on a huge plinth, is circular, or

---

40 See H. Stern, *Le Calendrier de 354* (Paris, 1953), p. 88.
41 Who killed Aëtius, victor over Attila on the Catalaunian Plains in 451.

perhaps hexagonal; contrary to the normal trend, it is wider than it is deep. Its upper part is decorated with a moulding. On either side are tall, narrow air pumps whose long handles, operating the crankshafts, are manipulated by figures so short in stature as to suggest that they are children. One of the levers is in a vertical position, while the other slopes at an angle of about 40°.

The wind-chest is of the orthodox type and supports ten or eleven pipes, though these are uncommonly tall—nearly twice the height of the cistern. They are held in place by two bars, one half-way up and the other at the bottom. They are graded in a gentle slant, with the treble pipes to the right of the organist, who is seen on the left-hand side of his organ. Whereas the organist's head generally towers over the organ pipes, here it reaches barely half-way up their length.

The man is dressed in a long straight tunic, and is bare-headed. He seems poised for action, for his gaze is fixed on what is going on, and the organ-blowers are already hard at work.

Allowing for the fact that the organ is slightly to the front of the organist, we can say that it must be at least 2·40 m. in height, and the average length of the pipes would be 1·50 m. It is not impossible that the instrument shown here is a new model, for, as we have seen, Ammianus Marcellinus, writing at this period, described a 'colossal' hydraulic organ. At all events it is the largest known hydraulis. The Peter mentioned in the description is probably a contemporary virtuoso.

This medallion, which cannot be much later than the reign of Valentinian III, is now in the Cabinet des Médailles in Paris.

18. *Nero contorniate* (Plate IX, no. 1). This fine specimen, also in the Cabinet des Médailles, has on its face a bust of Nero, accompanied by the following inscription:

IMP NERO CAESAR AUG P MAX

The Emperor, easily recognizable, is shown in profile, his head crowned with a wreath of leaves.[42] On the reverse face, we find the words 'LAU-RENTI NICA', and a hydraulic organ with a figure standing on its left. The instrument is of the usual type, with a hexagonal water cistern mounted on a similarly shaped base (though this is rather shallow) and decorated with mouldings which are clearly visible round its lower edge. The flat wind-chest supports seven pipes held in place by a slanting bar which in turn is held up by two lateral uprights. The manual is on the other side of the instrument, and is thus not visible; so that the treble pipes are to the right of the organist. The pumps are not shown; but on the right-hand side, and

[42] A. Alföldi, *Die Kontorniaten* (Budapest/Leipzig, 1943), Pl. XXXI, 2.

level with the wind-chest, there is a kind of lever jutting out obliquely which is undoubtedly part of the wind mechanism. The top of the player's body hides the left side of the organ, where the other lever is no doubt located.

This man is seen to be in a standing position, and is dressed in a long tunic. In his right hand he holds a triangular object which he seems to be displaying to the public. We do not know what this object is, or what to make of the large leaves on the ground to the right of the instrument. Perhaps they symbolize the attributes of victory, for in all probability the figure is Laurentius himself, the champion or favourite organist; his bearing exudes satisfaction. But whoever he is, his height enables us to calculate the dimensions of the organ. If, as seems likely, he is a young man, the overall height of the instrument is almost 2 m., the wind-chest measures 0·90 m. across, the longest pipe is approximately 0·90 m. in height and the smallest 0·80 m.

19. *Second Nero contorniate* (Plate IX, no. 2). In the British Museum[43] there is another contorniate somewhat similar in design bearing the effigy of the same prince and the same inscriptions. Here the Emperor's features are more youthful, and to the right of his face a palm is seen. The reverse shows a hydraulic organ, whose hexagonal water cistern is unadorned, and whose pumps and levers are not portrayed. It has eight pipes, with two uprights and a transverse bar. The treble pipes are to the right of the manual, which is on the other side of the instrument. The figure is more clearly depicted than on the previous medallion. He is wearing a belted, knee-length robe, and is holding out towards the public a triangular object grasped in his right hand. Behind him and to his right is what looks like an open cylindrical box and to the left of the organ are two large leaves.

20. *Caracalla contorniate* (Plate IX, no. 4). This medallion, which is also in the British Museum, is struck with the head of either Caracalla or Trajan.[44] The face expresses a certain nobility, but unfortunately the inscription is badly defaced and difficult to decipher. An intaglio palm tree seems to have been added later. The reverse face, which has no inscription, represents a hydraulic organ rather different from those we have seen. The water cistern, apparently equal in width and depth, is almost entirely obscured by a seated figure whose head is turned to the right and who appears to be offering someone an object held in his right hand, while his left rests on his knee. On either side of the instrument is a cylindrical pump, complete with its

43 Alföldi, Pl. XXXI, 3.
44 Alföldi, Pl. XXXIX, 8. I should like to express my thanks to the department of Roman Antiquities of the British Museum, which procured excellent casts of these medals for me.

handle. The musical section consists of eleven pipes, held in place by a horizontal bar, in turn supported by two lateral uprights.

The impression given here is that the figure—certainly the organist—is seated behind the organ and conceals the actual manual. The treble pipes would thus be on his right. Another point is that here he is playing sitting down, his body slightly turned round to greet his admirers who have come to offer their congratulations.

To either side of the instrument we see triangular objects placed one on top of the other—again, these are presumably the fruits of victory.

21. *Second Caracalla contorniate* (Plate IX, no. 5). The inscription on the face of this medallion (also in the British Museum), which bears the monogram P̄, is again difficult to decipher, though it appears to refer once more to Caracalla.[45]

The reverse face shows a different scene this time. In the centre is a hydraulic organ, whose water cistern, mounted on a plinth, is deeper than it is wide, and unadorned. Above the wind-chest, however, is a semi-circular object marked off in segments—rather like a half-wheel—which obscures the lower ends of the six middle pipes. It is impossible to tell whether this is a decorative motif or a functional part of the structure. The wind-chest supports nine or ten pipes, but has no bar or lateral upright supports; and here again the treble pipes are on the organist's right. On either side of the instrument two figures, of feminine aspect, are shown, the right-hand figure brandishing the familiar triangular object.

22 and 23. *Other Caracalla contorniates* (Plate IX, nos. 7 and 8). There are six more contorniate medallions almost identical with the last one,[46] all show-ing the same figures standing to right and left of the instrument, whose shape varies very slightly on each specimen, though none is fitted with the mysterious half-wheel. All these different examples certainly belong to the same era, if not to the same issue.[47]

24. *The Grenoble medallion* (Plate XI, no. 2). This contorniate, now in the museum at Grenoble (Cat. no. 6594), is struck in the name of Salustius Autor. The reverse face shows three figures, presumably actors, engaged in a theatrical performance. The central figure holds in his left hand a small instrument with pipes, which Sabatier[48] likens to an organ. We are able to

---

[45] ibid., Pl. XXXI, 4. For the significance of the monogram P̄, which occurs frequently on the contorniates, see H. Marrou, 'Palma et Laurus', *Mélanges d'archéologie et d'histoire*, vol. lviii (1941–6), pp. 109–31.

[46] Alföldi, Pl. XXXI, 1; XXXII, 12; XXXVII, 1; XXXVII, 2; XLV, 12; LVIII, 7.

[47] Alföldi, p. 126, no. 208.

[48] J. Sabatier, *Description générale des médaillons contorniates* (Paris, 1860), p. 69, no. 4.

distinguish five pipes held in place half-way up by a crossbar; but there is no evidence of any wind-chest. Judging by the stance of the figure, the instrument seems to be very light. While it is possible, as Degering suggests,[49] that this is a small-scale model of a pneumatic organ, it seems to me, as to Alföldi,[50] more likely that the object is actually a syrinx.

The words PETRONI PLACEAS, which run round the edge of the medallion on the reverse side, are again a dedicatory formula.

25. *The Orange medallion* (Plate XI, no. 1). The scene reproduced here resembles that just described, for it, too, is set in the theatre. This fragment of terracotta, which appears to have been used as a contorniate, is in the Saint-Germain Museum, Cat. no. 31673. Originally it came from Orange, and was acquired in 1889.[51] A similar motif, though smaller and badly mutilated, is preserved in the museum at Vienne, near Lyons.

This medallion is oval in shape, and measures approximately 10 cm. by 11·3 cm. It shows two people in stage costume. The figure on the right, wearing a long, sleeveless tunic, is holding a double thyrsus in his left hand, while with the right he triumphantly waves a theatrical mask. The other figure, decidedly smaller in stature, appears to be an adolescent. He is dressed in a long garment covering his legs, and a tunic with sleeves. In his left hand he grasps what looks like a roll of paper, and in his right a great palm leaf, the emblem of victory, which he is presumably offering to the triumphant actor.

In the foreground between these two figures is a small instrument with pipes, standing on the ground—and in this case there can be no doubt that it is an organ. A relatively deep wind-chest, patterned with decorative lines, supports seven pipes graduated from left to right and held in place by a gently slanting bar: there is no sign of lateral uprights, or of a manual, either because the latter is on the other side of the wind-chest or just as probably because the artist felt there was no point in reproducing it on such a small scale.

The wind-chest is mounted on a rectangular base a little narrower and scarcely as deep as itself. Perhaps this base is actually a water cistern, in which case the organ would be a hydraulis—or is it simply a plinth, making the instrument into a small 'pneumatic', fed by bellows and corresponding to the descriptions of Pollux and St. Augustine? It seems to me that the first hypothesis is the more likely one, and if, in fact, the absence of bellows is not in itself a sufficient argument to eliminate the second, the existence of such a base can only be justified if we compare it to the 'arca' or water reservoir. A

[49] op. cit., p. 81.
[50] Alföldi, p. 126, 212.
[51] J. Roulez, 'Trois médaillons de poteries romaines', *Gazette archéologique* (1877), p. 72.

further point to note here is the resemblance between this instrument and the organ on the Rheinzabern vase; and it should also be remembered that the vast proportions of a Graeco-Roman theatre would have been ill suited to the feeble, uncertain notes of a small instrument with no hydraulic compressor. Thus the argument put forward by Degering, who refuses to acknowledge this organ as a hydraulis because of the disproportionate sizes of the wind-chest and the cistern, is not at all convincing.[52]

Assuming that the actor is of medium height, the approximate measurements of the instrument would be:

Overall height: 80 cm.
Height of the lowest-pitched pipe: 42 cm.
Height of the highest-pitched pipe: 20 cm.
Width of the wind-chest: 40 cm.
Depth of the cistern: 18 cm.

It would seem, then, that this is a small hydraulic organ with a tessitura somewhere in the region of an octave. Possibly it was used to accompany the sung parts of the tragedy or comedy. The medallion bears the following inscription:

NICA PART[HE]NOPAEE

This hope for victory, addressed to the actor Parthenopaeus, together with the palm presented to him, suggests some kind of contest, and the fragment of terracotta, like the contorniates, is probably a goodluck token.

The medallion, which seems to be of local manufacture,[53] is said to date from the end of the second or the beginning of the third century.

26. *The St.-Maximin sarcophagus* (Plate X). In the crypt of the basilica of St.-Maximin (Var) stands a very fine marble sarcophagus, dating from the period of Constantine. On one of the lateral faces, which is unfortunately very badly lit, is a bas-relief 1 m. long by 0·78 m. in height. It represents a familiar Christian tableau, the resurrection of Tabitha, as related in the Acts of the Apostles (IX, 36–43). The dead woman has just seated herself on her bed, and Peter is offering her his hand. At the foot of the bed, behind a pillar, stands a hydraulic organ. The water cistern, which is decorated with grooves, appears to be cylindrical in shape, and is mounted on a small hexagonal plinth. The wind-chest is relatively deep, and supports eight pipes reducing in height from left to right. At the foot of each pipe the rings described by

[52] Degering, op. cit., pp. 84–5.
[53] An identical medallion, also found at Orange, forms part of a private collection: P. Wuilleumier and A. Audin, *Les médaillons d'applique gallo-romains de la vallée du Rhône* (Paris, 1952), p. 77, no. 108.

Vitruvius as securing them to the tabula summa are clearly visible. In this instance they are certainly flue pipes, for the slanting line of lips is plain to see. Furthermore, they are stopped, for we can see the ends of the tampons blocking the upper orifices. The whole pipe structure is held in place by a grooved transverse bar. The manual does not show, for it is at the other side of the organ. Nor are there pumps—though, as we have seen, these are often omitted. However, it is possible that what we see here is a fairly large pneumatic organ standing on a table.

The overall height of the instrument is almost equal to that of St. Peter, which would give the longest pipe a height of approximately 76 cm. from top to bottom, and the smallest 58 cm.

The most interesting aspect of this sculpture is that it shows an organ in a Christian mortuary, and though a number of explanations for this are possible, none is definite. Perhaps Tabitha has been depicted in the guise of a dead woman who in life was an organist by profession. Perhaps it was customary in those days for an organ to be played at the funerals of believers. Or it may simply have been used to accompany the singing of chants or psalms.[54] It is also possible, as Fr. Arbus[55] suggests, that the organ is here symbolic of the joys in store in the hereafter; though this hypothesis is rather difficult to sustain, since in actual fact the scene represents a return to life here on earth. I am tempted to think that it is an eschatological motif directly inspired by the traditions of Greece and Rome.[56]

27. *The Utrecht Psalter organ.* Although the instrument shown here is incontestably a hydraulic organ, the manuscript does not belong to ancient times, but to the later middle ages. It will be examined in a subsequent chapter.

28. *The organ in Autun Museum* (Plate VII, no. 1). This forms part of an uninscribed funeral stele, approximately 1·05 m. in height, originally from the Autun region and now preserved in the Autun Museum.[57] It shows the deceased, who must have been a professional musician, dressed in a loose mantle with wide sleeves, and holding in his hands a long tibia. To his right stands an instrument with six or seven pipes decreasing in height from right to left. It is legitimate to suppose that this is an organ, and not a large syrinx, since the pipes on the latter usually slant in the opposite direction. A windchest supports the pipes, and the whole apparatus appears to be standing on

54 This is the opinion of E. Le Blant, *Les sarcophages chrétiens de la Gaule* (Paris, 1886), p. 153.
55 *Une Merveille d'Art Provençal* (Aix-en-Provence, 1955), p. 32.
56 A lyre or a pandoura is often present near the image of a dead person. See H. Marrou's study, Μουσικὸς Ἀνήρ (Grenoble, 1937), pp. 154 ff. and pp. 216 ff.
57 E. Espérandieu, op. cit., iii, no. 1876.

a table—there is no evidence of either a cistern or a plinth. Presumably it is a small pneumatic organ.

The monument appears to date from the third century at the earliest.

29. *The lamp in the museum at Carthage* (Plate XII, nos. 1 and 2, and Plate XI, no. 6). This lamp, made in the shape of a hydraulic organ, is probably the most meticulously executed as well as the most perfect reproduction of the instrument that we have. At its meeting of 8 May 1885 the Académie des Inscriptions et Belles-Lettres received a communication from Fr. Delattre announcing its discovery:[58]

I am sending you [he wrote] a photographed sketch of a terracotta object recently found at Carthage, representing a complete organ. This object, probably a child's toy, is 0·19 m. in height.

In my opinion the value of the piece lies in the details which reproduce the special features of organs at the time when this terracotta was made. The finely traced inscription POSSESSORIS may be compared to a mark copied by me from the base of a Roman lamp, reading:

PVLLAEN

POSSESSOR

This enables us moreover to fix the date of our terracotta as somewhere around the 2nd century A.D., for the name PVLLAENI recurs frequently on Roman lamps unearthed in our two cemeteries which date back to the same era.

The terracotta, now in the Lavigerie Museum at Carthage, measures exactly 17·8 cm. high by 8 cm. wide by 2 cm. deep, and represents an elegantly designed hydraulic organ with its organist. The organ-blowers are not included. The work has been done with exquisite care, and we may suppose that the artist was copying an actual model. The organist, whose body has been broken off above the knees, and is missing,[59] is standing on a kind of platform consisting of an ordinary wooden plank fixed half-way up the pumps. The instrument matches Vitruvius's description exactly, with its solid, square base supporting the water cistern and its uprights, 'shaped like ladders', to which the cylinders are attached. Here again the cistern is hexagonal, with a sort of moulding at top and bottom. It is almost twice as deep as it is wide. It is flanked by two pump cylinders, each approximately half as deep as the cistern, which are held in place by three encircling bands, one at the top, one in the middle, and the third at the bottom, all three fixed to the uprights. There are neither piston-rods nor levers. The

---

[58] Académie des Inscriptions et Belles-Lettres, *Comptes rendus* (1885), p. 96.
[59] Fr. Deneauve, curator of the Lavigerie Museum in Carthage, has recently discovered the body of the organist among the reserves of the museum. The head is missing (Pl. XI, no. 3).

volume of these pumps in relation to the overall dimensions of the instrument is considerable, and implies a fairly large output of air. Indeed, the wind-chest supports three ranks of eighteen pipes, though the sculptor, in error, has made nineteen on the front of the organ, whereas the reverse shows only eighteen, and the manual has eighteen keys.

In the first rank, on the front of the instrument, all the pipes are clearly equal in diameter. They are held in place by a slanting cross-bar attached to two uprights, one on either side, by a decorative circular motif. This bar is missing on the reverse side.

The pipes are flue pipes, the lips quite clearly visible, the diamond-shaped orifices looking very much like those on modern organs. The effective length of the largest and smallest pipes, measured from the lip to the top, shows a numerical ratio of something like 16/27, roughly corresponding to the major sixth. Now, to fix eighteen notes at equal intervals, as indicated by the regular lengthening of the pipes, within the limits of a major sixth, necessitates the use of quarter tones. The wind-mechanism would consequently have had to produce a steady enough flow of air to guarantee such fine tuning. Experiments appear to confirm this. At all events, the statuette is modelled with some degree of accuracy, and we should beware of jumping to the conclusion that there has been any error of observation on the part of the craftsman.

Two more ranks of pipes, of different pitches, are shown on the same side as the manual. One is about half the height of the first rank, allowing for the fact that the manual masks the foot of the pipes; and the other about two-thirds. This means that the instrument represented here had three stops —a principal stop, an octave stop and perhaps a fifth stop, which, used together, must have resulted in a bright-sounding full organ (Plate XI, no. 6).

The manual is well shown, with its eighteen oblong keys, exactly in line with the pipes—an inevitable arrangement in any wind-chest with sliders. These keys, which are relatively broad, are set very low in relation to the organist, for they barely reach mid-thigh level. This anomaly, which would have needlessly complicated the playing of the instrument, is easily explained. The figure of the organist was not modelled with the organ, but made separately and joined with barbotine joints, which are clearly visible and are moreover rather clumsily contrived. Whoever was entrusted with this minor task was certainly not the modeller, and was not worried about this small point.

The front of the wind-chest, decorated top and bottom with mouldings, bears the word POSSESSORIS, traced in elegant characters—presumably the name of the maker. High on each side two large holes have been bored, whose significance has baffled many musicologists. Clément Loret[60] has

[60] op. cit., p. 26.

hazarded a guess that the pump handles were passed through them—an untenable hypothesis—while Degering[61] thought they might be sockets for decorative motifs. In fact, as J. Deneauve[62] has demonstrated, what we have here is a lamp made in the shape of a hydraulic organ, and these holes are the burners. This is further proved by the existence of the oil container, hollowed out inside the instrument, its base on a level with the middle of the water cistern. The oil was poured in through an opening to the right of the manual. This fully justifies Fr. Delattre's observation quoted above, and the mark PVLLAEN POSSESSOR is that of a manufacturer of lamps.

Assuming that the organist was of medium stature, the instrument would have had an overall height of 2·30 m., and a width of 1 m. The largest pipe on the principal set would have measured 90 cm. and the smallest 63 cm.; the water cistern would have been 0·90 m. deep by 47 cm. across, and the cylinders 45 cm. deep with a diameter of 24 cm.

The value of this Carthaginian terracotta for us lies in the fact that it shows an improved version of the original instrument, fitting the description given by Vitruvius and equipped with three ranks of pipes which, together, must have produced a warm, bright sound.

30. *The lamp in the Copenhagen Museum* (Plate XIII, nos. 1 and 2). This second lamp in the shape of a hydraulic organ, likewise from Carthage, is in many respects similar to the first, though it is much less skilfully modelled. Moulded in terracotta, the object has an over-all height of 15·7 cm., and its plinth is missing. The front of the hexagonal water cistern is decorated with a motif of leaves. Of the two pumps, only one remains, on the left-hand side; but it is similar in proportions to those on the instrument described above. The wind-chest is deeper, and has no inscription, though it is decorated with a kind of moulding running across it. On either side are the burners, simply cup-shaped hollows pierced by a round hole into which the wick was stuck.[63]

Like the instrument in the Lavigerie Museum, this organ has, in front, a rank of eighteen pipes whose lips are perfectly reproduced. These pipes are held in place by a slanting bar decorated at either end with a round motif. On the reverse side the organ has two more ranks, one about two-thirds the height of the front rank and the other only half as tall. Here again we have a

[61] op. cit., p. 69.

[62] 'Orgue et lampes romaines', *La Revue du Louvre et des Monuments de France* (1962), no. 4, pp. 151 ff.

[63] Two terracotta fragments in the Lavigerie Museum in Carthage certainly come from lamps of the same type. One represents a wind-chest very similar to that on the Copenhagen lamp, with two burners and part of the water cistern. The other forms the left half of the wind-chest and its burner; above it the foot of several pipes may be seen (Pl. XI, nos. 4 and 5). See Deneauve, op. cit., p. 152.

principal stop, an octave stop and a fifth stop. There is the merest suggestion of a manual,[64] and nothing remains of the organist but his legs and the front part of his thighs.

It seems certain that this lamp, which dates from the same period as the first, is another product of the POSSESSOR workshop. They suggest that the hydraulic organ was sufficiently established in the Numidian way of life for private individuals to want to illuminate their homes, on occasion, with a lamp whose shape reminded them of the organ.

THE ORGAN ALONE

31. *The Tarsus terracotta* (Plate XVI, no. 1). This terracotta, probably dating from pre-Christian times, was found during excavations at Kusuk-Kolah in 1852 by Mazoillier and Langlois. It is now in the Louvre.[65]

Fig. 4. Reconstruction of the Tarsus Terracotta

Though the piece is not intact, the workmanship is of a high standard. It measures 12·3 cm. across and 11 cm. high at its topmost point. It represents the upper part of an organ, and the design is most elegant. Fourteen or fifteen pipes, their height graduating downward in a regular progression from right to left, are held in place by a slanting bar decorated with a groove running its entire length. The bar is fixed to two lateral uprights, the one on the right being plainly visible, decorated with two parallel furrows. The pipes, whose lips are not shown, are set in a wind-chest gracefully embellished along the front with a pattern of leaves enclosed by mouldings.

Below and to the left of the wind-chest appears the head of a young boy, probably the organ-blower. It is impossible to conceive of this as being

---

[64] Niels Breitenstein, *Catalogue of Terracottas* (Copenhagen, 1941), p. 102, no. 972.

[65] W. Fröhner, 'Les musées de France', *Recueil des monuments↔antiques* (Paris, 1873), Pl. 32.

merely an ornament, for clearly it extends beyond the lower edge of the wind-chest. Moreover, a small fragment descending from the lower part of the wind-chest proves that the instrument did not stop there, and is, in fact, a hydraulic organ.[66]

The diameter of the pipes is not constant, the bass pipes being distinctly wider than the trebles. The tenth pipe from the bottom is half the size of the lowest-pitched pipe.

It is also worth noting that, since the decorative pattern on the wind-chest indicates the side facing the public, the organist had the treble pipes on his right.[67]

32. *The sarcophagus of Julia Tyrrania* (Plate XIV). This fine white marble sarcophagus, one of the treasures of the Musée Lapidaire in Arles,[68] preserves the memory of a young woman organist whose name and virtues are recalled in an inscription.

Juliae Luc[ii] filiae Tyrraniae vixit ann[os] XX m[enses] VIII quae moribus pariter et disciplina ceteris feminis exemplo fuit. Autarcius nurui, Laurentius ucxori.

(To Julia Tyrrania, daughter of Lucius. She lived twenty years and eight months. By her goodness as much as by her education, she was an example to other women. Erected by Autarcius for his daughter-in-law, and Laurentius for his wife.)

This young woman, cut off so early from her husband's love, pursued her studies primarily in the sphere of music, and musical instruments figure on each side of the inscription—on the left a hydraulic organ and a syrinx in its case. Beside the organ is an animal resembling a sheep, and in the background a small tree.

The organ is skilfully executed. The water cistern is mounted on a solid base, and is hexagonal in shape, with mouldings between each panel. The top of this cistern forms a kind of shelf, also hexagonal, with oblong sides ribbed round the edges. To either side of this shelf appear the two pumps, consisting of bulky cylinders, each with an air pipe leading from the lower end. This air pipe first falls vertically, then makes a right-angled turn to enter the cistern. Such an arrangement implies a piston acting from above: but there is no sign of a piston-rod or lever. The wind-chest is set on the platform top of the cistern, and has neither stop handles nor manual, though the latter is probably on the other side of the organ, since it was customary to show the front of the instrument, so that the public might

[66] See my reconstruction, fig. 4.
[67] The photograph reproduced by L. Nagy, op. cit., is the wrong way round.
[68] E. Espérandieu, op. cit., i, no. 181; L. A. Constans, *Arles* (Paris, 1928), pp. 82–3.

admire it. There are eight pipes, clearly equal in diameter, and rather tall, the bass pipe alone measuring as much as the wind-chest, cistern and base put together. No lips are visible; and if we take it that the front of the organ is shown, the bass pipes are to the organist's right. The relative heights of the pipes indicate a range of approximately an augmented fourth or a fifth, if they are flue pipes, so that eight notes would give roughly a chromatic scale.

Julia Tyrrania's favourite instrument is not without elegance, and it is easy to imagine the charming picture created by the young woman proudly ensconced behind the brazen pipes whose music she loved so much. As we look at the tomb of this young organist, we are reminded of the Aelia Sabina of the Aquincum inscription, likewise mourned by her husband, who recorded for posterity his pride in her musical talents.

It has been suggested that Julia was a Christian, and certainly the names Autarcius and Laurentius do frequently occur in Christian inscriptions. But while it is possible, there is not enough evidence to decide the question.

From the shape of the letters, experts have dated this sarcophagus to the second or third centuries. It was discovered locally, at the entrance to the church of St.-Honorat, in the Alyscamps.

33. *The Rusticus organ* (Plate XV). On the first floor of the monastery buildings of St. Paul-Outside-the Walls, in Rome, is a small museum containing Christian inscriptions discovered on the premises or in the immediate vicinity of the basilica. Amongst these is a large piece of marble showing a hydraulic organ. Thanks to the great kindness of one of the monks, I was able to see and examine this very fine specimen.

It consists of a rectangular plaque measuring 1·76 m. by 79 cm., described by A. Silvagni under the number 5466.[69] It is said to have been found under the altar of the Confession of St. Paul, and formed part of the basilica's pavement in the time of Sixtus V. It bears the image of a hydraulic organ, traced in the marble without any regard for perspective, but revealing a number of interesting details.

The water cistern, apparently cylindrical, is mounted on a plinth and decorated with somewhat unusual motifs. In the centre is a sun, surrounded by its rays; underneath, on each side, is a crudely executed figure; and above there are two small circles. According to the monks of St. Paul, the sun represents the divine light, which shines for all mankind.

To the top of the water cistern, which has no pumps, is fixed a most remarkable wind-chest. Its front, slightly slanting through the cistern is seen from the front, has two panels. The lower is almost horizontal, and the upper panel more or less vertical. Both are decorated with geometric patterns

[69] *Inscript. Christ. Urbis Romae* (Rome, 1935), ii, No. 5466.

consisting of bars or circles. The fact that this section of the organ is seen at an angle allows us a glimpse of the other side of the wind-chest, which is shaped rather like a box, with five small levers protruding from it, probably corresponding to register drawers.

Above and in front of the wind-chest the artist has depicted the manual, with fifteen keys longer than they are broad, and lying close together as in the modern manual. They do not appear to correspond exactly to the lie of the pipes, the reason being that there are only twelve pipes to fifteen keys. The pipes themselves are flue pipes, with the lips clearly shown. They seem to decrease in size from right to left, though this is perhaps a trick of perspective due to the angled position of the wind-chest. About two-thirds of the way up they are held in position by a crossbar with a small decorative circle at its centre point and a larger one on the left. These ornaments, already noted on the Carthaginian terracotta, are also present on the Aquincum organ. The tops of the pipes are attached to what looks like a straight bar, whose function is not clear.

The inscription, written in clear letters 4 cm. high, runs as follows:

> Rusticus se vibu feci

that is

> Rusticus se vivu[s] feci[t]

'Rusticus raised [this monument] in his own lifetime.'

He must have been either an organist or a builder of hydraulic organs, and was probably a Christian.

34. *Gentilla's organ* (Plate XVI, no. 2). In 1936 Fr. Bellarmino Bagatti published a *graffito* consisting of a Christian inscription and a somewhat mysterious design which he thought might have something to do with weaving.[70] The words:

> Gentilla
> in pace

would then refer to some woman who had plied the trade illustrated by the design.

The *graffito* is on a marble fragment found in the subterranean cemetery of Commodilla, near Ostia.[71] It measures 26 cm. by 19 cm., and the instrument shown on it is a little less than 15 cm. in height, by 9 cm. across. A slightly more careful examination reveals that the object is, in fact, an organ.

Sixteen pipes are clearly distinguishable, all of equal diameter and decreasing gently in size from left to right. Near each foot they appear to have flue apertures. On either side of this rank of pipes are two lateral uprights, one

[70] *Il cimetero di Commodilla* (Citta del Vaticano, 1936), fig. 123.
[71] Mercurelli, op. cit., pp. 73–86.

taller than the other, and to their tops the customary supporting bar is fixed, the point of contact being decorated with a circular motif reminiscent of those on the Rusticus organ. In the centre of the bar is a rectangular plaque, equal in width to five pipes. It may well have carried an inscription.

Two grooves run across each of the vertical supports, those on the left-hand upright being higher than those on the right, but in both cases they are the same distance apart. A narrow slanting bar, very lightly etched, joins the uprights at these two points.

The wind-chest is of the type found on pneumatic organs.[72] It broadens out at the base for greater stability, and is decorated with a frieze of geometric patterns. No manual is visible. This is a small table positive, the favourite instrument of a Christian woman.

35. *The organ in the Winghe manuscript* (Plate XVII, no. 2). In the course of his travels in the last quarter of the sixteenth century a young man from Louvain, Philippe de Winghe, copied a number of inscriptions in Rome and the principal Italian towns. The manuscript of his notes, which have never been published, runs to approximately three hundred pages, and the inscriptions appear to have been copied with considerable accuracy.[73] On page 22 recto he records the inscriptions he apparently transcribed 'in musino S. Maria de Navicolla'. At the top and on the right are two sketches of hydraulic organs, the instrument on the left being nothing more than a means of comparison, for Winghe has written beside it 'sic extat in nummo Caracallae et in alio Neronis', referring to two of the contorniate medallions described earlier in this study. The organ on the right is the one Winghe copied from the inscription.

The rectangular water cistern is decorated with a moulding round all four sides, and mounted on a plinth with a double-tiered base. The wind-chest is in two sections, one above the other, and supports ten pipes decreasing in height from right to left. These are held in place by a slanting cross-bar. Near the foot of the pipes is a line, running parallel to the wind-chest and apparently formed by the lips. There is no sign of either pumps or levers.

Below and to the left of the organ Winghe has drawn a dove holding an olive branch in its beak, and above it runs the inscription

ΣΕΚΟΥΝ[Δ]ΙΝΟΙΣ

possibly a reference to the Gallo-Roman family of the Secundini.

This may well have formed part of the tomb of a Christian organist.

[72] For no obvious reason, C. Mercurelli sees this as a hydraulic organ.
[73] I am most grateful to M. Fr. Lyna, curator of the Bibliothèque Royale in Brussels, who was kind enough to supply this information and obtain a microfilm of the manuscript.

36. *The fragment of pottery in the St.-Germain Museum* (Plate IX, no. 6). In 1948, while examining various shards of patterned pottery from Lezoux in the museum at St. Germain, I had the good fortune to come upon one bearing the image of a hydraulic organ.[74] This is a polygonal piece of terracotta measuring approximately 9 cm. by 6 cm., and is probably part of a pot about 20 cm. in diameter. Naturally, it is the convex surface which is decorated.

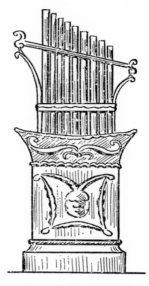

Fig. 5. Reconstruction of the Saint-Germain Fragment

Along the left-hand side of the fragment curves the upper section of a scroll, and the organ appears further to the right. Although the instrument is not shown in its entirety, it is possible to establish that it is a hydraulic organ. The water cistern, of which only the left-hand portion is visible, is decorated with curved lines and festoons near the edges, and in the centre with an oval motif. The wind-chest, which on its only visible side—the left—adopts a curious streamlined shape, is equally ornate, with scalloped edges and a graceful scroll running across it.

Six pipes are shown, held in place by two transverse bars supported in turn by a curving upright. The organ has neither pumps nor levers, and the manual is probably on the other side, since this is obviously the front of the instrument. Assuming that the oval motif on the wind-chest marks its central point—which it probably does—we may hazard a guess that the complete organ had nine pipes in all, with the bass pipes on the organist's right.[75] The last pipe shown on the shard, which is the sixth, is roughly

[74] Published in the revue *L'Orgue* (January 1949), no. 50.
[75] See my reconstruction, fig. 5.

three-quarters as tall as the end pipe, and must have sounded a fourth above it, if the design is accurate. Thus each pipe would sound a semitone above the preceding one.

This organ is clearly very stylized, and was probably part of a gladiatorial scene depicted on the original vessel, which can be dated back to the second or third century.

37. *The Rheinzabern terracotta* (Plate XVII, no. 1). This piece of terracotta, first described by Ludowisi in 1904[76] and now in the Speyer Museum, is extremely difficult to interpret, though it seems likely that it bears the image of an organ with a pneumatic wind-chest. It is 13 cm. high by 11·5 cm. across. The instrument has fourteen pipes, all equal in diameter, framed on either side by two solid upright supports decorated with a trellis pattern. There is no crossbar. The relatively large wind-chest is bordered with a band of the same design. It carries an inverted inscription reading

POTTALUSF.

Above the pipes, which describe a curve reminiscent of that on the Alexandrian terracotta, a round object may well be the organist's head, in which case the treble pipes would be on his right.

This piece appears to date from the fourth century.

38. *The glass vase in the Museo Nazionale in Naples* (Plate XVIII). This extremely pretty piece of glass, on view in room LXXXIV of the Museo Nazionale in Naples, is engraved with a Bacchanalian procession. It dates from the third or fourth centuries.

Various musical instruments are featured in the parade—cymbals clashed together by one dancer, a syrinx in the hands of another, a *lituus*, and also, it would seem, a small pneumatic organ standing on the ground. It has approximately twenty-five pipes held in place by a wide crossbar and set in a rather shallow wind-chest. The whole apparatus is strongly reminiscent of the upper section of the organ on the engraved gem in the British Museum. It has no water cistern or pumps, and the air pressure is probably maintained by bellows. The instrument has a strap by which the organist can sling it on his back.

It seems to me that this instrument is indeed an organ rather than a panpipe. Certainly it has an abnormally large number of pipes; but it should be borne in mind that the Nennig instrument is similarly well endowed. I feel that in both cases the artist was not so much concerned with the exact details of the organ as with its general shape. Furthermore, in relation to the

---

[76] op. cit., p. 137, no. 11.

human figures on the vase, the measurements of this object are those of an organ, for, assuming the dancers to be of medium height, the instrument is 70 cm. across, its lowest-pitched pipe 75 cm. long and its smallest 30 cm.

If this hypothesis is well founded, then we have here the first known illustration of a portative organ.

꧁꧂

CHAPTER FIVE

The Graeco-Roman Organ: Archaeological Evidence

THE 'ORGANS' IN THE MUSEO NAZIONALE, NAPLES

These two objects, discovered at Pompeii in the last quarter of the nineteenth century, set a difficult musicological problem which is still far from being solved. The archaeologists who found them took them to be syrinxes, but they are actually much too heavy to bear comparison with a panpipe.[1] In many respects they resemble each other; but only one still has its pipes.[2]

The first find, briefly described by Sogliano in 1899, is numbered 125187 in the catalogue. It consists of a heavy bronze plaque supporting eleven pipes.[3] The plaque, 39 cm. long by 32 cm. high by 2.5 cm. thick, is decorated on the front with three temple façades, each with two or four columns and a triangular pediment. These temple designs are 11.5 cm. in height, and their base is 10.5 cm. from the lower edge of the plaque. They indicate beyond all doubt the position in which the plaque should be placed—with the pediments pointing upwards (Plate XVII, no. 3).

There are eleven bronze pipes, decreasing in height from right to left and apparently firmly soldered to the upper edge of the plaque. The tallest measures 25.5 cm. and the smallest 11 cm. The latter is positioned more or less in the centre, while the former is fixed level with the right-hand edge. Their external diameter varies, from lowest to highest, from 19 to 17 mm.; their internal diameter measures approximately 9.8 mm. The metal is thus on average 4 mm. thick. These pipes seem to have been cast; several are slightly oval in shape, but this can be ascribed to the heat of the lava.

The fact that they are soldered to the edge of the plaque leads one at first

---

[1] In 1938 the catalogue of the *Mostra Augustea della Romanita*, 2nd ed., still described them as syrinxes (p. 678).

[2] Due to the great kindness of the authorities at the Museum, I was able to handle these pieces at leisure.

[3] A. Sogliano, *Notizie degli Scavi di Antichita* (Rome, 1899), pp. 442 ff. The instrument was found at a depth of 3.80 m. from the surface.

to suppose that the pipes were purely for decoration. But one detail at once invalidates this theory. On the front of the second, fifth, and sixth pipes from the treble end a vertical rectangular slit is clearly discernible. This slit, which certainly had some acoustic significance, is 17 mm. long and 1·5 mm. across, and its lower end is 9·3 cm. from the base of the pipes. It is similar to the hole in modern harmonic flue pipes, and to my mind proves beyond any doubt that the instrument was musical.

The second exhibit in the Museo Nazionale, no. 111055 in the catalogue, is curiously similar to the first. Again it is a rectangular bronze plaque, 35 cm. long by 9·6 cm. in height, thinner and lighter than the other, but again decorated with temples.[4] Though its musical apparatus is missing today, when it was discovered in 1877 by Mau it had nine pipes[5] fixed to the left half of the plaque's upper edge.

Contrary to what the pieces might suggest, they are not part of the same instrument—they were unearthed in different areas of Pompeii, the first in a house located outside the northern boundary of the city, and the second in a house belonging to region V.[6] But each one has a set of pipes arranged like those of a panpipe, on a plaque which could be the front of a wind-chest. Is it possible that they are organs?

This should not be ruled out *a priori*, though if they were organs, it is curious that not a single fragment of a manual, wind-chest, or wind mechanism was found near the instruments. However, such a negative argument is by no means conclusive, since the excavations were carried out at a time when archaeology did not demand the scientific discipline which it does today. And we should remember that the objects were immediately and without further discussion identified as syrinxes. We may therefore assume that any possible fragments of mechanism belonging to the wind-chest or the pumping system would not have been recognized as such, and would consequently have been overlooked, or at any rate scattered. The nine pipes of exhibit no. 111055 were irretrievably lost in this way.

The mystery surrounding these musical instruments remains complete. All that can be said is that if they really are organs—and there would surely have been organs in a popular holiday resort such as Pompeii—these were of quite a special type, unknown elsewhere, with their huge box containing both wind-chest and pumping mechanism. In all the iconographical evidence there is not one example of such a model. Perhaps these instruments should be regarded as the remains of musical automata of the type referred to in

---

[4] A. Mau, *Bulletino dell' Instituto di Correspondenza Archeologica* (Rome, 1877), p. 99.

[5] '. . . una syrinx in bronzo di nove canne con rappresentanza di tre tempietti . . .' ('. . . a bronze syrinx with nine pipes, decorated with three temples . . .').

[6] This information was supplied by the curator of the Museum, A. de Franciscis, to whom I am extremely grateful.

Hedylus's epigram. In any event, their weight would have made them extremely difficult to move about. It is to be hoped that somewhere in the excavations now in progress at Herculaneum a similar object may come to light in a more complete form and in a better state of preservation. Then it might at last be possible to solve this nagging archaeological and musicological problem.

THE ORGAN IN THE AQUINCUM MUSEUM

Our knowledge of the history of the Graeco-Roman organ was considerably advanced by the discovery in 1931, in the ruins of Aquincum in Hungary, of a small instrument with four sets of pipes, dating from the third century A.D. The find was important, although the instrument was not actually a hydraulic organ, but a very small positive designed for domestic use and of a little-known type. Fortunately it is possible to date the instrument exactly by means of its dedicatory plaque, which was recovered intact. An excellent analysis of this find has been made by Professor Lajos Nagy of Budapest, and this work, unobtainable today, has been used as a basis for much of this chapter.[7]

The circumstances which led to the burial of the instrument and its subsequent re-discovery deserve to be told. In the course of excavations designed to uncover the small Roman city of Aquincum, near Budapest, the ruins of the building of the Collegium Centonariorum, the company of weavers, came to light. When the cellar was being cleared, workers made the surprising discovery that it contained the fragments of an organ. The presence of the broken instrument in such surroundings came about in the following way. When the club-house of the guild was destroyed by fire towards the middle of the third century the floor burned and collapsed into the cellar, taking with it the little organ, which was already to a large extent destroyed by the flames. The falling beams probably added to the damage.[8] As a result, the parts made of wood and leather have almost entirely disappeared, but all the metal parts, though damaged, have been recovered, and from them we can piece together a relatively accurate picture of how the instrument was made and how it worked. So it is that because of a conflagration, which at the time was probably considered a public disaster, a

---

[7] *Az Aquincumi Orgona* (Budapest, 1934). The discovery was the subject of an article in the London *Observer* of 24 May 1932, of a study by W. Woodburn Hyde, 'The recent discovery of an inscribed Water-Organ at Budapest', *Trans. and Proceed. of the Americ. Philolog. Assoc.* (1938), and of a commentary by V. Sugar, 'L'Orgue hydraulique d'Aquincum', *L'Orgue*, 37 (March 1939).

[8] Contrary to all probability, Galpin (Grove's *Dictionary*, art. 'Hydraulis') assumes that the organ had been placed directly in the cellar, and a very hypothetical water cistern had been left in the upstairs room, because of its weight.

third-century organ, exactly fitting the technical descriptions, has come into our hands, after a sleep of seventeen hundred years.[9]

It is easy to imagine the considerable interest attached to the archaeological analysis of such an instrument. Although the pumping mechanism has been completely destroyed, there is still the wind-chest, which is easy to reconstruct in the light of the accounts left by Hero and Vitruvius. All the pipes are more or less shattered, but they comprise very nearly a complete set, and their remains enable us to estimate fairly exactly how they were made.

The date of the Aquincum organ is revealed by its dedicatory plaque, made of bronze, and measuring 16·7 cm. long by 9·5 cm. wide. It is inscribed with the words:

G . IUL . VIATORINUS
DEC . COL . AQ . AEDI
LICIUS . PRAEF . COLL .
CENT . HYDRAM . COLL .
S . S . DESUO . D . D . MODESTO
TO . ET . PROBO . COS .

that is to say:

G[aius] J[ulius] Viatorinus
Dec[urio] col[oniae] Aq[uinci] aedi-
licius praef[ectus] coll[egii]
cent[onariorum] hydram coll[egio]
s[upra] s[cripto] de suo d[onum] d[edit] Modesto et Probo co[n] s[ulibus].

(Gaius Julius Viatorinus, decurion of the Aquincum colony, aedile, prefect of the College of Weavers, has presented this Hydra to the College as a personal gift, under the consulate of Modestus and Probus.)

The presentation thus took place in 228,[10] and the organ, formally installed in that year, was evidently built early in the reign of Alexander Severus, who, as we have seen, was himself an organist. The motives behind this generous gesture on the part of Viatorinus are unknown—probably they were connected with the obligations inherent in his office. At all events, we may be sure that in offering the instrument to the College the prefect was conscious of the fact that it would be a particularly acceptable gift in the eyes of its members and of the whole population of the town. This would suggest that the popularity of the organ had spread even to this remote province. We have already seen how the young Aelia Sabina gave recitals on the hydraulic organ in Aquincum: but it is not clear how Via-

[9] I should like at this point to express my indebtedness to the Service for Cultural Relations of the Hungarian Government in Budapest, through whose good offices I was able to examine and study the remains of the instrument in April 1959.

[10] V. Sugar (op. cit.) puts forward the incorrect date of 229.

torinus's little instrument was used—perhaps it was played when members of the college held their meetings. It is unlikely to have been played anywhere but inside the building where it was discovered, for its thin tone would have been ill suited to open-air performances: and it is even possible that Aelia Sabina or one of her pupils may have used this small instrument at concerts given in the guild's headquarters.

The instrument is of the type known as 'tetrachordos', that is to say, it has four sets of thirteen pipes. The wind-chest was made of wood, but inside and out its walls were lined with thin sheets of bronze, probably to strengthen it. One of these sheets, corresponding to one of the sides, has remained in a good state of preservation, and tells us the approximate height of the wind-chest—13·4 cm. Its length and width may be exactly calculated from the length of the bronze table supporting the pipes: 27 cm. by 8 cm.[11]

The wind-chest has four channels along its length, corresponding to the 'canales in longitudine' described by Vitruvius. Rectangular in section, they are partitioned off by thin strips of bronze, half a millimetre thick, about 25·5 cm. long and less than 2 cm. in height, whose upper edges are soldered to the underside of a thick bronze slab forming the roof of the 'musical canon'. Below, the channels were shut off by small bronze plates bent round at the ends to seal off the lateral apertures.

There are two of these small plates to each channel, forming a floor, and between them, in the centre of the channel, a space of approximately 6 cm. long is left free. This space was closed off by a slider stop running inside a casing, and designed to control the intake of air. The casing measures about 8·8 cm. long by 1·7 cm. wide, and is pierced in the middle by a rectangular slit 2·8 cm. by 0·7 cm. The slider itself, which has a similar slit, measures 8·8 cm. by 1·6 cm., and is 0·2 cm. thick. A bronze shank approximately 15 cm. long is soldered to it and allows it to be manipulated at long range (Plate XX, no. 4). Three of these shanks are engraved with the numbers II, III, and IIII, indicating the relevant sets of pipes. All of them pass through the openings in a bronze side-sheet belonging to the outer envelope of the wind-chest and located to the right of the organist. These openings are roughly contrived and, to stop air leaks, circles of leather were stuck to them, of which some traces have been discovered. Probably the free end of each shank was fitted with a wooden knob for greater facility in operating the mechanism.

The thick sheet of bronze forming the roof of the four lateral channels, and measuring 27 cm. by 8 cm., is perforated by four sets of thirteen holes, each 6·5 mm. in diameter and spaced out 1·8 cm. apart. It is noticeable that the thirteen holes in each series do not lie in a perfectly straight line.

---

11 Several authors, following the example of J. Geyer (*Compte rendu du Congrès d'orgue de Strasbourg*, 1932), have written that the wind-chest measured 2·70 m. by 0·85 m.

On the upper surface of the sheet, between each group of four holes, and perpendicular to the channels, that is to say running from front to back, small bronze strips, 8 cm. by 0·4 cm., and from 0·3 cm. to 0·4 cm. thick, are soldered by one edge. In this way the larger sheet is divided on its upper surface into thirteen separate compartments (Plate XX, no. 3). Into these compartments run thirteen sliders, each corresponding to one degree of the manual and each measuring 12·4 cm. long by 1·5 cm. wide by approximately 1·5 cm. thick. Every slider has four holes, 0·7 cm. in diameter, 1·8 cm. apart, and exactly matching the four holes in each compartment. We recognize here Hero's πώματα and Vitruvius's plinthides. All the sliders are numbered off in Roman figures:

XIII XII XI X VIIII VIII VII VI V IIII III II I

These markings were, in fact, indispensable, since the holes on the bronze plaque are, as we have seen, not perfectly aligned, and each slider had to have its holes pierced so that they coincided with those on the plaque (Plate XXI, no. 2).

At the manual end of the sliders are two more narrow holes, to one of which was attached a small piece of iron shaped like a fish-hook and from 3 to 3·5 cm. long. A short length of cord was presumably slipped into the curl of the hook and attached by its other end to the corresponding key. The other hole was for the upper end of the return spring (choragium), consisting of a sliver of bronze averaging 9 cm. in length and tapering from 1·3 cm. in width at its lower end to 0·6 cm. at the top. The thirteen springs were held fast at the lower end by a horizontal bronze bar approximately 32·5 cm. in length, which was located half-way up the wind-chest, behind the keys (Plate XXI, no. 3). By exerting finger-pressure on one of these, the bronze strip was bent, and by its flexibility it pulled the slider vigorously, bringing it back again to a position of repose as soon as the pressure was released. The air stream was thus cut off, and it is fair to assume that the resilience of these bronze strips made the action sensitive and easy.

Above the sliders and their housing was the tabula summa, a solid rectangle of bronze actually made of two sheets soldered together. This slab is perforated by three ranks of thirteen holes, exactly corresponding to those in the lower sheet and in the sliders.

This meant that when the finger was applied to one of the keys a pull was exerted on the hook and consequently on the slider, whose four holes moved into line with the corresponding holes in the bronze sheet and the tabula summa, whereupon the air rushed in and made that particular pipe sound. What we see here, then, is the mechanism described by Hero. To limit the forward movement of the slider and to ensure that the holes always coincided perfectly, a small sheet of metal was riveted in place with a bronze nail at the distal end of the slider, and this struck the front edge of the tabula summa each time the key was depressed.

The keys forming the manual appear to have been shaped like angle-irons. Only fragments of these have survived, since they were made of wood and reinforced with small bronze bands. Judging by the size of one of these bands, the keys must have been approximately 1·4 cm. in width.

The wind-chest of this little organ is therefore made to the same design as that of Vitruvius's organ, apart from the replacement of the inlet valves (epitonia) by slotted sliders, which were easier to make and to operate, as well as being stronger. As in the modern instrument, the organist of the little Aquincum organ could immediately select the appropriate musical colour and use the various timbres and diapasons alone or as mixtures. It is clear, in fact, that if the four ranks of pipes had had to be used together all the time, the system of registers would have been useless, and Hero's wind-chest, much simpler in construction, would have been more suitable.

The remains of the pipes of the Aquincum organ are a fascinating subject for the scholar, since no other evidence throws any light on the manufacture or the characteristics of ancient organ pipes. Not one ancient writer thought fit to investigate the problems of practical acoustics.

All the pipes on the instrument are flue pipes, and are cast, not welded. There were fifty-two of them, arranged in four ranks of thirteen. All fifty-two have been found, but none is now capable of producing a note.[12] They nevertheless enable us to form quite an accurate idea of the technique involved in the manufacture of organ pipes at the beginning of the third century.

The first three ranks consist of stopped pipes, whereas those in the fourth rank are open. Each pipe has a body and a foot, which were found scattered among the debris.

First rank. All thirteen pipes were found. Without its foot, the smallest measures 13·7 cm. and the largest 24·1 cm. The external diameter varies from 0·9 cm. to 1·1 cm.

Second rank. Again all thirteen pipes were recovered. Without its foot, the smallest measures 17·8 cm. and the largest 32·5 cm. The diameter varies from 1·1 cm. to 1·4 cm. (Plate XXI, no. 1).

Third rank. Here, too, all thirteen pipes were found, but in an extremely bad state of preservation, making it virtually impossible to estimate their length. Their diameter varies from 1·3 cm. to 1·7 cm.

---

12 It is very difficult to study them nowadays, for they have been more or less repaired and reassembled in an attempt to reconstruct the organ. Fortunately, L. Nagy had measured and described them with a remarkable degree of accuracy.

All the pipes belonging to these three sets were stopped by wooden mandrels driven deep into the holes, whose calcined remains are in some cases still in place. Probably these plugs were movable, thus enabling the organist to modify the pitch-level of each rank of pipes. The problem of the tessitura of the various ranks is therefore impossible to resolve in any satisfactory way: but it is interesting that in the first two ranks—the only ones that can be used in this study—the largest pipe is almost twice the length of the smallest, 24·1:13·7 and 32·5:17·8. Consequently, the tessitura was probably something less than an octave—calculations put it round about the minor seventh. Assuming that the pipes are stopped near the top, the following notes would be obtained:

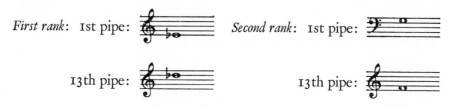

First rank: 1st pipe: *Second rank*: 1st pipe:

13th pipe: 13th pipe:

Naturally, if the plugs were inserted half-way up, the notes would sound an octave higher; and a third of the way up, the difference would be a fifth. These calculations, which are very rough, do not permit us to work out the progression of notes corresponding to the keys on the manual. At the most, we may assume that they proceeded by more or less equal semitones, though there is no proof of this. It might be thought that the stopped ranks of pipes, so easy to adjust, were able to sound in any 'harmony' the organist fancied—Dorian, Phrygian, Lydian, etc., without any need to transpose. But since the pipes in the fourth rank were open, and consequently produced fixed notes, it is difficult to see how notes on the other ranks could be variable, unless they could sound separately. The mystery of the long tampons on the first three sets of pipes has therefore never been cleared up.

The foot of almost every pipe in these sets was found. These are slightly conical in shape, narrowing towards the lower end. The top, cut at right angles, is closed by a sheet of bronze welded to it and pierced by a narrow, crescent-shaped slit. A welded sleeve joined the foot to its pipe, which was slotted at this level. The stream of air, passing through the foot, forced its way through the slit in the bronze and came up against the sharp edge of the slot, causing it to vibrate and produce a note whose pitch was determined by the length of the pipe. This type of lip is therefore very similar to its modern counterpart.

In addition, a double bronze sheath was fitted round the lower part of each foot, the outer sheath being welded or stuck to the tabula summa.

Fourth rank. This deserves to be examined separately, since its pipes are of a somewhat different nature from those we have just described. They are open, and their lips are of a special type, though they are unfortunately in a very bad state of preservation. The best of them measure from 22·6 cm. to 35·9 cm. in length, and their diameter varies from 1·6 cm. to 1·8 cm. Their tops are sheathed in bronze, doubtless for tuning purposes. At the bottom they are cut slantwise, with a bevelled edge, at an angle of approximately 40°. The lip and the foot are both of an unfamiliar type. The upper part of the foot is flattened and bent towards the horizontal at an angle of almost 50° at a point about 1·8 cm. from the top. In this angle is a vent 0·4 cm. across at its middle point.[13] Probably this had the same effect as the slits in the stopped pipes, and the air passing through it would presumably strike against the angled slot in the neighbouring pipe.

These curious pipes must have had a very special timbre which sometimes stood out from that of the others, and sometimes mingled with them. Probably their sound, more intense than that of the bourdons, was predominant.

The pipes were held in place by slanting bars, similar to those shown in the iconography, made of narrow strips of decorated bronze attached to lateral wooden uprights. Where they met the join was concealed on the side facing the audience by decorated medallions. One of these, a well-preserved motif 8 cm. in diameter, represents a winged cupid.

The case of the Aquincum organ was thus a perfect example, on a smaller scale, of that of the hydraulic organ, and the wind-chest complied in every way with Vitruvius's description. However, the wind mechanism made no use of water to compress the air—this seems to be indisputable. In Ktesibios's organ, both cistern and pnigeus were of metal, as were the feed-pumps. If this little organ had been a hydraulis, substantial remains of these parts would certainly have been recovered from the cellar among the debris of the wind-chest and the pipes. The fact that nothing of this kind was found is to my mind sufficient proof that the instrument was 'pneumatic'. Its air supply was undoubtedly furnished by bellows,[14] which, being made of wood and leather, were entirely consumed in the fire—unless they had been detached from the organ and kept in another room.

On behalf of the Budapest Museum, Dr. Hollendonner has analysed several fragments of calcined wood belonging to the organ which, doubtless

[13] Professor J. Chailley, who recently examined these pipes in Budapest, raises the possibility that this slit might be accidental, since it is not present on every pipe.
[14] On the left side of the wind-chest there was a metal socket which was found, into which fitted the bellows. The socket was 7·3 cm. long, with a diameter of 3 cm. (Nagy, p. 16, fig. 7).

for lack of air, had not been completely burned. A minute piece of charcoal which still clung to a nail from the lower part of the wind-chest has revealed that it was made of pine, while the mandrels plugging the stopped pipes were of oak. Another fragment, perhaps part of the bellows, is of elm-wood, as were the keys of the manual. The metal parts have also been subjected to analysis, and L. Sumegi and K. Franck have discovered the presence of the following elements:

$$\text{Metal from the pipes} \begin{cases} \text{tin } 0\cdot08\% \\ \text{lead } 0\cdot08\% \\ \text{zinc } 17\cdot83\% \\ \text{copper } 81\cdot80\% \end{cases}$$

$$\text{Metal from the dedicatory plaque} \begin{cases} \text{tin } 0\cdot06\% \\ \text{lead } 0\cdot06\% \\ \text{iron } 0\cdot26\% \\ \text{zinc } 14\cdot11\% \\ \text{copper } 85\cdot39\% \end{cases}$$

From the archaeological evidence concerning the Aquincum instrument several conclusions may be drawn. It is a very tiny organ, its proportions entirely different from those of the hydraules usually shown in the iconography. It is a modest 'positive', easily moved from one place to another, and its measurements appear to have been as follows:

Overall height: 60 cm.
Width: 35 cm.
Depth: 20 cm.

It would, I think, certainly have weighed more than the 8 kg. proposed by L. Nagy, thus ruling out the hypothesis that the organist was able to carry the instrument by a strap round his neck, playing with the right hand and pumping with the left, as was later done during the Middle Ages. It is none the less true that the similarity between the Aquincum organ and some of the portative organs of the thirteenth and fourteenth centuries is rather disconcerting.

This type of instrument corresponds to what Pollux calls a 'little organ'. The word *Hydra*, inscribed on the dedicatory plaque, has led several authors to the belief that the instrument is actually a hydraulic organ:[15] but as we saw earlier, the names applied to the organ from the third century onwards were often unrelated to its wind mechanism.

In ancient iconography, only the Orange medallion shows an organ comparable in size to the Aquincum instrument.

[15] V. Sugar, op. cit.; W. Woodburn Hyde, op. cit. Nagy, however, realized that the organ was fed by bellows.

PLATE I

The Nennig mosaic (*see p. 73*)

PLATE II

1. The first orchestra

2. The second orchestra

The Zliten mosaic (*see p. 75*)

PLATE III

1. The consular diptych of Verona (*see p. 79*)

2. The Via Appia graffito (*see p. 78*)

PLATE IV

1. Right-hand organ

2. Left-hand organ

The obelisk of Theodosius at Constantinople

PLATE V

The Alexandrian terracotta statuette (*see p. 77*)

PLATE VI

The uninscribed sarcophagus of Arles (*see p. 83*)

PLATE VII

. The stele in Autun Museum (*see p. 95*)　　　　2. The Rheims vase (*see p. 81*)

3. The Roman terracotta (*see p. 81*)　　　　4. The Copenhagen vase (*see p. 82*)

PLATE VIII

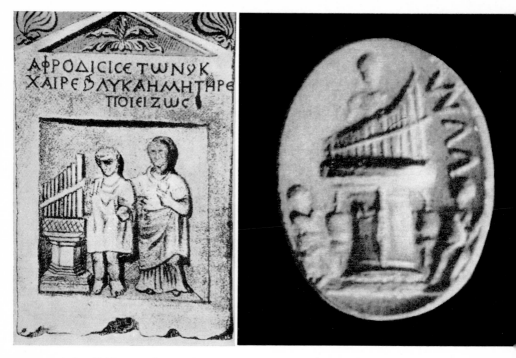

1. Aphrodisis' organ (*see p. 86*) 2. The British Museum gem (*see p. 84*)

3. The Rheinzabern vase (*see p. 85*) 4. The Tatarevo organ (*see p. 87*)

PLATE IX

4

7

Nero contorniates
(*see pp. 90–91*)

Caracalla contorniates
(*see pp. 91–92*)

5

8

The Valentinian III medallion (*see p. 89*)

6. The Saint-Germain fragment
(*see p. 104*)

PLATE X

The Saint-Maximin sarcophagus (*see p. 94*)

PLATE XI

1. The Orange medallion (*see p. 93*)

4 and 5. Terracotta fragments in the Lavigerie Museum at Carthage (*see p. 98*)

2. The Grenoble medallion (*see p. 92*)

3. The organist of the Carthage lamp (*see p. 96*)

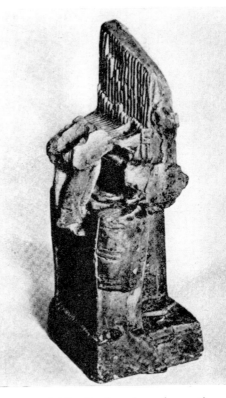

6. The Carthage lamp (*see p. 96*)

PLATE XII

The Carthage lamp (*see p. 96*)
1. Front view
2. Back view

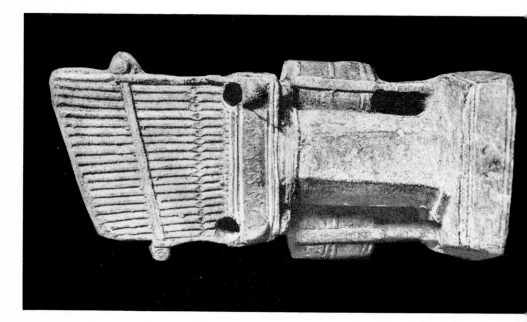

PLATE XIII

The lamp in the Copenhagen museum
(see p. 98)
1. Front view
2. Back view

PLATE XIV

The sarcophagus of Julia Tyrrania (*see p. 100*)

PLATE XV

The Rusticus organ (see p. 101)

PLATE XVI

1. The Tarsus terracotta (*see p. 99*)

2. Gentilla's organ (*see p. 102*)

PLATE XVII

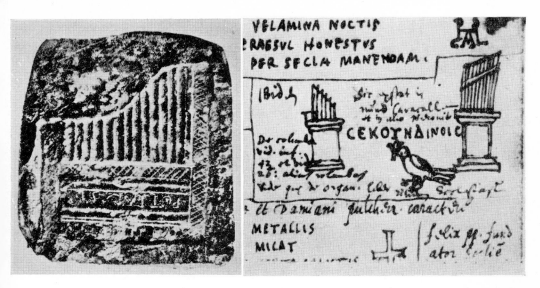

1. The Rheinzabern terracotta (*see p. 105*)   2. The organ in the Winghe manuscript (*see p. 103*)

3. One of the Pompeii 'organs' (*see p. 107*)   4. The author's reconstruction of a
hydraulis (*see p. 147*)

PLATE XVIII

The glass vase in the Museo Nazionale, Naples (*see p. 105*)

PLATE XIX

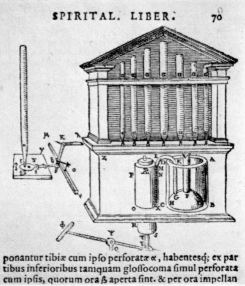

2. By Commandini (1575)

1. By Barbaro (1556)

Earlier reconstructions (*see pp. ix–x*)

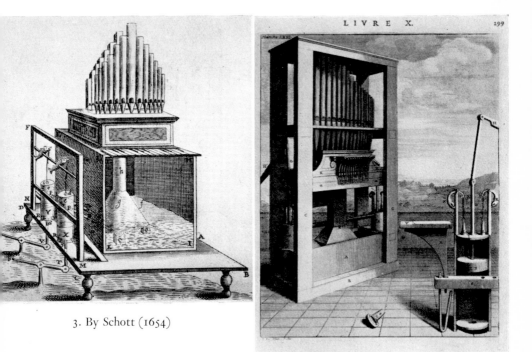

3. By Schott (1654)

4. By Perrault (1673)

PLATE XX

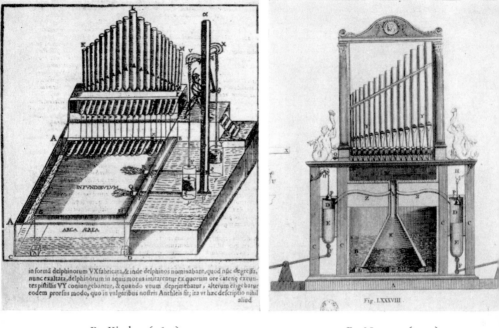

1. By Kircher (1650)   2. By Newton (1791)

Earlier reconstructions (*see pp. x–xii*)

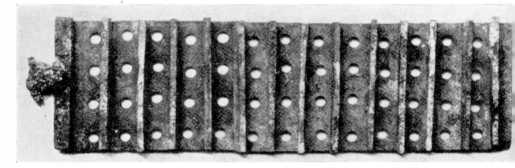

3. The tabula summa

4. The slotted sliders

The Aquincum organ (*see p. 109*)

PLATE XXI

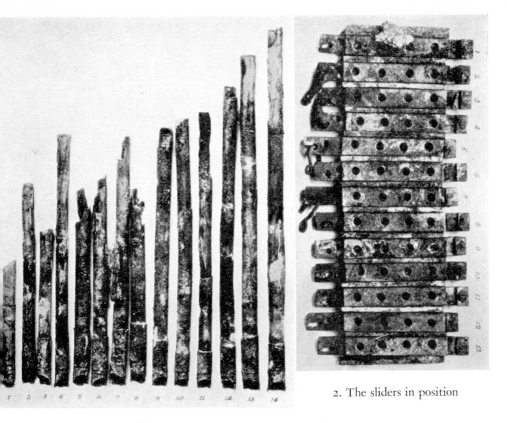

2. The sliders in position

1. Pipes

3. The springs

The Aquincum organ (*see p. 109*)

PLATE XXII

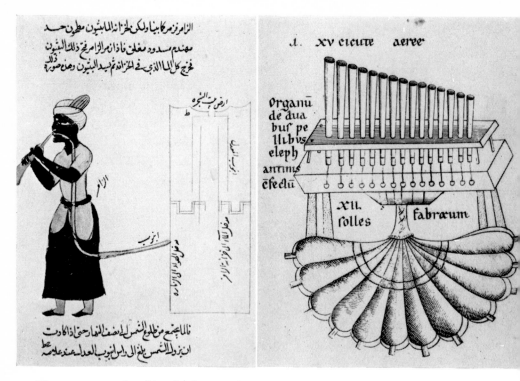

1. The automaton of Archimedes (see p. 202)   2. Illustration in the St. Blasien manuscript (see p. 2

3. The Grado wind-chest (see p. 243)

PLATE XXIII

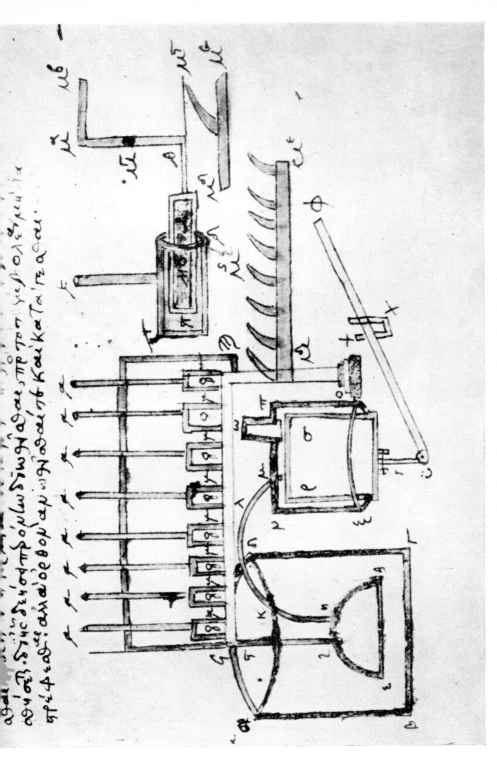

The illustration in the manuscript of Hero's *Pneumatics* (*see p. 28*)

PLATE XXIV

1. The illustration in the Utrecht Psalter (*see p. 278*)

2. The illustration in the Psalter of Eadwin (*p. 279*)

PLATE XXV

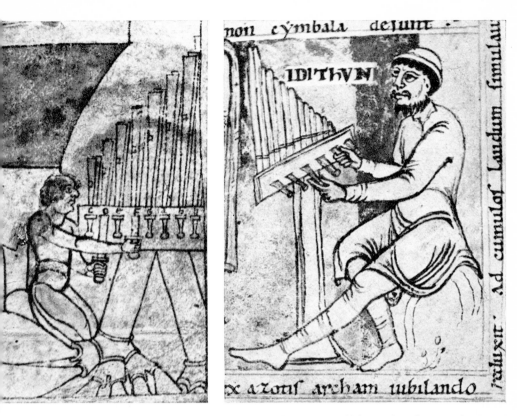

1. The Harding Bible (*see p. 280*)   2. The Pommersfelden Psalter (*see p. 280*)

3. The Cambridge Manuscript (*see p. 281*)

PLATE XXVI

The Munich Manuscript (*see p. 283*)

PLATE XXVII

1. The Cividale del Friuli Manuscript (*see p. 282*)

2. The Belvoir Castle Psalter (*see p. 282*)   3. The St. Blasien Manuscript (*see p. 179*)

PLATE XXVIII

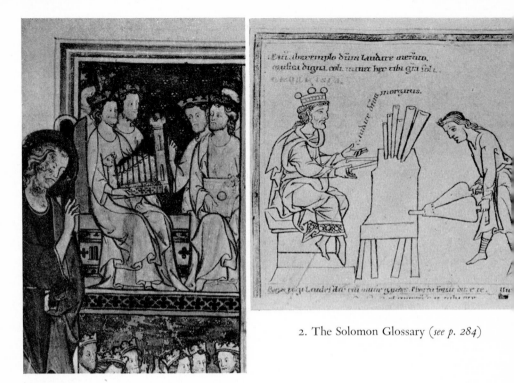

2. The Solomon Glossary (*see p. 284*)

1. The British Museum Manuscript (*see p. 269*)

3. The Arras Manuscript (*see p. 272*)

4. The Bibliothèque Nationale Manu
(*see p. 284*)

CHAPTER SIX

Graeco-Roman Music

Before approaching the specific problems relating to the tessitura of the classical organ manual, it is useful to recall briefly the principal elements of Greek musical theory as it was taught in the Hellenistic and Roman periods. Indeed, a rudimentary knowledge of the musical system of Antiquity, so different from our own, is indispensable if we are to try to visualize or understand the rhythmic and melodic possibilities of Ktesibios's instrument. In addition, the acoustic principles of pipes, which are analogous with those of vibrating strings so thoroughly studied by the Pythagorean school, will shed some light on the interpretation of iconographical evidence, and enable us at times to draw highly interesting conclusions.

It is also convenient at this point to take a brief look at certain wind instruments which the organ was to use for its own ends. Anything we can learn about their sound from literary sources is, with certain reservations, relevant to our subject. The seductive charm of the aulos, which Plato considered dangerous, will go some way to explaining the suspicion, not to say hostility, felt by the early Church Fathers towards the organ, while the martial overtones of the trumpet will justify the use of the organ as an accompaniment to fights in the arena. Finally, on a more general level, I shall try to determine the true place of music among the Greeks, who always infused it with their moral preoccupations, and among the Romans, who probably regarded it as nothing more than a source of physical pleasure.

It is a fact that not one work relating to instrument-making or the practice of music has survived from ancient times. However, this gap, so frustrating to musicologists, in no way implies that the subject was neglected. We know from Athenaeus, for instance, that Aristocles had made a study of the hydraulic organ and perhaps of its participation in vocal music, in his book *De Choris* (Περὶ χορῶν),[1] as had the grammarian Tryphon in a chapter 'On the aulos and musical instruments' in his dictionary (Περὶ ὀνομασιῶν). Unfortunately, every work of this kind has been lost, and any descriptions of organs which have survived are written by technicians whose interest is confined to the mechanical aspect of the instrument, so that the musical

[1] iv, 75.

part is always deliberately neglected. As regards the theory of music, antiquity has left us only short treatises, whose twin sources are the schools of Pythagoras and Aristoxenus. With the exception of Boethius's compilation, written in Latin at the end of the late Empire, all these works are in Greek, and are directed primarily at the teachers and trained musicians who, as we know, were nearly all Greeks.

MUSICAL THEORY AND NOTATION

The theory of ancient music owes its complexity to the fact that the ancients, though they regarded the octave as a consonance, never accorded it the fundamental role that it has today. And although Pythagoras's 'scale' is very near to our own, the basic melodic unit in Greek music is the tetrachord, four notes making up a perfect fourth. The origin of this tetrachord is the four strings on the primitive lyre, and the intervals separating the four notes are fixed, not at random, but by a logical process of reasoning.[2] Pythagoras (sixth century B.C.) is traditionally credited with having constituted the natural 'scale', so called because its intervals, unlike those of our own scale, are not tempered. In the Pythagorean philosophy, the universe is governed by simple numbers, and everything is referred to a rational relationship of sizes. The story of how Pythagoras discovered harmonic phenomena is certainly apocryphal: but the ancient writers on music attribute to him the basic principle of the division of vibrating strings into simple fractions to obtain the various consonances of the primitive scale. If the open string gives a certain note, then, if the tension remains constant, half of this string will sound an octave above, two-thirds of the string will give the fifth, and three-quarters the fourth.[3] Since the octave, the first harmonic in this system, is incapable of supplying a sequence of notes suitable for making a melody, we try the second harmonic, which is the fifth.

Let us take seven identical strings—seven being the most sacred number[4] —all subject to the same tension. If we give the second a length equal to two-thirds of the first, the third a length equal to two-thirds of the second, and so on, we shall obtain a series of perfect fifths. Here are the notes produced by these seven strings (assuming, for purposes of illustration, that the first string sounds F°).[5]

---

[2] Basing his theory on archaeological evidence, A. Machabey believes that Greek modality originally derived from the equidistance of the holes in the aulos (*Embryologie de la musique occidentale*, Paris, 1963, p. 10).

[3] Gaudentius, *Introd. Harmon.*, xi.

[4] Terpander, it was said, added three strings to the lyre, making it heptachordal. We know that Apollo's lyre had seven strings (Macrobius, *Saturn.*, i, xix, 15).

[5] Here I am following the demonstration given by P.-J. Richard (*La Gamme. Introduction à l'étude de la Musique*, Paris, 1930, pp. 29 ff.), who reproduces in a simplified form the teaching of Plato and the Greek theorists.

F⁰	C¹	G¹	D²	A²	E³	B³
I	$\frac{2}{3}$	$\frac{2}{3}$ of $\frac{2}{3}$	$\frac{2}{3}$ of $\frac{4}{9}$	$\frac{2}{3}$ of $\frac{8}{27}$	$\frac{2}{3}$ of $\frac{16}{81}$	$\frac{2}{3}$ of $\frac{32}{243}$
=	=	=	=	=	=	=
I	$\frac{2}{3}$	$\frac{4}{9}$	$\frac{8}{27}$	$\frac{16}{81}$	$\frac{32}{243}$	$\frac{64}{729}$

If we bring together these seven notes by means of octave transpositions (fraction $\frac{1}{2}$) and begin with C for reasons of clarity, we obtain the following:

C²	D²	E²	F²	G²	A²	B²
$\frac{2}{3}\times\frac{1}{2}=$	$\frac{8}{27}$	$\frac{32}{243}\times\frac{2}{1}=$	$I\times\frac{1}{4}=$	$\frac{4}{9}\times\frac{1}{2}=$	$\frac{16}{81}$	$\frac{64}{729}\times\frac{2}{1}=$
$\frac{2}{6}=\frac{1}{3}$	$\frac{8}{27}$	$\frac{64}{243}$	$\frac{1}{4}$	$\frac{4}{18}=\frac{2}{9}$	$\frac{16}{81}$	$\frac{128}{729}$

We then multiply these fractions by 3 in order to make C the unit:

$$\left|\frac{1}{3}\times 3=I\right|\frac{8}{27}\times 3=\frac{8}{9}\right|\frac{64}{243}\times 3=\frac{64}{81}\right|\frac{1}{4}\times 3=\frac{3}{4}\right|\frac{2}{9}\times 3=\frac{2}{3}\right|\frac{16}{81}\times 3=\frac{16}{27}\right|\frac{128}{729}\times 3=\frac{128}{243}\right|$$

As we have seen, this succession of fractions, which is characteristic of the Pythagorean scale, derives from simple numbers, and may easily be restated in simple numbers, despite its apparent complexity; since it may be written thus:

I	$\dfrac{2^3}{3^2}$	$\dfrac{2^6}{3^4}$	$\dfrac{3}{2^2}$	$\dfrac{2}{3}$	$\dfrac{2^4}{3^3}$	$\dfrac{2^7}{3^5}$

The Aristoxenian scale is very close to the preceding one. It derives from an observation made by the mathematician Archytas of Tarentum (*c.* 440–360) that a curious relationship existed between the characteristic fractions of the notes regarded as consonances, thus:

> the octave is represented by $\frac{1}{2}$;
> the fifth by $\frac{2}{3}$;
> the fourth by $\frac{3}{4}$.

Moreover, the 'tone', the difference between the fifth and the fourth ($\frac{2}{3}:\frac{3}{4}$), is numerically expressed as $\frac{8}{9}$. Hence all these fractions may be written as

$$\frac{n}{n+1}$$

Aristoxenus was consequently induced to simplify the Pythagorean scale. Certainly his figures are scarcely any different from those of his predecessor: for example, E is represented by the fraction $\frac{4}{5}$, or $\frac{64}{80}$, instead of $\frac{64}{81}$.

Each note therefore corresponds to a specific fraction which indicates the length of string to be used, in relation to the fundamental taken as the unit.[6] These laws of acoustics, being of general validity, apply also to resonating pipes. A flue pipe half the length of another will, all other things being equal, sound an octave higher;[7] a pipe two-thirds the length of another will produce the fifth above; three-quarters, the fourth and so on.[8] Moreover, for reasons of elementary physics which need not be restated here, a stopped pipe sounds an octave lower than the equivalent open pipe.[9]

It is easy to appreciate why Greek musicians did not contemplate using the octave as a basis. If we take the seven notes previously referred to, and add the octave of the fundamental, we observe that the last four constitute an exact reproduction, in their respective intervals, of the first four, a fifth higher. If we refer again to the previous figures.

C	D	E	F	G	A	B	C
1	$\frac{8}{9}$	$\frac{64}{81}$	$\frac{3}{4}$	$\frac{2}{3}$	$\frac{16}{27}$	$\frac{128}{243}$	$\frac{1}{2}$

we have only to multiply the last four by $\frac{3}{2}$ to obtain the first four:

$$\frac{2}{3} \times \frac{3}{2} = 1 \quad\Big|\quad \frac{16}{27} \times \frac{3}{2} = \frac{8}{9} \quad\Big|\quad \frac{128}{243} \times \frac{3}{2} = \frac{64}{81} \quad\Big|\quad \frac{1}{2} \times \frac{3}{2} = \frac{3}{4}$$

The two tetrachords are therefore exactly similar, the second being simply a transposition of the first. To a Greek, it was perfectly rational to employ the tetrachord as the melodic unit.

The tone (τόνος) is defined as the difference between the fifth and the fourth:[10] its characteristic fraction, $\frac{2}{3} : \frac{3}{4} = \frac{8}{9}$, was widely used from early in the Middle Ages for the tuning of organ pipes. The tone is divided into two semitones or hemitones, and half of the hemitone is known as the *enharmonic diesis*.[11]

The juxtaposition of tetrachords of different registers forms a system. The Greater Perfect Disjunct System (Σύστημα τέλειον μεῖζον) is composed of four tetrachords named, from top to bottom:

Tetrachord Hyperbolaion,

Tetrachord Diezeugmenon,

Tetrachord Meson,

Tetrachord Hypaton.[12]

[6] Plato takes Pythagoras's figures and inserts them in a philosophical context (*Timaeus*, 35–6).

[7] Theoretically at least. In practice one must take into account the disturbance due to the presence of the mouth.

[8] Nicomachus, Handbook of Harmonics, translated into French by Ch. Ruelle (Paris, 1881), ch. x, 49–50 and 51.

[9] Aristotle, *Musical Problems*, problem 23.

[10] Aristoxenus; *Elements of Harmonics*, i, 21.

[11] Bacchius, *Introduction to the Art of Music*, translated into French by Ch. Ruelle (Paris, 1895), p. 104.

[12] ὕπατος 'means "highest" to the hand on the tilted kithara; *nete* "lowest to the hand" —although in pitch *hypate* is the lowest note and *nete* the top.' I. Henderson, 'Ancient Greek Music', *New Oxford History of Music*; (London, 1957), p. 345. Generally the Greeks regard the sequence of sounds as running from the high to the low notes.

The whole is completed by the addition of a note at the lower end of the system, known as the *Proslambanomenos*. The system is said to be 'disjunct' because the tetrachord Meson and the tetrachord Diezeugmenon have no note in common. For example:

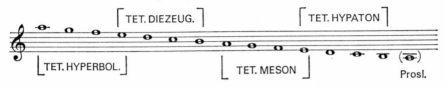

The Greater Perfect Disjunct System is thus limited by a consonance of the double octave.[13]

In addition to the Greater Perfect Disjunct System there is the Lesser Perfect Conjunct System (Σύστημα τέλειον ἔλαττον), made up of only three tetrachords, the tetrachord Meson being linked directly, without a hiatus, to the tetrachord *Synemmenon*. The compass of the Conjunct System is therefore an octave and a fourth:[14]

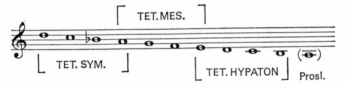

The Greeks did not give each of the notes in its system a specific name which was repeated from octave to octave. Their names merely defined the function of the note in its tetrachord. The principal note in each system, around the melody generally evolved,[15] is called the Mese because of its central position, and the function of all the other notes is revealed by their relationship to this note.[16] In the tetrachord Meson the three notes located below the Mese are called respectively Lichanos, or diatonic, Parypate, and Hypate. These names are also applied to the three lower notes of the tetrachord Hypate: we have observed that the note added to the bottom of this tetrachord is the Proslambanomenos, sounding an octave below the Mese. Above the mese, in the tetrachord Diezeugmenon, we have, going from top to bottom, the Nete, Paranete, Trite, and Paramese: and in the tetrachord Synemmenon the Nete, Paranete, and Trite. Finally, the tetrachord Hyperbolaion comprises, again in descending order, the Nete, Paranete, Trite, and Nete.[17]

---

[13] Cleonides, *Intr. Harm.*, translated into French by Ch. Ruelle (Paris, 1884), p. 35, no. 102.

[14] Cleonides, p. 34, no. 101.

[15] Aristotle, *Polit.*, i, 5, 1254, a.

[16] Cleonides, p. 36, no. 106.

[17] Gaudentius, vi.

GREATER PERFECT DISJUNCT SYSTEM

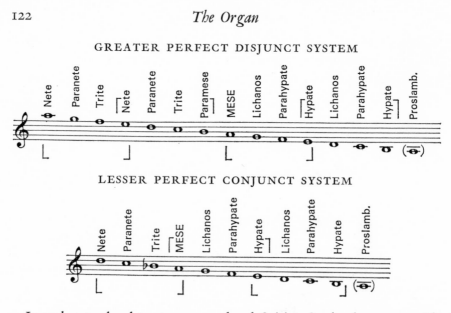

LESSER PERFECT CONJUNCT SYSTEM

In each tetrachord two notes are by definition fixed—the two outside notes. The two inner notes, the mobile notes, may be altered, thus lending the tetrachord a new character. In the forms transcribed above the tetrachords are said to be of the *diatonic genus*: in descending sequence the intervals are as follows:

tone — tone — semitone,

that is to say   A — G — F — E

If we lower the second note of the tetrachord by a hemitone, we have the following disposition, characteristic of the *chromatic genus*:

one and a half tones — semitone — semitone:

A   G flat   F   E

Finally, the tetrachord composed of the following intervals:

two tones — quarter-tone — quarter-tone
A — F — F flat — E

makes up the *enharmonic genus*.

The segment consisting of the three lower sounds of the chromatic and enharmonic tetrachords is called the Pyknon. The passage from one genus to another is effected by the alteration of the two mobile notes of the tetrachord:[18] and these modulations are called metabolae of genus. To lend variety to the melody the Ancients also practised metabolae of system, passing from disjunct to conjunct and vice versa, metabolae of tropos, and metabolae of rhythm.[19]

[18] Cleonides, p. 26, no. 56.   [19] Bacchius, pp. 121–2, nos. 50 to 59.

During the Roman and Hellenistic periods the diatonic genus is the most frequently employed, because it is the simplest and the most natural for the human voice.[20] The chromatic genus is used, especially in metabolae, to add expressiveness to the diatonic melody. The enharmonic genus, of auletic origin, reached its peak of popularity in the fifth century B.C. But a hundred years later it had to some extent fallen into disfavour in favour of the chromatic.[21] We cannot tell whether there were still many listeners capable of apprehending its intervals during the Roman era. The same is true of the nuances: the diatonic genus itself was capable of several varieties of intonation,[22] with the tone divided into thirds, sixths, and eighths. These academic subtleties, mocked by Plato in the seventh chapter of his *Republic*,[23] were certainly irrelevant to the organ, which was an instrument of fixed pitch: but, as we shall see in the following chapter, it seems likely that the enharmonic genus was sometimes employed on that instrument.

Rhythm was of cardinal importance—Plato even attributed an ethical significance to it.[24] The organ, above all other instruments, was capable of asserting it strongly; hence its role as an amphitheatre instrument. Bacchius tells us[25] that there were ten rhythmic formulae: the hegemon, the iambus, the choraea, the anapaest, the orthios, the spondee, the paeon, the bacchius, the dochmius, and the enoplion. In vocal and instrumental music the silences were known as diastoles.[26]

There remains the controversial question of what books on musical history continue to call the 'Greek modes'. It seems highly likely that such modes, in terms of our scale forms, never actually existed. Moreover, ancient texts give no accurate information on this subject, though in reading them we discover that place-names, 'Dorian', 'Phrygian', 'Lydian' were applied in the course of antiquity to fundamentally different melodic concepts. In the works of Plato and Aristotle, for example, such expressions as 'Dorian harmony' or 'Lydian harmony' refer to scales with characteristic melodic and rhythmic patterns, immediately perceptible to the listener. 'A harmony,' says Heraclides Ponticus,[27] 'must communicate a particular passion or character.' A moral influence is attributed to each one: virtuous gravity to the Dorian, unbridled passion to the Phrygian. Plato therefore selects the

---

[20] Aristoxenus, i, 19.
[21] Aristoxenus, i, 23.
[22] Cleonides, nos. 68–71, p. 27.
[23] 12, 531 b.
[24] *Republic*, iii, §11, 399 e, 400 a and b.
[25] Bacchius, nos. 100–1, pp. 138–9.
[26] Second Anonymous of Bellermann (M. Vincent, *Notice sur divers manuscrits grecs relatifs à la Musique*, Paris, 1847, p. 50).
[27] Quoted by Athenaeus, xiv, 19.

harmonies for the citizens of his Republic with great care, since he wishes to instil in them courage and integrity.[28] These formulated modes may resemble those in Oriental music (Hindu râgas, Arabian maqam, and so on).[29]

On the other hand, the tropes or tones (tonoi), which had the same place-names as the harmonies, define the respective pitch of the various systems within the scale of sounds. Having no moral overtones, they merely describe a 'species' of the octave, Greek musicographers actually present the consonances under their different 'species'; the fourth has three, the fifth four, and the octave seven, according to the placing of the semitone in the top register.[30] These various 'species' may be transposed on to all the degrees, in which case they acquire the name of 'tonoi' or 'tropes', the corresponding place-names having already been used for a long time in this sense in the Alexandrian era. Heraclides Ponticus was very critical of those who were unable to recognize these scales, and whose only concern was the relative pitch of the sounds, high or low.[31]

Greek musical notation seems to have been the exclusive preserve of composers and teachers, and it is unlikely that instrumentalists ever concerned themselves with it. The different notes are represented by letters, which vary according to whether the music is vocal or instrumental.[32] A complete list is given in the Tables of Alypius.[33] If the melody is accompanied, the upper signs represent the notes for the voice, and the lower ones those for the instrument. The Second Anonymous of Bellermann[34] tells us that 'There may, moreover, be a transition to a purely instrumental phrase, either inserted between the words, or added when the voice is still'.

THE STATUS OF MUSIC

The place occupied by music in the lives of the Greeks and Romans in the Hellenistic and Imperial periods is hard to determine, especially when two sources of information provide evidence of a somewhat contradictory nature. These are the writings of the moral philosophers and the glimpses of public life scattered through the literature of the time.

Plato and his school reflect the thinking of the intellectual aristocracy of

---

[28] *Republic*, 398 ff.

[29] See J. Chailley, 'Le Mythe des modes grecs', *Acta Musicologica* (1956), xxviii, part iv, pp. 137 ff.

[30] Cleonides gives a detailed list of these various 'species', pp. 30 ff.

[31] Athenaeus, xiv, 19.

[32] Alypius, *Introd. Music.*, translated into French by Ch. Ruelle (Paris, 1895), p. 2, no. 3.

[33] A. Quintilianus, Gaudentius and Bacchius also give some indications on this subject, though sometimes they are contradictory. See the article by H. Potiron, 'Les notations d'A. Quintillien', *Revue de Musicologie*, xlvii (December 1961).

[34] Vincent, op. cit., p. 35.

the ancient world, and their teaching, in its original form, still permeates the works of a man like St. Augustine. For these philosophers music is much more a science than an art—a special application of mathematics, like geometry. This concept accounts for the somewhat tedious complexity of Greek 'solfa'. Plato makes a point of warning his disciples that where music is concerned the mind must at all times have precedence over the ear,[35] for it is by disregarding this precept that the public deludes itself into thinking itself well informed on the subject.[36] Instruction in music should therefore be a part of every child's education, so that he may be guided towards an appreciation of the Beautiful[37] and his mind moulded towards Goodness.[38] However, the purely physical pleasure occasioned by an enjoyable concert is admitted by Aristotle, though with some reservations, and for adults only. This pleasure is conducive to a special state of mind known as catharsis, which can be beneficial.[39] Invariably, the professional musician is regarded by the moralists as essentially an inferior being, on a par with the common artisan.[40]

It should not be thought, however, that these harsh and austere ethical principles were blindly adopted by the man in the street. We have evidence of the enthusiasm shown by the people of Delphi for the virtuoso organist Antipatros, and the appreciation of Athenaeus's learned guests for their unexpected concert on the hydraulic organ. All the most popular songs came from Alexandria,[41] where many of the inhabitants not only played the aulos but played it well.[42] In Rome the discreet scorn poured by Cicero on organ music, which he rates on a par with the taste of a good piece of fish, is contradicted by numerous passages in his writings where he betrays the fact that he is not insensitive to instrumental music in general. Nevertheless, in those days no leading figure, even a Roman, would have dared to play an instrument in public. In the reign of Tiberius, the consul L. Norbanus Flaccus aroused indignation by practising his trumpet in full view of the people.[43] It was not long, however, before the emperors themselves set the example. Nero sang in public, and performed on both the lyre and the organ. From then on the aristocracy felt at liberty to study instrumental technique, and music, whatever its artistic level may have been—and this is very difficult to judge today—henceforth played a major role not only in public or religious ceremonies but in the intimacy of family life. The funeral

[35] *Republic*, vii, part 12, 531 a.
[36] *Laws*, iii, 700 d.
[37] *Republic*, iii, part 12, 403 c.
[38] Plutarch, *De Musica*, op. cit., 256, p. 98.
[39] *Polit.*, viii, part 7, 1341 a.
[40] Ibid., viii, 1341 b.
[41] Ovid, *Ars Amatoria*, iii, 318; Martial, *Epigr.*, iii, lxiii, 5.
[42] Athenaeus, iv, 79.
[43] Cassius Dio, lvii, 18, 3.

monuments of young female organists such as Aelia Sabina, Aphrodisis, or Julia Tyrrania further establish that during the Empire many young women unashamedly devoted themselves to playing the hydraulic organ.[44]

MUSICAL INSTRUMENTS

There is no need to discuss stringed instruments here. It is enough to remember that in the classical period they were more highly thought of than the aulos, which, in the opinion of Aristoxenus, distorted most of the melodic intervals.[45] Plato also commends the instrument of Apollo and rejects that of Marsyas.[46] However, during the Alexandrian era more and more people took up the study of wind instruments, in particular the aulos, and this upsurge in its popularity, which was to be of great advantage to the organ, continued unabated in the days of the Roman Empire.

The syrinx σῦριγξ or panpipe, which lent its shape to the musical part of the organ, is very ancient in origin, and is found among a wide range of peoples. Pollux[47] describes it as 'a collection of reeds bound together with a short cord and some wax . . . It is composed of a certain number of pipes placed side by side, stepwise, so that they grow gradually less from the longest to the shortest. At the open end they are all perfectly aligned; but at the other end, by virtue of their unequal length, they are graded, so that the whole looks like a bird's wing.'

On the syrinx, therefore, the pipes are stopped with wax, which means that they can be tuned.[48] They vary in number from seven to twelve—the instrument with a hundred pipes attributed by Ovid to Polyphemus is clearly mythical.[49] In its rustic form it had pipes of reed or hemlock, but they could also be of bronze or ivory. The overall measurements of the instrument are relatively constant, the average width was approximately 10 cm., and the longest pipe was a little shorter than this. Thus it produced a high, shrill sound. However, there is iconographic evidence that larger types of syrinx also existed, which, judging from the people playing them, could be as much as 40–50 cm. in height.[50] Perhaps it was the sight of instruments such as these which inspired Ktesibios to fit a set of pipes to his hydraulic machine and arrange them after the fashion of the syrinx.

The aulos or tibia was very widely used in the Graeco-Roman world. It has a vibrating reed, its basic principle being similar to that of the oboe.

---

[44] Plato admitted that 'some women are musically gifted' (*Republic*, v, part 5, 455 e).
[45] ii, iii, 34, p. 65.
[46] *Republic*, iii, 399 d.
[47] *Onomasticon*, iv, 69.
[48] Aristotle, *Probl.*, 23, p. 16.
[49] *Metamorphoses*, xiii, 784.
[50] As, for instance, the instrument shown in the diptych of Vernona (cf. p. 79), and Dionysus's organ on the Cologne mosaic.

Originally it consisted of a tubular reed pipe, varying in length, but as a rule not exceeding 50 cm. It is open at one end and fitted with a movable mouthpiece at the other, while all along the pipe are holes for playing. The aulos is made of a special type of reed, though Pollux says it may be of metal, lotus, boxwood, horn, ivory or laurel.[51]

The mouthpiece is a bulb with one or two reeds made from slivers of cane. The reed (γλῶσσα) is the most delicate part of the whole instrument, and the utmost care was taken in its manufacture. The reeds used for this purpose came from a particular locality, and might only be cut at certain times, in summer or a little later. The stems were laid out to dry in the sun for a fixed period of time, and then, from selected lengths, thin, smooth slivers were cut.[52] At the time of Pliny the Elder this process had developed to keep pace with changing tastes.[53] The artisan who made the reeds was known as the γλωττοποιός, and producing a finished instrument must have been a laborious task. Seneca, taking his ease at Baiae, rails against the noisiness of the neighbourhood, where a manufacturer of tibias and trumpets spends his time testing his reeds.[54]

The aulos is nearly always double. The auletes, or tibicen, holds two instruments, one in each hand, with both mouthpieces in his mouth—a practice said to have been initiated by Hyagnis: 'He was the first to separate his hands while playing; the first to play two tibias with a single breath; and, using the holes located to left and right, he was the first to produce a musical sound in which the high notes (acuto tinnitu) mingled with a low humming (gravi bumbo).'[55]

Originally the aulos has four holes, one for each finger, the thumb being kept tucked in under the pipe. Later, however, someone—it seems to have been the Theban Pronomius—had the idea of fitting ferrules round the tube to free certain fingers by continuing to stop the corresponding holes. This innovation meant that a greater range of notes could be obtained,[56] whereas before 'there were special auloi for each mode, so that at the Games all the auleti had to have an aulos for each mode. Pronomius of Thebes was the first to play all the modes on the same aulos.'[57] Pausanias offers some

---

51 *Onom.*, iv, 70.
52 Theophrastus, *Hist. Plant.*, iv, 2. On the Greek aulos see K. Schlesinger, *The Greek Aulos* (London, 1939).
53 *Nat. Hist.*, xvi, 66.
54 *Ad Lucil.*, vi, 56, 4.
55 Apuleius, *Florides*, 3.
56 The instruments discovered at Pompeii have from eight to ten holes, but the aulos in Candy Museum has twenty-four.
57 Athenaeus, xiv, 31. A certain Pythagoras of Xanthus had invented a 'musical tripod', consisting of three citharas tuned respectively to the Dorian, Lydian and Phrygian modes, so that the player could move instantly from one harmony to another. Athenaeus, xiv, 41.

information regarding the invention of this Theban, who was born around 475 B.C.:

For a long time it was customary for auletes to possess three types of aulos. On one, they played the Dorian mode, while another, different type was designed for the Phrygian mode; and the mode known as Lydian was played on yet another type. Pronomius was the first to invent an aulos for all these modes, and the first to play so many different melodies on the same instrument.[58]

These concepts of simultaneous and different musical lines played in the two pipes of the instrument, and its melodic polyvalence, are, to my mind, of great importance for the history of the organ. Indeed, it is most unlikely that, from the outset, the organ did not have the same musical possibilities as the auloi of which it was composed.

All the auloi did not have the same pitch. Aristoxenus[59] listed five distinct categories:

$$
\begin{array}{ll}
\left.\begin{array}{l}\text{the virginal aulos}\\ \text{the juvenile aulos}\end{array}\right\} & \text{trebles}\\[1.5em]
\text{the aulos in unison with the cithara—medium}\\[0.5em]
\left.\begin{array}{l}\text{the perfect aulos}\\ \text{the pluperfect aulos}\end{array}\right\} & \text{bass}
\end{array}
$$

Playing the aulos demanded not only agility in fingering,[60] but in addition considerable lung power, for a good supply of air was needed in competitions, for instance, at least for the lowest-pitched instruments. Perhaps it was the sight of the bulging cheeks and bloodshot eyes of the auletes in action which inspired Ktesibios to replace the human lungs with a mechanical wind mechanism.

The timbre of the aulos must be imagined as having been to some extent like that of the oboe,[61] although this varied, for example, according to whether a 'soprano' or 'tenor' aulos was involved. At all events, it was a pleasant, even a captivating sound: 'To begin with, it arouses passion; moves men to tears; and then, little by little, puts sorrow to flight.'[62] Aristotle also shares this view: 'Both those who grieve and those who are happy enjoy the sound of the aulos.'[63] Plato, however, finds it weakening,[64]

---

[58] ix, 12. Pausanias also says that he was honoured for this invention by having his statue erected.

[59] Quoted by Athenaeus (xiv, 36), according to Didymus.

[60] Philostratus, *Life of Apollonius of Tyana*, iv, 21.

[61] Under the Empire, the sound of the tibia sometimes emulated that of the trumpet. Horace, *Ars Poetica*, 202–3.

[62] Plutarch, *Quaest. Conviv.*, iii, 8.

[63] *Probl.*, 1. It is generally agreed that the Problems are probably not the work of Aristotle himself, but of several of his disciples.

[64] *Republic*, iii, 399 d.

and criticizes it for seeking only to induce pleasurable sensations.[65] Another accusation levelled at the aulos is that its volume too readily covers up mistakes made by the singer it is accompanying,[66] and cynics used to say that in Greece anyone who was incapable of succeeding as a citharist was only too happy to take up the aulos instead.[67] Some of these arguments were probably used against the organ in its early stages by the aesthetes and moralists.

The aulos was not only a solo instrument. It accompanied solo singing (auledia) or choruses (chorauledia) and combined with the cithara or with another aulos (synaulia). Frequently, too, it appeared in ensembles, on one occasion at an open-air banquet in honour of the Mother of the Gods, when 'the taut drums throb to the beat of the palms, the hollow cymbals clash around them, the trumpets shout their harsh threat, and the Phrygian rhythm of the tibia stirs the soul'.[68]

The other wind instrument which was soon to add new timbres to the organ was the flute (fistula), whose use in ancient times appears to have been confined to pastoral life. It could produce melodies described by Apuleius as softer than a murmur.[69]

★   ★   ★   ★

There remains the vital question of diaphony in antiquity: the problem of whether or not the ancients practised any true form of music in two parts. How far did the advent of a keyboard instrument, where both hands were involved as a matter of course, help to promote this particular aspect of musical thought? These are problems affecting the whole course of musical history, and which, if we cannot solve, we should at least attempt to clarify.

The practice of accompanying a melody with notes foreign to that melody is certainly a very ancient one, and appears to have been in current use in the time of Plato, who refers to such a technique only to condemn it, at least in teaching.

The teacher of the lyre and his pupil should exploit the precision of the notes produced by the strings by seeing to it that the notes exactly accompany the voices. But to make the lyre sound separately by multiplying each note so that the strings give forth their melody, different from that written for the voice: and to combine small and wide intervals, quick and slow notes, treble and bass notes: to complicate the rhythms in the lyre's accompaniment in every way—all such affectations should be banned from the teaching repertory.[70]

[65] *Gorgias*, 501 e.
[66] Aristotle, *Problem* 43.
[67] Cicero, *Pro Murena*, ch. xiii: 'eos auleodos esse, qui citharoedi fieri non potuerint'.
[68] Lucretius, *De Nat. Rer.*, ii, 618–20.
[69] *Florida*, 17, 8: 'fistula susurru jucundior'.
[70] *Laws*, vii, 812 b.

We have seen that Hyagnis, father of Marsyas, had in his possession a double aulos, which combined treble with bass. Varro says more specifically that the right-hand pipe played the melody, while the left took care of the accompaniment,[71] and we know from Alypius and the Second Anonymous[72] that different forms of notation were used for the melody and the accompaniment. Ovid, in his *Metamorphoses*, is probably referring to this early polyphony in the lines:

> Ut satis impulsas tentavit pollice chordas,
> Et sensit varios quamvis diversa sonarent,
> Concordare modos . . .[73]

What of the intervals used in this accompaniment? It seems likely that it was often improvised, as in contemporary jazz: but the principal consonances came together at the various punctuation marks in the voice part. The comic poet Damoxenus puts the following words into the mouth of a cook: 'I blend the food harmoniously, as with the diatessaron, the diapente, and the diapason.'[74]

But the accompaniment was more than a series of consonances. The note that was foreign to the melody (κροῦσις) could, for instance, be the nete, sounding in a dissonance with the paranete, though in consonance with the mese or paramese.[75] Clearly a vocal line accompanied in this way by consonances or passing notes did not constitute a true counterpoint, in which each voice would have had a character of its own. Here the melody, whether it was given to the voice or to an instrument, always predominated.

Again, it seems that the ancients appreciated a certain style of 'vertical' polyphony, where the vocal line was doubled at the octave, the fifteenth, and perhaps at the fifth. Aristotle remarks that the octave falls more sweetly on the ear than the unison,[76] and Macrobius is struck by the sound of a mixed choir with instrumental accompaniment:

Consider how many voices go to make up a choir: and yet all of these combine to make but a single voice. Some are high, some low, and some fall between the two, the women singing with the men. The flute adds its voice, and all these different elements form a harmonious ensemble.[77]

Such considerations naturally apply to the organ, which is by its very

---

[71] *De Agricultura*, i, 2: 'Et ut dextera tibia alia quam sinistra, ita ut tamen sit quodam modo cunjuncta, quod est altera ejusdem carminis modorum incentiva, altera succentiva.'
[72] Vincent, op. cit., p. 34.
[73] x, 145.
[74] Quoted by Athenaeus, iii, 60. He is referring to the fourth, the fifth, and the octave.
[75] Plutarch, *De Musica*, op. cit., 175–6, p. 77.
[76] *Probl.*, 39, p. 25.
[77] *Saturn.*, i, 9. Seneca had already said much the same thing (*Ad Lucil.*, xi, 84, 9).

nature a polyphonic instrument, since from the first it was equipped with a series of pipes and a manual. At the organ congress in Strasbourg in 1932 Canon Mathias declared:

From the first, organ-playing was polyphonic . . . Besides, we have only to picture to ourselves an intelligent man faced with so many pipes, and so many keys unlocking the musical treasures of these pipes. It would be against all human reason and ingenuity not at least to try and play with both hands simultaneously, particularly since the way had long since been prepared for this by playing the bagpipes, which produced a perfect heterophony.[78]

Without going so far, it is worth noting that, in the iconographical evidence, the organist appears in most cases to have both hands on the manual: we can take it as certain that he did not play with one hand only. Either he was playing in parallel octaves or twelfths, or else—and this is the most likely hypothesis—he was playing his own accompaniment to the melody he had to interpret, like the tibicen with his two pipes.

[78] *Compte Rendu du Congrès d'Orgue de Strasbourg* (Strasbourg, 1934), pp. 166 ff.

CHAPTER SEVEN

The Graeco-Roman Organ: the Pipes and their Tuning

Very little indeed is known about the sounding part of the organ of antiquity. We know nothing for certain about the number of pipes, their sound quality, their pitch, or how they were made, for not one contemporary text tackles any of these even briefly. Thus the historian is reduced to hypothesis in his attempts to find a solution to what are for us problems of abiding interest.

The ancients attached much less importance to manufacturing processes than we do today: such matters were left to the artisan. The intellectuals affected to despise them, though they did consider the arithmetical relationship between the sounds, and indulged in subtle speculations on their various systems. Not a single treatise on the measurement of pipes, of the type that has survived from medieval times, has come to light; probably because ancient theoreticians considered it to be self-evident that flue pipes were subject to the same general rules as vibrating strings. Nicomachus of Gerasa[1] tells us that Pythagoras himself had verified these rules on the syrinx, while, in the third century A.D., Porphyry specifically quotes the pipes of the hydraulis as an example of how sounds vary in pitch according to the length of the pipe.[2]

Nowhere is there any reference to the number of pipes normally present on the organ. Tertullian's allusion to an army drawn up in battle order (tot acies tibiarum) is his way of painting a verbal picture of the serried ranks of pipes making up the stops. What we should like to know is the number and nature of the degrees covered by the manual. Nicomachus's statement[3] that instrument-makers used twenty-eight notes[4] is obviously no proof that any one instrument, be it lyre, aulos, or hydraulis, could produce all of these. For want of other evidence, it is the iconography alone which enables us to glean a relatively precise idea of the number of pipes that went to make up each stop on the organ, and then only so far as the different artists have reproduced their models faithfully.

---

[1] *Handbook of Harmonics*, vi, 32.   [2] Düring, op. cit., p. 120.   [3] *Fragments*, vii, 1.
[4] This number is made up of the different mobile sounds peculiar to the three genera.

If we take the thirty-one most carefully executed representations of the hydraulis, we notice immediately that a set of eight pipes recurs most frequently (six times), closely followed by instruments with seven, nine, and ten pipes (four times each). And while too much weight should not be attached to such deductions, it does seem that the organ equipped with from seven to ten pipes was the most common, whereas the eighteen-pipe model was probably much rarer.

Deciding the tessitura of the manual is still more arbitrary. It would seem logical to infer *a priori* that a hydraulis with fifteen pipes might have a range covering the Greater Perfect Disjunct System, extending over two octaves and four tetrachords, from the proslambanomenos to the hyperbolaion nete.[5]

An organ tuned to this scale, whatever the genus, would have been unable to play, within a given register, the different species of octave, each of which necessitates alterations easily obtainable on the aulos, but practically impossible here. These different modes—Lydian, Phrygian, or Dorian, for instance, could only be achieved if the proslambanomenos were located on the appropriate degree of the manual.[6] But in any case none of the illustrations shows an instrument whose first pipe is four times the height of its last, to give the double octave between the extreme notes of the Greater Perfect System. On the British Museum gem the lowest-pitched pipe is three times the size of the highest, so that they sound only a twelfth[7] apart, giving a tessitura of an octave and a fifth, or twelve notes for a total of thirteen or fourteen pipes. In this particular case we may have an example of the Greater Perfect Disjunct System minus its final tetrachord and enriched by the characteristic note of the Synemmenon. On this instrument the manual would therefore have been laid out approximately in this order:

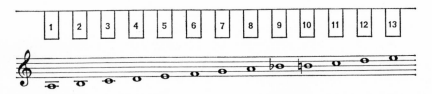

[5] Cleonides, *Introd. Harm.*, part 102.
[6] As indicated by Gaudentius (*Introd. Harm.*, xx) in relation to strings.
[7] For Bacchius (*Introd. to the Art of Music*, ii) the twelfth constitutes the fifth consonance.

The Tarsus terracotta, again a carefully made piece, represents a fifteen-pipe organ on which the respective heights of the two extreme pipes stand in a ratio of roughly $\frac{3}{1}$, suggesting a manual of the following type:

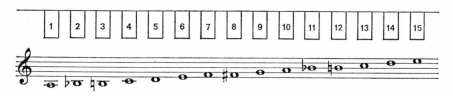

The Carthaginian lamp sets a much greater problem. The instrument it represents has an eighteen-key manual, and the pipes, carefully modelled, have lips which allow us to take exact acoustic measurements. By noting the respective heights of the vibrating columns of the first and eighteenth pipes, we find a numerical ratio of approximately $\frac{27}{16}$, implying an interval of a major sixth. We must therefore assume the existence of sixteen inter-mediate notes, necessitating the division of the canon into enharmonic dieses, more or less equal quarter-tones. Even allowing for a slight error on the part of the potter, we have no choice but to accept a certain number of these dieses, so that the manual may possibly have looked like this:

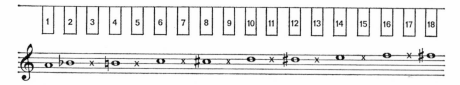

Equally narrow intervals between the two extreme pipes are shown on the instruments in the Nennig mosaic ($\frac{4}{3}$), the Valentinian III contorniate ($\frac{4}{5}$) and the St. Maximin sarcophagus ($\frac{5}{4}$) as well as the organ on the tomb of the unknown musician at Arles ($\frac{4}{3}$). It is difficult to concede that the same type of mistake was made by so many artists and sculptors of different eras. We must therefore assume that the hydraulis was sometimes equipped with pipes proceeding by intervals equal to or smaller than a semitone. My own experience has moreover verified the practicability of feeding a set of pipes as finely tuned as this by means of a hydraulic wind mechanism.

But, as I have said, most of the iconographic documents show organs with seven, eight, or nine pipes, and here, too, it is interesting to try to establish their tessitura. Looking closely at the bas-relief of Julia Tyrannia's organ, which may be analysed quite accurately because of the meticulous workman-ship, we see that the eight pipes stand in a ratio of about $\frac{3}{2}$; that is to say they span an interval of a fifth. If they are indeed flue pipes, then presumably the manual proceeded by intervals approximating to a semitone:

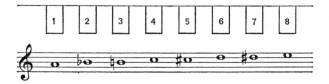

The archaeological remains of the Aquincum organ may also be used for such measurements. This particular instrument is, of course, a very special case—extremely small, with four ranks of thirteen pipes, three of them composed of flue pipes. Though considerably damaged, most of the pipes could nevertheless be measured.[8] In each of the first two sets, less ravaged than the others, the lowest-pitched pipe is roughly twice the height of the highest. Assuming that each plug was located at the top of its pipe, we can say that the compass of these sets, and therefore probably of the whole organ, was in the vicinity of an octave. Within this interval there would have been eleven notes, and the simplest division of these implies the use of semitones:

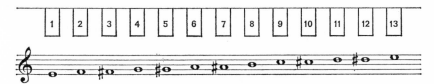

Such a pattern, though it is purely hypothetical, would have allowed the use of the system of transposition by 'onomaseis', described by Claudius Ptolemy in the second century A.D. If we adopt the suggestive comparison made by J. Chailley[9] between this procedure and the mobile manual of transposing harmoniums, it is easy to see the advantage of spacing out the sounds by equal semitones. The label stuck to the front of the manual on the harmonium to identify the notes corresponds to the fixed or theoretical names of the notes in a given trope, for example the Dorian. The transposing manual corresponds to the mobile or dynamic names of the notes. On the harmonium, if the keys of the central octave coincide with the sounds indicated by the label, they play the real notes. If the manual is displaced, this octave will give the same intervals, but transposed to other degrees.

In the example chosen here the extreme notes on the organ manual mark the limits of the central part of the diatonic Dorian. To play a different trope, let us suppose that the mese is the same, but a special key signature will be used so that certain notes will change. If, for instance, we consider

[8] L. Nagy, op. cit., pp. 24 ff.
[9] J. Chailley, *L'imbroglio des modes* (Paris, 1960), pp. 20–21.

the octave 'species' specified by Cleonides[10] and named by him Dorian, Phrygian, and Lydian, we obtain this pattern:

	1	2	3	4	5	6	7	8	9	10	11	12	13
	E	F	F♯	G	G♯	A	A♯	B	C	C♯	D	D♯	E
Dorian	★	★		★		★		★	★		★		★
Phrygian	★		★	★		★		★		★	★		★
Lydian	★		★		★	★		★		★		★	★

Hypat.   Mese   Nete

Division by approximately equal semitones appears to have been foreseen by Aristoxenus himself, by the assimilation, implicitly admitted, of the notes E♭ and D♯.[11] This modulation, by allowing the usual transpositions, widened the range of small instruments. Further, we have seen that the first three ranks on the Aquincum organ were stopped by movable tampons inserted into the pipes. It is tempting to liken these adjustable plugs to the rods studied by Curt Sachs in connection with the lyre,[12] and to invest them with the same function, that is to say modifying the tuning of certain pipes by one or two enharmonic dieses, thus enabling the player to use three genera. My reconstruction of this instrument has certainly revealed the possibility of tuning the stopped pipes to the quarter-tone, and indeed for demonstration purposes two enharmonic tetrachords have been introduced into the scale of the third rank of pipes.

No inquiry into the notes used on the manual of the classical organ would be complete without an analysis of the famous text of Bellermann's Anonymous.[13] Having said that wind instruments more often use the Phrygian mode (ἡ ↔ φρύγιος ἁρμονία), the author states categorically that hydraules play in none but the following tropes (μόνοις . . . τρόποις): Hyperlydian, Hyperiastian, Lydian, Phrygian, Hypolydian, and Hypophrygian.

Thus the 'confusion of the modes', denounced by J. Chailley, occurs even in antiquity. The two pieces of information given by Anonymous really have no connection. The Phrygian mode played by wind instruments is a scale with 'ethos', that is to say it has a special character, easily recognizable and capable, it was said, of arousing excitement and even passion.[14] On the other hand, the tropes mentioned later indicate the real pitch ratios of the various sounds. For instance, Aristides Quintilianus places the two octaves

---

[10] *Introduction to Harmonics*, 88.

[11] Th. Reinach, *La Musique Grecque* (Paris, 1926), p. 22. See also H. Potiron, *Boèce, théoricien de la musique grecque* (Paris, 1961), pp. 74ff.

[12] J. Chailley, op. cit., p. 21.

[13] See below, p. 183.

[14] Each of the 'harmonies' was certainly characterized by a special rhythm. Lucretius speaks of the 'phrygian rhythm' of the tibia (Phrygio stimulat numero . .. tibia mentis), *De Nat. Rer.*, ii, 620.

spanned by the voice in the Dorian trope, while the third fragment of the Hagiopolites quotes the favourite tropes of the trumpet, the aulos, the voice, the cithara, and the pteron. If we refer to the tables of Alypius, therefore, the tessitura of the hydraulis would have contained the following notes, according to Bellermann's Anonymous (if we adopt the convention that C=LA):

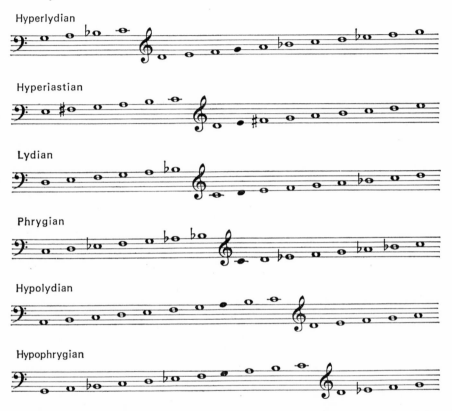

By suppressing the doubled notes, we are left with the following scale:

At this point the question arises as to whether the hydraulis did, in fact, have all these notes, which would have required a manual of thirty-two keys. The iconography categorically argues against any such interpretation. Not one of the instruments illustrated actually shows more than eighteen pipes in any rank. Gastoué's hypothesis,[15] according to which each register would have supplied air pressure to a specific trope, does not stand up, for

---

[15] *L'orgue en France*, op. cit., p. 17.

if this were true many of the pipes would have been doubled, making the instrument needlessly complicated and top-heavy. It seems to me that the Anonymous text suggests a different theory, namely that there were various types of hydraulic organ, with different pitches, probably distinguished by their mese, in G, E, D, C, A and low G, just as today we have clarinets in C, F or B flat.[16] It is also quite possible that some instruments included the notes that went to make up two or three of these tropes; or again they may have been provided with the notes belonging to all six tropes within the compass of a single octave. This last appears to have been realized on the manual of the Aquincum pneumatic organ. But it will not have passed unnoticed that in the complete range of notes belonging to these six tropes there are no degrees corresponding to the C sharps (still adopting Bellermann's convention), that is to say the sounds Ⅎ, λ and K' in the diatonic genus. The omission does not appear to be fortuitous. According to this same Anonymous, the aulos, which used seven tropes (Hyperaeolian, Hyperiastian, Lydian, Phrygian, Iastian, Hypolydian, and Hypophrygian), had a range of three octaves with all the semitones—this particular instrument was famous for the number of notes it could play.[17] Does the systematic omission of the C sharps on the hydraulis imply respect for an 'ethos' specifically associated with the instrument?[18] It seems highly improbable, since we know that the organ frequently played in consort with the horn, trumpet, or vocal ensembles. Moreover, if we write down the complete series of notes forming the six tropes, not in the diatonic genus, but chromatically—still in accordance with the Alypian tables—we find that every note in our chromatic scale is included. Furthermore, there is nothing to suggest that the organ manual did not have the conjunct trite characteristic of the Synemmenon tetrachord, which, in the Phrygian diatonic, is none other than the note λ, the second C sharp in our series. It becomes obvious that, given the present state of our knowledge, a measure of uncertainty must attach to the information in Anonymous, and the value of the text should not be overestimated. Since it is the only one of its kind, it is clearly very precious, but it may reflect a local tradition rather than a widespread practice.

An analysis of the illustrative evidence reveals, then, that the manual of the hydraulis embraces a somewhat restricted number of tetrachords. A nucleus of 'fixed' notes (hypate, mese, paramese, and nete) probably formed the framework of the melodic scale, and these, with the addition of certain 'mobile' notes (parypate, lichanos, trite, and paranete) enabled the organist to perform in several tropes, thus introducing a little variety into his play-

---

[16] As we saw, there were five distinct types of aulos in Aristoxenus's day.

[17] Plato, *Republic*, iii, 399 d; Plutarch, *De Musica*, 293, p. 114.

[18] On the assumption that we are certain of the exact scale of the sounds given in the Tables of Alypius. On this dubious point, see J. Chailley, op. cit., pp. 19 and 22.

ing. We know that the so-called 'instrumental' notation which in Alypius's treatise specifies the notes of the fifteen tropes in the three genera, was used above all by pedagogues and composers. Although this notation is very probably of Alexandrian origin,[19] like the hydraulis itself, it is by no means certain that the artisan organ-builders were very deeply concerned with all its various subtleties. Probably it was enough that the instrument should be capable of modulating a tune in the diatonic genus, certainly the most widely used in Roman times, and possibly in the chromatic genus, whose intervals were still used in Vitruvius's time for tuning theatre vases.[20] The organist could therefore change 'genera', passing from one to the other in the course of the same piece of music. As well as this, he could add variety to his music by changing 'systems', combining the Disjunct with the Conjunct; by changing 'tropes' and, of course, by varying his 'rhythms'.[21]

It seems to me out of the question that 'nuances' could have been achieved on the classical organ—such pedantic refinements certainly meant nothing to the great mass of the Roman people. Moreover, even today an organ pipe cannot be tuned to $\frac{3}{8}$ or $\frac{11}{6}$ of a tone. It remains within the bounds of possibility, however, that some instruments were fitted with pipes progressing by quarter-tones or thirds of a tone, at least for several pyknons. But it is most unlikely that the hydraules destined to form part of an amphitheatre orchestra were encumbered with such intellectual refinements. In all probability they pumped out popular, easy-to-remember airs moving in the diatonic or chromatic genus and adding some variety by resorting to metaboles, especially changes in 'tonoi', as in the case of the air from the *Mysians*, which, according to Plutarch, went from the Hypodorian to the Dorian by way of the Myxolydian, Hypophrygian, and Phrygian.[22] This may well be what Tertullian means when, writing about the organ, he boasts of the frequently interchanging 'modes' it can produce (tot commercia modorum);[23] and it is perhaps also uppermost in the thoughts of the author of the *Aetna* poem[24] when he attributes to the instrument the practice of varying the 'modes'. However, it would have to be proved that in both texts the term 'modus' means the same as 'trope'. For Boethius, at any rate the words are synonymous.[25]

[19] A. Bataille, *Remarques sur les deux notations mélodiques de l'ancienne musique grecque*; i: *Recherche papyrologique*, i, p. 19 (Publication of the Faculté des Lettres de Paris, Série Recherches).

[20] *De Architectura*, v, 5.

[21] Bacchius gives a detailed list of all the changes used by musicians in his day in *Introduction to the Art of Music*, 50 to 58.

[22] Op. cit., xvii, p. 143.

[23] *De anima*, 14.

[24] Line 296: imparibus . . . modis.

[25] '. . . ex diapason igitur consonantiae speciebus existuunt, qui appellantur modi, quos eosdem tropos vel tonos nominant': *De Inst. Musica*, iv, 15.

It will be realized how very fragile all these hypotheses relating to the sound of the ancient organ really are. But one thing is certain: in those days, as in our own times, no two instruments were exactly alike. Though from the iconography it might appear that the overall proportions of the instruments altered only slightly, there can be little doubt that the palette of sound was extremely varied. There were the reed instruments, built for the amphitheatre and for public spectacles, and here the words 'aulos' or 'tibia' are frequently used to describe the pipes. Constantine Porphyrogenitus invariably selects the verb 'αὐλέιν' in speaking of the sound made by the organ during official ceremonies. There were other instruments made with flue pipes, whose more intimate sound was better suited to the palace or the homes of the rich. The lipped pipes are always recognizable by their keyhole, and they are clearly shown on some of the evidence already discussed. It is also certain that hybrid instruments, in which both timbres were mixed, made an early appearance and were widely used.

Little is known as to how many sets were fitted to hydraulic organs—that is to say the number of ranks of pipes corresponding to each degree of the manual. If Vitruvius is right—and he seems well informed—there were four, six, or eight. However, technical considerations, which will be studied in due course, tend to suggest that the organ-builder generally restricted the number to four. Furthermore, it is not clear whether every instrument was fitted with a wind-chest with registers, though the tiny Aquincum organ was.

To sum up, it would seem that ancient organs may be classified in a few characteristic ways:

1. According to the number of pipes: instruments having eighteen or more pipes (Carthaginian lamp); instruments having thirteen, fourteen or fifteen pipes (British Museum gem, terracottas from Tarsus and Alexandria, Aquincum hydra); instruments with seven or eight pipes (Roman terracotta, Julia Tyrannia's sarcophagus, St. Maximin relief, Nero contorniates).

2. According to register. Some organs were built to produce high tones (Aquincum organ), some had a medium register (Julia Tyrannia's organ), and some had a low register (Valentinian III contorniate). The following is a list drawn up from the illustrations, giving the approximate length of the lowest pipe on three instruments. The measurements have been calculated in relation to the stature of the human figures represented with them, assuming that these are of average height. The lips of the pipes, clearly shown in all three cases, enable us to make a fairly accurate estimate of the diapason of the organs.

Carthaginian terracotta (open pipes). Height of vibrating column: 72 cm.

Note approximates to

St. Maximin sarcophagus (stopped pipes). Height of vibrating column:

60 cm. Note approximates to

Valentinian III contorniate (open pipes?). Height of vibrating column:

140 cm. Note approximates to

The diapason was thus relatively high, and rarely went below our 'four-foot' pipes. The use of lower-pitched notes would necessitate a greater and more regular air supply than either the pumps or the wind-chest of the hydraulis as they were at that time could have generated or stored.

3. According to the compass of the manual and its melodic progression. From this point of view three types of instrument are distinguishable:

(*a*) Diatonic type (Fig. 6). With thirteen, fourteen, or fifteen pipes the ambitus is approximately a consonant twelfth. The notes of both the Conjunct and Disjunct Systems are represented (British Museum gem, Tarsus terracotta, St. Sebastian graffito).

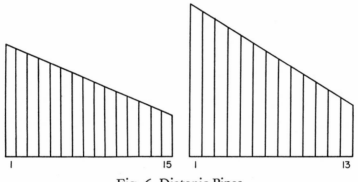

Fig. 6. Diatonic Pipes

(*b*) Chromatic type (Fig. 7), involving a progression, by more or less equal semitones of a fifth in the case of Julia Tyrannia's organ and on the Aquincum instrument of an octave. This division, which allows the various octave species to be transposed, was probably widely used during the late Empire. The height or depth of a note, says Pachymeres,[26] in no way alters its nature.

(*c*) Enharmonic type (Fig. 8). The enharmonic genus, described as austere and majestic by Sextus Empiricus, was practically abandoned in Roman times. Much earlier, Aristoxenus had been forced to admit that it took a trained ear to discern the intervals.[27] This makes it all the more astonishing to find such a scale being used on the hydraulic organ. However,

[26] *Treatise on Harmonics*, xxi.   [27] *Elements of Harmonics*, x.

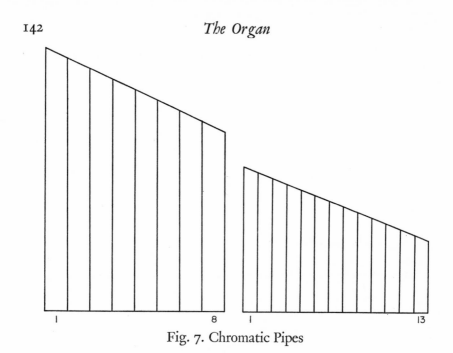

Fig. 7. Chromatic Pipes

as we have seen, the silhouette of the pipes on the Carthaginian instrument and a number of others implies a manual proceeding by intervals smaller than a semitone. Nevertheless, it is most unlikely that an organ of this type, given the instability and delicacy of its tuning, would have been in common use.

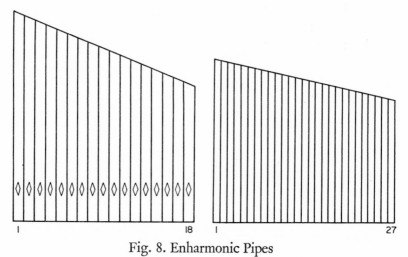

Fig. 8. Enharmonic Pipes

CHAPTER EIGHT

〜〰〜

The Hydraulic Organ (2)

The following considerations are based neither on archaeological evidence nor on historical texts, and they form a chapter which stands slightly apart from the actual history of the instrument. Their aim is, by calculation and experiment, to settle certain questions concerning the mechanism of the hydraulis about which the technical treatises are either silent or uninformative.

The mathematical analysis of the compression of the air in the wind-chest sheds some light on the hydrostatic phenomena present in the cistern and the pnigeus when the instrument is being played; and this in turn helps to explain the layout or shape of particular organs. The theoretical work is complemented by a direct observation of the working organ, which allows one to make tests and measurements. A working model seemed inadequate; I have therefore built a full-scale hydraulic organ, in order to obtain as accurate an idea as possible of how it was made and how it worked.

SOME THEORETICAL CONSIDERATIONS

The principle which inspired Ktesibios, when he decided to try to feed a set of auloi with air under pressure, is based on the compressibility of air, 'the most elastic of all the elements'.[1] A large volume of air can become smaller, and vice versa.[2] Strato of Lampsacus, who synthesizes the ideas of Democritus and Aristotle, claims that air owes its elasticity to numerous void interstices. If it is compressed into a volume smaller than its original volume, it will expand again as soon as the compressing agent is removed, and will resume its initial volume. In his Βελοποιϊκά, Philo enlarges on this basic property of air.

The hydraulic compressor made by Ktesibios in the third century B.C. was a most ingenious device designed to supply air, at a constant pressure, to any type of machine. As we have seen, its component parts are a πνιγεύς, a receptacle of variable shape, with a wide opening at the bottom, immersed in a water-filled cistern. It is not impossible that this system was the result of

[1] Seneca, *Ad Lucilium*, v, 50, 6.   [2] Aristotle, *Physics*, iv, 9, 217 b.

experiment, perhaps with the aim of proving the corporeal existence of air. The problem was tackled by Philo of Byzantium, and was still very much in vogue in Hero's day.[3] The hydrostatic phenomena employed by Ktesibios stem directly from the ideas and experiments of Archimedes.[4] It is interesting, therefore, to make a theoretical analysis of how this original compressor worked.

If we take first of all a cistern containing water, cylindrical or hexagonal in shape,[5] and if S is the area of the base measured in square centimetres and H the height of the water level in centimetres, then the total pressure, in grammes, exerted on the base of the cistern, is equal to P, the weight of the water:

$$P = SH$$

The pressure pr, in grammes/square centimetre or, in the terminology of organ-builders, in centimetres of water, will be numerically equal to the height of the water:

$$pr = \frac{SH}{S} = H$$

If the πνιγεύς, sealed at the top and filled with air, is placed on the bottom of the cistern (Fig. 9), the air pressure inside it will be equal to the weight of a column of water whose height is H and whose section is equal to the surface s of the lower opening:

$$pr = sH$$

and, in centimetres of water:

$$\frac{sH}{s} = H$$

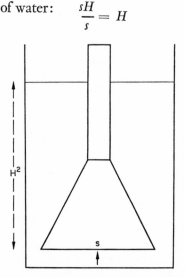

Fig. 9. The Pnigeus in the Cistern

[3] *Pneumatica*, ch. 1.
[4] Archimedes, Περὶ ὀχουμένων ed. Teubner (Leipzig, 1912), ii, pp. 323 ff.
[5] These are the shapes most frequently shown in the iconography, but the receptacle can be any shape.

If the pnigeus does not reach the bottom of the cistern, the air pressure will be equal to the weight of a column of water whose base is s and whose height is H^2, this height H^2 being the difference between the level of the base of the pnigeus and the height of the water in the cistern.[6] In other words, the pressure exerted inside the pnigeus full of air, expressed in centimetres of water, will not depend on the shape of the pnigeus, on the open surface or on the shape of the cistern. It will always be numerically equal to the difference in the levels of the water in the cistern and in the pnigeus, expressed in centimetres.

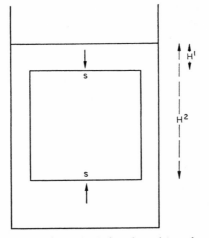

Fig. 10. The Principle of Archimedes

It will be seen that Ktesibios's hydraulic apparatus is a special manifestation of the 'principle' of Archimedes. We know that a cylinder plunged into a vessel filled with water is exposed on its top and bottom surfaces, marked s, to opposing pressures.[7] A downward force equal to sH^1 is exerted on the top surface, where H^1 is the height of the water above this surface; while the lower surface is subjected to an upward thrust equal to sH^2, where H^2 is the height of the water above it. Since H^2 is necessarily greater than H^1, the cylinder is subjected to an upward thrust (Fig. 10):

$$F = sH^2 - sH^1 = s(H^2 - H^1)$$

Now $s(H^2-H^1)$ is, in fact, the volume of the cylinder, so that the resulting pressure is always equal to the weight of the volume of water displaced.

---

[6] In fact, since the air is compressible, the level of the water does not correspond exactly to the base of the pnigeus. The volume of water contained in the pnigeus decreases in inverse proportion to the pressure exerted inside it, according to Mariotte's law.

[7] The lateral pressures cancel each other out. It goes without saying that the demonstration may be made with any solid, and not merely a cylinder.

In the case of the pnigeus, a receptacle closed at the top and fixed to the base of the cistern, the only thrust which will be exerted will be sH^2, and the air pressure will correspond to the pressure of water at the level of its base.[8]

These steps are easily verified by experiment, using, as I did, a glass funnel whose neck was connected to a pressure guage. All that was necessary was to immerse the glass funnel in a transparent cistern filled with water, and, varying the degree of immersion, compare the pressures indicated with the difference between the levels. The figures were always identical. The height of the pnigeus has no effect on this, nor does its shape, hemispherical in Hero, conical in Vitruvius, or cylindrical. It is also possible to connect the neck of the funnel to a small organ pipe, and pump air into the apparatus using a small bellows. The resulting sound is perfectly stable if the pnigeus and cistern are large enough in relation to the pipe.

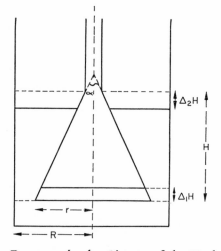

Fig. 11 Pressures in the Cistern of the Hydraulis

Let us now take a hydraulic organ fitted with a wind mechanism adapted to the number and size of its pipes, and observe how the pressure will vary if the blowers fail to pump sufficient air into the pnigeus, or—what amounts to the same thing—if the wind-chest's consumption of air should happen to exceed the output of the pumps (Fig. 11). When this happens the water falls in the cistern by a height of $\mathit{\Delta_2H}$ and rises in the pnigeus by a height of $\mathit{\Delta_1H}$. The normal pressure H will decrease, and become H':

$$H' = H - (\mathit{\Delta_1H} + \mathit{\Delta_2H})$$

The volume of water $\mathit{\Delta V}$ which has risen inside the pnigeus clearly

[8] Pascal took up the study of hydrostatic phenomena in his *Traité sur l'équilibre des Liqueurs* (1647).

depends on the dimensions of the pnigeus and the cistern. If R is the radius of the cistern (which we shall assume to be cylindrical in order to simplify the demonstration), r the radius of the base of the pnigeus and a the apex angle of the cone of the pnigeus, then the decrease in pressure may be calculated as roughly corresponding to the following equation:[9]

$$(\Delta_1 H - \Delta_2 H) = \Delta V \left(\frac{1}{\pi r^2} + \frac{1}{\pi R^2 - \pi(r\text{-}H \text{ tg } \frac{a}{2})^2} \right)$$

In order that this fall in pressure ($\Delta_1 H - \Delta_2 H$) should be as slight as possible, the denominators of the formula should be raised to the maximum, thus:

1. R and r should be made as large as possible; that is to say both cistern and pnigeus should have an adequate diameter.

2. $\left(r\text{-}H \text{ tg } \frac{a}{2} \right)$ should be made as small as possible, i.e. the cistern should be filled right up to the neck of the pnigeus, which itself should be appropriately wide.

Briefly, these calculations applied to the hydraulic compressor allow us to form two practical conclusions. (1) It is possible to obtain the desired pressure in the wind-chest[10] simply by giving a corresponding value to the difference in water levels inside and outside the pnigeus. (2) If the air pressure is to remain as constant as possible, the cistern and pnigeus must be sufficiently large in relation to the consumption of the wind-chest, and the water in the cistern should be level with the neck of the funnel.

THE HYDRAULIS RECONSTRUCTED

If I was to produce a genuine reconstruction of the hydraulic organ and carry out tests of historical value, I felt bound to follow step by step the original technical descriptions. The text used was actually that of Vitruvius, since it analyses a much more sophisticated instrument than that of Hero of Alexandria. It describes a wind-chest with register stops, enabling the player to use his various ranks of pipes separately or together, and two lateral pumps, with pistons sheathed in leather, working alternately. For the manual, however, Hero was the guide, since his account of the keys and their springs is much more detailed than Vitruvius's. When it came to the external appearance of the instrument, I relied on the considerable iconographical evidence discussed earlier, particularly on the Carthage terracotta, which is certainly the most carefully executed replica of Ktesibios's organ.

[9] My friend Dr. J. Lequeux was kind enough to supply this formula.
[10] This does not take account of the inevitable air leaks, which assume considerable importance in this part of the instrument.

This work of reconstruction created a great many problems, especially since I felt it necessary, in order to recreate as far as possible the techniques used in classical times, to use only simple tools, as well as somewhat primitive materials. The difficulties involved in such a task will be explained later; but it should be said at once that the greatest and most recurrent problem is that of air leaks. A wind-chest with sliders can never be absolutely airtight, particularly when we realize what the standard of mechanical finish would have been at that time in an ordinary workshop. Undoubtedly a substantial volume of air was wasted, and to compensate for this loss the bellows output had to be greatly increased.

The condensed, fragmentary nature of Vitruvius's text is often an embarrassment to the experimenter. The architect warns his readers that he will deal with the organ 'as briefly as possible' (quam brevissime potero), and is aware of the shortcomings of his account—he concludes by saying that it is better to examine the instrument for oneself if one wishes to understand fully how it works. Also, while giving a lucid explanation of the mechanism's main components, he deems it unnecessary to enter into any detail of interest only to a craftsman. For instance, he uses the term 'arcula' to describe the small reservoir which distributes the air to the longitudinal channels through the epitonia, but omits to give any indication as to its shape, its location, or the material of which it is made. The same is true of the manual: not a word is said about how the keys were articulated, how they were joined to the sliders, or what was the shape of the spring. For this part of the instrument, I referred to the remains of the little Aquincum organ. But in the absence of adequate evidence one is frequently obliged to resort to intuition to fill in any gaps in the texts.

A further obscurity in the texts concerned the nature of the materials employed. Hero tells us that the cistern was 'bronze', and Vitruvius that the plinth was made of wood, the cylinders and the dolphins of 'bronze' and the shafts and springs of iron. But the materials used for the arcula, the wind-chest, sliders and pipes are nowhere indicated. Here again one has to work by rule of thumb, and choose what seems best. I used wood as far as possible in making all the parts not subjected to great stress—wind-chest, arcula, and pump handles. Lead and zinc were used for the air ducts, iron for the cylinders and pistons, and, by a pardonable anachronism, sheet iron for the cistern, duralumin for the tabula summa and the sliders, and permali[11] for the upper casing of the canon. These last were adopted for purely practical reasons; their use cannot influence the actual working of the instrument.

One final and unexpected difficulty caused a considerable delay in the undertaking. It was vital that we should be able to dismantle the completed

[11] A compound of hard woods, used in aircraft factories and as resistant as oak, though much more economical.

instrument, if only to ensure that any mechanical failure might be speedily repaired. Certain originally simple parts thus had to be altered, though this resulted in not inconsiderable risks of further air leaks.

The painstaking work of reconstruction enabled me not only to experiment with the hydraulic organ as it was made in Vitruvius's day, but to realize at first hand the difficulty of making such an instrument at a time when the techniques involved in small-scale mechanics were still relatively coarse. I include here some information connected with the reconstructed instrument;[12] the details are given in my complementary thesis.

The plinth is made of deal. It is square, each side being 1·20 m. long by 0·165 m. deep. The floor-boards used were found to be not quite strong enough to bear the instrument's weight, and had to be reinforced.

Bearing the results of the earlier calculations in mind, I chose to have a large cistern. It is a cylindrical drum made of sheet metal, 58 cm. in diameter and 92 cm. deep. Its total capacity, which proved excessive, is more than 200 l. One end was removed, and on each side, near the upper rim, a hole was made, 8 cm. in diameter. These holes were for the air ducts. A drainage hole was made in the base of the cistern.

The cylinders are made of two sections of iron pipe, with an external diameter of 21·5 cm. and a depth of 34 cm. The metal itself is 4 mm. thick. The bottom end is open, but the top is sealed by an iron disc soldered to the pipe. Attaching the cylinders to the cistern proved difficult in view of their considerable weight (each weighed 10 kg. without piston or valve) and the movement of the shafts.

The cistern was enclosed in a hexagonal wooden casing, solidly anchored to the plinth. Strong iron brackets, each fitted with a claw designed to fit round the lower rim of each cylinder, were screwed to two of the lateral ribs of the hexagon. In addition both cylinders are held in place top and bottom by two metal bands, similar to those on the Carthaginian model, and screwed to the brackets. In this way the cylinders are perfectly stable.

Each piston consists of two iron discs gripping a pump leather. In the centre of the piston is fixed the piston-rod, an iron bar 1·8 cm. in diameter and 30 cm. long, passing through a small block of hardwood located at the lower end of the cylinder, so that the rod is always on the same axis as the cylinder. The rod is hinged to the pump handle, which is simply a piece of oak 1 m. long firmly bolted to a small iron support screwed to the plinth.

In the top of each cylinder are two openings. One of these, 4·6 cm. in diameter, is designed to allow the passage of air into the cylinder. A cup-shaped cymbal, made of duralumin and larger in diameter than the hole, hangs down inside the cylinder on a chain dangling from the snout of a

[12] Pl. XVII, no. 4.

dolphin 11 cm. long, made of the same alloy. The cymbal and dolphin represent the inlet valve and its counterweight, as described by Vitruvius. The air duct leading to the pnigeus is attached to the other opening in the cylinder. This pipe, made of lead, is 4.5 cm. in diameter. It rises vertically from the cylinder, then, turning at right angles, passes through the hole in the cistern and fits into a zinc tube soldered to the neck of the pnigeus. In this zinc tube is the cone-shaped escape valve, whose function is to prevent the air from returning to the cylinder on the upstroke of the pump.

The pnigeus is a large zinc funnel, conical in shape, 46 cm. in diameter at its base and 38 cm. in height. The tube is 10 cm. in diameter. The pnigeus is raised 10 cm. from the floor of the cistern on three zinc lugs.

The wind-chest is by far the most difficult part of the organ to make. Here two essentials must be borne in mind, though frequently they are incompatible. The wind-chest must be flexible; and air leaks must be prevented at all costs.

The function of the arcula, or small box, which Vitruvius barely mentions, is to distribute the air rising from the neck of the pnigeus into the various longitudinal channels. In my reconstruction it is a box, made of wood, 30 cm. long, 18 cm. wide and 8 cm. deep, with a wide hole in its base into which the neck of the funnel fits tightly. The top consists of a much larger, hexagonal piece of wood, which seals the top of the wooden casing housing the cistern. It is pierced by three holes, since the organ is designed to have three sets of fifteen pipes. These holes, 35 mm. in diameter, are 10 cm. apart, and into them fit the lower pipes of three stopcocks, whose square-cut control valve protrudes on the right-hand side and is held in place by a piece of wood glued to the upper surface of the hexagonal wooden top. One end of a wooden rod is fastened to each of these valves, the other being fitted with a metal handle which appears on the right flank of the wind-chest. Thus each handle controls a stopcock.

Located above the arcula is the κανὼν μουσικός, a long, flat box made of a stronger type of wood. It is 108 cm. long by 28 cm. wide and 6.4 cm. deep. Inside, two lengthwise partitions divide the canon into three equal compartments, the 'canales in longitudine'. In the centre of each channel holes 35 mm. in diameter are bored, to take the upper pipes of the stopcocks.

The roof of the canon is a strong piece of permali, 120 cm. long, 40 cm. wide and 1 cm. thick. It is perforated by three ranks of fifteen holes, 7 cm. apart and 1 cm. in diameter. These ranks are 10 cm. apart, and each opens into one of the channels, whence it receives the air for one set of pipes. On the roof of the canon are the sliders, which run at right angles to the long channels. Each duralumin slider is 39 cm. long, 2.5 cm. wide, and 0.4 cm. thick, and moves between two narrow metal strips nailed to the case. Three holes, 1 cm. in diameter, perforate every slider, exactly matching those in the canon. To limit the movement of the sliders in each direction, each is fitted with two iron pins set in a long groove in the permali.

The pinax, or tabula summa, is fitted on top of the sliders. This is a sheet of duralumin cut to the same measurements as the roof of the canon and perforated in a similar way, so that the feet of the pipes slot into it. Thus when none of the sliders is pulled the air remains trapped between the roof of the canon and the pinax; but if one is moved so that its holes coincide with the holes above and below it the air rushes into the pipes, provided, of course, that the stopcocks for the required ranks have been opened. To minimize air leaks, soft leather was placed between the roof and the sliders, and again between the sliders and the pinax.

The manual consists of fifteen 'pinnae' or ἀγκωνίσκοι, simple angle brackets of duralumin with the horizontal leg 10 cm. long and the vertical leg 8·5 cm. long; the overall width is 2·5 cm. At the angle of the vertical and horizontal legs was soldered a small iron socket, to take a rod, also of iron, which acts as a pivot. This rod, fixed horizontally to the back of the wind-chest, is 1 cm. in diameter and 120 cm. long. Both keys and rods were found to be a little weak, and had to be reinforced. The pinnae, fitted to their axles, are placed facing the sliders. They are joined to the sliders by small squares of leather, flexible, silent, and strong. When the horizontal leg of the angle bracket, which is the key proper, is depressed the whole device pivots on the rod and pulls the slider.

The springs (choragia), of which Vitruvius merely says that they are 'made of iron', were modelled on those of the Aquincum organ, and consist of springy strips of steel 10 cm. long and 0·8 cm. wide. At their lower end they are held by a metal bar screwed to the back of the wind-chest as in Viatorinus's organ. They limit the movement of the sliders by means of a simple little pin screwed in 1·7 cm. from the end of the latter. The whole system functions perfectly well.

More experimentation was needed when it came to making the pipes, for none of the texts gives even a brief account of the techniques adopted.[13] The only information was that provided by the iconography and the remains of the Aquincum organ.

It was decided to make three sets of pipes, differing in timbre and in height: a trumpet set, a set of flues, and a second set of flues sounding an octave above the first. The trumpet pipes have a metal reed and the flue pipes are of the type made today. It should be borne in mind that the reconstruction carried out within the scope of this work was designed purely as a series of scientific experiments centred on an ancient mechanism, and purposely excludes any study of organ pipes as they might have been in the time of Augustus—this would in any event be a most difficult undertaking,

[13] Neither do we have any account of how the lyre or the trumpet were made.

for lack of any relevant data. All the pipes on my organ are made of an alloy of tin, and are arranged as they would be on a modern organ, and indeed as they appear on most of the illustrated documents we know: bass pipes to the left and trebles to the right of the organist.

For the tessitura I chose to proceed by equal semitones, though fully aware of the arbitrary nature of such a scale. The compass thus obtained is a ninth, from ♪ to ♪ It is possible to tune the tetrachords in the enharmonic genus, as on the reconstruction of the Aquincum instrument; but though this is relatively easy on the flue pipes, it is practically impossible on the trumpets because of their instability.

The first set of flue pipes was placed at the front, its two extreme pipes measuring 98 cm. and 55 cm. respectively, including the feet. Behind this comes the octave set, and, by the manual, the set of reeds. A piece of wood perforated with forty-five holes holds the pipes steady near the top, and is screwed firmly in a slanting position to two transverse bars, one behind and one in front of the pipes, as in the iconography.

Experiments carried out with the apparatus revealed the various merits and demerits of the hydraulic organ. By and large it is surprising how well the mechanism actually functions. The air pumps are easy to work, and may be confidently entrusted to children 10–12 years old, thus confirming the textual and documentary evidence. They must simply take care to pump alternately. It was possible to verify that, using a single rank of pipes and with the compass reduced to seven or eight degrees, a single pump was more than adequate to feed the wind-chest. It is the system of registers, the source of many air leaks, which calls for the double pump described in the *De Architectura*. Here are some figures. With 80 l. of water in the cistern (the level reaches approximately 10 cm. below the neck of the pnigeus), a moderate rate of pumping gives a pressure in the arcula of about 30 cm. of water. A trumpet pipe placed directly on the tube of one of the stopcocks then utters a deafening sound. But if new measurements are taken on one of the openings on the tabula summa, the pressure falls to 11 cm. if only one channel is open and to 8 cm. if the two others also have pipes playing. These figures are thus quite close to those still used by organ-builders at the beginning of this century.

The sound from the pipes is quite steady if the blowers are careful to adjust their rate of pumping to meet the demands of the moment. But if the three sets are used together there is occasionally a degree of vibrato which is unpleasant to the modern ear.

The manipulation of the keyboard is relatively smooth, and allows for some rapid passages. It is as easy as playing a classical organ without the Barker action, the only inconvenience being the spacing of the keys, for the key must lie directly beneath the corresponding pipe. In my organ the distance separating the keys is 7 cm. from spindle to spindle, virtually the minimum distance, for even at that the pipes are very close together. The virtuoso players of the time were in all probability trained in the appropriate manual technique.

The stopcock registers are practical and airtight, and though the efficiency of the valves is not perfect, they perform quite satisfactorily. It was found that the dolphins do not really serve as counterweights, for the cymbals are immediately pushed up by the thrust of air when the pistons rise, and the dolphins appear to do no more than limit the downward movement of the cymbals. Another point is that the cymbals make a small sharp sound when they come in contact with the top of the cylinder, but this is drowned by the sound of the pipes. Experience also showed that when there is too little water in the cistern, and the pressure of air from the pumps exceeds the weight of liquid displaced, the air escapes through the water with a loud and extremely unpleasant gurgling noise. This does not happen if the cistern is well filled.

Thus the hydraulic organ, a complicated piece of machinery, is in addition a musical instrument in the true sense, comparable on a smaller scale with the organ we know today. The sounds it produced, ear-splitting when the pipes were working under full pressure, are very similar to those we know. A standard of virtuosity in playing was attainable which would justify its participation in the festival at Delphi and account for the success of the personalities represented on the contorniate medallions. On the reconstructed organ it was found that, by working the sliders at the foot of each pipe so as to cut off the supply of air abruptly, striking rhythmic effects could be obtained, of the type used on the modern cinema organ. This would in part explain the frequent appearances of the instrument in the amphitheatre.

The hydraulic organ is, however, difficult to build. The pumps can only have been made in a few special workshops where fire pumps were also produced. Making the canon was a hard and thankless task, for the air was always only too ready to escape between the sliders. The making and tuning of the pipes involved still another set of craftsmen; and even when it was completed the instrument was far from strong. The leather in the pumps wore out quickly unless the cylinders were perfectly true, and that in the sliders was even more perishable, if the debris of the Aquincum organ is any guide. To these disadvantages must also be added the corrosion of various parts due to the presence of the water in the cistern and the passage of the humid air through the entire mechanism. In the arcula of my own hydraulis the humidity was at one time observed to be more than 80 per cent.

It is worth noting that in my reconstruction of the Aquincum organ a single bellows gave a steady air pressure of 4 cm. of water, sufficient to feed the fifty-two small pipes correctly.

❦

CHAPTER NINE

The Graeco-Roman Organ: a Synthesis

Having now made a systematic study of the organ of antiquity using the texts which describe it and the illustrations which show it, and by actual experiment, I feel that this is an appropriate stage at which to make a brief synthesis. It has already been pointed out that the greater proportion of documentary evidence, both literary and iconographical, relates to the hydraulic organ and deliberately neglects the bellows organ. The most plausible reason for this apparent disparity is that the former virtually disappeared with the fall of the Roman Empire in the West, and that in the Byzantine world no writer thought it worth his while to give an account of the mechanism and technique of the pneumatic organ—probably they were regarded as too elementary. One must remember, too, that Byzantine painting and mosaics are essentially religious in character, and very few works relating to secular life have come down to posterity.

An interesting point about the bellows organ is that it was made in a wide range of sizes, from the tiny Aquincum instrument to the mighty palace organ belonging to the Eastern emperors. The hydraulic organ seems on the contrary to have varied little in its proportions from the time of its invention until its disappearance: or so the iconography suggests. We shall look at the two types of instrument separately.

THE HYDRAULIC ORGAN[1]

General dimensions and weight. The instrument is 1·80 to 2 m. in height, occasionally slightly more. Only Aphrodisis's hydraulis is smaller, seemingly not more than 1·60 m. high. The widest part of the instrument, the windchest, measured on average from 1 to 1·20 m. across. The weight of the assembled instrument was certainly considerable, and from my reconstruction I would estimate it at more than 200 kg.

[1] The reader who feels that there is some duplication between this section and the last section of the previous chapter is reminded that the latter is a description only of my own reconstruction. What follows is a general summary of our knowledge concerning the hydraulis in antiquity.

The base. According to Vitruvius, this is made of solid wood, and it always features in the illustrations. Sometimes rectangular, but generally hexagonal, it varies in height from 10 to 20 cm. It is always considerably wider than the cistern it supports, for it is more than just a means of raising the instrument a little higher so that the sound may carry further and the public have a better view. Experiments, have, in fact, revealed that its primary function is to give the cistern a solid base, since the latter would tend to rock under the stress of the movements of the blowers and the organist, if it rested on the ground.

The cistern. Designated βωμίσκος by Hero, and *ara* by Vitruvius, this part of the instrument is made of brass.[2] Its most common shape is that of a prism with a hexagonal base, though occasionally it may be rectangular, and on the Rusticus organ and that shown on the British Museum gem is cylindrical. Very frequently it is decorated with motifs—mouldings on the Nennig and Zliten instruments, foliage on those of the Copenhagen lamp and the Roman terracotta, a sun and its rays on the Rusticus organ, scrolls on that of the St.-Germain pottery. I have reason to believe that these decorations were not always applied to the actual cistern, but to a wooden casing enclosing it. Indeed, it would be difficult to keep the two heavy pumps, when they were in action, perfectly stable in relation to the cistern, without such a casing, firmly anchored to the base. However, in certain cases where the 'ladder-shaped uprights' as described by Vitruvius were solidly attached to the base and the wind-chest, and the cylinders were well soldered to the cistern, it might be possible to dispense with the casing. The ancients knew how to join two pieces of brass together by soldering with tin;[3] but this presupposes a very strong receptacle, very heavy and hence extremely expensive. Such a cistern is apparently shown on the British Museum gem and on the Rusticus marble.

As a rule the cistern is deeper than it is wide. This is easily explained by the fact that the air pressure results solely from the difference in the water levels, so that it is desirable to increase this as much as possible. From the iconographical evidence in which a figure is present to provide a scale, it would appear that the average depth of the cistern ranged from 0·80 m. to 1 m. with a diameter of from 0·60 m. to 0·80 m., so that its capacity might be around 100 l.

The pumps. Where these are represented, they are invariably two in number, one on each side of the cistern, though occasionally one is hidden by a figure

[2] Pliny claims that Campanian bronze is best for making vessels (*Nat. Hist.*, xxxiv, 20, 95).

[3] Lucretius, *De Nat. Rerum*, vi, 1079.

(e.g. on the Alexandrian terracotta, of Alexandria and Rome). Vitruvius says they are attached to solid iron uprights, presumably mounted on the base. Their size, always in proportion to that of the organ, varies from one instrument to another. On the Carthaginian organ their diameter is approximately 24 cm. and their height 45 cm., which would allow each pump to send about 10 l. of air into the wind-chest at each upstroke of the piston. Allowing for air leaks in the mechanism, this does not appear excessive for a wind-chest supporting three sets of pipes. Usually the cylinders are coupled to the cistern or to its casing, as this increases their stability. However, on the organ depicted on the sarcophagus at Arles, they are located some ten centimetres from the wall of the cistern. Each cylinder, cast in brass and turned on a lathe, is attached to its support or supports by metal bands, which are clearly visible on the Carthaginian lamp.

Vitruvius states that the pistons are sheathed in leather to render them airtight and reduce wear and tear. These leather coverings would certainly have been oiled, and indeed Pliny tells us that straps and leathers were greased with a special emollient known as amurchus, a by-product of olive-pressing.[4] The piston-rods, rarely shown, were of iron, and Pliny says that this metal was protected from rust by coating it with white lead or tar.[5] The pump handles, probably made of wood, are plain to see on the gem, the Caracalla contorniate, the St. Sebastian graffito, the Verona diptych and the Valentinian III medallion. Their average length appears to have been 1 m.

The air ducts. Their function is to lead the air from the cylinders into the pnigeus, and they very rarely figure on any of the illustrations. On the gem and on the Arles sarcophagus they are located above the cylinders, whereas on Julia Tyrannia's instrument they are underneath. Vitruvius says that the inlet valves, which are never shown, are simply cups balanced by a counterweight shaped like a dolphin.[6] Nothing definite is known about the outlet valves.

The pnigeus. Hemispherical in Hero's text, and shaped like a rounded funnel in Vitruvius, this part of the organ was certainly made of some type of rust-proof metal, either lead or some lead alloy, since it is in a state of continual immersion. The two air ducts lead into lateral apertures in the neck of the funnel—Vitruvius uses the plural form 'cervicibus' to describe these apertures.

Possibly the pnigeus was fixed to the bottom of the cistern, for when the

---

[4] *Nat. Hist.*, xv, 8, 34.

[5] *Ibid.*, xxxiv, 43, 150.

[6] The cups were certainly made of bronze. In the Museo Nazionale in Naples there is a bronze 'cymbal' of this type, 75 mm. in diameter and 10 mm. high. In the middle of the convex curve there are signs that it was once soldered to something, but there is nothing to prove that it is the valve of a hydraulic organ.

wind mechanism is operating it has to withstand a strong thrust from below because of the compressed air inside it. However, it could have been held stable sufficiently by its own weight together with the arcula and air ducts.

Arcula and stopcocks. There is nothing to be said about the arcula except that it must have been more or less as it is in my reconstruction. The register stopcocks (epitonia) were probably no different from the stopcocks used to control the inflow of water in baths and fountains. Archaeology has given us a number of these water taps,[7] also called 'epitonia'[8] by Seneca. In the organ the fact that they were operated from a distance suggests a shank that was turned by means of an iron handle (manubrium ferreum), projecting from one side of the wind-chest, though these handles are never shown in the iconography. An interesting point about the little Aquincum organ is that the air is allowed to enter the canales by a sliding window controlled by a brass rod, an innovation which is a decided improvement on Vitruvius's device. Besides being easier to make, the window also provides a wider passage for the air. It is probably the sliders of windows of this type which appear to the right of the manual on the Rusticus organ.

The wind-chest. In the documents this is represented as a wide, flat box lying athwart the cistern and supporting the pipes. In size it appears to have ranged from about 1 m. to 1·20 m. in length, and from 8 to 15 cm. in depth. Its width clearly depended on the number of ranks of pipes it supported. Almost invariably rectangular in shape (though on the Nennig mosaic it is hexagonal), the wind-chest frequently shows a decorated front panel: circular motifs on the Rusticus organ, a trellis pattern on the organ on the Copenhagen vase, mouldings on the Copenhagen lamp, scrolls on the St.-Germain pottery. For the sake of stability, it had to be firmly set on a cistern which was itself adequately moored to its base.

We are familiar with the workings of the wind-chest from the technical descriptions of Hero and Vitruvius, in addition to which the canon of the Aquincum instrument coincides with the facts given in these texts. The case of the wind-chest was made of strong boards nailed together. Experiments have shown that air leaks are easily prevented by first smearing the parts that are to be joined with glue, and for this the ancients used the 'bull glue' that was so highly recommended by Aristotle,[9] Lucretius,[10] and Pliny[11] because of its great strength.

---

[7] On this point see Fr. Kretzschmer's admirably documented article 'La robinetterie romaine', *Revue archéologique de l'Est et du Centre-Est*, xi (1960), pp. 89 ff.

[8] *Ad Lucil.*, xi, epist. 86, 6.

[9] *Hist. Anim.*, iii, 29, 517 b.

[10] *De Nat. Rer.*, vi, 1069–70.

[11] *Nat. Hist.*, xxviii, 17, 236.

The manual. The manual virtually never appears in the iconography, since the organ is normally viewed from the other side. It can, however, be seen on the Rusticus instrument, though the artist has completely ignored the realities imposed by the mechanism—the keys, placed side by side, are irregularly arranged in respect of the pipes they control. On the other hand, we can easily distinguish their oblong shape, which lends the manual an aspect very similar to that of a modern instrument without its black keys. The manual is again well defined on the Carthaginian lamp, with its eighteen oblong keys laid out in line with their respective pipes. The row of keys lies some 12 cm. higher than the foot of the pipes; and if this is an accurate reproduction—as seems to be the case—then the angled keys have their horizontal leg pointing upwards. Thus the finger playing the note pushes the slider by pressing on it, and the spring brings it back; this procedure coincides with Vitruvius's description (pinnae . . . manibus tactae, *propellunt et reducunt* regulas); and Hero indicates a similar device. I feel there was a reason for the high position of the manual, for it is shown very clearly on the Nennig mosaic as well as on the lamp. It enabled the organist, who was thus in a more elevated position himself, to watch the spectacle he was supposed to enliven with his playing, by looking over the tops of the pipes. Most of the illustrations do, in fact, show the head of the organist rising above the pipes; the attitude is entirely characteristic of the Graeco-Roman hydraulic organ.

Metal was certainly used in making the plinthides. These were brass rods, generously oiled to avoid friction and minimize air leaks. As we have seen, the Aquincum organ still had its plinthides, which correspond exactly to Vitruvius's description of them.

The keys on the manual were either of metal or of wood (Cassiodorus)—if the latter, they were reinforced with bronze strips (Aquincum organ). Originally they were pulled back to their normal position by horn spatulas (Hero), and later by steel springs (Vitruvius). These springs must have been strong enough to overcome the frictions to which the slider was subjected in its movements. Those on the Aquincum instrument are made of bronze.

The manual was played with the fingers, as Theodoret specifically says (. . . τοῦ τεχνίτου δακτύλων). This called for real virtuosity, and Julian speaks of 'nimble fingers' (θόα δάκτυλα), Claudian of fingers 'straying' over the keys (erranti digito), Cassiodorus of 'masterly fingers' (magistrorum digiti). As Porfyrius Optatianus says, the keys must be frequently depressed, so that the sliders are 'continuously in motion' (Vitruvius). Furthermore, the organist had frequent opportunities to display his talent (Boethius).

The pipes. An analysis of the illustrations reveals that these vary in number from seven to eighteen in each set, and in most cases the front row of pipes are all of equal diameter.[12] This implies slight differences in timbre between bass and treble pipes, though these are almost imperceptible where the range is small. The compass of each set of pipes appears not to have exceeded a twelfth, and generally varied from a fifth to an octave. These acoustic deductions, based on a study of the iconography, are valid only for open flue pipes, for reed pipes remain outside the scope of this investigation, as do the stopped pipes whose plugs can be driven a variable distance into the interior of the pipe, as in the first three ranks of the Aquincum organ. It seems reasonable, on the basis of what has been said above, to assume that the scale of notes controlled by the manual proceeded in most cases by intervals somewhere near the semitone, though smaller intervals appear to have been used on occasion.

The number of stops must have varied according to the instrument and the date, but in view of the mechanical problems involved, there could hardly have been more than three or four. The octochordos quoted by Vitruvius was probably more theoretical than real. For a hydraulic organ of the usual dimensions, the diameter of the pipes as depicted in the iconography would necessitate a minimum space between the axes of 5 cm. for each degree of the manual. If there were eight ranks of pipes, the slider would have to be approximately 50 cm. long, counting the two ends. It is obvious to anyone who has experimented with a hydraulis's wind-chest that friction would have made it impossible to manipulate such a slider, however well greased it might be. In addition, the air leaks would have assumed disastrous proportions.

Sets of reed pipes were widely used—Hero of Alexandria, Julian, Simplicius of Cilicia and St. Athanasius all refer to the 'auloi' of the organ, while Tertullian calls them 'tibiae'. It is not known whether the vibrating tongue was made from a reed, as it was on the aulos; but I think it was of metal, probably not very different from the reeds used in modern organs. Flue pipes were also common, and Cassiodorus and the Pseudo-Prosper both refer to the 'fistulae', whereas Prudentius calls them 'calami'. The keyhole mouths of such pipes are clearly visible on the Carthaginian instruments, the Copenhagen lamp and the Rusticus and St. Maximin organs. As far as stopped pipes are concerned, their use is authenticated by the archaeological remains at Aquincum.

We have no information as to how these pipes were actually made or tuned. Those on the Naples Museum and Aquincum organs are cast; but they are very small indeed. The larger pipes may have been rolled and soldered—Pliny tells us that as a rule the soldering was done with an alloy of lead and tin.[13]

---

[12] However, on the Tarsus terracotta and Aphrodite's stele the treble pipes appear to be thinner than the bass pipes.

[13] *Nat. Hist.*, xxxiv, 48, 160.

Those authors who do refer to the organ's pipes nearly always specify that they are of bronze, and as we have seen, those on the Aquincum organ are made of an alloy whose principal component is brass (about 80 per cent, with 18 per cent zinc and small quantities of lead and tin).

The position of the pipes in relation to the organist varies in the illustrations, but for the most part it conforms to modern usage—treble pipes to the right, bass pipes to the left. I am convinced that this arrangement, which is purely arbitrary, dates back to the very origins of the organ, and the tradition has been maintained right up to the present time, just as the appearance of gaming dice has remained unchanged from ancient times until today.[14]

The question of how the pipes were held in place on the tabula summa has never been fully answered. It is true that the majority of the illustrations show two vertical uprights standing one on either side of the pipes, with a slanting bar (on rare occasions two are visible) running from one to the other. I think there must have been a board pierced with holes—really a false wind-chest—fixed parallel to this slanting bar to keep the tops of the pipes steady, unless the slanting bar is itself the false wind-chest seen edge-on. Frequently the points where the bar was joined to the upright were decorated with a circular motif, as on the Carthage, Copenhagen, Rusticus, and Aquincum organs.

The pipes were not simply set on top of the wind-chest as they are today. Vitruvius says they were fitted into 'anuli', ring-like sockets soldered to the pinax opposite each hole. These anuli are clearly visible on the St. Maximin sarcophagus, and several were unearthed among the remains of the Aquincum organ.

It is not known how the inevitable process of tuning organ pipes was carried out, but it cannot have been very different from that used today. In the case of flue pipes, it is a matter of increasing or reducing the height of the vibrating column. A tuning strip, attached to the upper end, is the simplest solution for open pipes. Stopped pipes are regulated by the movement of their cap or their tampon. Reed pipes can only be tuned by varying the effective length of the vibrating tongue.

Timbres. The hydraulic organ could produce two main categories of timbre. On the one hand it had its noisy reed pipes, endowed with a 'most ardent voice' as Pollux puts it, or capable of producing 'thunder' in Claudian's words. By contrast there was the soothing sweetness of the flue pipes, whose dulcet sound was so greatly admired by Julian, whose harmonious and rhythmic song was extolled by Theodoret, and whose subtle sweetness so enchanted the Pseudo-Prosper. Generally speaking, it seems certain that an organ designed for the amphitheatre was fitted mainly with heavy reed

[14] Surprisingly modern-looking dice may be seen in the Antiquarium at Pompeii.

pipes capable of filling the vast stretch of the arena with their music—[15] noisy concerts are known to have been very popular with Roman audiences. At the funeral of the Emperor Claudius, if what Seneca says is true,[16] there was a great concert given by an ensemble of trumpets, horns, and all kinds of brass instruments; and under Carinus a hundred trumpets played together in the course of a popular entertainment.[17] The epithets suggested by the grammarian Pollux[18] to describe the sound of the trumpet may certainly be applied to the shattering din of the amphitheatre organ: exciting, heartening, robust, solemn, harsh, powerful, violent, terrifying, martial, bellicose, stormy, steady, dignified, primitive, noisy. The need for a type of music that was rousing, clamorous, and able to 'inject some measure of heroism into the hearts of the citizens' partly accounts for the presence of the instrument, so frequently demonstrated by the evidence—in the vicinity of gladiators locked in combat (Nennig and Zliten mosaics; Copenhagen and Rheinzabern vases; Tatarevo monument; Petronius's *Satyricon*).

But the hydraulic organ had other roles, and among these was that of theatre instrument. Towards the end of his reign it was Nero's intention to bring a new type of instrument into the theatre. The author of the *Aetna* poem refers to its presence 'in the great theatres'. The Alexandrian model preserved in the Louvre, and the Orange medallion, both show the instrument in theatrical surroundings.

In addition to the violent and powerful sounds that were so well suited to large enclosures, the hydraulic organ could provide the soft, sweet music that was so highly praised by the guests at *The Learned Banquet* and was quoted by Cicero as being one of the most exquisite of all worldly pleasures. There can be little doubt that the instrument played by Antipatros at the Delphic contest was equipped to produce such music, or that the organ which stood in Nero's apartments was also of this type.

THE BELLOWS ORGAN

Though first mentioned by Pollux in the second century A.D., the bellows organ had in all probability already existed for some time before then. In its original form it is described as a 'small instrument' as opposed to the 'great instrument', that is to say the hydraulic organ. Even by St. Augustine's day, however, the newcomer had grown to more solid proportions (organum . . . quod grande est) and the instrument mentioned by the Emperor Julian at approximately this period is obviously a large one, since the air-bag is made from bull's hide.

---

[15] Aristotle's recommendations (*De Audibil.*, 802 a) for making the sound of the aulos hard and bright are certainly in some measure applicable to the organ pipe, since they relate to the reed.

[16] *Apocolocyntosis*, xii, 1.   [17] Vopiscus, *Life of Carinus*, xix.   [18] *Onomasticon*, iv, 85.

Since Homeric times craftsmen had known how to make a blacksmith's bellows, and in the Roman world this was such a commonplace object in the trade that Vitruvius does not feel obliged to describe it: 'Machines . . . such as blacksmiths' bellows (folles fabrorum) are too familiar to warrant discussion.'[19] The idea of fitting them to the organ must have occurred to more than one organ-builder, but in my opinion—and here again this is based on experiment—the pneumatic organ can only have begun to present a serious threat to the hydraulis when some unknown inventor devised the regulating bellows (which was incidentally already used in the bagpipe).

As we have seen, this regulator was already known in the time of Augustus. Without such a stabilizing device, and because of the considerable air leaks from the wind-chest sliders, the sound tails off between each new influx of air; and even when the instrument is fitted with two bellows the sound from the pipes lacks firmness, and still quavers.[20] If we have until now given little thought to the necessity for such a system in the Roman and Byzantine pneumatic organ, this is because ancient authors habitually use the same term, 'follis', to describe the generating and the regulating bellows. In fact, the 'cavern of bull's hide' in Julian's organ is not the source of the air supply, but the storage-bag-cum-regulator. In analysing the organ-siren as he knew it, the Pseudo-Jerome distinguishes clearly between the fifteen generating bellows on the one hand, and the regulator, made from two elephant hides sewn together, on the other. The Byzantine organ described by the Arab Muhammad ibn Ahmad, as well as the first Muristus instrument, is fitted with regulating skins. And finally, the organs shown on the Obelisk of Theodosius are equipped with two great bellows whose function is clearly to offset the irregularities in the influx of air. In a word, the pneumatic organ truly became a musical instrument from the moment when a regulating device was perfected that worked as effectively as the water in the cistern of the hydraulis.

We can appreciate the immense simplification that resulted from the development of this new component. It cut out the need for the liquid element, and all that was required under the wind-chest of the instrument was a regulating bellows fed by a blacksmith's bellows. The heavy bronze cistern, the pumps that wore out, the corroding water—all of these were things of the past. At the same time the instrument became much lighter and therefore easier to move; and it could be made either very large or very small, a small pair of bellows being much easier to make than a small pump. This raises the question of why people continued right up to the Middle

---

[19] *De Architectura*, x, I.

[20] W. and T. Lewis (*Modern Organ Building*, London, 1939) show that they have understood perfectly the problem of regulating the air in the classical organ (pp. 227 ff.).

Ages to describe bellows organs as 'hydraulic organs'. The anomaly is, however, hardly surprising, and is due purely and simply to habit. We ourselves persist in calling one of the manuals on the modern organ the *positive*, though the instrument of that name, which it operated, died out seven or eight hundred years ago.

It seems likely that the Byzantines used only the bellows organ, since it was easily moved during processions and within the confines of the arena. The hydraulic organ, known only to scholars, was no longer in general production, and was probably regarded as a museum piece. The Arabs, who may well have used a water compressor in their war sirens, also concentrated on building bellows organs, such as the instrument sent by them as a gift to the Chinese Emperor Shih Tsu.

THE ORGAN AS A SOLO AND ORCHESTRAL INSTRUMENT

Essentially a solo instrument by virtue of its varied sound spectrum, the organ played alone on numerous occasions. It appeared thus in musical festivals of the type held at Delphi, where Antipatros covered himself with glory, and those which were commemorated on the contorniate medallions. It also featured in recitals such as those given by the young Aelia Sabina in Pannonia, and it was played as a solo instrument in Nero's palace, or at the end of the Deipnosophists' banquet, or under the nimble fingers of the organist described by Julian. But in both its hydraulic and pneumatic forms the organ of the ancients appears on occasion in the company of other instruments—trumpets, horns, lyres (Corippus), and probably also with the tibia and the cymbals, in the theatre (Alexandrian terracotta) and in private houses. It was probably used to accompany singing, particularly in Byzantium.[21] But the known iconographical evidence shows orchestral scenes only in the context of the amphitheatre or the circus. We know that a gladiatorial fight without music was unthinkable, and it is interesting to recall, in explanation of this fact, that in the time of Plutarch the aulos was played during the pentathlon,[22] while Athenaeus tells us that the same instrument was used to accompany boxing matches.[23] There is therefore nothing remarkable in the fact that a small orchestra often features in gladiatorial scenes. But there were other reasons why the organ was indispensable to the amphitheatre games. The first was its ability, thanks to its mechanism, to mark out clearly defined and complicated rhythms to co-ordinate the gestures and movements of the combatants in the arena, at

[21] We have only to recollect that the organ was mentioned in Aristocles's treatise *De Choris*.

[22] *De Musica*, 262, pp. 100–1.

[23] iv, 39–40.

least while the parade was taking place.[24] Furthermore, the effect created by the sound of its many pipes was intoxicating and spellbinding. We have only to look at the attitudes of the organists on the documents previously quoted to realize how very true this was. Their eyes never leave the struggling gladiators in the final stages of their combat; and it is reasonable to assume that at this crucial moment the organ, with or without the accompaniment of trumpets and horns, struck up some martial air which whipped up the emotions of the crowd, thirsty for blood and excitement, into a real frenzy. It is interesting to note that in the early days of the Empire, whenever a public execution was carried out in the Forum in the presence of the Praetor and the people, the executioner, having tied the condemned man's hands behind his back, ordered the crowd to be silent. Then the formula fixed by law was pronounced, while a trumpet fanfare rang out just before the axe fell.[25] Military regulations likewise prescribed the practice of the *classicum* when a soldier suffered the death penalty.[26] These traditions account for the presence, on a bas-relief in the Munich Glyptothek, of two tubicines playing while one of the combatants is about to receive the fatal blow. Another bas-relief, this time in the Chieti Museum, shows four tubicines and four cornicines in similar circumstances. A small orchestra appears on a mosaic in the Bardi Museum in Tunis, and further examples are in the process of being verified.[27] Small wonder, then, that from the time of the Antonine emperors the organ began to participate in these instrumental ensembles. Each of the two orchestras represented in the Zliten mosaic consists of a trumpet, two horns, and an organ, though that on the Nennig mosaic has only a horn and an organ. On the St. Sebastian graffito we have a horn, a trumpet, and an organ. It is logical to suppose that 'great orchestras' were used in very large enclosures, when important combats were on the programme, for in other examples the organ is shown on its own during the spectacle (Rheinzabern, Rheims, and Copenhagen vases; evidence of Petronius), when the games were presumably on a more modest scale.

Orchestras with an organ also appeared at the circus. On the diptych of Verona, for instance, it accompanies the syrinx during a juggling act, and on the Obelisk of Theodosius it is shown with the syrinx, the recorder, and the double aulos.

THE ORGANISTS

Despite the unfavourable prejudice to which he, like the auletus, was very likely subjected in comparison to the citharist, the professional organist

---

[24] The presentation of the combatants, mentioned by Cicero (*De Orat.*, ii, 80, 325), was often accompanied by music: see above, p. 88.
[25] Seneca (the rhetorician), *Controversiae*, ix, 11, 10.
[26] Vegetius, ii, xxii.
[27] G. Ville, op. cit.

was nevertheless an able performer. He had to possess a very specialized manual technique in order to operate the keyboard, a new contrivance consisting of keys that had to be depressed by the fingers. He was consequently obliged to spend long hours practising so as to bring off quick-moving passages without smudging or execute strongly marked rhythmic patterns. The latter were probably in common use, especially at the circus; their importance in Greek music has already been observed. Thanks to the precision of its attack and its silences, the organ was the ideal instrument for giving full value to such rhythms. Moreover, it seems entirely probable that in his position facing the manual, and with both his hands free, the organist was frequently tempted to add some kind of accompaniment to his melody, in this way effecting a rough form of two-part counterpoint similar to that improvised by the auletus on his instrument's two pipes.

Most of the iconographical evidence reveals that the organist played in a standing position, propping himself up on a small stool which may be clearly seen on the Carthage statuette. The manual, which was frequently raised up in relation to the wind-chest, allowed the player to follow the course of events over the tops of the pipes. I think that it was this need to watch the progress of the combat closely and fit his music to it which caused him to perch so high up, even though this involved a number of small mechanical adjustments.

As a rule the blowers stand on either side of the instrument. They are generally two in number, and they are pictured hard at work on the British Museum gem and on the uninscribed Arles sarcophagus. In some cases only one blower is shown, as on the Rheims vase, the Roman terracotta and the diptych of Verona. The actual task of pumping the bellows appears to have been greatly eased, at least in the first half of the fifth century, by an innovation mentioned in a curious text by Theodoret of Cyrrhus, where he tells of a bellows organ whose organist pumps the air with his feet. This piece of information, which leaves no room for doubt, would seem to imply that the player was seated, as at a harmonium,[28] since it is difficult to imagine how he could operate both manual and pedals in a standing position. Is it perhaps just such a wind mechanism, operated by the organist's feet, which explains the absence of blowers on a number of second-century illustrations, for example the Nennig and Zliten mosaics? It seems to me unlikely, but the question is none the less reasonable.[29]

History has preserved the names of some of antiquity's organists. Thaïs, wife of Ktesibios, was allegedly the first to take up the new instrument—it

[28] One of the Caracalla contorniates shows the organist seated at his instrument.

[29] It has been suggested that in Claudian's poem (see p. 60) 'pedibus' should be substituted for 'penibus'. But I am not sure if the script in the MSS. would allow such an interpretation (see D. Batigan Verne, 'The Water-Organ of the Ancients', *The Organ*, 1922–3, p. 242).

is worth noting that the first organist was a woman. Then there was the virtuoso Antipatros, who made the journey to Delphi to compete on the hydraulic organ, and carried all before him. Next we have Nero, a sincere and enthusiastic amateur, who spent one of the most tragic evenings of his life studying the new instrument he had just acquired. Two other emperor-organists were Elagabalus and Alexander Severus. We know, too, of Julia Tyrannia in Gaul, and the young Aphrodisis in Macedonia, both mourned by their mothers; and Aelia Sabina, who also died in the flower of her youth, and who gave concerts in the garrison town of Pannonia where her husband, a musician like herself, followed his curious calling of military organist. In Egypt there was Gorgonius, who received his wages in kind; and the two virtuosi Laurence and Peter, victors in the contests commemorated by their contorniate medallions. It appears that women were particularly ready to devote themselves to studying the organ, and this is often borne out by the iconography (Alexandrian terracotta, Zliten mosaic, Rheinzabern vase, St. Maximin sarcophagus). It is also clear that, after Nero, the upper classes in Rome and the provinces were no longer ashamed to play the organ or the tibia—a far cry from the sarcastic gibes of Aristotle, for whom all instru-mentalists were objects of scorn. 'The study of an instrument is no occupa-tion for a free man . . . such tasks are for hired men.'[30]

In classical times some men—such as Antipatros or Titus Aelius Justus—made organ playing their whole life, devoting themselves exclusively to one instrument. But as we have seen, Julia Tyrannia and Aelia Sabina, Nero, Elagabalus, and Alexander Severus played other instruments as well as the organ.

[30] *Polit.*, viii, 1341 b.

PART TWO

The Organ
in the Middle Ages

CHAPTER TEN

∽⚬∾

The Organ and the Eastern Empire

THE HISTORICAL BACKGROUND

By the beginning of the fourth century the long struggles against the barbarian invasions had clearly exposed Rome's vulnerability and her perilous geographical situation. Constantine accordingly cast about for an alternative site, geographically strong, and more central, which would allow him to keep a watchful eye on his vast domains and dispatch his armies to trouble-spots with greater speed. His choice fell on the little town of Byzantium, standing on the borders of Europe and Asia. The centuries that followed were to justify Constantine's clear-sightedness, since the new Rome, which took its founder's name, repulsed repeated attacks for over a thousand years.

By the end of the fifth century the Eastern Roman Empire had already assumed its own distinguishing characteristics; 'Roman in its traditions, Hellenistic in its culture, Oriental in its methods of government'.[1] An original civilization developed both in Byzantium and in the great provincial cities, rich, traditionalist, showing little development, but for this very reason homogeneous from one period to another. The study of this civilization is of enormous importance to the musicologist, for the capital became a new focal point in world culture at a time when the West was plunged in darkness. The cosmopolitanism of Greek Alexandria found a new home there, and every tongue, every race was represented in the streets. Despite occasional periods of eclipse, occasioned by the interminable theological wrangling, the town remained the undisputed intellectual centre of Europe and Asia. Music occupied an important place in its life, as it did in the other great cities of the Empire—Antioch, Ephesus, Alexandria—which were also famous for their schools and for their great libraries. But the great vogue for abstract studies led to a neglect of the sciences (with the exception of mathematics) in favour of the literary and oratorical arts and of theology: it is useless to explore Byzantine history for signs of any decisive steps in

[1] L. Bréhier, *La Civilisation Byzantine* (Paris, 1950), p. 16.

scientific progress. Physics, chemistry, and applied mechanics appear to have been consistently disregarded. This explains why the technique of organ-building remained virtually static during these ten centuries.

However, the Eastern Empire performed a great service to history by copying, translating, and commenting upon a vast number of literary and scientific works dating from Graeco-Roman antiquity, thus rescuing from perhaps total oblivion centuries of culture and research. Furthermore, Byzantine technology filtered through to the Arabs by way of the Syrians. Thus certain Greek scientific treatises, among them Philo's *Pneumatics*, Hero's *Mechanics*, and the *Automata* of Apollonios of Perga, have survived only in Arabic translation. Conversely, the Byzantines took note of scientific advances among their neighbours, and the scholarly Psellus (1018–78) speaks highly, if somewhat bitterly, of the knowledge acquired by the Arabs in this field.[1]

THE BYZANTINE ORGAN

The principal Byzantine writers on music—Psellus, Pachymeres, Manual Bryennius, and the author of the *Hagiopolites*, are almost exclusively concerned with musical theory. This is entirely in keeping with the Hellenistic tradition: instrumental technique is the province of the artisan and beneath the notice of the educated man. Consequently, we have to look elsewhere for material which might throw some light on the history of the organ during this period, for, as will readily be understood, it is in the last analysis to Constantinople that the modern world owes the survival and development of the organ. In western Europe the instrument quickly disappeared, and by the eighth century it had been completely forgotten, but it continued to be played in the East. And though organ-building made little progress in the course of the next thousand years, and indeed seems even to have slipped back by comparison with Vitruvius's time, at least the organ's popularity and usefulness did not suffer an eclipse. This meant that the secrets of its construction were able to find their way back to the West long before the destruction of the Byzantine Empire in 1453.

A contributory factor to the organ's long survival in Byzantium may have been the musical tastes of some of her emperors. Julian the Apostate composed an epigram on the instrument; Constantine Copronymus sent an organ to Pepin the Short; and Theophilus built his own instruments. Constantine Porphyrogenitus decreed that it should be played in the Palace on many occasions.[2] But its survival was essentially due to the fact

---

[1] Quoted by Sathas, ed. of the *Chronographie de Psellos*, and reported by E. Renauld in his edition of the 'Belles Lettres' (Paris, 1926), p. xi.

[2] Psellus tells us (*Chronographie*, cxxxviii) that, on the contrary, Constantine IX was not interested in music, and 'was indifferent to the sound of the organ'.

that, by a tradition that never lapsed, the instrument was an integral part of imperial pomp, its sound in some way symbolic of the majesty of power.[3] It seems, however, that the organ never found its way into the Church, for the clergy, influenced by the Fathers,[4] remained stubbornly opposed to all instrumental music. Only vocal music was tolerated in divine worship, a practice which has been maintained in the East right up to the present day.[5]

I would like to be able to give an accurate technical description of the Byzantine organ. Unfortunately, no text comparable to those of Hero and Vitruvius has survived, and the treatise of Muristos related, as we shall see, to very special instruments. By now the hydraulis had disappeared: nowhere is there a reference to anything but bellows organs, and the only known iconographic evidence shows two instruments of this type. Not that it was completely forgotten, for its tradition was maintained by the treatises of Hero and Vitruvius, and it was again referred to in Syria in the ninth and tenth centuries. But in general all organs are bellows organs, nearly always described by the single word ὄργανον.

The external aspect of the instrument is briefly described by the Arab Harun ben-Jahja, who was brought to the capital in 867 as a prisoner of war. The scene takes place at a banquet given for the Muslim captives on Christmas Day by the Emperor Basil I:

The Muslims are led towards a table set forth with a great number of hot and cold dishes. Then the herald makes this proclamation: 'By the head of the Emperor, this repast contains no pig's flesh'; whereupon the food is brought in on platters of gold and silver. After this an object called *al-urgana* is introduced; it is made of wood, square in shape, and looks rather like an oil-press. This press is covered with very strong leather, and supports sixty copper pipes. That section of the pipes extending above the leather is plated with gold, but only part of this is visible, since each pipe is slightly taller than its neighbour. At each side of the square object there is a hole, and into these bellows are inserted, like those of blacksmiths. Two men apply themselves to pumping

---

[3] According to Ermold le Noir, one of Louis the Pious's court poets, the instrument was the pride of Byzantium. See below, ch. 15, p. 279.

[4] Especially St. John Chrystostom, in Antioch: A. Puech, *Saint Jean Chrysostom et les moeurs de son temps* (Paris, 1891), pp. 56 ff.

[5] E. Wellesz, *A History of Byzantine Music and Hymnography* (Oxford, 1942), p. 42. Gastoué (*Revue de Musicologie*, February 1930), with reference to M. Raghib, writes that the organ was used in Byzantine churches at the time of its capture by the Turks in 1453. But, in fact, M. Raghib is much less positive about this, and is alluding to certain orthodox churches of the sixteenth and seventeeth centuries (*Revue de Musicologie*, May 1929). It is significant that, according to a scholium on one of the manuscripts of the *Letters* of the Emperor Julian, it was after worshipping in the church of the Apostles in Constantinople that he composed his epigram on the organ which we saw earlier (J. Bidez, *L'Empereur Julien, Oeuvres complètes*, Paris, 1960, i, part 2, p. 215, note 1). See also the text of the Syrian Josua bar-Bahul, below, ch. 13, p. 237.

these, and then comes the organist, who makes the pipes sing. Each pipe gives out a note in proportion to its height, to the glory of the Emperor, while the whole company is seated at table. Next a score of men enter, bearing cymbals in their hands, and these men play throughout the banquet.[6]

The instrument is obviously a mobile organ easily carried from one room in the Palace to another—a 'table positive' comparable to those familiar to western Europeans in the Middle Ages. It is fed by two bellows, each requiring the services of a man to work it. They are thus probably fairly large; but the fact that they are detachable makes the instrument lighter and easier to move. The bellows are primed a few moments before the organist appears—a point not without some significance, for it seems to prove that there is a regulating bellows inside the organ. Indeed, this warming-up process would have been pointless if the air from the bellows had been pumped straight into the wind-chest.

The instrument has sixty copper pipes, arranged in panpipe formation, since each pipe is partly concealed by its neighbour. Their gold casing shows, as we shall see, that this organ is the Emperor's personal instrument. Its sixty pipes are divided up into several ranks, perhaps three or four.[7] No mention is made of their timbre—are they flue pipes or reeds? Possibly both types are used. The leather covering the outside of the wind-chest is presumably to prevent air leaks. All that is said regarding the actual playing of the instrument is that the organist first plays on his own, and the cymbalists who are introduced later appear to play with him, loudly beating out the rhythm of the music right through the meal.

A further reference to the bellows organ of the Byzantines occurs in the writings of the Arab historian Al-Mas'udi (tenth century). He quotes Ibn Khurdadhbih, author of a work on musical instruments: 'And the Byzantines have the Urghanun, with leather bellows and [pipes of] iron.'[8] An equally concise definition of the instrument is given by an annalist of the court of Constantinople, Nicetas Choniate (late twelfth century, who records that the Basileus Alexis III (1195–1203) caused a theatre to be built: 'the bellows of the organs with their many pipes are fitted at the sides . . .'[9]

There is a fuller reference by Muhammad ibn Ahmad al-Khwarizmi, in his book *The Keys of the Sciences*, dating from the middle of the tenth century. 'The organ is an instrument of the Greeks and Byzantines. It is made of three large bags of buffalo skins, one being joined to another. And there is

---

[6] This Arabic text is translated into German by J. Marquart in *Osteuropäische und ostasiatische Streifzüge* (Leipzig, 1903), p. 218.

[7] The organ on the Carthaginian statuette has three ranks, and the Aquincum instrument four.

[8] Barbier de Meynard's translation of Mas'udi *Les Prairies d'Or* (Paris, 1874), viii.

[9] Bonn ed., p. 674.

mounted upon the head of the middle bag, a large skin. Then there are mounted upon this skin, brass pipes having holes upon recognized ratios, from which proceed beautiful sounds, pleasing or melancholy, according to what the player desires.'[10]

It seems very likely that the middle bag acted as a regulating reservoir, and the lateral bags were the bellows generating the air, while the skin supporting the pipes is none other than the wind-chest. Experiments show that it is actually impossible in these conditions to obtain stable sounds of a musical nature without such a regulator.

THE CEREMONIAL USE OF THE ORGAN

In his treatise *De Ceremoniis*[11] the emperor-historian Constantine Porphyrogenitus (912–59) frequently mentions the organ, which has to play on certain occasions at rigidly predetermined moments. It is fascinating to explore the intricacies of this unbending protocol, for it gives us some insight into the role played by the instrument in a society where ceremonial counted for so much. When moving in procession to the *great church*— Hagia Sophia—after the third reception in the Chalke, the sovereigns proceed towards the Augusteon by way of the bronze door.[12] 'It is there, in fact, that the organists take their places to right and left, to pay homage to their sovereigns, according to the ritual procedure.'[13]

On Easter Monday, after the religious ceremony, special acclamations were sung. 'When the sovereigns sit down at table, the organ of the Blue faction plays, and the crowd sings: "Holy Grace". Then, when the organ has ceased, the precentors shout: "Thrice Holy, let the sovereigns reign with you."'[14]

This passage reveals a number of interesting details. The organ plays while the crowd is singing, as though to support them and heighten the effect.[15] It is worth noting that each time he refers to the organ Constantine Porphyrogenitus invariably uses the verb αὐλεῖν, presumably implying that the instrument is sounding its reed pipes, similar to those of the aulos, and more fitting, by reason of their vibrant timbre, to mark the solemnity of the moment.

On Easter Saturday, towards the ninth hour, the Basileus is present at the

[10] Farmer, op. cit., pp. 59–60.
[11] These are not religious ceremonies, but those that took place in the Palace or at the Hippodrome.
[12] See the plan of the Palace in A. Vogt, *Le Livre des Cérémonies* (Paris, 1935), Commentaires, i.
[13] Book i, ch. 1.
[14] Book i, ch. 5.
[15] J. Thibaut ('La Musique instrumentale chez les Byzantins', *Echos d'Orient*, iv, pp. 339 ff.) is mistaken when he says that the organ never accompanied the voices.

ceremony held in the Church of the Theotokos of Pharus. At the end of the service the precentors standing at the doors of the sanctuary cry out 'May God strengthen our Emperor'; and immediately thereafter the organ, stationed in the Tripeton, begins to play, and continues until the sovereign has gone out and has had time to seat himself, with his guests, at the table laid in the Chrysotriclinos.[16] The Tripeton was a room situated to the north-west of the Chrysotriclinos and communicating with it. Assuming that the distance separating the Chrysotriclinos from the Pharus Church was approximately 100 m., we may conclude that on that day the organ played for more than a quarter of an hour.

It is this passage from the *De Ceremoniis* which has led more than one author to believe that there was an organ in the Pharos Church; but the instrument is not actually inside the church, and is only heard when the service is over.[17]

At the nuptial coronation of a Basileus, celebrated in the Church of St. Stephen, near the Hippodrome, the cortège proceeds after the ceremony towards the Grand Consistory. The factions are posted near at hand, in the Triclinos of the Candidates, one on either side. When the newly married pair come through the doors of the Grand Consistory, 'the organs of the two factions play, the factions being drawn up on the left at the foot of the steps'.[18] The phrase indicates clearly that the two organs play together briefly as the sovereigns pass by.

At the coronation and marriage of one Augusta the ritual is different. On the third day the Blue faction takes up its station under the right-hand portico of the Magnaurus, while the Greens stand under the left-hand portico. 'The organ [of the Blues] is in the arbour, and the other [belonging to the Greens] at the entrance to the stable close by. Another organ is positioned beyond the threshold of the baths . . . When the Augusta appears . . . the organs play.'[19] Here we have the implication that the three instruments play in consort for a few moments while the sovereign is passing by. In certain circumstances the organist is obliged to pay close attention to the order of the ceremony. For instance, when there is a reception at the Golden Hippodrome on Easter Monday, the Emperor, standing before his throne, blesses the people three times, and takes his seat as soon as the crowd shouts 'Holy'. When the deme has repeated this acclamation, 'while the organ plays near the phiala,[20] the praepositus receives a sign from the

[16] Book i, ch. 44.
[17] J. Reiske (Constantine Porphyrogenitus, ed. Bonn, *Commentaires*) pointed out this error more than a hundred years ago (p. 203).
[18] Book ii, ch. 48.
[19] Book ii, ch. 50.
[20] The 'phiala' is a font which was at the entrance. Vogt (op. cit.) points out that this gathering is very much like a concert (pp. 105 ff.).

emperor, whereupon he himself makes a sign three times with his hand; the organ falls silent.'[21]

Obviously what the organist has to do is play short interludes at given moments, rigidly defined by protocol, and he must be able to break off correctly at a simple sign from the praepositus. The nature of these interludes is occasionally specified for certain types of ceremony, as, for instance, the drawing of lots to decide the order of running for the chariots, horses and drivers at the start of the races. Following an endless exchange of acclamations, 'the Kractae [singers] chant: "Thrice Holy, succour the Lords", while the organ plays the Trisagion.'[22] The same ritual is repeated when a driver has won: the organ accompanies the acclamation sung by the Kractae.

Before every race meeting the organs are carried to the Hippodrome, and afterwards they are stored in predetermined places. If the meeting is cancelled because of the wind, the programme is held over until the next day, as long as the flag is still hoisted, even if the organs have already been put in store. But if the flag is taken down, the programme is cancelled altogether, even if the organs are already in place at the Hippodrome.[23]

But it is not only the silver organs belonging to the factions that are heard at the Hippodrome. At the race meeting on 11 May, the anniversary of the city's foundation, as soon as the two-horse teams have reached the Cathisma, 'the actuarios, acting on an order, gives a signal, and the imperial organ (τὸ βασιλικὸν ὄργανον) rings out while the drivers dismount from their chariots.'[24] This was the golden[25]—or at least gilded—organ (τὸ χρυσοῦν ὄργανον) which was the Emperor's personal property and was heard only on special occasions. The organs of the two factions, on the other hand, might be heard all over the city. Since they were probably smaller in size, they could be more easily moved from place to place. When celebrations were arranged in honour of the demarchos the demesman goes to the courtyard of the house where the demarchos lives, taking his organ with him.[26] Likewise, when a newly betrothed girl is taken to the house of her future husband, she is accompanied by both factions together with their respective organs.[27]

Working the bellows of Byzantine organs appears to have been a task allotted to special people. Constantine Porphyrogenitus indicates that, in the Hippodrome at least, Slavs were employed for this purpose.[28] These were either slaves or prisoners of war who were required by the regulations to stand clear of the doors leading to the racecourse.

It is reasonable to suppose that these organs produced a penetrating sound, since they could be heard all over the Hippodrome, which was

[21] Book ii, 73. [22] Book ii, 78. [23] Book ii, 78. [24] Book ii, 79.
[25] Book ii, 48. [26] Book ii, 89. [27] Book ii, 90. [28] Book ii, 81.

500 m. long.[29] When the races or contests were in progress it must have been a wonderful sight. On one side was the imperial box, where the sovereigns and their retinue sat in their sumptuous robes; and on the other was the densely packed, milling crowd, ready to voice its acclamations in response to the slightest signal. Under the official stands stood the precentors, the instrumentalists, and the organists, each performing in turn. The scene is brought to life in the stone of the Obelisk of Theodosius, which can still be seen. The Emperor, standing before his throne, holds the garland for the winning driver in his right hand. Beside him are the high court dignitaries, and below him the representatives of the two factions, with their organs and musicians.[30]

Concerts were not confined to the Hippodrome and the Palace, however, and might also be heard in the streets of the capital. A contemporary eyewitness, the poet Corippus, gives his impression of one such occasion from his own time:[31] the young people laugh, dance, and cheer the royal couple, singing all manner of songs of homage and praise. Plectra, lyres, and organs are heard throughout the city.[32] At other times the organ is dragged along the Triumphal Way.[33]

It has been claimed repeatedly that the hydraulic organ played at the court baths:[34] but this is a misconception which originated in a faulty interpretation of a mediocre and obscure poem by Leo Magister (early ninth-century). Here is a rough translation of the passages concerned:

Throughout the town strike up the sound of instruments. What is that? Let him who discerned it speak up, let someone say, if he knows. In this work, the Basileus Leo[35] has surpassed the intelligence of Daedalus . . . Here is the edifice of the Baths: let the sound of the instruments ring out . . . The sound of the doors, by some mechanical device, produces a song of exquisite art and pronounces these words: Glory to thee, O king of kings! . . . Leo has even now revealed himself to be a skilled engineer: the ceaseless running of the waters causes instruments to sound by a secret device, with no master, composing a song of praise to the Basileus. By this art a serpent rears its head, a lion roars with a shattering din . . . A sapphire-coloured bird charms with its piercing cry . . . The beauty of a much-laved body obtains the benison of perpetual health, while the rhythm of the music keeps sickness at bay and gives men strength . . .[36]

[29] A. Vogt, 'L'hippodrome de Constantinople', *Byzantion*, x (1935).
[30] Pl. IV, nos. 1 and 2.
[31] More or less coinciding with the reign of Justinian (527–65).
[32] *In laudem Justini*, iii, 71–5; *Iohannidos*, 575–9.
[33] Theophanes, ed. Boor, i, p. 383.
[34] Among others by Thibaut, op. cit.; Gastoué, op. cit., and others who have blindly copied them.
[35] Leo 'the Wise' (886–912). K. Kraumbacher, *Geschichte der Byzantinischen Litteratur* (Munich, 1897), p. 723.
[36] P. Matranga, *Anecdota* (Rome, 1850), ii, pp. 565 ff.

There can be no doubt that these baths, whose therapeutic properties were so renowned, were a source of perpetual amazement to the Byzantine peoples and were greatly admired by foreign visitors to the city. The lion that roared, the bird that sang, the doors that talked as they swung open, must have been a never-failing attraction for the public. The very existence of these wonders indicates that the treatises on automata by Philo and Hero were well known to the court architects. However, there is no mention of the hydraulic organ, though it might be possible to translate the expression 'μέλος ὀργάνων', which occurs twice, by 'the music of the organs'. It is conceivable, since these instruments were so popular at court, that they did, in fact, play in such a sumptuously appointed establishment as the baths. But of the hydraulis there is no mention whatsoever, and the apparatus described in the poem is really a musical machine of the type that Ktesibios had constructed for the Temple of Arsinoë-Zephyritis more than a thousand years before. It is not a musical instrument in the true sense, but a musical automaton, in which a steady stream of air is achieved by the alternate pumping of water into two closed vessels; this air is then forced into a kind of fixed aulos provided with holes to give several notes. A mechanism operated by a paddle-wheel plays the melody, which is, of course, repeated indefinitely. As we shall see, the Arabs showed an intense interest in such automata, whose invention they attributed to Apollonios of Perga. The very phrases used by Leo Magister, far from suggesting a hydraulic organ, apply beyond all possible doubt to this mechanism. The continuous movement of the water (ῥόος ὑδατῶν ἀπείρων) generates the stream of air which, by a hidden device (ἀφανῶς) plays a ritornello without any outside assistance (ἄνευ κρατοῦντος).

ORGANS AT THE PALACE: THE GOLDEN TREE

The Emperor's Palace, on the other hand, possessed both organs and automata, which were at once part of the interior decoration and a means of impressing foreign ambassadors. In the time of Constantine VII and Romanus I the grand Triclinium of the Magnaurus contained the Emperor's two great golden organs, installed between the columns of the portico.[37] On the right, towards the east, stood the silver organ of the Blue faction, and on the left that of the Greens.[38] During a state banquet given in 946 in honour of the Saracen ambassadors, choirs concealed behind the hangings sang songs of homage to the Emperor; as each course was served the singing ceased, whereupon the sound of the organs rang out, causing great pleasure among the guests.[39]

Was it these palace organs that were dragged through the streets to the Hippodrome and carried by the young Constantine VI in his baggage train

[37] *De Cerem.*, Bonn ed., i, p. 580.   [38] *De Cerem.*, Bonn ed., i, p. 571.   [39] Ibid., p. 585.

when he went travelling with his mother Irene?[40] We have no means of knowing for certain. The imperial apartments probably housed larger instruments, less mobile, but lavishly decorated in keeping with the rich surroundings for which they were designed.[41] At all events, it was a golden organ which played when newly-weds walked through the doors of the Chrysotriclinos.[42] On other occasions, one of the palace instruments played from a concealed position, just as the choirs were hidden away behind their purple curtain. On the Feast of the Annunciation, after divine worship in the Pharos Church, the senators repaired to the vestry to change their robes, while a hidden organ thundered out its music.[43]

The Emperor Theophilus (829–42) was passionately devoted to the organ. He was a real musician, and had received a good education at the hands of John the Grammarian. He composed hymns which he sang himself at divine worship,[44] and donated a sum of money in order that the monks should regularly practise their singing.[45] He built sumptuous organs to adorn his palace, which his architect Patrikios was determined should rival those of the Caliphs of Baghdad. 'The emperor at that time, Theophilus, who loved luxury, built the whole of the Pentapyrgion[46] and the two very large organs, entirely of gold, inlaid with all kinds of precious stones.'[47] Another author is a little more specific: 'The most striking outward sign of [Theophilus's] magnificence is the fact that he was skilled in the manufacture of splendid golden organs, in which the air, supplied by a machine, produces music that is serene and full of charm.[48]

It is not known whether the Emperor confined his activities to the external embellishment of the organ or whether he actually made the mechanism of the instrument. Perhaps he was helped in the technical work by one Leo, an engineer known as 'the prince of philosophers', whose fertile mind had created among other things an optical telegraph for military use.[49]

---

40 Theophanes, ed. Boor, i, 457, 8.
41 See O. Tiby, *La Musica byzantina* (Milan, 1938), p. 160.
42 *De Cerem.*, book ii, 48.
43 *P.G.*, cxii, col. 1395.
44 Zonara, xv, 27.
45 Cedrenne, Bonn ed., p. 118. Five centuries earlier, the Emperor Julian, in a letter to the Prefect of Egypt, had already shown a lively interest in pagan sacred music. He ordered that young singers should be recruited in Alexandria and that they should be encouraged and subsidized (*Lettres*, ed. Bidez, Paris, 1960, p. 186, no. 109).
46 An enormous cupboard crowned with five towers, in which works of art were displayed.
47 Simeon Magister Logothetes, ed. Bonn, p. 627, 4.
48 Constantine Manasses, Bonn ed., p. 205. Michael Glycas says virtually the same thing, Bonn ed., p. 537.
49 Manasses, 5275 ff. It is difficult to see why E. von Muralt (*Essai de chronographie byzantine*, St. Petersburg, 1885, p. 423) describes what is undoubtedly an optical apparatus as a 'telegraphic organ': Cedrenne, ii, p. 174.

This Theophilus had also constructed a musical tree which he had installed in one of the great reception rooms in the Palace. According to Simeon Magister,[50] it consisted of a golden tree with small birds perched on its branches, twittering musically by means of a pneumatic mechanism which sent air through concealed tubes.[51] Manasses also writes a glowing account of this marvel, which seems to have been fairly large:

Besides these, were gilded trees, shining in the distance with a ruddy glow of yellow gold, whereon perched musical birds, fashioned of gold, just as though they were among the leaves of some pine or lofty fir tree, twittering forth a sound sweet as honey by means of a mechanism . . .[52]

It was Ktesibios who first invented these musical birds, like the automata at the baths, which he made to sing by forcing a stream of air into them by water pressure.[53] In Hero of Alexandria's *Pneumatics* there is an even more sophisticated version, where the birds take it in turn to sing;[54] here the water, entering a closed vessel, expels the air from it through tubes placed at staggered levels. These tubes, concealed among the branches of the tree, end in whistles fitted into the beaks of the birds. It seems unlikely that the necessary air pressure was supplied by bellows, as shown in a twelfth-century manuscript from St. Blasien published by Gerbert.[55]

But, however it was fashioned, this musical tree was fated to be destroyed, like the organs, by Theophilus's son Michael III:

Michael rapidly squandered this great wealth with his mimes, his toadies, his charioteers . . . He exhausted his treasures, and there was nothing he did not destroy: the golden plane-tree . . .[56] and the organs, all made of gold, the trappings of majesty, which were the envy of foreigners. He had them melted down and handed them over to be made into coins.[57]

We may assume that the two marvels constructed by Theophilus, the organ and the tree, were quickly replaced, for Liutprand, Bishop of Cremona, saw the famous 'plane tree'—no longer of gold, but of gilded bronze—when on a mission to the court at Constantinople in 931.[58] As for the organs,

---

[50] Bonn ed., p. 627.

[51] It is interesting to speculate whether the Pseudo-Jerome is in fact describing this tree when he refers to the 'bunibulum aereum', *P.L.*, xxx, 214.

[52] Bonn ed., p. 205.

[53] Vitruvius, *De Architectura*, x.

[54] Ed. Teubner, pp. 218 ff.

[55] *De Cantu*, op. cit., ii, Pl. XXVII. See Pl. XXVII, no. 3, in this book.

[56] Trees made of metal were traditionally Oriental. Athenaeus (xii, 53) quotes Phylarchus as saying that up to the time of Alexander the Great, the kings of Persia held audiences in their palace under magnificent golden plane trees studded with precious stones.

[57] Zonara, Bonn ed., iii, p. 393.

[58] *P.L.*, cxxxvi, col. 895.

Constantine Porphyrogenitus testifies that they were certainly in the Palace during his reign. From the evidence, however, it would seem that this tree was not a musical instrument, and it is mentioned here solely because the majority of musical writers describe the trees as 'tree-shaped organs'.[59] In fact, there is nowhere any indication that these musical machines had either pipes or a manual, so that it is legend alone that has transformed them into organs. As an example of this, here is how the poet of the *Titurel* describes the fabulous instrument installed in the temple of the Grail:

Above the western door, inside the temple, is an instrument that plays subtle melodies that caress the ear. It is an organ, used to accompany the celebrations of the Mass on the great feast-days . . . In shape it is like a tree of gold, decked with branches and foliage, in which there are birds whose sweet voices are much admired. The air is led into them by bellows, so that each sings its own particular note . . .[60]

ORGANISTS

Of the Byzantine organists nothing is known, and history has not preserved the name of even one of them. Constantine Porphyrogenitus refers to them simply as 'οἱ ὀργανάριοι';[61] but they had to be well versed in court procedure in order to have the instrument moved to the place where it was due to be played, and to strike up at the precise moment hallowed by custom. As we have seen, the blowers had to fill the reservoirs a few moments beforehand, after attaching their bellows: and it is not impossible that on some instruments it was the organist himself who worked the bellows with his feet. The text of Theodoret, a Syrian bishop who lived during the reign of Theodosius II, strongly suggests this.[62]

The organists of the two factions are clearly distinguishable on the Obelisk of Theodosius in Constantinople. Their hands poised on the manuals, they are craning their necks past the pipes to watch the ceremony and start playing at the given moment. The blowers are not shown: but we can see the stabilizing bellows on each organ, with small children on them in place of a weight.

The organists are even better depicted on a drawing illustrating the celebrated Utrecht Psalter. We shall see later, however, that this must not be taken as representing a Byzantine organ, but simply as the drawing of an educated monk.[63]

[59] For example Barbier de Montaux, *Annales Archéologiques*, xviii (1858), pp. 90–5.
[60] From the translation of O. Van den Berghe, *Annales Archéologiques*, xvii (1857), pp. 293–4.
[61] Book i, ch. 1.
[62] See p. 63.
[63] Pl. XXIII, nos. 1 and 2.

APPRECIATION OF ORGAN MUSIC

The frequent participation of the instrument in the life of the capital shows how widely appreciated organ music must have been. The popular epic of Digenis Akritas, dealing with events of the ninth and tenth centuries, tells how the silver organs sounded when the hero and his betrothed arrived at the house of the strategus.[64] It was even said that the sound of the organ exercised a strange power over the minds of its hearers, and a curious text on this very theme is contained in a treatise on alchemy generally assumed to be from the eighth or ninth century.[65] Having attempted to establish a parallel between chemistry and music, the anonymous author goes on to say: 'As for those that we call "instruments par excellence", the Ancients called these the "auletic plinthion without strings". [This instrument] is in tune with divine powers and is in perfect harmony with the soul; equipped to fortify bodily strength; and to soothe the soul and to promote fellowship with God.'[66]

The rest of the text is obscure. It lists a number of 'auletic' instruments, that is to say wind instruments: 'Wind instruments of bronze include the auletic psalterion, known as the "Very Great Organ", the hand organ (χειρόργανον) . . . the trumpet and the horns.'[67] The terms 'Very Great Organ' and 'hand organ' are interesting if they actually refer to our instrument, as seems likely; and so, too, is the expression 'psalterion or auletic plinthion without strings', which does not recur elsewhere. The Greek word πλινθίον means a square brick, or any object having that shape. The psalterion had a quadrangular resonating chamber, as some of the frescoes in Kiev Cathedral show; and the Byzantine pneumatic organ has this same shape (the Muslim prisoner quoted earlier describes a 'square object'). This may account for the unusual expression 'auletic plinthion.'[68]

An Arabic text discussing the Byzantine organ recounts with gusto the extraordinary effects of its music. The passage is contained in the *Kitab al-aghani*, or Book of Songs, written by Abu'l-Faraj al-Isfahani (died 967). The scene takes place somewhere between 813 and 825:

There informed me Muhammad ibn Yahyā, on the authority of 'Awn ibn Muhammad, on the authority of Abu Ahmad ibn al-Rashid, and [in addition] I copied the story from a book by Muhammad ibn al-Hasan, who got it from

---

64 Quoted by Bréhier, *La Civilisation Byzantine* (Paris, 1950), p. 394.

65 According to G. Reese, op. cit., p. 85, the author was a certain Zozimus of Panopolis in Egypt, not later than the fourth century.

66 Berthelot and Ruelle, *Collection des Alchimistes Grecs* (Paris, 1887), p. 438.

67 Ibid., p. 438.

68 The fourth fragment of the *Hagiopolites* mentions the plinthion in a group of musical instruments which includes the cithara, the aulos, the trumpet and the hydraulis (Vincent, op. cit., p. 266).

'Awn ibn Muhammad, who got it from Abu Ahmad ibn al-Rashid, the following: He [Muhammad ibn Yahya] said, Isma'il ibn al-Hadi entered one day into the presence of Al-Ma'mun, when he heard music which diverted his attention. Then Al-Ma'mun said to him, 'What ails you?' He replied, 'I have heard something that has bewildered me, and yet I have been the most strenuous in denying that the Byzantine organ (urghan al-rumi) killed with delight, but now I declare that to be true.'[69]

Still in the realm of anecdote, we hear of an original therapeutic application of the instrument at the Byzantine court. In the third part of his *Ecclesiastical History*, John, Bishop of Ephesus, reports this curious fact apropos of the madness of the Emperor Justin II (574–8), the nephew of Justinian:[70]

In this disordered state of the king's intellect, those about him devised various kinds of amusements, both to divert his attention, and in the hope of restoring him to the use of his reason. The most successful of these was a little wagon, with a throne upon it for him to sit upon, and having placed him on it, his chamberlains drew him about, and ran with him backwards and forwards for a long time, while he, in delight and admiration at their speed, desisted from many of his absurdities. Another was an organ, which they kept almost continuously playing day and night near his chamber; and as long as he heard the sound of the tunes which it played he remained quiet . . .

Another surprising use for the organ is said to have been devised by Belisarius, commander-in-chief of Justinian's armies. He ordered an organ to be played in military posts during the night watches to prevent his soldiers from falling asleep.[71]

Scarcely anything is known as to what timbres were available; but it would seem that two types of music were played on the organ. There was first of all the ceremonial music, grandiose, brilliant, solemn, designed for court occasions and alternating with the acclamations of the people and the choruses of the precentors. For this the reed pipes were called into play. By contrast, there was the more intimate style, better suited to the smaller apartments or to the private concert, and for this the flue pipes were generally used. Probably it was this second type of music that was thought by the alchemist to dispel the anguish of the spirit, turn men towards the love of God, and, if we are to believe al-Isfahani, cause men to die of joy. But from the general corpus of existing texts it appears that the Byzantine organ, 'the ornament of royalty', was above all designed to enhance the sacred majesty of the imperial palace. It was essentially an instrument of

[69] Quoted by Farmer in *The Organ of the Ancients*, pp. 57–58.
[70] *The Third Part of the Ecclesiastical History of John, bishop of Ephesus*, translated by R. Payne Smith (Oxford, 1860), p. 169.
[71] F. M. Feldhaus, *Die Technik der Antike und des Mittelalters* (Leipzig 1931), p. 226. The author does not quote his source.

pomp and prestige. When, on the eve of the destruction of the empire, the Emperor Constantine XI Dragses sent Phrantzes to ask for the hand of an Iberian princess, the ambassador was dispatched with magnificent gifts, with an organ featuring high on the list. On reaching Spain, the organists who had come along as part of the retinue hastened to unpack their instruments and start playing. The people came running to listen, and there was universal astonishment at the sound of this new music.[72]

We know nothing of the tessitura of the eastern organ. If however the text of Bellermann's Anonymous, quoted above,[73] is accepted as representing Byzantine science, one may conjecture that in the Eastern Empire, as at Rome, different types of organ used one or more tropes, but none used all. This hypothesis may find support in the third fragment of the Hagiopolites, whose author was an oriental living in Jerusalem, probably during the time of the Comnenas.[74]

The range of sounds perceptible to the ear is substantially represented by five types of instrument, which is why it is divided into only five tropes, i.e. the trumpet, the aulos, the voice, the cithara, and the pteron.[75] The names of the tropes are as follows: the Dorian, which is the lowest; it suits the trumpet. The next, the Phrygian, suits the aulos. The Lydian, the middle one, suits the voice. Finally, the Aeolian is for the cithara and the Iastian for the pteron. In addition, instruments of each type can differ in size and pitch, either high or low, as one desires.[76]

This fragment, which has obvious resemblances to the Anonymous of Bellermann, shows that each of the instruments mentioned developed a definite tessitura, represented by a trope. But, the author adds, there are different varieties of each type of instrument—as archaeology has shown in the case of the trumpet, aulos, and syrinx. It is thus very likely that in Byzantium various models of organs were in use, with very different diapason, tessitura, and size, from the great Palace organ to the little portative organs mentioned above.

[72] Phrantzes, Bonn ed., iii, p. 207.
[73] See above, p. 137.
[74] A Gastoué, *L'importance musicale, liturgique et philosophique du manuscrit Hagiopolites* (Byzantion, 1929), p. 347.
[75] Probably the syrinx.
[76] Vincent, op. cit., p. 264.

CHAPTER ELEVEN

༄ཡཿ

The Organ in the Arab World

THE HISTORICAL BACKGROUND

The evolution of the organ in the Islamic world of the eighth, ninth, and tenth centuries, at the zenith of the three Caliphates, constitutes a strange episode in the instrument's history with which we are still imperfectly acquainted. In the light of the published documents (and there are others still in manuscript form) it seems unlikely that in this world it was the object of luxury and pomp that it was in Byzantium. It was probably studied more from the mechanical and technical point of view.

In the closing years of the Umayyad dynasty (660–750), with its capital at Damascus, the Muslim Empire reached its widest territorial limits, stretching from Spain to the valley of the Indus, and from Arabia to the edge of the plains of Turkestan. But this period, though productive in art and architecture, saw little progress in the sciences. They were destined to flourish with dazzling brilliance under the next dynasty, that of the Abbasids (750–1258), founded by Aboul' Abbas. The unity of the Empire was now at an end, but with the three Caliphates of Cordova, Cairo, and Baghdad, Arab culture entered its golden age. The first, set up in 750, reached its peak in the tenth century. During the same period the second, descended from the Fatimids, lived through its most splendid period since the capital was founded. But the most glorious era in the history of the Caliphat of Baghdad belongs to the second half of the eighth century and the first half of the ninth.

The court of Baghdad was even richer than that of Damascus, and enjoyed considerable revenues from her agriculture, industry, and commerce. Under the enlightened patronage of the Caliphs, literature, the arts, and the sciences were cultivated with great ardour: here, unlike Byzantium, the scholars worked in a spirit of research and discovery that was to ensure substantial progress in every field. The State itself encouraged such study. The Caliph al Ma'mun (813–33) founded a 'House of Science' in Baghdad, furnished with a well-stocked library,[1] and, perhaps taking the Ptolemies as his example, he attracted many scholars to Baghdad, even enticing some from

[1] Ch. Diehl and G. Marçais, *Le Monde Oriental de 395 à 1081* (Paris, 1944), p. 373.

Byzantium. Advances were made in astronomy, and also in chemistry, medicine, and mathematics. The translators of scientific documents were no less active, and as early as the end of the eighth century the celebrated Haroun al-Rashid tried to make Baghdad a great translation centre,[2] though most of the Greek manuscripts translated into Arabic date from the ninth century. The Arabs' curiosity also embraced music, an important branch of the 'quadrivium', and a number of treatises by Greek musicians were known in the Arab world at a time when their existence was unknown in western Euorpe. Among these were the *Harmonics* and the *Treatise on Rhythm* of Aristoxenus; the *Problems* of Aristotle; the *Harmonics* and *Canon* of Euclid; and the *Harmonics* of Ptolemy and of Nicomachus. In Baghdad it was possible to read a work by Pythagoras concerning music which has survived neither in Greek nor in Arabic.[3] Thus there appeared in the libraries of the Caliphate quantities of translated material comprising much of the scientific literature written by the Alexandrian scholars and carefully preserved by the Byzantines.[4]

THE ORGAN PRESENTED TO SHIH TSU

References to the organ in Arabic texts are generally meagre. The celebrated Ibn Sina, known in Europe by the name Avicenna (late tenth century) had heard tell of the organ: 'Wind instruments may be used together to form an ensemble, like the Byzantine instrument called *urganun*.'[5]

The following text is also attributed to Avicenna: 'One branch of musical science is the art of building marvellous and extraordinary instruments such as the organ and its like.'[6]

We have a definition of it from the lexicographer Asho bar'Ali, professor at the House of Science in Baghdad, towards the middle of the ninth century: '*Hedhrula* (hydraulis): [it is] the organ (*urghanun*) . . . skins, on which they play.'[7] Another lexicographer, Bar Saroshwai, writing at the beginning of the tenth century: says: '*Hydraules* are instruments of music on which one plays, such as reeds (one MS. has 'skins') which men work.' A few years later Isho bar'Bahlul offers the following explanation: 'The hydraulis of bronze is explained as a certain oven (*tannur*).'[8] To which the Arab commentator adds: '[It is] the musical skin (bag), the organ (*urghanun*).'

[2] De Lacy O'Leary, *How Greek Science passed to the Arabs* (London, 1948), xii.

[3] H. G. Farmer, *Historical Facts for the Arabian musical Influence* (London, 1930), p. 64.

[4] See A. Mieli, *La Science Arabe* (Leyden, 1938), pp. 52 ff., and O'Leary, *Arabic Thought and its place in History* (London, 1922), pp. 2 ff.

[5] R. d'Erlanger, *La Musique Arabe* (Paris, 1935), ii, p. 234.

[6] From the Latin translation of A. Bellunens (Venice, 1546), pp. 142–3.

[7] Farmer, *The Organ of the Ancients*, pp. 52–3. The three following quotations are taken from the same work. Here again the word 'hydraulis' is used to describe both the bellows and the hydraulic organ.

[8] The Greek origin of the comparison is clear: oven = πνιγεύς.

Another writer, Elias bar'Shinaya, living at the same time, gives his own slightly different version: '*Hydraules* are instruments which they play like reeds and what resembles these.' The Arab commentary runs: '[It is] the musical skin (bag), like the flutes and wooden contrivances and the like.'

These observations have the air of being made by scholars who never actually set eyes on a hydraulic organ. However, in the twelfth century organs were still manufactured at Damascus; the scholar Abu'l-Majd, a doctor and musician residing in that city,[9] 'had knowledge of the science of music and played the lute; excelled in the song, the rhythms, the reed-pipe, and other instruments. And he constructed an organ (*urghan*) in which he attained perfection.' Also during this period Abu Zakariyya, an Andalusian by birth, who was in the service of Saladin, was active in the same sphere: 'Abu Zakariyya . . . made for Ibn al-Naqqash many instruments of a composite nature, which he derived from engineering . . . was an excellent player on the lute, and he constructed an organ (*urghan*), and sought by artful contrivance the playing of it.'[10]

The best proof that the Arab organ-makers were perfectly at home with Graeco-Byzantine techniques is contained in a fourteenth-century Chinese document which tells how, between 1260 and 1264, a sizeable organ was sent to the Emperor Shih Tsu[11] by the 'Muslim kingdoms' (this probably meant the authorities in Baghdad). The descriptions given by the Chinese chronicles enable us to form quite an accurate idea of what could still be achieved by the Arabs at this time.

Instruments for Feast Music:

Hsing lung shêng. It is made of *nan* wood (*machilus nanmu*). The shape is like a double screen, pointed above but with a smooth face; inlaid with gold wire and carved with *loquat*, roses, peacocks, bamboos, trees, clouds, and mists. At the two sides decorated boards are placed sideways, each occupying one-third of the width of the back. Inside is a hollow chest like the air-chamber of the *shêng*.[12] Above are ninety pipes of purple bamboo set upright. The ends of the pipes are filled with sheaths of *mu lien* wood (ficus pumila). Outside the chest fifteen small rods (or drumsticks) project, and small pipes are set upright above, the ends of the pipes being filled with brass apricot leaves. Beneath is a stand surrounded with lions and elephants. On the stand and in front of the chest one decorated board carved like the board at the back is set. Two leather wind-mouths project between [this board and the instrument]. When the instrument is in use they place a small red lacquer frame in front of the stand and tie wind-bags to the wind-mouths. The [wooden] face of these bags is like the *p'i p'a*

---

[9] Farmer, *The Organ of the Ancients*, p. 75.

[10] Farmer, op. cit., p. 75.

[11] This Shih Tsu, none other than the Mongol Kublai Khan, was the grandson of Genghis Khan. He set himself up as the patron of literature and the arts.

[12] The *shêng* is a mouth organ. See p. xix.

(lute), red lacquered with various flowers, and with handles. One man manipulates the little pipes, one man sets the wind-bags in motion, and then the reeds speak naturally following the tune.

The instrument presented by the Moslem kingdoms in Chung-t'ung (1260–1264) used bamboo for the reeds, and produced sounds but no scale.

Chêng Hsiu, *p'an kuan* of the Yü chên Music Office, after examining the notes and scales and distributing the high and low notes properly, added to and changed the instrument until it was constructed as at present.

On the two sides of the shield-head of the instruments used inside the Hall they set two carved wooden peacocks, decorated with real peacock feathers, with mechanism arranged inside. On every occasion three men were employed to play. One man set the wind-bags in motion, one man handled the notes, and one man moved the mechanism and then the peacocks flapped their wings and danced in time with the music. The *shêng* for the palace were ten . . .[13]

. . . The *Hsing lung shêng* stood outside the Ta ming Hall. The construction: fit a number of pipes into soft leather shaped like a large gourd. The performers set two leather bellows in motion, and touch the pipes, and then the reeds sound. On the ends of the cross-bar of the frame are two peacocks. When the organ sounds mechanism moves and then they respond and dance. On all feast days the whole orchestra plays as soon as this *shêng* sounds, when it stops the orchestra also stops.

. . . Now our Emperor Shih Tsu [Kublai], received the clear mandate of Heaven and included Hsia [China] in the universal union, with divine merit and holy virtue surpassing all kings. When his work was completed and his rule established, he planned to make large musical instruments to be used at Court. The instruments included this one called *hsing lung shêng*. It is really one which his Majesty made himself, though some say it was just an offering from the lands of the West and that the Son of Heaven added improvements to it. It is made with ninety pipes arranged in fifteen ranks, each rank with six pipes arranged across. The pipes are fitted below into a chest, and at the back of the chest it is filled with air by means of bellows. From the foot of the chest to the tops of the pipes it is about five feet high. And moreover there are carved boards shaped like the phoenix and painted with gold and colours, to surround the pipes on three sides; about three feet wide, and with inscriptions added to ornament them. At all great Court gatherings it is set between the eaves and the steps, and is played together with all the instruments. Two musicians are always employed, one to manipulate the pipes, one to move the bellows so as to drive the air and produce sounds in unison with all the notes . . .

The greatness and excellence of its construction are not found in the ages of antiquity. It is indeed fitted to manifest merits and virtue and to hand them down to the generations of eternity. . . . The influence of its magical notes [makes men] sedate and pure. . . .

---

[13] This passage, and the two following excerpts, are published in English by A. C. Moule, 'A Western Organ in Medieval China: the Chinese Texts', *Journal of the Royal Asiatic Society*, ii (April 1926), pp. 193 ff.

For all their grandiloquence and abstruseness, these texts succeed in painting a relatively accurate picture of the Arab organ and its use. It must have been a fairly large instrument, since it measured 1·50 m. high and a little less than a metre in width. According to one chronicler, its ninety pipes, made of bamboo,[14] divided up into six sets and fifteen degrees of sound, and though originally they were tuned to the Arabic musical scale, as soon as the instrument arrived in China they were re-tuned to the Chinese scales by one of the palace musicians. Some of the sets, if not all, must have been reed-pies, the reeds being made of a special wood known as *mu-lien*. The wind-chest, made of *nan* wood, was lacquered and inlaid with scenes representing animals, trees, and flowers. It has been suggested that these decorated panels could not have been of Arabian origin, since Islamic law proscribed such illustrations.[15] However, it is likely that only these panels were made of the *nan* wood, since this would be specifically Chinese. Inside the wind-chest was the regulator, a skin bag shaped rather like a plump gourd. Leading into this regulator were the two tubes to which the bellows were attached. The bellows themselves were richly decorated, and required the services of only one blower.

The manual was somewhat primitive, with a small tube soldered perpendicularly above each of the fifteen drawers. These must certainly have been joined to sliders perforated with six holes corresponding to the feet of the six pipes tuned to the same degree of the scale—this is the device described by Vitruvius. But there is no mention here of the little angled joint enabling the slider to move back and forward, and it is quite possible that this organ was played by pulling and pushing the tubes of the various keys. One passage in the description, not included here because of the vagueness of the Chinese text and its translation, seems to imply that the tube was pushed with one finger when the note was played, and had then to be pulled towards the player, using two fingers, to cut off the sound.[16] It is also not clear if there was any system of stops which allowed the player to separate the different ranks of pipes.

Obviously this Arab organ is not far removed from the Byzantine organ. The air, supplied by bellows, is compressed and regulated in a supple, elastic skin bag, and subsequently directed towards the pipes under the control of a manual. There can be no doubt that an instrument of this type was a most lavish gift, and we shall see what excitement was aroused when the Byzantine Emperor Constantine Copronymus sent an organ to Pepin the Short.

[14] Possibly these bamboo pipes are Chinese reproductions of the original pipes.
[15] F. W. Galpin, 'Some Notes on the original form and source of the Hsing lung Shêng', ibid., p. 208.
[16] Moule, op. cit., p. 202, note 3.

As with the Byzantine instrument, this organ is transportable, and was hoisted up to the topmost rooms in the palace every time an important reception was given—an operation only made possible by the lightness of its wind mechanism.

However, the organ sent to the Emperor Shih Tsu was probably not the only one made by Arab craftsmen. Around 963 a Syrian writer, Joshua Bar-Bahlul, describes something rather different:

There are two types of organ, the first being shaped like a weaver's loom. It is fitted with a great number of strings [?] and may be heard at a distance of seven stadia. The second is composed of two slender hollow columns, made of superb marble, positioned vertically and designed with admirable skill. Underneath are bellows, like those of blacksmiths, but smaller and prettier. The player is seated above them, and those who take part in the singing, whatever it may be, stand to right and left. And then is heard an exquisite concert, with which nothing on earth can compare. It is said that such an instrument is to be found in the Church of Byzantium.[17]

Possibly the author is here describing an instrument of which he has heard, but which he himself has never seen, or perhaps this is actually the imperial organ from the Grand Triclinium. We know for a fact that there were no organs in Byzantine churches, and the marble columns supporting the instrument recall only too well those of the great reception room in the palace. They are the tall columns of the portico, between which, as we saw earlier, the organ of the Basileus was positioned. An interesting point about this text is that Joshua bar-Bahlul ranges the choristers on either side of the organist, as is customary in organ lofts today.

A further intriguing feature of this text is that it refers to a second instrument, entirely different from the organ, despite its name, and characterized by its loud sound, which can be heard from a very great distance. The author is probably mistaken in describing it as an instrument with strings, for what he is actually writing about is a kind of organ siren.

MURISTUS AND PSEUDO-JEROME

This hybrid hydraulic organ, of enormous size, is described by one Muristus, whose name I have mentioned more than once. The historical significance of this man, who figures only in the Arabic texts, stems from the fact that apparently his instrument derives directly from the *Commentaries* of Ktesibios. For this reason it would seem indispensable to reproduce in full the description of two devices, each called organs.

[17] Translated from Syriac into Latin by R. Payne Smith, *Thesaurus Syriacus* (Oxford, 1868), i, p. 91.

Muristus has always been surrounded by an aura of mystery. It is not certain exactly when he lived; and his name, not to mention his personality, is a subject of some controversy. His first historical appearance dates from the middle of the ninth century, in a quotation from Al-Jahiz (773–868), but there is no reference to his works before 988, when Ibn al-Nadim writes:[18] 'Murtus or Muristus. And among his books are, *Book on the Musical Instruments called the Flue-pipe Organ (urghanun al-buqi) and the Reed-pipe Organ (urghanun al-zamri); Book on the Musical Instrument which may be heard Sixty Miles.*'

A later Arabic treatise (first half of the thirteenth century), entitled *Ta'rikh al-hukama*, and written by Ibn al-Qifti, says: 'Murtus or Muristus, a Greek sage, skilled and ingenious. And among his literary works is a *Book on the Musical Instrument called the Flue-pipe Organ and the Reed-pipe Organ which may be heard Sixty Miles.*'[19]

It has been suggested that this Muristus and the Greek mathematician Ameristos (640–555 B.C.) are one and the same, basing the theory on no more tangible evidence than the similarity between the two names. Another theory makes him a contemporary of Philo of Byzantium (third century B.C.), because the name Muristus varies from one manuscript to another, so that we find him as Muristos, Muristus, or Ariston. Now, it so happens that Philo of Byzantium dedicated several of his works to one Ariston, among them the Syntax of Engineering: Φίλων Ἀρίστωνι χαίρειν. It could be that this Ariston, Philo's friend, is identical with Muristus,[20] but there is no evidence to prove this. Moreover, there is a further problem, and one which cannot easily be brushed aside. In the title of the relevant texts the Arabic particle *li* is translatable by both 'from' and 'to'.[21] Thus the title might be 'Epistle *from* Muristus the Sage' or 'Epistle *to* Muristus the Sage'. The text must date at the very earliest from one or two centuries before the first appearance of his name in the Arabic encyclopedias. I am inclined to think that the author of these treatises is a Muslim of Baghdad, a compiler of the works of Philo and Ktesibios. The Greek Muristus would seem to my mind to have been a Byzantine, for one of the texts we are about to analyse strongly suggests this.[22] There are also the words of the Arab Al-Jahiz, whom we have already mentioned:

What a distance! Archimedes to Muristus![23]

[18] Farmer, *The Organ of the Ancients*, p. 60.

[19] Farmer, op. cit., p. 60.

[20] Carra de Vaux supports this theory, *Le Livre des appareils pneumatiques et des machines hydrauliques, par Philon de Byzance* (Paris, 1902), pp. 13–14.

[21] Carra de Vaux, *Mémoires Scientifiques de P. Tannery* (Paris, 1915), iii, p. 296.

[22] Below, p. 197: 'Muristos says: the Greeks carried this instrument when they went to war . . . to warn the inhabitants of the King's city'.

[23] Farmer, op. cit., p. 13.

At all events, the descriptions bearing Muristus's name are adapted from an earlier work, and revised and corrected in the Arab fashion. The writings of the Byzantine author were certainly compiled from those of a Greek engineer, probably Ktesibios himself. As I have said before, the graphic resemblance in Arabic writings between the names Muristus and Qatasibiyus —that is to say Ktesibios—has been noted.[24] The Arab editor was very likely an inhabitant of Baghdad, for the custom of using the word 'epistle' to denote musicological treatises had become established there from the time of the first Abbasid rulers.[25]

Under the name of Muristus, two descriptions of machines have survived which, despite their name, are certainly not organs in the modern sense. One is a curious musical instrument activated by the breath of four men and fitted with twelve pipes; while the other is a type of siren essentially designed for military use, though it does have some musical potential. The first of these is in some respects analogous with the pneumatic organ, and in the second we again encounter Ktesibios's wind mechanism. These texts were first published in Arabic by Fr. L. Cheïkko, in 1906.[26] The manuscript, apparently dating back to the twelfth century, contains some twenty essays on geometry, astronomy, dynamics, music, and other subjects, accompanied by drawings, some of them in colour. Apart from the manuscript used by Fr. Cheïkho, we know of two others.[27] The translation given here draws on material from two of them.[28] Here is the first treatise:

Epistle to Muristus on the construction of the reed-pipe organ for all the wonderful sounds.

And it is that which makes you hear a wonderful sound, causing you to weep violently. And makes you hear a sound compelling sleep, for he who hears it falls asleep where he stands. And makes you hear a sound to grieve or amuse you. And makes you hear a sound that causes you to be merry and to dance. And makes you hear a sound that ravishes and carries away the senses. So, when you wish to make this instrument, take three skin bags, well tanned and very soft, and do not let bitumen (?) come near them. Next, sew up the heads of two of these skins thoroughly, so that they are air-tight, and leave the third skin with its head unsewn. In the middle place the skin that has its head unsewn, with one of the other two skins to right and left of it. Then, on the [inner] side of the skins lying to either side of the middle skin, pierce four holes; similarly pierce four holes on each side of the middle skin, exactly

---

[24] Farmer, op. cit., p. 19.

[25] D'Erlanger, op. cit., i, p. xxiii.

[26] Al-Mashriq, Beirut, p. 444–58.

[27] The Beirut Manuscript is in the Greek Orthodox College of the Three Moons. The second is in the British Museum (Or. 9649), and the third in the Hagia Sofia Library in Constantinople (2755, iii–iv).

[28] From the Three-Moons manuscript translated by a learned Lebanese and Farmer's translation of the British Museum manuscript (op. cit., pp. 63–70).

opposite to the holes in the lateral skins. The three skins are marked A, B, and J; and the middle skin is B.[29]

Then take pipes of strong brass, about the thickness of a stick, and approximately a *dhira*[30] in length, and use them for joining one skin to another. And these pipes are known as 'the Wind Passages'. And let these holes and these pipes be of different size in their measure and arrangement, according to the ratios I shall describe to you.

Let the first hole of the right-hand skin, which is opposite to the middle skin, be of whatever width you desire. The size of this first hole will govern all the others and the corresponding tubes. This first tube is marked D. The second, which lies next to it, is twice the diameter of the first, and is marked H. And the third is three times the diameter of the first, and is marked W. The fourth is four times the diameter of the first, and is marked Z. And the diameter of each pipe is equal to that of the corresponding hole. Let this be understood.

The holes of the skin lying on the left-hand side should also be according to these ratios. If the diameter of the first hole on the left-hand skin is equal to the diameter of the first hole of the skin on the right, the others will increase in size accordingly. But if you make the diameter of the first hole in the left skin half that of the first hole in the right skin, then again you will make the other holes in proportion. And if you make the first hole in the left skin wider than the first hole in the right skin, then you will keep the same proportions for the other holes. This means that for the pipes D and K, the diameter is optional: they may be either equal or unequal. Then we make the ratio of pipe H to pipe D 2/1, and similarly with pipes Y and K. Then the ratio of pipe W to pipe D will be 3/1, and similarly with pipes Ṭ and K. And the ratio of pipe Z to pipe D will be 4/1, and the same will be true for pipes Ḥ and K. And these are the respective proportions of the pipes which are called 'the Wind Passages'.

Then on the head of the middle skin mount a pipe one dhira in length, projecting out. Its diameter is that of a *dirham*.[31] Fix it so that there is no escape of air: this is the pipe BL.

Then perforate the body of each skin with four holes, so that the distance between the holes is exactly equal. These holes should be, in their size, width and measure, equivalent to the width of the tubes known as the 'Wind Passages', and observe the same ratios. Then mount upon these holes brass pipes, whose diameters and ratios correspond to those of the holes. Let each of these pipes be 1 *dhira* in length. Arrange these pipes vertically in relation to the skins: and they are twelve in number. Those in the skin A on the right are marked M, N, S, X; those of the skin B, in the middle, are marked F, Ṣ, Q, R; and those in skin J, on the left, are marked Sh, T, Th, Kh.

---

[29] These letters correspond to the Arabic characters on the diagram given in the British Museum manuscript (see fig. 12).

[30] Farmer says that the *dhira* is equivalent to 54 cm.

[31] Farmer says this was a silver coin equivalent to and about the same size as a sixpence.

Then, at the extremity of each pipe, firmly attach a 'sound box',[32] and you will obtain twelve sounds. Then, half-way up the length of these twelve pipes equipped with their 'sound boxes', you insert stoppers, firm and tight, which open and shut in order to change the sounds. This is the chief requisite in the construction of the instrument. Understand that.

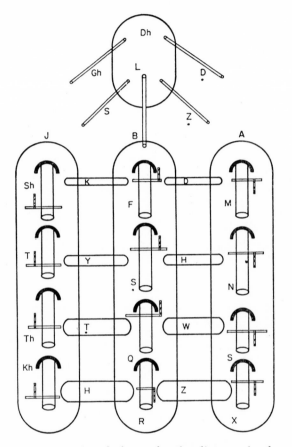

Fig. 12. Muristus's 'organ'. The diagram in the
British Museum manuscript

Then, to return to the pipe which was fixed in the head of the middle skin (and marked BL), this is where the wind enters. Mount upon it a small skin, firmly fixed to the extremity L of the pipe. This skin is marked Dh. Then insert in this small skin four pipes, each three *shibr*[33] in length, of a width convenient for the lips of the blowers. These pipes are marked Ḍ, Ẓ, Ṣ and Gh.

Then place the whole instrument on a frame, and prepare places on which the blowers may sit. If you are disposed to play sorrowful music, close the

[32] This probably refers to the reed, placed at the lower end of the pipe.
[33] 81 cm. (Farmer).

stoppers in the pipes so that no air escapes, except from the hole of the second pipe in the second skin, the same pipe in the first skin and the same pipe in the third skin. This means that you close all the stoppers with the exception of N, Ṣ and T.[34] And when the men blow, their breath should come gently,

Fig. 13. Muristus's 'organ'. The diagram in the
Beirut manuscript

moderate in intensity, for no one can hear these sounds without himself feeling sorrowful. Then calm prevails, and sleep so overcomes him that he sleeps where he stands.[35]

And if you wish to play music conducive to vigilance and courage, then open the hole in the first pipe, which is the upper one in the first skin, the second pipe in the second skin—again the upper pipe—and the third pipe in

[34] Here and later on the text is obviously in error, and I have corrected it to comply with the diagram.
[35] Note the similarity of effect between this music and that of the aulos, as described by Plutarch (see above, p. 128).

the third skin. This means that you open the stoppers M, Ṣ, and Th. This time the blowing should be violent, so that the sound produces an effect conducive to courage and vigilance.

And if you wish to engender delight and activity in a man until his senses are carried away, so that he weeps and groans, then open the holes in the pipes of the second rank and those of the pipes in the third rank, that is to say the stoppers N, Ṣ, T, S, Q, Th. Regulate the sound by blowing with moderation, and the man will experience the onset of joy and gladness, and his intelligence will be numbed, so that he weeps without knowing the cause.

And if you desire to torment your listeners until their spirit is softened and their body grows weak, then open the holes of the upper pipes on all three skins (those of the high notes) and those of the lower pipes on the three skins (those of the low notes), that is to say the stoppers M, F, Sh, X, R, Kh. Then you will see something marvellous, for this complex effect is alien to man's temperament, since, hearing it, a man does not grasp what we have just described.

And the ears of the blowers should be stopped so that they themselves are not exposed to what the listeners hear, otherwise their work would be ill-done.

And it would also be more effective, if a greater volume of sound were desired, and the notes would be of greater strength and length and duration, if the blowers were to be twelve in number, like the pipes. If you should wish this, then insert twelve pipes into the small skin, for twelve men.

Furthermore, those who blow must be intelligent and experienced in the art of singing and scansion of melody, for they may be called upon to play the melody, just as the player on the flute or the reed-pipe phrases his tune. And their larynxes should be wide and resonant.

And we may compare the composition of this instrument to the disposition of the organs in the human body. This organ is one of the best composite productions among the instruments of sound, with its many uses, giving all the sounds that one might desire, in all the languages of the earth and of the creatures of the sea. And no one will be able to build these instruments, so well adapted to man and affording all the sounds we have described, except by following the instructions given here.

This curious instrument bears little resemblance to the Byzantine organ except that its skins function as regulating air reservoirs. It is fed, not by blacksmith's bellows, but by the combined lung power of four men seated round a small receiver.[36] The air, led into the skins through a long pipe, is compressed and regulated by the weight of twelve sounding pipes. These are reed pipes, if the title is correct, of equal length and producing twelve sounds, probably all different. We are told that the upper rank gives the

[36] Perhaps this system was more common than might be expected. A painting by Tintoretto in the Castelvecchio Museum in Verona, entitled 'Concerto di dame all' aperto', shows a two-rank table positive fitted in front with a thick, curving pipe into which a young woman is blowing as hard as she can.

high notes and the low rank the bass notes. The intervening ranks presumably fill in the middle register. As in modern organ-building, the bass pipes are wider than the trebles[37] and receive more air through their wider conduit. The author further specifies that the blowers must perform their task intelligently, blowing harder or softer to vary the effect, and above all phrasing the melody in a proper manner.

We have now to attempt to explain, from the information given in the text, how this 'organ' worked. It seems out of the question that the sounds obtained could have been uniform and stable, and even less likely that they could play a fixed 'harmony'. But if we bear in mind that the air is distributed to each pipe by a kind of valve,[38] we have then only to assume that this valve is operated by a 'key'. This, by controlling each rank of pipes, gives the overall effect of a miniature three-note manual. Consequently, having selected his 'console', that is to say the rank or ranks he wishes to sound, the player manipulates the 'key-valves' with his fingers in order to obtain a strongly rhythmic monody. This ritornello, consisting of only a few notes, intelligently phrased by the breath of the four blowers, would thus have been capable of producing the extraordinary effects described in the texts.[39] If such a hypothesis is correct, then the instrument might validly be assimilated to the organ, with its wind mechanism, its manual and its pipes: but the completely original conception appears to be specifically Arabic.

The other apparatus described by Muristus, primarily designed to produce very penetrating sounds, is based on a totally different principle. Historically its interest is twofold; in the first place its wind mechanism is analogous with that of the hydraulis; and in the second its existence seems to have appealed to the popular imagination at the time. It has been said that a similar instrument—the Magrephah—is mentioned in the Babylonian Talmud, and the *Dardanus Letter* of Pseudo-Jerome describes an apparatus of the same type, with certain details adapted for the purpose of edification. These traditions have a common origin, certainly Middle Eastern, of which Muristus's organ siren appears to represent the true core. Consequently it seems hardly right to summarize the Arabic text, despite its occasional long-windedness and obscurity.[40]

[37] Here the illustration contradicts the text.
[38] The British Museum manuscript shows the valves stupidly placed in the middle of the pipes.
[39] Farmer (*Hist. Facts for the Arabic Musical Influence*, pp. 104–5) has observed that the letters used to name the pipes here correspond to certain notes referred to by the Arab theoretician Ibn Zaila. The sounds conducive to sorrow would thus be la-la-doh, and those conducive to vigilance and courage la-fa sharp-re.
[40] I have drawn on the translations of a Lebanese friend, of Carra de Vaux (*Revue des Etudes Grecques*, xxi, 1908, pp. 326–40) and of Farmer (*The Organ of the Ancients*, pp. 128–35).

Epistle to Muristus on the Construction of the Flue-pipe organ, that can be heard sixty miles.

Muristus says: the Greeks carried this instrument with them when they went to war, for their country was surrounded by many enemies. And when they had occasion to alert their allies or ask them to help by sending cavalry or provisions, or warn the inhabitants of the King's capital[41] or that of any other territory, they sounded this instrument, which is the 'Great Organ', nick-named 'The Great Mouth with the Loud Voice' because its sound carries for sixty miles.

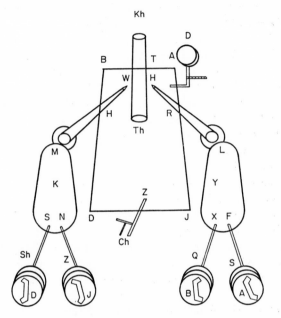

Fig. 14. Muristus's 'Great Organ'. The diagram in the British museum manuscript

If you would make this object, you must first take an 'apparatus' of brass, the size depending on the distance the sound is to carry—this may be longer or shorter than the distance I have mentioned. In the case of the one I person-ally made for the King of the 'Inner Franks', the distance was as stated. Its capacity is 1,000 *qist*; its height is 12 *dhira* and the circumference of its base 35 *shibr*.[42] This base should be broad, and the apparatus should narrow as it rises, until its diameter at the upper end is no more than 3 *shibr*.[43] Its shape recalls that of an oven,[44] and it is shut by a lid. Near the apex, 1 *shibr* from the

41 Byzantium.
42 7 and 9 m. respectively (Farmer). The diameter is thus slightly less than 3 m. The value of the *qist* is not known. See fig. 14.
43 This is Hero's pnigeus, and Vitruvius's '*infundibulum inversum*'.
44 A literal translation of πνιγεὺς.

top, three holes are pierced, forming a triangle, and the holes are equidistant from one another, a third of the circumference apart.

Next take three skins, each made from the hide of a great buffalo, and tan them with care so that the hide is soft, thin, and smooth. Into the mouth of each skin insert a brass pipe, the same length as the apparatus, so that if the end of this pipe is inserted into the skin at the top, the other end would reach to the bottom. These pipes should be flexible (=bent), and wide at the bottom, narrowing as they rise, as I shall describe.

The end of the pipe which reaches up nearly to the head of the instrument should have an opening measuring 1 *aqd*; the opening at the lower end should measure 4 *isba maftuh*.[45] The narrow ends of these pipes should fit into corresponding holes in the head of the instrument. Then take each of the three skins and fix the head of each very firmly to one of these pipes projecting from the top of the instrument, so that there shall not be the slightest leak of air.

The apparatus is marked A B D J, and the lid is A B and the bottom D J. As the design represents a flat surface we show, instead of three holes forming a triangle, two only, R and H. And of the three skins we show only two, marked Y and K; and of the three pipes we show only two, L H and M W. And their upper ends H and W are inserted in the apparatus,[46] and their lower ends are in the heads of the skins.

Then, in the back of each skin, pierce two wide holes, each one 4 *isba madmum* in diameter. And to each hole there shall be fitted a pipe 1½ *shibr* in length, narrowing towards its other end to a diameter of 1 *aqd*.[47] And these pipes should be firmly fixed in place so that there shall be no leak of air. Then, to each of these pipes fits a Greek bellows—this is a round bellows used by goldsmiths when they make seals—so that the bellows are mounted on the ends of these small pipes protruding from the backs of the skins. Understand that.

And the holes in the skin Y are F and X, and those in the skin K are N and S. The pipes fitted into these holes are marked S—Sh, N—Z, X—Q, F—Ṣ; and the Greek bellows are A, B, J, and D. Know that.

Now take a receptacle of a shape consistent with that of the instrument. At the lowest part its width should be . . .[48] and at the top . . .[49] And the length of this receptacle should exceed that of the apparatus by one-third. Then pierce the head of the apparatus and insert it into this receptacle, so that the head of the apparatus will rise 1 *shibr* above the top of the receptacle. Solder it well with lead, so that no air shall leak out of it, and let the bottom of the receptacle be solid.[50] At a distance of 1 *dhira*³ from the top, pierce a hole

---

[45] 2·25 cm. and 27 cm. respectively (Farmer).

[46] The copyist of the British Museum manuscript has omitted to indicate this join, which is correctly shown in the Beirut manuscript.

[47] 18 cm., 40·5 cm., and 2·25 cm. respectively (Farmer).

[48] The figures given in the text are undoubtedly wrong, since they completely contradict what is said later.

[49] This phrase reminds Carra de Vaux of Vitruvius's 'de materia compacta basi . . '

[50] 54 cm. (Farmer).

for pouring in the water: this is a funnel mounted on a strongly-made stopper. Water is poured in by the opening Dh and the funnel D, and the outlet hole, at the bottom of the receptacle, is Z, and the stopper Gh.

Then water is poured into the receptacle in the quantity I state here, that is to say until it reaches half-way up the instrument which will produce the sound. Then close the stopper Dh-D.

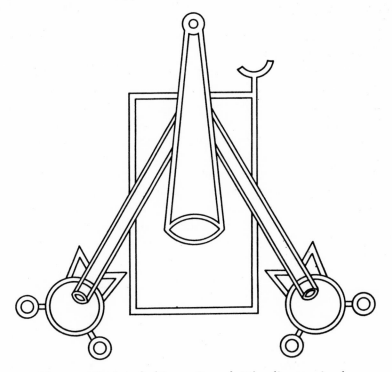

Fig. 15. Muristus's 'Great Organ'. The diagram in the
Beirut manuscript

When you desire to make the instrument sound, supports should be placed around the receptacle, and these should come as high as the skins, so that these skins rest on them. Stools should be fitted to these supports in order that the blowers may be seated, and they will begin by attaching the Greek bellows to their pipes.

Then they blow until the skins are filled with air, and this air enters the water and disturbs it, raising its level (in the receptacle), and circulates, seeking an outlet, escaping at the last through the opening in the pipe of the instrument with a loud and terrifying sound, so violent as to tear at the hearts of its hearers, and is heard the distance I have stated. The men who blow should moreover have their ears stopped with cotton covered with wax, so that they do not swoon or lose their hearing.

Furthermore, this instrument does not produce only one sound, as I shall explain in detail, if it please Allah. To obtain further sounds attach to the pipe from which the wind goes out three or four other pipes, each provided with a flue opening, and then you will obtain other wonderful sounds. And if the men blow harder, the sound will be stronger, and if they blow softer, the sound is gentler. In this way different kinds of sounds are obtained, producing effects that are pleasing, moving or otherwise. But the original purpose of this instrument is to project sound to a great distance, if Allah wills.

Without embarking on a detailed analysis of this long description, we may note the following points:

The first step is to make 'the brass apparatus', which is none other than Hero's pnigeus. Three air pipes are then inserted into the upper part of this, their free ends attached to three skins, each of which is in turn fed by two cylindrical bellows—probably piston pumps. The pnigeus is then placed in a large, hermetically sealed receptacle, leaving only its neck protruding. It would appear that at this point there is a gap in the text, for there is no description of the sound mechanism. Is there a thick reed on the air outlet pipe, or does the pipe simply narrow at the end so that the air, escaping at a high velocity, produces a kind of whistling?[51] It seems certain that the final part of the account is incomplete, for the author, having promised a detailed explanation of the process by which 'various wonderful sounds' may be obtained, rounds off his description in three lines. However, we are at liberty to assume that the organ pipes were attached only to small instruments of this type, with moderate air pressure.

If we accept the figures given here literally, the pressure generated would have been tremendous. The pnigeus would have had a capacity of approximately 10 c.m., and to fill it with air each bellows would have had to produce 1,600 l. Pressure at the outlet would thus easily have been equivalent to the weight of a column of 6 m. of water, since the pnigeus is 6.48 m. in height. This pressure is further increased by the fact that the receptacle is hermetically sealed. Indeed, the water, rising in the cistern under the thrust of the air filling the pnigeus, itself compresses the air above it and is subject to a counterpressure whose effect is to increase still further the force of the air issuing from the apparatus. The skins serve the same purpose. By closing the neck of the pnigeus by some undefined process, the skins swelled out with the air from the bellows; their elasticity and their weight added new impetus to the outflow of air when the siren was required to make a very loud noise.

This account mentions one fundamental detail which is omitted by both

---

[51] The second hypothesis appears much more likely, from Ktesibios's experiment: 'Ita pundus . . . cum premeret caeli crebritatem, vehementi discursu per fauces frequentiam caeli compressione solidatam extrudens in aerem patentem effusione acuti sonitus expresserat claritatem' (Vitruvius, *De Arch.*, ix, 8).

Hero and Vitruvius—the stopper for emptying the cistern. Briefly, if we imagine such an instrument built to a reasonable scale, and if we add the set of flue pipes mentioned in passing at the end of the text, we have the Graeco-Roman hydraulis as it appears in the iconography, give or take a few details. As for the 'King of the Inner Franks', said to have commissioned Muristus to build him a siren of this type, we have no means of identifying him. Possibly he is a Merovingian.

This is a suitable point at which to examine the much-quoted text of the 'Letter to Dardanus', long attributed to St. Jerome, but in fact anonymous. The Latin is rather careless, and the text probably dates from the late Empire.

First of all I come to the organ, because it is reckoned to surpass these in sound, with its tones of extreme loudness. A hollow container is made up of two elephant-hides sewn up together: air is squeezed into it from fifteen blacksmith's bellows, and with twelve bronze pipes of formidable power, it roars like thunder, so as to be distinctly audible at a thousand paces or even further. It is acknowledged that the organs of the Hebrews sound so loudly that from Jerusalem they can be heard on the Mount of Olives and even beyond it.[52]

At the beginning of the ninth century the Bishop of Mainz, Hrabanus Maurus, takes up the same text, though in better Latin, and adds a symbolic commentary:

The second division of music is organic [instrumental] music, which includes . . . the wind instruments: trumpets, pipes, flutes, organ, pandoura and the like . . . I take first of all the mighty voice of the organ (because it is reckoned as greater than all these types by virtue of the extreme brilliance of its sound). Two elephant hides are put together to form a reservoir: air is squeezed in by twelve blacksmith's bellows. Twelve bronze pipes, capable of greater sonority, roll like thunder, so that they are perfectly audible at a thousand paces and more, as, it is said, are the organs of the Hebrews, which may be heard distinctly from Jerusalem to the Mount of Olives, and even beyond it. There are said to be two kinds of organ, the first being that of which we have just spoken. The other is that quoted by the Prophet in connection with the wanderings of Israel before Babylon, saying: 'By the waters of Babylon' (Psalm 137). All this symbolizes the Gospel of Christ in the figurative and spiritual sense: the Gospel is made up of two things—the harshness of the two Laws. The twelve smith's bellows are the Patriarchs and the Prophets. Through the twelve bronze pipes, that is to say the Apostles, it sends forth a mighty noise, as it is written: 'Their noise is gone out through all the earth' (Psalm 19), signifying that the voice of the Gospel has been heard over the entire surface of the earth, as it is written: 'The voice of thy thunder was in the heaven' (Psalm 77). The thousand paces signify the perfect number ten, the number of the Words of the Law that go to make up this voice.[53]

[52] P.L. 30, 213.   [53] P.L. 111, 496–7.

The pseudo-Jerome of the *Dardanus Letter* was certainly acquainted with the instrument referred to by Muristus, at least through his reading. In giving it twelve musical pipes, fifteen pairs of bellows, and two skins he is, as we have seen, doing so in the interests of apologetics; but the fact that these skins bags are made from elephant hides seems to confirm the Byzantine-Arab origin of the machine. This again emerges in his parable of the assembly trumpet, fed by three pipes and producing a deafening clamour through four brass pipes.

The existence of the instrument is likewise noted in the *Book on Government*, supposedly a translation from the Greek through Syriac, dating from the ninth century:[54]

And it is necessary that there should be with thee the instrument which Yayastayus invented for warning people. And it is a pneumatic instrument used for various purposes, because it enables you to warn all your country, and prepare the troops the same day for advancing or retiring, or any other purpose necessary in a mighty army. And its sound will be heard sixty miles.

In the thirteenth century Roger Bacon again refers to this curious military machine, which he attributes to a certain Temistius.[55]

MUSICAL AUTOMATA

The Arabs' skill and knowledge in organ-building extended to musical automata, following the principles outlined by Ktesibios, Philo, and Hero. The most elementary of these devices, attributed to Archimedes in the Arabic text, consists of a simple closed tank into which water falls (Plate XXII, no. 1). This water forces the air into a pipe which ends in a flute, the flute being held by a figure whose body and neck conceal the pipe.[56] It is not impossible that this toy was indeed contrived by Archimedes himself, since he was interested among other things in pneumatic phenomena,[57] as a phrase of Zosimus seems to confirm: $τὰ$ $πνευματικὰ$ $Ἀρχιμήδους$.[58] The musical tree that graced Theophilus's reception chamber probably operated on this extremely simple principle. Less than a century later the Caliph Al-Muqtadir proudly displayed a similar instrument in his Palace in Baghdad, and an Arabic text describes this strange apparatus in the context of a visit paid to the Caliph by envoys from the Basileus in A.D. 917:

When the Ambassadors entered the Palace of the Tree and gazed upon the

[54] Farmer, p. 121. The author is unknown. Compare also the illustration from the 6th-century manuscript of St. Blasien, Pl. XXII, No. 2.

[55] *Secretum Secretorum*, ed. R. Steele (Oxford, 1920), v, 151.

[56] Farmer, p. 80.

[57] A Reymond, *Histoire des sciences exactes et naturelles dans l'Antiquité gréco-romaine* (Paris, 1924), pp. 71–2.

[58] Daremberg-Saglio, art. 'Hydraulus'.

Tree, their astonishment was great. For this was a tree of silver, weighing 500,000 *dirhams*[59] . . . and this is standing in the midst of a great circular tank filled with clear water. The tree has eighteen branches,[60] every branch having numerous twigs, on which sit all sorts of gold and silver birds, both large and small. Most of the branches of this tree are of silver, but some are of gold, and they spread into the air carrying leaves of divers colours. The leaves of the tree move as the wind blows, while the birds pipe and sing.[61]

The system of producing air by letting water into an ordinary tank has the great disadvantage that it stops once the tank is full. A much more ingenious device, giving not only a constant stream of air but a real melody, is attributed by the Arabs to Apollonios of Perga. This apparatus is described by one of the Banu-Musa (ninth century), the three scholars who worked in the House of Science in Baghdad under the enlightened patronage of the Caliph Al-Ma'mun. Probably the author has added some of his own improvements to the mechanism, for his account is extremely lengthy.[62] It begins thus:

In the name of Allah the merciful, we desire to show how to construct an instrument which automatically plays the flute, and in a continuous fashion, giving the desired melody, and capable of achieving either a slow rhythm or a rapid one.

This text, which is hardly relevant to the history of the organ, is preserved in a manuscript in the Greek Orthodox College of the Three Moons, in Beirut, and has been published in Arabic by Fr. Collangettes.[63] The instrument is described as box-shaped, and measuring, according to the data, 1 m. across and 1.50 m. in height. It consists of two cisterns, filling and emptying alternately by means of a system of valves controlled by a paddle-wheel. The air generated in this way is channelled into a flute pierced with nine holes to give nine sounds. A cylinder with suitably placed cogs operates small levers as it rotates, and these in turn open and close the holes in the flute, on the principle of our musical boxes. It was most likely an instrument of this type which graced the temple of Arsinoë-Zephyritis, and aroused the admiration of the poet Hedylus; and equally likely that an identical automaton played 'without a master, by a hidden device' in Byzantium's imperial

---

[59] Approximately 1,417 kg.

[60] The author of this account alternates between the imperfect and the present tense, for, though he is writing a hundred and fifty years after the events he is describing, he is borrowing material from an earlier chronicler.

[61] Translated from the Arabic by Guy Le Strange, 'A Greek Embassy to Bagdad in 917 A.D.', *The Journal of the Royal Asiatic Society* (1897), pp. 40–2.

[62] This apparatus has been reconstructed by E. Wiedemann, who has published a German translation of the document ('Ueber Musikautomaten bei den Arabern', *Centenario della nascita di M. Amari*, 1909, pp. 169 ff.).

[63] *Mashriq*, ix, 444–58.

baths. Fr. Kircher describes an apparatus somewhat similar to the Banu-Musa automaton as an automatic hydraulic organ,[64] and a similar machine was still entertaining visitors to Tivoli in the sixteenth century.[65]

In the twin capitals of Damascus and Baghdad, then, the Arab organ did not evolve significantly. More precisely, it evolved in a very special way, in the direction of the automaton, that ingenious, amusing and even amazing instrument that also originated in Alexandria. In Syria, however, the real tradition of the organ seems to have been maintained, as we shall have occasion to observe.

Curiously, the State organ used in Byzantium also failed to establish a tradition in after years. From that day to this no palace or official reception chamber has provided an organ to accompany the pomp of ceremonial occasions. Instead, a different future lay in store for the organ. Though strictly excluded from the churches of the East, it was destined to find its way into those of the West, and to become so much a part of them as to disappear almost entirely from secular use.

---

[64] *Musurgia Universalis*, op. cit., ii, p. 334.
[65] Montaigne, *Journal de Voyage*, 'Séjour à Rome'.

CHAPTER TWELVE

The Organ in Western Europe from the Eighth to the Tenth Centuries

The Carolingian organ and its early descendants are of great historical interest to the musicologist, not so much by virtue of any evolution in technique—this was actually quite rudimentary—as because of the curious circumstances surrounding the reappearance of the organ in western Europe. The darkness which descended in the wake of the great invasions had caused even the memory of the Graeco-Roman hydraulis to be erased. It was only with the arrival in France, in the middle of the eighth century, of a Byzantine organ, that the instrument became known again. Its resulting fresh growth was not a purely musical phenomenon, but the chance outcome of political and diplomatic events which must be outlined at this stage.

In Western Europe the onslaughts of the barbarian hordes had brought ruin and disaster. For three centuries after the last Roman emperor was deposed no substitute was found for Rome's authority, and instead a multitude of chiefs—Franks, Lombards, Visigoths, Ostrogoths, and Vandals —each controlling small territories, waged constant war among themselves. There was widespread distress, and intellectual life practically disappeared. In the arts there was little or no activity, with the sole exception of music, which flourished in the monasteries. Instrumental music indeed, both in manufacture and technique, fell far short of that of Rome and Byzantium. But religious vocal music, nurtured in the tranquil atmosphere of the monastic communities, blossomed in a most extraordinary fashion: this was the golden age of vocal monody, known today as Gregorian chant.

Pope Gregory I (540–64) is known to have taken a lively interest in Byzantine liturgical chant in the course of a long sojourn in the capital of the Eastern Empire, and on his return to Rome he undertook sweeping reforms in religious music. Later Pepin, and more especially Charlemagne, sent cantors to Rome in order to perfect their art and thus improve the Gallican liturgy and vocal music. As a sequel to this, schools of religious music were established in Gaul, first in the palace at Aix-la-Chapelle, then at Metz and St. Gall.[1] In certain monasteries—St. Gall in particular—the monks soon became interested in the making of instruments; thus when the organ appeared in Europe it was swiftly reproduced and fostered in the religious communities. This accounts for the fact that the two treatises on organ-building which have come down to us from the later Middle Ages are the work of ordinary monks.

It is difficult to trace the history of the organ during this period because of the scarcity of relevant documents. In addition, one has to distinguish carefully between the different meanings of the word 'organum'. It is used even more ambiguously now than in ancient times, and can be applied both to the pipe organ and to other things more or less closely connected with music. 'Organum' means 'organ'; but it also means 'any musical instrument'. In the texts inspired by Psalm 150, 'Laudate eum in chordis et in organo', it has no exact sense. A more formidable problem arises from the introduction of a certain style of vocal music which appeared in the ninth century under the name 'organum'; the various words deriving from this, 'organalis', 'organarius', 'organista', should be translated with caution, and only after a considered assessment of the context. I am convinced that the term 'organum', as applied to vocal writing, was no arbitrary choice; but this point will be discussed in due course.[2] It should also be noted that the word 'organa' was used to describe the religious services at which this music was performed. Thus the letter from Amaury, Bishop of Meaux, dated 1221, refers to church worship and cannot be taken as evidence that there were organs in the cathedral at this time,[3] any more than there were organs in the cathedral at Clermont-Ferrand in 1270.[4]

THE RETURN OF THE ORGAN

It was in the dawn of the Carolingian era that the organ made its dramatic re-entry into western Europe. It came from Constantinople as a gift from the Emperor Constantine Copronymus to Pepin the Short, King of the Franks. The sending of this precious instrument was more than a mere gesture of friendship from one monarch to another: it was, in fact, the outward manifestation of far-reaching political design.

Pepin was proclaimed King in 751 by the assembly of the Franks, and—most important—was anointed and crowned by Archbishop Boniface at the instance of Pope Zachary. By this flattering gesture, an honour never accorded to any of the Merovingian rulers, the Pope hoped to persuade the

[1] Th. Gérold, *La Musique au Moyen Age* (Paris, 1932), pp. 13 ff.
[2] See Chapter XVI.
[3] Du Cange, *Gloss. Med. et Inf. Latinit.*, art. 'Organum'.
[4] A. Tardieu, *Histoire de la ville de Clermont-Ferrand* (Moulins, 1870–1), p. 237.

Franks to help him ward off the threat from Lombardy.[5] Only scattered areas of Italy remained in the Eastern Emperor's possession, among them the Exarchate of Ravenna and the Duchy of Rome. Now the new Lombard king, Aistulf, had seized Ravenna and menaced Rome itself. Pope Stephen II, Zachary's successor, sent a delegation to Constantinople to ask for help; but it was a fruitless errand, for the Emperor Constantine V had no armed force in Italy worthy of the name, besides which he was entirely preoccupied with his iconoclastic campaign. Stephen II thus had to turn to Pepin for assistance. The danger from the Lombards was so acute that he made the journey to France himself to solicit the intervention of the Frankish armies. Pepin dispatched two expeditions, which easily won back the Exarchate and delivered Rome. Then, instead of restoring the territories to the emperor, he did homage for them to the Pope.

The emperor could hardly take military action in reply, since this was beyond his powers. Instead, he resorted to a somewhat surprising diplomatic manoeuvre. Between 756 and 769 he sent three delegations to Pepin, in the hope of persuading him to turn iconoclast.[6] These missions were accompanied by various gifts, and it was thus that, in 757, the organ arrived at the court of the Frankish king.

The arrival of this organ in the West appears to have captured the imagination of contemporary observers. All the Frankish chronicles of the time, and there are more than twenty,[7] record it as a highlight of the year 757. The *Annals of Fulda*, for instance, report the two outstanding events for that year:

DCCLVII. During a hunt, Aistulf, as the result of a fall from his horse, loses his kingdom and his life in one stroke. The Emperor Constantine sends, among other gifts to King Pepin, an organ (organum).[8]

Other chroniclers even go so far as to record nothing for that year except the arrival of the organ:

DCCLVII. The organ reaches France.[9]

Eginhard gives a little more detail:

DCCLVII. The Emperor Constantine sent numerous gifts to King Pepin, among them an organ (inter quae et organa), which reached him in his domain at Compiègne, where the general assembly of his people was then in progress.

[5] F. Lot, *Naissance de la France* (Paris, 1948), pp. 322 ff.

[6] L. Bréhier, *Vie et Mort de Byzance* (Paris, 1948), pp. 84 ff.

[7] They may be found in the *Recueil des Historiens de France*, by Dom Martin Bouquet (Paris, 1744), vol. v.

[8] The *Chronique de Frégédaire* merely records the fact that gifts were exchanged when the embassies arrived, without going into any detail (*Monumenta Germaniae Historica*, p. 186).

[9] *Chronicle of the Monastery of St. Gall.*

This piece of information, which is repeated in the *Chronicles of St. Arnulph* and the *Annals of the Franks*, has inspired several musicologists to write that the instrument was placed in the royal abbey of St. Corneille. The abbey did not even exist at the time, only being founded a hundred years later by Charles the Bald. However, this pious tradition has survived in the shape of a Latin inscription placed above the manuals of the organ in the Church of St. Jacques recording the restoration of 1768 and stating that 'in the opinion of the ancients' the present instrument contains fragments of Pepin's organ.[10]

Some texts contain an additional detail which is of greater historical import. In the Chronicle of the monastery of St. Arnulph, for example, we read:

The year of the incarnation of the Lord DCCLVII. The Emperor Constantine sent to King Pippin, among other gifts, an organ, an instrument never before seen in France (quod antea non visum fuerat in Francia).

Other texts reiterate this: 'Organum primitus venit in Franciam',[11] 'organa primum missa sunt Pipino'.[12] Thus all memory of the Gallo-Roman organ had been lost.

Of the instrument itself—how it looked, its size, its ultimate role, its mechanism—we know nothing. Presumably it was a bellows organ of the type then made by Byzantine craftsmen. At all events, it was well received. A thirteenth-century chronicle, referring to an earlier source, describes it as 'admirable',[13] and it may be this same source which is translated into French in the *Chronicle of St. Denis* in connection with the 'Gestes du Roi Pepin': 'En ce tens vindrent au roi le message de l'empereour Constentin . . . Entre les autres choses li ot envoié uns orgues de trop merveilleuse biauté. . . .'[14] (At that time came an embassy to the King from the Emperor Constantine . . . Among other things he sent him an organ of the most marvellous beauty. . . .)

A further text would appear to throw a little more light on the instrument received by Pepin. The monk of St. Gall, author of a narrative entitled *De gestis Caroli Magni regis Francorum et Imperatoris* and identified today with Notker the Stammerer, records, with considerable unction, the details of various embassies sent to Charlemagne. We read how in the year 812 the 'King of Constantinople' dispatched a delegation to the 'Most Glorious son of Pepin'. The ambassadors

brought with them all manner of musical instruments and divers objects; all

[10] Canon Delvigne, *Guide du Visiteur de l'église Saint-Jacques de Compiègne*, 1942, p. 17.
[11] *Ex Mariani Scoti Chronicorum . . .* anno 757.
[12] *Ex chronico Lamberti Schafnaburg*, anno 757.
[13] *Chronica Albrici monachi Trium Fontium*, M.G.H., 24, p. 710.
[14] *Recueil des Historiens de France*, v, p. 221.

were examined virtually in secret (dissimulanter) by the workmen of the most cunning Charles, and assembled with the utmost care, in particular this splendid musicians' organ (et praecipue illud musicorum organum praestantis-simum) with its cisterns wrought of bronze and its bellows of bull-hide, breathing sounds in a most stupendous fashion through its bronze pipes. It made a sound like the rumbling of thunder, or the trembling of the lyre, and had the charm of a peal of small bells (cymbalum). As to where it was installed, how long it lasted, how it was destroyed together with other objects of State, this is hardly the time or place to relate such matters.[15]

Notker's narrative is fascinating; but, although a number of people have accepted it as it stands, it appears to be based on some misapprehension. As far as we know to date, no other author mentions this episode, not even Eginhard, who misses no opportunity to record the slightest fact or incident that might enhance the glory of Charlemagne. The error may be explained by the following passage from the *Annals of the Kingdom of the Franks*, which describes an Arab embassy to the Emperor:

Year 807. The legate of the Persian king, named Ab'della, accompanied by monks . . . named Georgius and Felix (this Georgius being abbot at the Mount of Olives, his native country being Germany and his real name Egibald), came into the Emperor's presence bearing gifts . . . There was a pavilion and reception tents of all colours and of wondrous size and beauty . . . And there were also . . . many precious stuffs from Syria, perfumes, ointments and balm, and besides this a clock which struck the hours, a marvellous example of mechanical ingenuity . . . in which the twelve-hour cycle turned as in a water-clock. There was an equal number of small brass balls which fell with the passing of each hour, causing a bell to ring . . . All these things were brought to the Palace at Aix.[16]

Among the other gifts listed by the chronicler there is no trace of an organ. Either Notker unintentionally confused this delegation to Charlemagne with that received by Pippin, or he is going beyond the facts in order to enrich his narrative.[17] Strangely enough, there is no reference in Arabic sources to these exchanges of delegates and presents.[18]

It appears quite likely that the instrument described by Notker is none other than Pepin's organ. But the great virtue of this text is that it offers us a few precious scraps of information relating to the impact made by the organ

---

15 *De Gestis Caroli Magni Regis Franc. et Imper.*, book ii, *Recueil des Historiens de France*, v, p. 124.

16 *Annales Regni Francorum*, ed. Kurze (Hanover, 1895), pp. 123–4.

17 This is the origin of a great variety of errors reproduced by Dom Bédos, op. cit., p. viii; R. Brancour, *Histoire des Instruments de Musique* (Paris, 1921), p. 199; W. Apel, 'Early History of the Organ', *Speculum* (April, 1948), etc. . . .

18 Th. Houtsma and others, *Encyclopaedia of Islam* (Leyden/Paris, 1916), book 18, p. 228.

on the courtiers at Compiègne and Aix when it reached the Frankish court at the end of the eighth century or the beginning of the ninth. It was a magnificent instrument (praestantissimum), probably lavishly decorated and set with precious stones in the Byzantine tradition. The palace artisans, curious to know how it worked, examined it secretly. It was a pneumatic organ, with metal tanks fed by several pairs of bellows made of strong leather (doliis ex aere conflatis follibusque taurinis). The pipes, whose number is not specified, were of bronze and produced a wonderful sound.[19]

Still more interesting is the reference to the different timbres available on the organ—the rumbling of thunder (boatum tonitrui), the light quivering sound of the lyre (garrulitatem lyrae), and the charming tinkle of small bells (dulcedinem cymbali). Even allowing for poetic licence, it is possible that here three entirely different timbres are involved, produced by three distinct stops. It has been suggested[20] that the sound of thunder implies a heavy set of reed pipes, and the lyre effect a small set of flue pipes, while the tinkling of small bells could quite easily be obtained on a small mixture; and, although it has not been proved, this hypothesis has much to recommend it. As we have seen, the Byzantines were perfectly familiar with reed and flue pipes, and mixtures may have been in use since the time of the Antonines, as the Carthaginian lamp described earlier suggests. It should be said that the cymbalum referred to here is not the bronze cymbal whose loud percussive sound enlivened the cults of Dionysos and Cybele. This cymbalum was a row of small bells, often featured in the iconography of the later Middle Ages.[21] We shall meet it again in another context.[22]

From all these accounts it is evident that the organ was destined for the palace and not the church, exactly as it was in Byzantium. Historically it is unfortunate that the author of the *Gesta Caroli* did not pause to comment on the circumstances that led to the destruction of the instrument. He implies, however, that it did not perish alone, but in the company of other 'State' objects. But we have no idea whether they were destroyed as an act of war or perhaps consumed by fire.

GEORGIUS THE ORGAN-BUILDER

The second event marking the renaissance of the organ in the West took place half a century later, in the reign of Louis the Pious. Contemporary chroniclers record an incident of cardinal importance in the history of

[19] It seems to me that the Ingolstadt Chronicle, written in the sixteenth century and quoted by H. Riemann (*Präludien und Studien*, ii, Leipzig, 1900, p. 193), who refutes it, need not be taken seriously. It says that Pepin's organ had manuals that were played 'manuum peduumque digitis'!

[20] A. Gastoué, *L'orgue en France*, p. 32.

[21] Du Cange, op. cit., art. 'cymbalum'.   [22] p. 275.

music, namely the arrival of the first organ-builder at the court of Charlemagne's son. The craftsmen of the 'cunning Charles' had probably proved unequal to the task of reconstructing the instrument which had been destroyed; but it was still fondly remembered by the ruling family, so much so that when an unknown man boasted in the sovereign's presence of his ability as a maker of organs, he was immediately supplied with materials, workmen, and funds. This is how the incident is recalled in the Annals of Eginhard:

826. With Baldric there came a certain priest of Venice, named Georgius, who proclaimed himself able to construct an organ (se organum facere posse asserebat). The emperor despatched him to Aix with his Treasurer Tanculf, commanding that he should be given all that was necessary to make the instrument.[23]

Eginhard gives another, more detailed, account of this in his *Translation of the Holy Martyrs Marcellinus and Peter*:

Such are the miracles and prodigies that Our Lord Jesus Christ, by the merits of his Blessed martyrs Marcellinus and Peter, thought fit to bring about, in the village of Valenciennes, for the good of mankind. The celebrated priest Georgius has carefully preserved these events in writing, by collecting them in a small book. For our own part, we have thought it fitting to relate them in our own work. This Georgius, a native of Venice, came from his own country to the court of the emperor, where, at the palace of Aix, with consummate skill (mirifica arte), he constructed an organ, an instrument known in Greek as the *hydraulicon*.[24]

The author of the *Life of Louis the Pious* expresses himself in similar terms:

During this period . . . Baldric brought to the lord-emperor a certain priest named Gregory [*sic*], a good-living man, who proclaimed that he could build an organ in the Greek style (more Graecorum). The emperor received him joyfully; and, because he was introducing to the Frankish kingdom something that was as yet unknown there (illa quae antea inusitata erant), he thanked him publicly, commending him to Tanculf, minister of the Sacred Treasury, and ordered that he should be supported by public moneys. Then he decreed that he should be supplied with everything that he might need for his enterprise.[25]

Another version gives an additional detail:

826 . . . A certain Georgius, a priest from Venice, who arrived with Baldric, Count of Frioul, constructed a hydraulic organ at Aix.[26]

[23] Eginhard, *Annales, Recueil des Historiens de France*, op. cit., vi, p. 187.
[24] A. Teulet, *Oeuvres complètes d'Eginhard* (Paris, 1840), ii, p. 340.
[25] *M.G.H., Script.*, ii, p. 629.
[26] *Annales de Fulda, Recueil des Historiens de France*, vi, p. 209.

In 826 Louis the Pious was forty-eight years of age. According to Eginhard, he spent the summer at Ingelheim, where he received envoys from the Pope, the King of the Danes, and the Breton chieftains, and did not return to Aix until the onset of winter. Presumably, then, it was at Ingelheim, a small place near Mainz, that he received this unknown priest who professed himself able to build an organ. But who was this mysterious Georgius? It has been suggested[27] that he may be the Georgius Monachus who was a member of the embassy sent by Haroun al-Rashid to Charlemagne; but this is highly unlikely. Georgius Monachus was a German, whereas Georgius the priest was a Venetian. He had a knowledge of organ-building, but where had he learned his craft? Venice was at this time in constant commercial contact with the Levant, and in particular with Syria, where the organ was well known. Theoretically, however, it was still a dependency of Constantinople, and, this being so, it was just as probable that the priest Georgius gained his knowledge of organ-building in Constantinople itself. Moreover, he undertook to construct an instrument 'in the Byzantine style'.

Was it as a reward for his success that he received from the emperor the Abbacy of St.-Sauve? This may have been what happened, though Eginhard does not specifically say so:

In the palace of Aix the priest Georgius requested and received from the Abbot Eginhard relics of the blessed martyrs of Christ Marcellinus and Peter, which the Abbot had but lately received from Rome, whence his servants had brought them. Georgius then enclosed them in a shrine appropriately decorated with gold and precious stones, and had them taken by his deacon Theothard to the Basilica of St. Sauve the Martyr, which he then held as a benefice from the king.[28]

. . . Georgius, priest and Abbot of the Monastery of St. Sauve the Martyr, located in the village of Valenciennes,[29] in the Fomars district, on the bank of the Escaut . . .[30]

A further point is that Georgius arrived 'de sua patria'; but it is not clear whether the emperor, having heard of his skill, summoned him to the court, or whether he came of his own accord to offer his services. His reception, however, is curiously flattering, for the emperor immediately puts him in touch with his finance minister and orders that he is to be supplied with workmen and materials. What prompted this eagerness?

Travellers who had witnessed ceremonies at the Byzantine court had presumably brought back tales of the marvellous music made by the instru-

---

[27] H. G. Farmer, *The Organ of the Ancients*, p. 152.

[28] From *Hist. Transl.*, translated by Teulet, op. cit., ii, ch. 69, p. 333.

[29] Clearly it is not Saint-Savin in Poitou, as Gastoué writes (op. cit., p. 33). This mistake has been copied by a number of musicologists.

[30] *Hist. Transl.*, op. cit., ch. 68, p. 329.

ments with the pipes. But the reason underlying this slightly unexpected haste on the emperor's part was apparently not a purely musical one. We shall see that at this time the organ was considered by the Franks to be one of the most notable attributes of the glamour and prestige of the Eastern Empire, and we know that the Carolingians strove desperately to emulate the pomp of Constantinople.[31]

The texts suggest that the court of Louis the Pious was exceedingly proud of the fact that there was an organ in the Palace at Aix-la-Chapelle, and the Frankish sense of inferiority *vis-à-vis* the splendour of oriental ceremonial must have been somewhat diminished thereby. This, at any rate is the impression given by a poem glorifying Louis, written by a contemporary poet named Ermold le Noir. The piece has 2,649 lines, and is called *In honorem Hludowici Christianissimi Caesaris Augusti*. The reference to the organ built by the priest Georgius comes at the end of the episode describing the baptism of the Danes. Herold, their king, who has declared himself willing to become a Christian, arrives at Mainz, where Louis is holding court. After a banquet, followed by a hunt and an al fresco meal, Herold announces that he is placing his kingdom under Frankish protection. Then he sets off down the Rhine to return to his own country. The poet continues:

> Thus, Louis, do you bring your conquests to Almighty God
> And spread your aegis over noble kingdoms.
> The realms your forebears could not gain by force of arms
> Beg you of their own accord to seize them today.
> What neither mighty Rome nor Frankish power could crush,
> All this is yours, O Father, in Christ's name.
> Even the organ, never yet seen in France,
> Which was the overweening pride of Greece
> And which, in Constantinople, was the sole reason
> For them to feel superior to Thee—even that is now
> In the palace of Aix.
> This may well be a warning[32] to them, that they
> Must submit to the Frankish yoke,
> Now that their chief claim to glory is no more.
> France, applaud him, and do homage to Louis,
> Whose valour affords you so many benefits.[33]

Even allowing for the hyperbole of the text, which grossly exaggerates an event of minor importance, we can still gauge the importance attached by contemporary opinion to the presence of an organ in the Palace of Aix. For

[31] For the effects of Oriental influence on Gaul, see H. Pirenne, *Mahomet et Charlemagne* (Paris, 1937), pp. 112 ff.

[32] For the poet, the presence of the organ at Aix is sufficient justification for this threat.

[33] E. Faral, *Ermold le Noir* (Paris, 1932), 2515–27.

the Franks the whole concept of grandeur and majesty was bound up with this great instrument and its noble, hieratic music. This explains the emperor's ardour when presented with an unknown man claiming the ability to make such an instrument, and likewise the somewhat naïve pride of the courtiers who henceforth regard themselves as equal if not superior to the Byzantines.

Another text from the same period expresses the same idea, and adds some curious details to the picture of the imperial instrument. The author, better known than Ermold le Noir, is the Swabian Walahfrid Strabo, a monk of Fulda and preceptor of Charles the Bald. The work in question is rather an obscure poem of 268 lines, entitled *On the Statue of Theodoric*. It exalts Louis the Pious, comparing him with Moses and Solomon, while abusing the king of the Ostrogoths, whose statue, brought from Ravenna as a prize of war, has been erected by Charlemagne in front of the Palace at Aix.[34] Strabo, conversing with his Muse, whom he refers to as his 'star', paints a picture of the royal residence and its vast domain, where splendid buildings are set in gardens and parks, where game abounds and wild animals roam at will, and where the air is full of birdsong.[35]

But elsewhere, shining with a brilliant light,
A gilded knight capers, surrounded by a band of foot-followers.
One plays the bells, another the organ.[36]
A subtle melody sets their light hearts dancing
Till, losing consciousness, a woman
Breathes out her life under the music's spell.
Rome, let the vast image of your Colosseum[37] admit defeat!
This is far greater. Our great Caesar has but to state his wishes,
And all the achievements of this wretched world
Shall be transported to the Frankish citadels.
The organ, once the pride and joy of Greece
Is no marvel now to our great king.[38]
But if ours comes to no harm and continues to play as it has begun,
He who often disturbs the air with his hammer[39] will be idle.
But first he will cast his cloak, spurning its warmth,

[34] J. Calmette, *Charlemagne* (Paris, 1951), p. 38.

[35] This zoological park is also described by Ermold le Noir. It was located near the palace: 'Est locus insignis, regali proximus aulae' (op. cit., 1836).

[36] For reasons based essentially on the iconography, I think that this refers only to two instruments; see Chapter XV.

[37] When this poem was written the word 'Colossus' was applied to the amphitheatre and not to the huge statue of Nero. See H. Jordan, *Topographie der Stadt Rom Altertum* (Berlin, 1871), ii, p. 510, and iii, p. 285.

[38] That is to say, he no longer ranks it among the inaccessible wonders of the East.

[39] *Plectrum*, says Du Cange, is the term applied to the clapper of a bell. Here it means the hammer used to play a set of bells.

And, running mad, wielding an iron bar,
Will shatter the sounding trunks and the pipes with their unequal sounds.
It will not be in vain, for, though he goes unrewarded for his music,
At least the outer surface of the yellow gold
Might paint his dusky limbs to give him his reward.[40]

Though difficult to interpret and laced with hyperbole, these verses have some interest for the musicologist. In the course of a military parade (the gold-clad knight is probably the emperor himself)[41] the organ is heard in company with a chime of small bells—this type of instrumental ensemble was, as we shall see, very popular in the later Middle Ages. The scene is set in the courtyard of the palace, and the poet, having described the imperial park and gardens, now turns his attention to a different part (*alia de parte*) of the domain. It is quite inaccurate to claim, as Schubiger has done,[42] that the organ was installed in the chapel, for Walahfrid Strabo's text indicates that, on the contrary, it played outside the buildings. As for the effect created by this music on the listeners, this clearly reflects the instrument's prestige and the marvellous reports brought back by travellers in the East. The sudden demise of the woman listening to the concert is surely reminiscent of an Arabic text we saw earlier,[43] where it was claimed that the music issuing from the organ's pipes could cause people to die of joy.

The monk-poet gives evidence of an attitude of mind very similar to that expressed by Ermold le Noir, in that he somewhat passionately accuses the Byzantine Empire of having been excessively proud of the organ. Louis, secure in the knowledge that now he, too, had one in his apartments, feels that the instrument should not be the pretext for so much boasting. However, adds Strabo, if nothing happens to our organ,[44] then the musician who plays the bells must expect to lose his audience if he is to compete with the organist, whose glamorous instrument has such power to seduce. But is what happened next real or imaginary? The cymbalist, filled with envy and jealous of his companion's success, seizes an iron bar and, in his rage, shatters the graded pipes.[45] The closing lines may be interpreted as follows. By wantonly smashing the gilded organ pipes[46] (the pipes are known to have been covered in gold at the Byzantine court) the rejected musician stirs up a cloud of golden dust, which settles on his clothes—an absurd and totally unexpected reward!

[40] *M.G.H., Poetae Latinorum Medii Aevi*, ii, p. 374.
[41] See Ermold le Noir (2349–50): Caesar . . . aureus (2349–50).
[42] *Musikalische Spiciligien über das liturgische Drama, Orgelbau und Orgelspiel* (Berlin, 1876), p. 79.
[43] See above p. 181.
[44] Possibly an allusion to the destruction of Pepin's organ.
[45] The synecdoche recalls Prudentius's phrase: organa disparibus calamis (*Apoth.*, 389).
[46] 'Aurum fulvum' is reminiscent of Virgil, *Aeneid*, vii, 279.

'ORGANUM HYDRAULICUM' IN MEDIEVAL TEXTS

The use of the phrase 'organum hydraulicum', which occurs in several chronicles probably copied from one another, should not be allowed to mislead us. By the ninth century the hydraulis had completely disappeared, and survived among scholars purely as a literary memory. The system of hydraulic compression devised over a thousand years earlier had been abandoned for reasons which have already been given, and there is no doubt in my mind that the instrument constructed by the priest Georgius was a pneumatic organ similar in every way to those made by the Byzantine craftsmen of that era, with two bellows, air-bags, a manual and several ranks of musical pipes of distinctive timbres. The epithet 'hydraulic' is a literary relic borrowed from Vitruvius's treatise, which Eginhard knew intimately, having made a personal study of it, as is proved by a letter he wrote to his son Vussin: 'I have sent you those words and abstruse terms used by Vitruvius which I have been able to note so far, so that you may seek to establish their meaning. I think you will find the solution to most of these difficulties . . .'[47]

Eginhard is not alone in referring to the 'hydraulic organ'. Walahfrid Strabo, in an even more puzzling poem than the previous one, credits the instrument with a most amazing range of sounds.

> If thousands of flutes washed me with waves of sound,
> They could not compete with you.
> I offer what praise I can to you, from a fervent heart,
> For you deserve to be praised in ringing tones.
> Let the semitones sing for you in symphony, three by three,
> Let all the glory of harmony ring out for you.
> Let fourths be played on instruments with triple songs,
> Let the octave and the fifth sing in turn for you.
> Let an artist shout your praises on the loud hydraules,
> May you have a Colchian witch, fashioned from adamant.[48]

The poet Eugenius Vulgaris is the author of the following 'adonic metre' describing Linus, son of Apollo and teacher of Orpheus, filling the cisterns of his hydraulis with water:

> Sing, O ye peoples,
> Sing his praises everywhere
> With cunning tongues
> And learned poems.

[47] A. Teulet, op. cit., ii, letter XXX.

[48] Δίστιχοι πρὸς τὸν ἀρχὸν τῶν ἀγαθῶν, *M.G.H.*, p. 397. The last line is borrowed from a misinterpreted poem by Propertius, in which Medea of Colchis drives her bulls under a yoke of steel: 'Colchis flagrantis adamantina sub iuga tauros . . .' (*Eleg.*, iii, ii, 9). This piece of verse by Walahfrid Strabo undoubtedly alludes to a style of vocal music called *organum*, where the melody was doubled at the octave, fifth, and fourth, and here supported by the organ. See Chapter XVI.

> The group of musicians
> And the whole assembly,
> Even Orpheus himself
> Setting his instruments a-quiver,
> While Linus is carefully
> Filling his hydraules;
> Let them echo each other, saying:
> Leo Caesar,
> The one great emperor,
> Resplendent on his throne,
> Honoured as a god,
> Made happy by Providence,
> May he live for ever![49]

Several further allusions to the hydraulic organ are scattered through a number of texts dating from the Middle Ages. The monk Aurelianus Reomensis (ninth century), who had read Boethius, writes in his *Musica disciplina*:

The third species of music is played upon certain instruments, e.g. organs, citharas, lyres, and a number of others . . . [A distinction should be drawn between those that are played] by the degree of tension, as are the stringed instruments; or by blowing, as in the case of the tibia; and those that are activated by water, like the organs.[50]

The author of the treatise attributed to Hucbald and written during this same period mentions the hydraulis as having an interval of a tone between its first two bass pipes and a semitone between the third and fourth;[51] but he is clearly thinking of the bellows organ, since little or nothing was known at this time about the exact working of the hydraulic organ. The author of the Anonymous treatise of Berne (probably eleventh century) rounds off an excellent description of the bellows organ as it was at that time with the observation that 'these pipes may be hydraulic. All that is necessary is to fix a receptacle filled with water underneath them. The air sucks up the water, which it causes to flow into the pipes, making a sound.'[52]

At the end of the chapter dealing with the size of the pipes this anonymous author again refers to the hydraulis, but the text is so corrupt as to defy translation.[53] And finally, in the thirteenth century, Marcheti of Padua writes that water had to be poured into the pipes to make them sound: 'For water is very favourable to the formation of musical sounds, as is

[49] *M.G.H., Poet. Latin.*, iv, p. 425.
[50] Gerbert, *Script.*, op. cit., i, p. 33.
[51] ibid., pp. 109, 110 and 113.
[52] W. Nef, 'Der sogenannte Berner Orgeltraktat', *Acta Musicologica* (1948), vol. xx, p. 18.
[53] ibid., p. 15.

manifestly borne out by organ pipes, which are filled with water as they make their sound.'[54]

Jerome of Moravia is no better informed: 'The hydraulis is the sound of the organ . . . organ pipes are known as hydraules.'[55] The drawing in the Utrecht Psalter (ninth century), which is discussed elsewhere, reveals the same ignorance of the hydraulic organ.

THE CHURCH'S ATTITUDE TO THE ORGAN

Georgius is of prime importance on two counts: he was the first organ-builder in the West for some five centuries; and he passed on his knowledge to his pupils, who spread his teaching throughout Europe.[56] This coincided with a remarkable phenomenon whose consequences are still felt to this day. At the court of Constantinople the role of the instrument was strictly secular, and the organs of Pepin and Louis the Pious, too, were primarily designed for the royal palace. Henceforth, however, the organ in the West becomes increasingly involved with the Church. For almost three hundred years there is scarcely a mention of instruments being built for secular use. This naturally leads us to seek the reasons for such a development. The main one, as I see it, stems from the fact that during this period the monks were virtually the only group of people competent to make the pipes the correct size, and tune them, since both these operations called for a certain degree of instruction in arithmetic and acoustics. Moreover, Georgius was a priest, and soon retired to a monastery. His original pupils were therefore most probably monks. Thus it is hardly surprising that these pupils were tempted to dedicate the new and wonderful instrument to the exclusive service of the Christian religion.

The problems concerning the organ's first introduction into religious ceremonies have never been satisfactorily explained, and we may never know the truth of the matter, since at present there is no known official text among the pontifical archives which authorizes the use of the instrument in church.[57] There is a possible reason for this curious silence. As we have

[54] Gerbert, *Script.*, op. cit., iii, p. 67.

[55] Coussemaker Ch., *Script. de Musica*, i, pp. 5 and 6.

[56] There is no proof that Judith, Louis the Pious's wife, ever learned to play the organ, as Degering believes (op cit., p. 63), on the strength of an ambiguous line from W. Strabo: 'Organa dulcisono percurrit pectine Judith' (op. cit., p. 376).

[57] The question of when the organ was admitted to religious ceremonies is discussed by Dom Bedos (op. cit. Preface, pp. vii and viii): 'The illustrious Duranti, First President of the Parlement of Toulouse, examines this question in his excellent Treatise on the Rites of the Catholic Church. He believes that organs were first introduced into the Churches a long time ago. He bases this view on what is said by a Commentator of the Holy Scriptures who, he says, lived before the time of St. Gregory the Great, when interpreting a verse of Job: that *the use of Organs was not forbidden, for it is possible to use them in a spirit of piety, and they are even employed in the Churches.* I do not know the name of this writer.'

seen, the Church Fathers regarded all instrumental music as suspect; and when, on feast days, the faithful brought to the services a small portable organ which they used to accompany their singing, the helpless clergy turned a blind eye to what, for those who know their St. Augustine, was both improper and dangerous. But later, after the success of Georgius, who was a priest, many clerics probably succumbed to the charm of the new instrument and were attracted by its sustained sound, which was to some extent religious in character and was certainly more appropriate to the liturgy than stringed instruments or cornets. And so the organ, though never officially acknowledged in the pontifical decrees, and tolerated rather than accepted by the hierarchy,[58] gradually established itself until, by the fourteenth century, it was the established servant of Christian worship. Those documents purporting to prove that the church organ was accepted by authority even before Pepin's time are historically worthless. Platina, librarian of Sixtus IV, attributes to Pope Vitalian (656–72) the reform of ecclesiastical chant and the use of the organ in divine worship.[59] The poet Battista of Mantua, a contemporary of Platina, is even more specific:

> The Signian[60] added organs forged in soft metal,
> Which rang out to accompany the religious ceremonies on feast days.[61]

However, both Platina and Battista were writing around 1480, more than eight centuries later, and both based their assertions on tradition. Platina makes no secret of this, and qualifies his words by the phrase 'some say'. There can be little doubt that, if organs had been heard in Rome during the second half of the seventh century, the poets at Pepin's court and at that of his grandson Louis would not have written in the vein they did, and their enthusiasm would have been more moderate. For this reason the famous passage written by Fortunatus, Bishop of Poitiers in the sixth century, should not be taken literally. It seems to me more a scholarly recollection of his reading in the classics than a true description of the choir school at Notre-Dame de Paris in the time of St. Germanus, who had died in 448, a hundred and fifty years previously:

> In their midst is Germanus, honourable master,
> Now keeping the young men in order, now raising up the old.
> The deacons go before, there follows the important order [of singers?] . . .

---

[58] Dom Bédos also says (though this time he fails to reveal his sources) that the church organ was opposed in the twelfth century by the Petrobrusians, forebears of the Albigensians (Preface, p. xviii).

[59] *De Vitis Pontificum* (Venice, 1479): '. . . et cantum ordonavit adhibitis consonantiam (ut quidam volunt) organis.'

[60] Vitalian was born at Signia in Campania.

[61] Gerbert, *De Cantu*, op. cit., ii, p. 141.

Here a child plays upon instruments with small pipes;[62]
And here an old man blows into a large trumpet;
The sound of the cymbalum mingles with that of the high pipes . . .
The flute sounds sweetly, varying its modes,
The children's oboes join soothingly with the harsh drums of the old men,
The words of the men, by their music, revivify the lyre.
Here the melody goes sweetly on, and here it is full of fire,
The effect varies according to sex and age.[63]

The tone of the poem clearly suggests that it is to be regarded as an imaginative word-picture of the different instruments and voice registers which combined within the choir school.[64] Similarly the phrase—certainly of Biblical origin—used in telling of the death of St. Lambert in 708 in no way implies the actual presence of an organ.

The appearance of the 'great organ' in churches was to provoke varied reactions, some idea of which is given in a document dating from a later century. This is the latter addressed by Baldric, Bishop of Dol, to the people of Fécamp, following a visit he made to the town. The text, written some time between 1114 and 1130, reveals that occasionally feelings of envy and spite filled the hearts of the faithful whose church had no organ:

In this church [of the Abbey at Fécamp] there was something which caused me no small pleasure . . . which David included in his psalms to praise God and stimulate us: 'praise the Lord upon the strings and the organ' (Psalm CL). Since there indeed I saw a musical instrument made of bronze pipes (fistulis aeneis) and set in motion with blacksmiths' bellows (follibus fabrilibus); and it gave forth pleasant music. Low, medium, and high notes mingled in a continuous unison and a symphony of sound, and it was as though a choir of clerks sang together with the voices of children, old men and youths united in a joyful sound and persisting therein. They called this instrument 'organ', and it was played at fixed times (certis temporibus).

I am not, however, unaware that there are many people who, having nothing resembling this in their churches, cast stones at those who have them and upbraid them. We have no hesitation in describing such men as slanderers and detractors, incapable of explaining what the organ means to us. Perhaps they have not read that the most blessed David calmed the transports of Saul, who was possessed of the devil, with the sound of his lyre . . . For myself, I take no great pleasure in the sound of the organ (ego siquidem in modulationibus organicis non multum delector); but it encourages me to reflect that, just as divers pipes, of differing weight and size, sound together in a single

---

[62] 'Organa exiguis cannis' could also mean a syrinx.
[63] *M.G.H., Auct. Antiqu., Fortunatus*, pp. 38–9.
[64] Gastoué shares this view (*L'orgue en France*, p. 24). However, J.-E. Bertrand (*Histoire de l'orgue. Son introduction dans le culte chrétien*, Paris, 1958) and W. Apel (op. cit., p. 191) thought that the lines referred to a full-scale orchestra with an organ.

melody as a result of the air in them, so men should think the same thoughts, and inspired by the Holy Spirit, unite in a single purpose . . . All this I have learned from the organs installed in this church. Are we not the organs of the Holy Spirit? And let any man who banishes them from the church likewise banish all vocal sound, and let him pray, with Moses, through motionless lips . . . For ourselves, we speak categorically—because organs are a good thing, if we regard them as mysteries and derive from them a spiritual harmony; it is this harmony that the Moderator[65] of all things has instilled in us, by putting together elements entirely discordant in themselves and binding them together by a harmonious rhythm . . . Therefore if we possess organs we undertake to use them in accordance with ecclesiastical custom; and if we have none, we can do without them without committing sacrilege. As we listen to the organs, let us be drawn together by a deeper harmony, and be cemented together by a two-fold charity . . .[66]

As early as the twelfth century, therefore, the Abbey of Fécamp housed an instrument of some importance, permanently installed in the church, where, as in the case of St. Oswald's organ, it was played only on feast days. Baldric's letter seems to have been aimed at soothing the discontent that was rampant in those parishes where there was no organ, and, in making his appeal, he uses the time-honoured symbolism of the Church Fathers. But the hostility directed at the organ was by no means always motivated by envy. Even at this stage its misuse during divine worship may well have antagonized a number of clerics and convinced them that it disturbed prayer. This was certainly the feeling of an English monk living at this time; St. Aelred, Abbot of the Cistercian abbey of Riévaulx in Yorkshire, who in 1166 delivered an impassioned diatribe against the abuses of instrumental and vocal music during services:

Let us now turn to those who, under cover of religion, conceal the care they lavish on their pleasures . . . I ask you why, when statues and images are being abandoned, why, I ask you, do we see in the Church so great a number of organs and sets of bells (tot organa, tot cymbala)? What use, pray, is this terrifying blast from the bellows that is better suited to imitate the noise of thunder than the sweetness of the human voice? . . . During all this [distorted singing] the people, standing trembling and speechless, are amazed by the throb of the bellows (sonitum follium), the jingling of the little bells (crepitum cymbalorum), the harmony of the flue pipes (harmoniam fistularum) . . . It is as though the crowd had assembled, not in a place of worship, but in a theatre, not to pray, but to witness a spectacle.[67]

[65] Play on words: 'moderator' is also applied to the organist.
[66] *P.L.*, clxvi, 1177–8.
[67] *P.L.*, cxcv, 571, *De vana aurium voluptate*. Writing at the same time, John of Salisbury (*P.L.*, cxcix, 401 ff.) also fulminates against singers, but makes no mention of the organ.

This tirade is, in fact, directed not so much at the organ as at the singers;[68] but it brings two interesting points to light. The bellows, roughly made, are noisy, and from the nave they can be heard almost as clearly as the music from the pipes. Further, the organ in this instance plays in the company of a set of small bells known as a *cymbalum*: the iconography of the period frequently illustrates this association. According to the chronicle of the Abbots of Lobbes (in Belgium), the Bishop of Arras had the organ and bells of the Abbey transferred to his own church:

1134. The organ which Abbott Fulcuin, of blessed memory, had given to be used in the divine worship of the church, had to be removed from thence; the Bishop of Arras, himself an accomplished organist,[69] had it transferred to his own church. Likewise the set of bells, which . . . were used in divine worship, were removed.[70]

THE ORGAN IN THE NINTH AND TENTH CENTURIES

From the last quarter of the ninth century the pupils of Georgius dispersed all over Europe, and certain regions quickly acquired a great reputation for organ-building. Thus Pope John VIII (872–82) commissioned Bishop Anno of Freising in Bavaria to find him an organ and someone to play it:

. . . If the revenues have not reached us by the due date, we shall be forced to ascribe this specifically to your slothful negligence, and not to that of another. Furthermore I charge you to send us, for the purpose of teaching the science of music, an excellent organ (optimum organum) together with an organist capable of playing upon it and drawing the maximum amount of music from it.[71]

The implication is that if the pontiff looks so far afield for a good organ this was because none were being built in Italy, whereas Bavaria's reputation in this sphere was established. Moreover, centres of organ manufacture evidently also trained organists and musicians. John VIII makes it quite plain why he wants the organ—not to be played in church but to be used in the teaching of music in its theory and practice. In fact, the oldest known treatises on pipe measurement date from the end of the ninth century. He may perhaps have intended to train organ-builders for Italy and at the same time teach organists to accompany chants. But this is pure hypothesis, for there are no documents dating from this time to prove that the organ was ever used in

[68] On the attitude of the Church towards cantors, see S. Corbin, *L'Eglise à la conquête de sa musique* (Paris, 1960), pp. 51 ff.

[69] For Du Cange, 'incentor' sometimes means the precentor. Here, however, 'huiusmodi maxime incentor' suggests that it is the quality of the instrumentalist which is involved.

[70] *M.G.H.*, xxi, p. 326.

[71] *M.G.H., Epist. Merov. et Karol. Aevi.* v, anno 873, p. 287.

divine worship. (It is very doubtful whether the church at Tona, in Cata-
lonia, possessed such an intrument in 888—the relevant text is ambiguous.[72]

It is certain, however, that the chronicle of the monk Ademar (998–1034)
refers to the art of vocal organum. It tells how Charlemagne, anxious to
promote ecclesiastical chant, sent for two excellent Roman musicians,
Theodore and Benedict, who came to France to train Charlemagne's own
singers 'in arte organandi'.[73]

But from the beginning of the tenth century the organ makes its appearance in monasteries for the liturgical service. This is proved by the
Liber de Temporibus of Albert Milion, where the gifts of a certain rich bene-
factor are enumerated:

The year of Our Lord 915 . . . Count Atto set up the said monastery on the
summit of Canusina, in honour of St. Apollonius the confessor. He endowed it
with many ornaments and obtained for this same monastery gold and silver
vessels and ornaments for the celebration of divine worship. He installed an
abbot and monks, and caused an organ to be built in honour of the confessor.[74]

The *Life of St. Oswald the Younger* records the following events, dating
from the year 992:

In honour of God and St. Benedict, and for the glory of the Church, he commissioned a wooden panel to be made for the front of the high altar . . .
Moreover, he paid out thirty pounds to make copper organ pipes (ad fabric-
andos cupreos organorum calamos). These were arranged in close ranks,
[their lower orifice] set in a socket, and vibrated on feast days to the somewhat
fierce blast of air from the bellows, giving out a sweet cantilena or a loud burst
of sound which may be heard afar off (clangorem longius resonantem). And
all this was duly accomplished as the result of a vow, for the former dedication
had disappeared with the old building.[75]

The instrument described here seems to have had at least two sets of
pipes, one of which was probably made up of strong reeds. He says categorically that it was only played on feast days. During this same period
England's St. Dunstan (*c.* 924–88) provided an organ for the monastery of
Malmesbury:

In his deep generosity to this place, he frequently gave objects regarded at
that time as truly marvellous in England, and which bear witness to the quality
and intelligence of the giver. Among them were . . . organs, in which a

---

[72] 'Ad ipsus dedicationem tradimus nos: ego Albarus prbr. calicem et patenam,
Missalem, Lectionarium et organum . . .' (Higini Angles, *La Musica a Catalunya
fins al Segle XIII*, Barcelona, 1935, p. 82).

[73] *P.L.*, cxli, 27–8. A seventeenth-century edition adds 'Imo Romanos Organistas
advocat in Galliam, qui Francos organa pulsare doceant' (*Hist. Franc. Epitome*, Paris,
1652, p. 126–7.)

[74] *M.G.H., Script.*, *Liber de Temporibus*, CLVII, p. 431.

[75] *Acta SS Bened.*, xxvii, p. 755–6.

bellows is tortured into belching forth blasts of air, and as soon as they are produced, they are fed through bronze pipes, made according to musical measurements. And there he had this couplet engraved on a bronze plaque:

These organs [were made] by Bishop Dunstan in honour of St. Aldhelm; He who removes them hence, may he forfeit the Kingdom of Heaven.[76]

St. Dunstan was himself a musician, and his biographer claims he was skilled in all the arts, and played several instruments, 'like David, taking up his psaltery, plucking the cithara, playing the organ, beating the cymbalum.'[77]

There is good reason, too, for the presence of St. Aldhelm's name on the dedicatory plaque, for he is said to have been another passionate music-lover, and certainly his works are liberally punctuated by allusions to the art,[78] while his knowledge of the organ is indisputable. It is not known whether he had had the opportunity of hearing the instrument in the course of his travels, or had simply heard tell of it from people who had visited Constantinople and the Middle East. But in his long poem *De Virginitate* he speaks of it with eloquence and even emotion:

The babbling poem is perhaps not strong enough to do full justice to
A boundless chastity in its raucous verses,
Although all mouths extol it with a thousand tongues,
Just as organs are made to breathe with the air from bellows
And the music sings songs with short broken notes.

And elsewhere:

Let us then sing hymns to Christ on the strings of the cithara.
But if perchance this music is rejected,
If more is wanted than the strings quivering under the plectrum,
Those strings on which the good Psalmist used to accompany himself
    long ago,
If a man longs to sate his soul with ardent music,
And spurns the solace of a thin cantilena,
Let him listen to the mighty organs with their thousand breaths,
And lull his hearing with the air-filled bellows,
However much the rest [of it] dazzles with its golden casings
Who can truly fathom the mysteries of such things,
Or unravel the secrets of the all-knowing God?[79]

Aldhelm also takes the organ as the subject of his thirteenth Riddle:

[76] William of Malmesbury, *De gestis Pontif. Anglorum*, P.L., clxxix, 1660.
[77] *Vita Santi Dunstani auctore Osberno*, P.L., cxxxvii, 420.
[78] J. H. Pitman, *The Riddles of Aldhelm*, New Haven, 1925, p. 69.
[79] *M.G.H.*, *Aldhelmi opera*, pp. 466 and 355–6. It is possible that the following passage refers to the organ: '. . . licet organica bis quinquagenis et ter quinis sonorum vocibus concreparet armonia . . .' (ibid., p. 292).

The heralds may sound their horns of hollow bronze,
The citharas twang, the trumpets blow their bright note,
My entrails blast forth a hundred songs;
In my presence, nothing speaks; nor voice, nor [instrument] of fibrous
gut.[80]

The detailed accuracy of the first two texts is perplexing, and prompts us to ask ourselves if the organ did perhaps exist in England as early as the second half of the seventh century, a hundred years before Constantine's gift to Pepin. The lack of any documentary evidence precludes any definite conclusion, but the possibility remains. Whatever the truth may be, the organ rapidly gained in popularity in England, for in the middle of the tenth century a monumental instrument was built in the Church of St. Peter at Winchester, by order of Bishop Elphege, who died in 951.[81]

In France, the churches followed the general trend, and even though it is doubtful whether the monastery of St. Florent at Saumur had been endowed with an organ by the efforts of the Abbot Sigon[82] by the end of the tenth century, it has been established that several centres of organ-building were in existence at this time. A letter from Gerbert, a native of Auvergne, Abbot of Bobio and future Pope, to the monk Bernard, suggests that during this period an organ-builder of repute was working at the Abbey of Fleury (St.-Benoît-sur-Loire):

If one of you were interested in making a thorough study of music and those matters concerning organs (*et in his quae fiunt ex organis*), I should arrange for him, since I cannot do so myself, to fill the gaps in his knowledge by studying with Constantius at the Abbey of Fleury, on condition that I have the assurance that the Lord Abbot, Raymond, to whom I owe everything, agrees to this. [This Constantius] is very distinguished man of learning, and very well educated, who is firmly bound to me by the ties of friendship . . .[83]

This organ-building monk, who had possibly learned his craft from Gerbert himself, held the position of grand cantor at the Abbey and is thought to be the author of a hymn on the translation of St. Benedict's remains.[84]

---

[80] ibid., p. 103.

[81] *P.L.*, cxxxvii, 110–11. A detailed description will be given later.

[82] The much-quoted lines: 'Karitate Sigo noster plenus atque gratia . . . singularis organali regnabat in musica' would appear to refer to the art of vocal organum. Fr. Bösken's assertion (*Beiträge zur Orgelgeschichte des Mittelrheins bis zum Beginn des 16. Jahrhunderts, Kirchenmusikalisches Jahrbuch*, 1961, xlv, pp. 82 ff.), that the cathedral of St. Stephan, at Mainz, possessed an organ in the tenth century, is purely hypothetical and is not based on any documentary evidence.

[83] *P.L.*, cxxxix, 224–5, epist. 92.

[84] This information was supplied by Fr. Médard-Louillet, former organist at the Abbey, who is preparing a book on the history of Fleury. This Constantius is perhaps also the Constantine mentioned by Malmesbury as having been the 'conphilosophus et studiorum socior' of Gerbert (*De Gestis Regum Angl., Recueil des historiens de France*, x, p. 244).

A further letter, written from Rheims—Gerbert was appointed arch-bishop of that town by Hugh Capet in 992—concerns an organ which a certain Gerald had asked him to procure. The instrument appears to have been built in Italy, perhaps by Gerbert himself while he was still at the Abbey of Bobio: 'As to the organs you have enjoined me to send you, they are in Italy, where they are being maintained with great care. As soon as peace returns you shall have them, as you desire.'[85] The Abbot Gerald having died, his successor, Raymond, sent a renewed request for the instrument to Gerbert, who was at the time on a journey to the 'land of the Saxons' with Theophania, wife of the German Emperor Otho II:

Since my sovereign lady Theophania, my most august empress, commands me to accompany her on a journey to the country of the Saxons; and since I have asked some of my monks and soldiers to join us there from Italy, I am for the time being unable to write with any certainty of the organs stored in Italy, or of the monk who must be sent to install them. Above all, in the absence of my sovereign lady, I should not venture to rely on the loyalty of my soldiers, since they are Italians.[86]

The organ was still not forthcoming; and when Raymond again wrote to inquire about it Gerbert replied that events prevented him from attending to the matter: 'Circumstances have further postponed my journey to Italy, where I have left the organs and most of my effects. I have had no means of parrying such strokes of fate; and God has even now not made it clear to me at which port I am to stop.'[87]

It is not known if Raymond ever received his instrument; but his reiter-ated requests show that the monastery of Aurillac, of which he was the head, stood in real need of an organ. The episode also testifies to the great reputation that Gerbert had acquired as an expert on organ-building. But where did he learn this complex art? Presumably at the monastery of Aurillac, where he had pursued his studies; but he could also have learned it from the Arabs. We know that he lived for a long time in Spain, probably in Cordova, then ruled by the Caliph Al-Hakam II..[88] According to William of Malmes-bury, he went there with the intention of furthering his scientific and musical knowledge, and certainly in his sixties he was still devoting his life to research in mechanics. One passage even claims that he knew the work of Hero of Alexandria, and attempted to reconstruct a hydraulic organ:

. . . Subsequently Robert, king of France[89] . . . appointed him Archbishop of Rheims. In that church there is still evidence[90] of his scientific knowledge;

[85] *P.L.*, cxxxix, 220, epist. 61.   [86] ibid., epist. 91.   [87] ibid., epist. 170.
[88] Farmer, op. cit., *Gerbert and the Arabian Contact*, pp. 177 ff.
[89] Robert II, son of Hugh Capet.
[90] Malmesbury was writing in the first half of the twelfth century, and Gerbert died in 1003.

a clock constructed on mechanical principles, and a hydraulic organ (organum hydraulicum) in which the air, displaced in an amazing way by the violence of heated water (per violentiam aquae calefactae) fills the hollow interior of the instrument, and bronze pipes emit harmonious sounds through passages with many apertures.[91]

Commentators have been intrigued by the words 'aquae calefactae'. Is this strange instrument to be regarded as some kind of steam organ? Presumably not, for he says clearly that it is the air propelled by the water (ventus emergens) that causes the pipes to sound. Is it an aeolipyle (a type of steam turbine described by Hero), as Gastoué believed?[92] No, for the words 'modulatos clamores . . . aereae fistulae' invalidate such a hypothesis. The text only makes sense if instead of the word 'calefactae' we read 'calcatae', deriving from the verb 'calco' 'I press'—the water is pressed by the wind. Seen in this light, Malmesbury's account becomes perfectly clear: the air, produced by the agitation of the water, makes the bronze pipes sing melodious strains.

The learned Gerbert had therefore successfully reconstructed Ktesibios's hydraulic organ: but had he fully understood the extremely technical treatises of Hero and Vitruvius, or had he been given the opportunity to see such an instrument among the Arabs of Cordova? The first hypothesis is the more likely one. The astonishing thing is that he had no hesitation in installing this hydraulis in his church, which suggests that the music it produced was not unworthy to be heard in the sanctuary.

The organ is said to have been played in Cologne Cathedral in 953 at the consecration of Archbishop Bruno, brother of Otho I, Emperor of Germany: but the text of the life of St. Bruno, which reports this fact, is ambiguous. It tells of the joy that reigned among the faithful and expressed itself in all kinds of rejoicing, on the organs, and also the 'cymbala' (organis nihilominus et cymbalis). The context obliges us to ask whether this is not perhaps a Biblical formula.[93] Likewise the reference in a short poem by Walahfrid Strabo in honour of the visit of Charles the Bald to the Monastery of Reichnau in 829 is probably a poetic image:

> Bring the harps and flutes,
> The organ with the cymbals;
> Whatever music's art provides
> With air, mouth, and beat.[94]

[91] *De Gestis Regum Anglorum,* op. cit., x, p. 224.
[92] *L'orgue en France,* p. 34. It is out of the question that a steam-driven organ could have been constructed at that time. See F. M. Feldhaus, *Die Maschine im Leben der Völker* (Basle-Stuttgart, 1954), p. 177.
[93] *M.G.H., Script.,* iv, p. 259.
[94] *M.G.H., Poet. Latin.,* ii, p. 406.

A more exact account is that of the consecration in 972 of the church of the monastery of St. Benedict of Bages, in the diocese of Vich, in Spain: 'The priests and deacons joyfully sang their praises to God; and near the entrance, the organ poured forth music that could be heard from afar, praising and blessing the Lord.'[95]

Two ancient charters published by Ugelli led Du Cange[96] to believe that the church at Verona possessed organs from the time of Charlemagne. However, Murator explains this misapprehension by the fact that one of the gates of the city was known as 'the organ gate', and that a convent was established near by which took the name of 'St. Mary of the Organ.'[97] But this still does not tell us why the gate was given its name in the first place.[98] Perhaps it was a relic of the late Empire. A different kind of error misled Grattan Flood, and others who have reproduced it without checking its origins. In Flood's *History of Irish Music* he writes that, according to the *Annals of Ulster*, the church at Cloncraff had been endowed with an organ which was destroyed by fire in 814.[99] Here the confusion arises from a faulty translation into Latin of these Irish annals, and a fanciful interpretion by Gratton Flood himself. The real story tells of the sacking of a church and the murder of a man—but there is no mention of either a fire or an organ.[100]

Where seventeenth and eighteenth century authors speak of events in the distant past, these should be accepted only with considerable reservations. Thus Ziegelbauer alleges the existence of an organ in the church at Augsburg about the year 800 and Praetorius one at Halberstadt and Erfurt in the tenth century.[101] As early as the tenth century, however, we do find genuine evidence of the spread of the organ in Europe—the Winchester instrument and those of St. Oswald and Gerbert have already been quoted. From this time, too, date the first treatises on the measurement of organ pipes, and the state of organ-building is broadly outlined in the poem by the monk Wulstan to be discussed in the following chapter.

---

95 *La Musica a Catalunya*, pp. 80 ff.

96 *Glossarium*, art. 'organum'.

97 Quoted by Gerbert, *De Cantu*, ii, p. 142.

98 I was unable to consult Ugelli's work.

99 Grattan Flood, *A History of Irish music* (Dublin, 1906), p. 31.

100 The Erse word *orgain*, depending on the accent, can mean either organ or pillage— hence the error. This information was supplied by R. A. Wilson of the British Museum.

101 E. Buhle, *Die musikalischen Instrumente in den Miniaturen des frühen Mittelalters* (Leipzig, 1903), p. 59, note 3, and p. 66, notes 5 and 6. According to G. Frotscher (*Geschichte des Orgelspiels und Orgelkomposition*, Berlin, 1935, i, p. 16), who does not give his sources, the Frauenkirche in Augsburg had an organ in the ninth century, thanks to Bishop Wicterp. This is probably mere legend.

CHAPTER THIRTEEN

Techniques in Organ-building in the Tenth and Eleventh Centuries

From the later Middle Ages two treatises on organ-building have survived—short didactic accounts dealing as much with the making of the pipes as with the wind-chest, manual, and air ducts. These two texts, though written in sometimes obscure Latin, are extremely valuable in helping us to trace the history of organ-building in those centuries about which we know so little. Moreover, they are more complete and in a way more precise than those of Hero and Vitruvius, which discuss only the wind-chest and the wind-mechanism. Indeed, these treatises discuss important topics lacking in the ancient texts, namely the materials used and the actual manufacturing processes. Reading them through, however, it becomes strikingly apparent that the instruments discussed are fitted with a rather clumsy mechanism, making them not at all easy to play—their whole conception seems in more ways than one to represent a step backward from Vitruvius. At first sight this is astonishing; but the phenomenon is entirely in keeping with the poverty of the times. Nevertheless, the organ of the tenth and eleventh centuries is particularly interesting, since it was the direct precursor of that complex and wonderful ensemble, the great cathedral organ of the Renaissance.

THE ORGAN AT WINCHESTER

Before discussing the texts of these treatises, I should like to quote from a long poem dedicated by the monk Wulstan to his bishop, Elphege. This refers to the installation in the church at Winchester[1] of an organ which, for its time, was of monumental size. It is not a technical account in the true sense, but rather a literary description, full of imagery, yet sufficently detailed to take its place beside the treatises. The poem was written a little after 966.[2]

[1] Not Westminster, as Dom Bédos has written, op. cit., Preface, p. xi.
[2] M. Manitius, *Geschichte der Lateinischen Literatur des Mittelalters* (Munich, 1923), ii, pp. 442–6.

Here you have built organs greater than may be seen elsewhere;
They are set solidly on a double plinth.
Above, twelve bellows are set out in a row;
While fourteen lie below.
Their alternating blasts supply vast quantities of wind,
Worked by the might of seventy strong men,
Labouring with their arms, running with sweat,
Each urging his companions to force the wind up
With all his strength, filling
The wind-chest's vast cavity that it may rumble.
It alone supports four hundred 'musics', ranged in order,
And ruled by a skilled hand of melodious skill.
When closed, it opens them, and when open, he closes them,
To produce the varied sound the muse requires.
And two like-minded brothers sit at the instrument,
Each master of his own manual (alphabetum suum).
Moreover, there are holes hidden by forty tongues (linguis),
Ten holes along each tongue.
Some tongues slide forward, others back,
Giving each note (singula puncta) its proper value.
Thus the seven notes of the scale mark the 'Jubilum' in cadence,
Mingling with the sound of the lyric semitone (lyrici semitoni).
Like thunder, the strident voice assails the ear,
Shutting out all other sounds than its own;
Such are its reverberations, echoing here and there,
That each man lifts his hands to stop his ears,
Unable as he draws near to tolerate the roaring
of so many different and noisy combinations.
The music of the pipes is heard throughout the town,
And their winged fame goes forth through the land.
Thy solicitude has dedicated this ornament to the mighty Church,
And has built it in honour of Peter, the Blessed Turnkey.[3]

For all its poetic style, this report, in which technical matters bulk large, provides a number of details—not all symbolic—about the instrument. This organ, which replaced another, much smaller, instrument (talis et auxistis . . . organa), is of considerable size, and the only one of its kind in England (qualia nusquam cernuntur). The bellows, arranged on two levels, are located in the base of the organ, and their great number—twenty-six in all—implies that the organ required a vast supply of air, and that the output of each bellows was very small. Presumably these bellows were hard to operate since it took seventy strong men to move them—more than two to each bellows, unless the men were divided up into teams working in rotation.

---

[3] *P.L.*, cxxxvii, 110–11.

The poet does not specify the shape of the bellows, but presumably they were similar to those used by blacksmiths.

The air duct is vertical, and leads into a huge wind-chest supporting four hundred pipes (musas) ranked in order (ordine). This 'order' does not apply to one single rank of pipes, as Willi Apel believes:[4] what follows indicates beyond all possible doubt that there were ten ranks of forty pipes. Probably these represented ten ranks of varying timbres and pitches, which always sounded together and could not be isolated, since the organ had no draw stops. These were not developed until the fourteenth century—though it will be remembered that the instrument described by Vitruvius was fitted with a special device which allowed the organist to select his timbre. The nature of the pipes is not specified here; but the word 'musas' suggests sets of reed pipes.[5]

The slider mechanism is familiar, being absolutely identical to that of Hero and Vitruvius. The instrument has forty sliders (linguae), each perforated with ten holes. The 'hidden holes' (occulta foramina) are those in the wind-chest. It was not clear whether there was a recoil spring or whether the organist had to push the slider back into place after use: both possibilities appear in the treatises of the following century. However, it is logical to suppose that in this case the keys had to be pulled out and subsequently pushed back manually—otherwise there would be no reason. for the simultaneous presence of two organists. The two 'like-minded brothers' (duo concordi pectore fratres)[6] are actually seated on the same bench, each playing his own manual. From the data given here on the construction of the wind-chest, it would appear that one manual is a continuation of the other, and that the organists are seated side by side. This curious arrangement, arising from the slow and complicated manipulation of the sliders, is found again in the illustration from the ninth-century Utrecht Psalter, which will be discussed later. There are also two organists at the manual of the organ in the Munich manuscript.[7]

The term 'alphabet', as applied to the manuals, derives from the letter inscribed on the tip of each slider, to remind the player of the pitch of the note it controls. This special feature of organ-building, which is mentioned in both treatises, is shown in the illustration of the instrument in the Harding

---

[4] *Early History of the Organ*, p. 206.

[5] 'Musa' is used from the eleventh or twelfth century to describe a type of bagpipe with a bellows: J. Cotton (*De Musica*, Gerbert, *Script.*, ii, p. 233) mentions the organ in connection with it.

[6] Aldhelm used this expression in a similar sense (*P.L.*, lxxxix, 290):

> Fratres concordi laudemus voce Tonantem
> Cantibus et crebris conclamet turba sororem.

[7] See Chapter XV.

Bible. We can only assume that in those days organists were poorly trained.[8]
A reasonable assumption here would be that each of the two players controlled twenty keys, one playing the bass notes, the other the treble; thus
great care would be needed to co-ordinate their movements. There are forty
notes, since there are forty sliders, and the poet points out that in addition
to the seven notes of the scale (septem discrimina vocum—the expression is
Virgil's)[9] 'lyric' semitones were included. It is not clear exactly what these
were. If all the semitones were present—which is most unlikely—the
instrument's tessitura would have been slightly more than three octaves.
Judging by what is said in the treatises on pipe measurement, a range of
this size was in any case quite common.

The second part of Wulstan's letter is also interesting, though from a
historical rather than a technical point of view. It is impossible to miss the
similarity between the author's hyperbole and that developed by Muristus
in each of his two treatises. The 'strident voice', the music that can be heard
throughout the town, the necessity to stop up one's ears when approaching
the instrument—all these things are directly in line with the description of
'the organ with the wonderful sounds', and suggests that Muristus's Arabic
text must have been known in English monasteries in the tenth century.
This would be most surprising, did one not know that in France about the
same time Gerbert was greatly interested in Arabic science. The unusual use
of the adjective thunderous to describe the Church of St. Peter is simply
an example of an ancient application of a word being brought back into
fashion.[10]

THE TREATISES OF THEOPHILUS AND THE ANONYMOUS OF BERNE

Wulstan's poem, though detailed, is not a treatise on organ-building: it
simply gives a description of an instrument without any pretence of explaining how it was made. The two texts which follow, however, were both
written for strictly didactic purposes, by monks who were also organ-
builders. The instruments discussed are practically identical in type, with a
few minor variations in respect of the materials involved.

Though of unequal importance, these treatises are conceived in the same
spirit. Both are addressed to the craftsman as yet unfamiliar with the art of
making organs. The author of the first is a religious who gives his name as

---

[8] Even today the names of the seven notes of the central octave on the harmonium
are often inscribed above the corresponding keys.

[9] *Aeneid*, vi, 646.

[10] It is also applied to Zeus (*Iliad*, ii, 478, 781), Jupiter (Apuleius, *Metam.*, vi, 4), and
to God (Ermold le Noir, *In Hon. Hlud.*, 799). Contemporaries may have been struck
by the powerful reverberation created by the organ pipes in the small Anglo-Saxon
churches of the time. See D. Knowles, *The Monastic Order in England* (Cambridge,
1950), pp. 559 ff.

Theophilus, and of whom nothing is known. Presumably he lived in Germany or in eastern France, and, though his dates are uncertain, a number of points suggest that he belongs in the first half of the eleventh century.[11] The construction of the organ takes up only one chapter of a vast encyclopedia entitled *Diversarum Artium Schedule*, which describes the processes involved in making everything to do with a church: windows and paintings, gilding, the forging of metals, the moulding of a censer, the casting of a bell and so on. Its purpose is twofold, as the reader is informed in the Preface:

Theophilus, a humble priest, servant of the servants of God, unworthy of the name and profession of monk, [dedicates this treatise] to all those who desire to ward off and drive out a slothful spirit and mistaken ideas by useful manual work and pleasurable study . . .

From the moral aim, he passes to the practical object: the treatise will instruct a man how to make 'all those things which until now are lacking in the House of God . . . without which neither the Mysteries nor the serving of the Masses may be carried out . . . There are the chalices . . . and other objects indispensable to the ecclesiastical function.'

We will see that the organ is included among the objects necessary to the proper celebration of worship, but frequently absent at the time when Theophilus is writing.

The author of the second treatise is anonymous. Attention was first drawn to this manuscript in 1875 by H. Hagen, and it was published by Schubiger in the following year. It is usually referred to as the *Anonymous of Berne*, since it is preserved in the library of that city, where it is catalogued as Cod. B 56. In origin, however, it is not Swiss, but is believed to have come from the Abbey of Fleury, which was, as we have seen, at one time a famous centre of organ-building, even in Gerbert's day. The majority of musicologists date the treatise as from the eleventh century: it is not impossible that it was the work of the celebrated Constantius, friend and pupil of the future Sylvester II.

For clarity's sake those chapters in each treatise which relate to the same parts of the organ have been grouped together, since this makes it considerably easier to effect a useful comparison between the two. A text by Aribo (eleventh century) on making pipes has been added.

MAKING THE PIPES

Theophilus, *De Organis*.[12]

He who would make organ pipes should first provide himself with a Treatise

---

[11] M.-J. Bourassé, *Dictionnaire d'Archéologie Sacrée*, ed. Migne (1851), ii, 736.
[12] Here 'organa' refers to the organ pipes. Vitruvius uses the same term when describing the pipes on his instrument.

on Measurements,[13] wherein he will find the specifications for the low, high, and very high pipes.[14] Thereafter he is advised to make himself an iron [mandrel] of the same length and diameter as the pipes he intends to fashion. This mandrel must be rounded, and should be filed and polished with the utmost care, and made thicker at one end, then tapering slightly, so that it may be inserted into another piece of curved iron, which will encase it as an auger (runcina) is enclosed by the piece of wood in which it turns. At its other end, the mandrel should be slender, corresponding to the diameter of the lower end of the pipe, which will rest on the wind-chest.[15]

Next take a quantity of very pure copper, of excellent quality, and beat it flat, to the point where the pressure of a fingernail leaves a visible mark on the reverse surface. When it has been fitted[16] and cut to the size of the mandrel, which is the size of the longer pipes which are called the bass pipes,[17] an aperture (foramen) is made following the instructions given in the treatise, and in it the plectrum will be placed. This aperture should be slightly filed round its circumference, according to the dimensions of the pipe, and thereafter plated with tin, using a soldering iron (atque superlineatur stagnum cum ferro solidario).

One of the long edges (of the sheet of copper) is filed on its inner surface, and the other on its outer surface, to the same degree, and then they are lightly tinned (superstagnetur tenue). Before this plating is set it is smeared with a coating of fir-resin (resina abietis) while the filed surfaces are still fresh, the copper having been first of all heated slightly so that the tin adheres to it more easily and quickly.

This done, the sheet of copper is rolled round the iron mandrel and firmly secured with metal wire of medium thickness, so that the tinned edges exactly correspond. First the wire should be threaded into a small hole in the narrow end of the mandrel, wound around it twice, and continued up the length of the mandrel in a spiral (deduci involvendo) until it reaches the other end, where it is fastened off in the same thorough fashion (as it was below). Then, having seen to it that the joins exactly correspond and are carefully held in place, you set the ligatured mandrel near a furnace of glowing coals which an apprentice, seated beside it, is gently blowing up. In his right hand he holds a stick, with one end split, and into the split is thrust a rag soaked in resin. In his left hand he holds a long tin rod. When the pipe is hot, the apprentice passes the resin-soaked rag over the solder;[18] then the tin he applies liquefies, enabling him to make a well-soldered joint (ipsamque juncturam diligenter consolidet).

Later, when the pipe has cooled, the mandrel is placed on an instrument

[13] *Lectionem mensurae.* These treatises on measurements will be examined later.
[14] Presumably Theophilus plans to have three octaves.
[15] By mistake, the text reads 'on the wind-collector'.
[16] I agree with W. Theobald (*Technik des Kunsthandwerks im zehnten Jahrhundert*, Berlin, 1933, p. 144), that this should be read as 'lineatum' and not 'limatum.'
[17] The organ-builder makes all the pipes in the same rank equal in length; then they are cut to fit each note.
[18] Just as nowadays plumbers use candles.

prepared like that of a turner[19] (instrumento tornatoris modo parato); and when the wire has been removed, the curved iron is laid on it. One (of the workmen) revolves the curved iron (with his hands), while the other, wearing gloves,[20] keeps a firm hold on the pipe so that the (curved) iron is turned round while the pipe is held steady, until it emerges gracefully for all to see, as if it had been turned on a lathe.[21]

After that the mandrel is removed and the pipe itself hammered with a medium-sized mallet in the vicinity of the aperture[22] above and below until the circumference (rotunditas) is beaten in to a depth of two digits, so that it almost reaches the middle point.[23] The plectrum[24] is made from slightly thicker copper, cut in a half-wheel (quasi dimidia rotula). It must be soldered with tin on its curved edge (circa rotunditatem), like the pipe (whose soldering is described) above, and placed in the lower part of the aperture, so as to lie in a central position under the lips of the aperture and projects neither above nor below it. You should also have a soldering iron the same width and curvature as the plectrum; this iron, well heated, allows you to place small particles of tin upon the plectrum, together with a little resin. While still hot, it is passed carefully all round, and you must see to it that the plectrum does not move. It should adhere, by means of the melted tin, so that round its circumference no air may pass, save only towards the front part of the aperture.[25]

Having done this, you place the pipe in your mouth and blow, moderately at first, then more strongly, and finally very strongly indeed. And according to what your ear tells you, you adjust the sound in the following way: if the sound is to be fuller, the hole must be enlarged;[26] and for a thinner sound, it should be narrowed.

All the pipes are made in this manner. Each will be measured from the plectrum upwards, (a plectro superius), according to the instructions in the treatise; but from the plectrum downwards, all will be the same height and thickness.[27]

Anonymous of Berne, *De fistulis organicis, quomodo fiant.*

A quantity of very pure copper (cuprum purissimum) is hammered very thin (ad summam tenuitam), and then rolled round an iron [mandrel]. The mandrel

---

[19] E. Buhle, op. cit., p. 106, is mistaken in taking this to be a vice. It is actually a type of lathe which holds the mandrel at each end in a horizontal position.

[20] For fear of marking the brass with his fingers.

[21] The metal was not planed smooth, as E. Buhle suggests. The thinness of the brass would rule this out.

[22] Which was made before the pipe was soldered.

[23] That is to say almost to the axis of the pipe.

[24] The 'bevel', a metal disc positioned horizontally, which all but closes the pipe and forces the air forward.

[25] I think that here the text should read 'anteriori' instead of 'superiori.' This passage dealing with the mouthpiece is rather puzzling, but it seems to differ very little from the lip on a modern pipe.

[26] That is to say, the 'light'.

[27] Théobald, op. cit., pp. 143 ff.

is appropriate to this use by virtue of the fact that all the pipes will then be of equal diameter; it is almost four feet in length and should be well rounded, like a cylinder (in modum chilindri bene rotundo).

Approximately a palm's[28] length from one end, it gradually narrows to a point, so that a pigeon's egg may be inserted into the interior of each pipe at its upper end, and lark's egg at its lower end.[29] At the place where the diameter becomes constant[30] (ubi incipit equalis grossitudo) the copper of the pipe is cut open crosswise into a semicircle: then, on the inside, a valve bevel (uva) is soldered. For the note to sound, it is important that the pipe should press hard against this all the way round.[31]

Aribo, *Qualiter ipsae congruenter fiant fistulae.*

Since the pipes have the same diameter, the metal sheets (laminae) of which they are made are of equal width. It has previously been established, following Dom Willelm, how the circumference of these pipes is calculated. We should make careful and circumspect examination of the relationship existing between this circumference and this width. Macrobius, commenting on the *Dream of Scipio*, says: 'The diameter of any circle, multiplied by three, plus one seventh (diametrum . . . triplicatum cum adiectione septimae partis suae) gives the circumference of the circle;'[32] these are the words of Macrobius.[33] By his method the diameter of the circle is tripled, and to this is added one seventh of the diameter. The resulting figure will give the width of all the metal sheets to be used in the making of the pipes.

These sheets should be beaten very thin along their lateral edges, and then —this is the important point—the ends, bent round by the smith's hand, are brought face to face, not overlapping, but just touching (non superponantur sibimet, sed osculo tantum collidantur coniunctissimo) the two lips juxtaposed. To cover this join, metal strips (laminellae) are prepared, the width and thickness of a straw (festucae); and these are soldered to the join with a solid layer of tin or some other 'lotarium', less quickly applied but stronger.[34] While the sheet is still open, the length of the pipe is fixed by points marked at either end; then a transverse line is traced from one point to the other. The extremities of this line mark the (upper) orifice of the pipe and the (position of) the mouthpiece.

The mouthpiece will be cut out above this line, so that it lies midway across the width of the pipe; and at the end of the line the bevel will be

---

[28] Approximately 7 cm.
[29] The crosswise diameter of a pigeon's egg is approximately 3 cm., and that of a lark's egg 1 cm.
[30] That is, where the foot is joined to the body of the pipe.
[31] W. Nef, op. cit., pp. 13–14.
[32] $3 + \frac{1}{7}$ gives π the very satisfactory value of $3 \cdot 14$.
[33] Aribo is quoting from memory. Macrobius's exact words are: 'Item omnis diametros cuiuscumque orbis triplicata cum adjectione septimae partis suae mensuram facit circuli . . .' (*Comm. in Somn. Scip.*, book i, xx, 16. Ed. Teubner, p. 567).
[34] It is not known which metal or alloy is meant by this.

soldered, using great care. The upper lip of the mouthpiece will be separated from the bevel by the width of a medium-sized straw.[35]

Some conclusions may be drawn from these three texts, which help to clarify the making of organ pipes in the eleventh century.

Materials. Though Aribo does not specify what materials he uses, Theophilus and the Anonymous of Berne state explicitly that they use pure copper. The other texts examined refer to the metal by the somewhat vague term *aes*—but it is not clear whether this is pure copper or some alloy. The astonishing thing about the instructions given by Theophilus and the Anonymous is the beating of the metal 'until it is very thin'; the pipe lost in strength what it gained in elegance. Perhaps such a practice was prompted by reasons of economy.

Shapes and sizes. There appears to be a difference in the shape of the pipes as described by Theophilus and Anonymous. The former implies that the pipe is a regular cone, since the mandrel and the 'curved iron' must be placed in position and then withdrawn. The latter, however, suggests a cylindrical pipe with a detachable conical foot, the join being at the point 'where the diameter becomes constant'. There is no indication that the foot was soldered to the body of the pipe. Conical pipes are featured on the organ shown in the Harding Bible,[36] while cylindrical pipes appear in the Cividale del Friuli manuscript. The three descriptions do, however, have something in common: all the pipes in the same rank are of equal diameter. This is the classical tradition; we have already seen that the differences in timbre resulting from this uniformity of calibre are scarcely perceptible unless the range exceeds the double octave.

Only the Anonymous of Berne gives a few figures relating to the dimensions of the pipes.[37] The mandrel, that is to say the largest pipe, is, he says, almost 4 ft long, or a little more than a metre. Taken separately, the foot of the pipe measures 7 cm. The lower orifice is approximately 1 cm. in diameter, and the upper 2·5–3 cm. The bass pipe is thus quite narrow, while the highest treble pipe is relatively wide.

Aribo gives a simple formula for calculating the length of the metal sheets, given the diameter of the relevant pipe.

Soldering. The pipes are not cast, but soldered. To join the two free edges of the sheet of metal, two processes are suggested—that of Theophilus, where

[35] The width of the 'light'.

[36] See Ch. XV. In folio 43 of the Latin MS. 12949 in the Bibliothèque Nationale there is a drawing at the top of the page of six organ pipes, lying horizontally, with distinctly conical feet and clearly visible lips.

[37] There are also some in Notker Labeo's treatise on measurement's which will be discussed later.

the edges of the sheet are rolled one over the other (as in rolling a cigarette), and the more elegant procedure advocated by Aribo, where the edges are juxtaposed, and joined by a thin strip of metal. This second method of soldering is very similar to that still used today.

Mouthpieces. Unfortunately all the texts are rather vague as to how this essential part of the pipe is contrived. It consists of a rounded aperture whose edges, top and bottom, are bent inward towards the axis of the pipe; a semi-circular bevel is soldered horizontally inside the aperture. Such lips, apparently similar to those made nowadays, were known in Roman times and are perfectly distinguishable on the Carthaginian model and the St. Maximin sarcophagus. Theophilus states categorically that the feet of all his pipes are the same height: therefore the lips on every pipe in the same rank are in line.

Theophilus further tells us how the tone-quality of his pipes could be adjusted. The 'light' of the lips should be widened or narrowed according to whether a loud or thin sound is required. This 'light' is on average 0·4 cm. in height (the thickness of a straw).

THE WIND-CHEST AND MANUAL

Theophilus, *De domo organaria*:

Before constructing the wind-chest on which the pipes will be fixed, decide whether it is to be of wood or copper. It if is to be of wood, take two thick planks of the wood of the plane-tree, perfectly dry, two and a half feet long, something more than a foot wide and four digits thick for the first plank, and two for the second.[38] The wood should be free of knots and flaws.

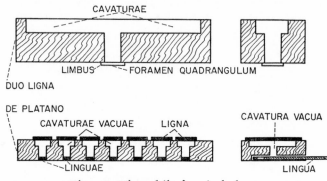

Fig. 16. Theophilus's wind-chest

The utmost care should be exercised to make sure that these planks fit together exactly. Then, in the centre of the lower surface of the thicker plank, a square hole is made (foramen quadrangulum) measuring four digits across,[39]

[38] Approximately 81 cm., 35 cm., 8 cm., and 4 cm. respectively. See fig. 16.
[39] Approximately 8 cm.

and furnished round its perimeter with a frame (limbus) of the same wood, a digit in height and width,[40] into which will be fitted the air collector (conflatorium). In the upper part of the side, cavities (cavaturae) should be hollowed out on either side, through which the wind may pass into the pipes.

The other plank, which should also be uppermost (quae et superior esse debet), has the same internal dimensions, and in it are hollowed out[41] seven or eight channels into which the sliders (linguae) are fitted exactly, so that they may run easily back and forth (educendi et reducendi) without the slightest escape of air. In the upper surface, hollow out channels corresponding to those underneath, but slightly wider, and on these you will fix a like number of small strips of wood, in such a way as to leave between these strips and the plank [literally the thicker plank] an empty space, through which the wind may flow upward into the pipes. And these small strips should have holes, into which the [feet of the] pipes will be fitted.[42]

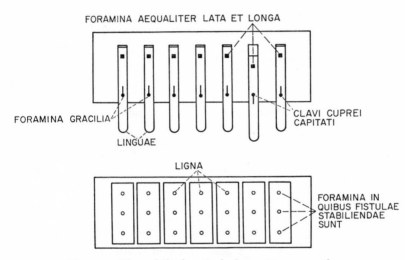

Fig. 17. Theophilus's wind-chest. Upper surface

The channels into which the sliders are fitted should project towards the front like a slanting window (quasi obliquae fenestrae), through which the sliders may be pushed and pulled. Further back, the sliders are perforated, not far from the end, by holes two digits square,[43] through which the wind coming from below will pass upwards; so that, when the sliders are pushed, the holes are automatically blocked; and when they are pulled, they open again. The small strips of wood fixed above the sliders will be perforated carefully and symmetrically, according to the number of pipes corresponding to each note

[40] Approximately 2 cm.
[41] In its lower surface.
[42] See fig. 17.
[43] These holes are therefore approximately 4 cm. square.

(secundum numerum fistularum unius cuiusque toni).[44] These pipes will be placed in the holes so as to be solidly anchored in them while receiving the wind through their lower end.

The handle of each slider is marked with the letter appropriate to its position in the scale, enabling you to know where this sound or that is located. In addition, each slider should have a narrower hole, half as wide as the little finger, towards the front, near the handles and lengthwise. In each of these holes fix a copper-headed nail, bisecting the small windows through which the sliders pass, from the height of the sides of the wind-chest right to the bottom (?). Above, the heads of the nails are visible, and by this means, when the organ is played, the sliders may be pulled without coming right out.

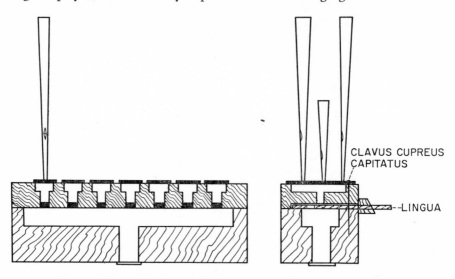

Fig. 18. Theophilus's wind-chest. Frontal and cross sections

When this has been done, the two planks which constitute the wind-chest of the organ are stuck together with cheese glue (glutine casei);[45] and thereafter the small strips of wood pierced with holes and joined above the sliders are also carefully filed and scraped.[46]

Theophilus, *De domo cuprea* (The copper wind-chest):

Calculate the length and width of your wind-chest according to the number of pipes (to be fed); then construct a mould (forma) of clay beaten soft (in argilla macerata). When this is dry, cut it exactly to the desired measurements and cover it entirely with wax which has been carefully rolled thin with a

[44] He is allowing for several pipes to each key.
[45] Theophilus (i, xvii) tells us that this glue is made from soft cow's cheese mixed with quicklime. 'Wooden boards joined together with this glue are stuck so fast that neither humidity nor heat can sunder them.'
[46] Théobald, op. cit., pp. 146–7. See figs. 18 and 19.

wooden roller, between two rods of equal thickness. Next drill the grooves for the sliders in the wax itself, and also the hole underneath through which the wind enters. Having added the airholes and their funnel[47] (*additis spiraculis cum infusorio*), cover them with the same clay once, then a second and a third time. When the mould is dry,[48] pour the copper as for the censer mould described earlier[49] . . . when the wind-chest has been cast, place within it, about one digit from the bottom, a sheet of beaten copper, evenly fixed under

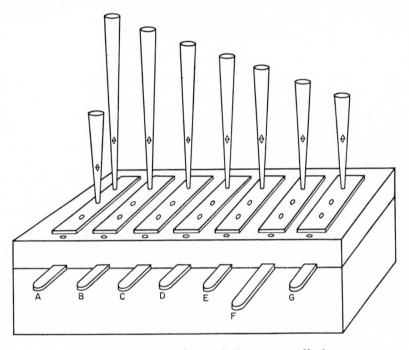

Fig. 19. Theophilus's wind-chest. Overall view

the housings of the sliders, which should lie immediately above, and be able to slide freely back and forth. The sliders themselves should be covered with a thin layer of clay, and molten lead should be poured over the rest (of the upper part) of the wind-chest, above the sliders, right to the top.

Having done this, you will carefully remove the sheet of lead, and mark upon it the positions of the orifices of the pipes made in the sliders. Then you will drill holes in the lead itself, with the utmost caution, and using an iron awl or a brace and bit. Next you will fashion ducts under the sliders,[50] by

[47] Smelting openings which are also laid down for the casting of the censer: 'deinde unicuique parti suis infusoriis atque spiraculis imposito' (*De thuribulo fusili*, iii, lxi).
[48] To get rid of the wax the mould is placed near the forge, so that the wax liquefies (*De thuribulo fusili*).
[49] Chapter LXI, where the casting of metal is described in great detail.
[50] i.e. under the sheet of copper.

which the wind may enter, and you will slide the sliders, one by one, into their housings; then, replacing the sheet of lead, you will hammer it down to the wind-chest, so that no air shall escape save by the holes in which the pipes are set.[51]

Anonymous of Berne:

The box in which the pipes are set must be square, or longer on one side;[52] at each of the four corners . . . there is a receptacle, hollowed out to a greater depth[?], so that the wind, distributed equally, pours into all the holes[53] . . . From the centre of this box the principal air-duct (fistula maxima) leads down, and is fed on four sides with (the wind from) double bellows . . . The box is covered with a thin, flat sheet, fine and quite straight, and on both sides of this are pierced lines of holes equidistant from one another, and corresponding in number to the number of pipes.

Under this sheet provision should be made for another,[54] facing (the orifice of) the principal air-duct, not so as to block it up, but to ensure an even distribution of the wind. Across the opening of the box, running from front to back above the (upper) sheet, thin sliders are set in place, level, light and quite straight, pierced with holes corresponding to all of those in the sheet. These holes should be linked together, so that they appear to form a single orifice. Having plugged these holes in such a way as to unstop them after-wards, molten lead is poured on the box, above the sheet and the sliders. If these sliders are subsequently pulled, they will be mobile in their housing and will run freely (cursoriae).

Next the pipes are set up in a row, and the rank must be graded upward from the right towards the left of the organist.[55] But above each slider only single or double pipes may be placed (simple et duple fistule):[56] each thus gives the same sound, high or low. There may be as many sliders[57] as you wish, five, six, or what you will. In the dimensions in which we are working, there are fifteen sliders.

Thereafter the remaining parts (of the instrument) are made, (which will be arranged) on a wooden bar fixed in front of the box. For each slider a semicircular horn spatula is made, and a wooden key (lamine ligneae) re-inforced at the end with an iron spike joined to the centre of an iron rod linking the head of the semicircular spatula to the slider, so that when the key is depressed from above (a tergo depressa lamina) the entire slider is pushed back to the point where it is attached to the iron rod. If the wooden key is then released (laxa lamina lignea), the slider is brought back (extrahatur) to the

[51] Théobald, op. cit., pp. 150–1.
[52] i.e. rectangular.
[53] Here the text has been considerably altered, and does not lend itself to a coherent translation.
[54] Inside the box.
[55] So that the trebles are to his right.
[56] That is to say the fundamental and its octave below.
[57] 'His' refers to the sliders and not to the pipes, as the rest of the sentence shows.

middle of the first hole.[58] But the greatest care should be taken to avoid any gap (*aliqua rima*) in the joins of the box through which air might escape.

The wooden keys are marked with the letters of the alphabet,[59] twice over, in the following way: A.B.C.D.E.F.G.A.B.C.D.E.F.G.H.[60] in order that the organist may more easily recognize the key he must operate.

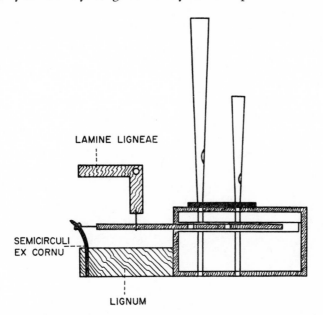

Fig. 20. Anonymous of Berne's wind-chest. Cross section

The three wind-chests just described have one striking common denominator: they have no draw stops, so that the organist is denied the possibility of selecting one rank of pipes rather than another. Though several pipes are meant to be controlled by each key, these pipes sound together and cannot be separated. The organ described by the monk Wulstan was certainly of this type, with its ten pipes to each note.[61] One wonders why the system of distribution outlined by Vitruvius was abandoned, since it constituted a

---

[58] What the author obviously means is that the other end of the slider is brought back to the middle of the first hole. See fig. 20.

[59] i.e. the scale.

[60] Earlier in the text fifteen sliders were mentioned, so that we have two diatonic octaves with the eighth note sharpened and doubled.

[61] Like the wind-chest examined by Zarlino in 1588 (*Supplementi musicali*, viii, p. 291); Forkel has reproduced the drawing that accompanied the text (*Gesch. der Musik*, ii, Pl. V, fig. 16; it shows the wind-chest the wrong way round). This wind-chest came from the town of Grado, destroyed in 1044. 'It was an ell long and a quarter of an ell wide, and had places for thirty pipes without a register . . . in two ranks of fifteen . . .' says Pierre Trichet, quoting from Zarlino's account in his *Traité des Instruments de Musique* (1640). See F. Lesure, op. cit., p. 34. Pl. XXII, n. 3.

considerable improvement on Hero's instrument. The reason for such a regression is probably purely technical: medieval organ-builders were dogged by the problem of air leaks, and their equipment was inadequate to cope with this. An additional piece of apparatus channelling air under each rank of pipes multiplied the risk of leaks by two or three, and we can appreciate that, with their primitive bellows and no stabilizing reservoir, they could not afford to waste any air. This very likely explains why the technicians of that period were unable to reproduce the organ sent to France by Constantine Copronymus, which could probably produce three separable timbres. Not until the fourteenth century did the wind-chest with draw stops reappear, in principle identical with that used in ancient times, although somewhat different in practice.

Theophilus's wooden wind-chest was easily made, since it consisted basically of two parts glued together to give a hollow receptacle, provided on the underside with an orifice through which the air enters. In the upper part this cavity communicates with the channels which open above the housings for the sliders. These mobile sliders are perforated, and are in every way similar to those on Ktesibios's instrument. Above, each channel is closed off by a perforated strip of wood supporting all the pipes controlled by the same key.

Every slider, marked with a letter for easier identification, acts as a manual key at its forward end, and it operates purely on a horizontal plane. It is pulled towards the player when in use, and pushed back again afterwards. To prevent it from pulling right out of its housing, a copper-headed nail limits its forward movement. Sliders of this type are clearly visible on the miniatures of the Cividale del Friuli manuscript and the Harding Bible,[62] and the position of the hands manipulating them probably gave rise to the common belief that the keys were played by striking them with the closed fist.

The copper wind-chest subsequently described by Theophilus is based on the same principle. The chest itself is cast in a clay mould, and the resulting shape is closed above by laying over it, horizontally, a sheet of copper on which the sliders run. The whole thing is covered with molten lead, providing a strong and relatively airtight covering. Air holes are then drilled through the lead, metal sheet, and slider.

Though certainly more costly to make than its wooden counterpart, this metal wind-chest has the advantage of being stronger, and above all of being impervious to humidity. The wind-chest described by Anonymous of Berne is a compromise between the two: but in some respects it represents a decided improvement on both. It must have been apparent that the pipes positioned in the centre of the wind-chest, that is to say directly above the

[62] Chapter XV.

mouth of the air duct, received too much air, whereas the supply to those set out towards the sides was inadequate. To rectify this uneven distribution, the anonymous organ-builder places a small sheet of copper opposite the mouth of the air duct, to ensure a more even dispersal of the air. But the main improvement concerns the manual. Here the sliders, moving under a lead cover, are no longer manipulated by traction, but by pressing on a separate key. This key, shaped like an angle iron and entirely similar to the keys described in Hero's text, moves on an axle placed in its angle. The end of its lower leg is hinged to an iron rod which moves horizontally, attached at one end to the slider, and at the other to a semicircular spring made of horn. Again this is exactly the system outlined by Hero. The organ is made to play by depressing the keys, which automatically return to their original position as soon as the finger is removed. This technical advance, which gave the performer greater freedom in his playing, undoubtedly made possible the evolution of compositions specifically designed for the organ.

Anonymous of Berne states quite clearly that the bass pipes are to the organist's left, and the trebles to his right, as they are today. Provision is made for two pipes to each key, one sounding an octave above the other. The tessitura is fifteen notes, forming two diatonic scales.

The keys themselves are of wood, but the material used for the sliders is not specified. Probably they were of metal, though they, too, might have been of wood. There is also no indication as to how the pipes were fixed to the wind-chest—perhaps they were simply stuck into their sockets.

THE BELLOWS AND COLLECTOR

Neither treatise describes the bellows: they are taken for granted, since they are the same as those used by blacksmiths.[63] Theophilus outlines briefly and very vaguely, how those used in a foundry[64] are constructed. They are made from ram skins,[65] well dried and carefully tanned. Through the nozzle, which is made of wood, passes an iron tube, and the boards are made from wooden planks. The number of bellows required to supply air for an organ obviously varies according to the size of the instrument. Anonymous's wind-chest has four sets of double bellows: the Winchester organ needed twenty-six; but the more modest instrument illustrated in the Cividale del Friuli miniature has only two.[66]

Though by Wulstan's account the actual pumping involved a great deal

---

[63] Baldric of Dol: 'follibus . . . fabrilibus'.

[64] iii, iv.

[65] Or bullhide, recommended by the monk of St. Gall: 'follibus taurinis'.

[66] The organ in the St. Blasien manuscript (Gerbert, *De Cantu*, ii, pl. XXVII) has twelve bellows; though this is probably a symbolic representation of the Dardanus letter: see Pl. XXII, no. 2.

of hard work, the various people represented in the iconography—often adolescents—do not appear to find it taxing. However, it was an exacting task, for, in the absence of any stabilizing reservoir, the blower had to see to it that he regulated the supply of air to suit the fluctuating demand. Hence the advice of the poet of the Benedictine Abbey at Engelberg: 'Follibus praevideas—Bene flantes habeas.' Large instruments had to have a copious supply of air and a high degree of pressure;[67] and in such cases the action of the wind mechanism could produce sufficient noise to distract the faithful who were present at divine service.[68]

But the organ bellows cannot be wholly similar to a forge bellows, for the following reason. Whereas the latter can admit air freely through its nozzle while it is filling up, the organ bellows must perforce be equipped with a device to prevent any return of air from the organ. This special valve, without which the wind-chest would never have filled, is located by Anonymous in the collector, while Theophilus describes it as being in the head of the bellows:

At the narrow entrance of the nozzles [of the bellows], a span from the main air-duct, [the collector] is fitted with a copper or iron valve (uvam ex cupro vel ferro) capable of opening and shutting . . .[69]

A further detail should be executed with the utmost care: in the head of each bellows, before the opening of its nozzle, hang a thin sheet of copper (cuprum tenue) which blocks the entry of air so that when the bellows, in action, empties itself, the metal sheet lifts and allows the air to pass freely; and when it fills up again, with the air entering through its inlet valve (ventilabrum), the sheet is lowered, and completely seals the opening, thus preventing the re-entry of air (ventum quem emisit redire non permittat).[70]

The air produced by the combined forces of the bellows is pumped into a collector leading to the wind-chest. Theophilus uses the term 'conflatorium' to describe this collector, and suggests methods of making it either in wood or cast brass.

Theophilus, *De conflatorio*:

To make the air-collector, take as before[71] two thick planks of the wood of the plane-tree, a foot long, one a span thick and the other three digits.[72] Both should be rounded at one end, like a shield (in modum scuti) a foot and a half wide, and the other end should be blunt and measure a span across.[73] Having fitted these planks carefully together (diligenter coniuncta), make as many

---

[67] *Life of St. Oswald*: 'spiramento fortiori follium'.
[68] St. Aelred: 'Terribilis ille follium flatus . . . sonitum follium.'
[69] Anonymous of Berne.
[70] Theophilus.
[71] Thoroughly dry and having no knots, as for the wind-chest. See fig. 21.
[72] Approximately 32 cm., 7 cm., and 6 cm.
[73] Approximately 48 cm. and 7 cm.

holes as you require on the rounded surface of the thicker plank, one for each bellows, and in the blunt end a single hole, but larger. Then, proceeding from each hole, hollow out tapering cavities converging on the large hole (in the blunt end), to make passages for the air produced by the action of the bellows. Then you must join the two pieces of wood with cheese glue, and wind around them a length of strong new linen cloth (*panno lineo novo et forti*) coated with the same glue to make it stick fast.

Further, you will make strong iron clamps (*ligaturas ferreas fortes*), plated inside and out to hold them firmly on the wood, and fix them on with nails made with long, plated heads, so that between each hole there is a clamp holding the two planks together top and bottom.[74]

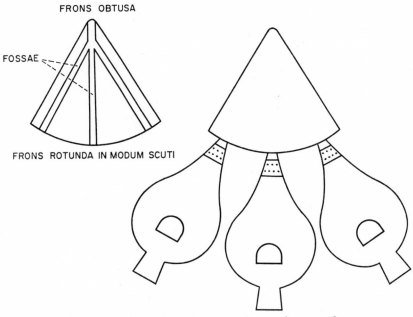

Fig. 21. The conflatorium. Section and upper face

(The principal air-duct.)

Thereafter take a curving oak log (*lignum curvum de quercu*), sound and strong, a foot long in its concave arc and two feet in the other.[75] In the cross-section at either end of this branch make a hole with the heavy drill used to pierce the hubs of plough-wheels. But since these holes cannot meet, by virtue of the curve, make an iron tool with a rounded head in the shape of an egg and a long, thin stem, fitted with a handle, slightly curved near the head. When this tool is heated, it will burn the wood, thus enabling you to fashion curving channels inside the branch, until the two holes meet. Having done this, cut (one end of) the branch in a square, each side a span long,[76] to fit the blunt end of the air collector.

[74] See fig. 22.   [75] Approximately 32 cm. and 64 m. See fig. 23.   [76] Approximately 7 cm.

Next fit the other end to the lower aperture in the wind-chest of the organ, so that a kind of shank, cut from the branch and approximately an inch thick[77] is placed in the hole and driven well home. See to it that this join is carefully finished, so that no air may escape through it. Likewise fit the other end to the air-collector, and stick the wood itself in place with cheese glue; roll a linen strip round the whole branch and its joints, and then add a further broad covering of sheet copper extending to the seam between the two planks.

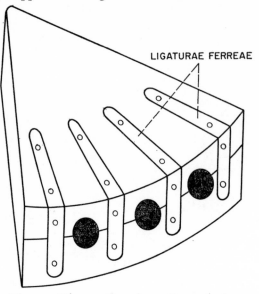

LIGATURAE FERREAE

Fig. 22. The conflatorium. General view

Theophilus (The copper conflatorium)

You will also make a clay mould of the air-collector, with the air-channels converging from all directions below, like the roots of a tree (*radicis unius arboris*), and meeting at the top in a single orifice. When you have done this according to the instructions, cut (the mould) with a knife, cover it with wax and proceed as before . . .

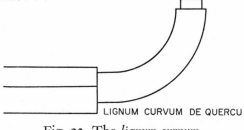

LIGNUM CURVUM DE QUERCU

Fig. 23. The *lignum curvum*

When the air-collector has been cast and filed down, the nozzle of each bellows should be affixed to its own conductor: then it must be joined and

[77] Approximately 2·7 cm.

firmly attached underneath to the wind-chest, so that the air may find its way in freely, and does not escape in any way through the other joints.

Anonymous of Berne (The bicorn collector)

. . . The principal air-duct (fistula maxima) runs down from the centre of the wind-chest, fed on four sides (per quattuor partes) by (the air from) twin bellows (geminos folles). But before these bellows join the aforesaid air-duct, they are attached to a hollow receptacle with a double orifice (bicorni instrumento perforato) . . .

The wooden air duct described by Theophilus curves through an angle of approximately 90°, judging by the iconography. This curvature allows the bellows to lie horizontally, making them easier to operate. An air duct of this type is represented in the Cividale del Friuli miniature, while Anonymous's double device may be seen on the Cambridge miniature. However, the air duct need not be curved, and the organ illustrated in the Harding Bible has two straight ducts which incidentally act as feet for the instrument, and are each fed by three pairs of bellows.[78]

SITING THE ORGAN

Theophilus alone offers advice on the actual installation of the organ in a monastery church, and the placing of its various component parts—wind-chest, pipes, console, and bellows:

Having done this, should you wish to set up the organ beyond the masonry of a wall, so that inside the monastery church only the wind-chest and pipes are seen, the bellows being on the other side of the wall, you would so orientate the wind-chest that the sliders may be pulled out in the direction of the bellows.[79] Then you must make an archway (arcus) in the wall itself, where the organist (cantor) would sit, his seat so placed that his feet would be above the air-collector.

Then a square opening is cut in the centre of the archway beyond the masonry, through which the wind-chest appears, with its pipes, rising above the neck of the collector, which is fixed in the wall with stones below the opening. It is supported at its junction and rests on two long iron nails hammered an equal distance into the wall. The opening has a wooden door[80] which shuts with a lock and key, so that anyone who passes by has no means of knowing what it conceals, unless he is privy to it.

Outside, a thick curtain (pannus spissus) is hung above the organ, extended inside by wooden rods, like a small tent (in modum domunculae). This curtain is suspended from a rope fixed to the ceiling, and its role is to protect the

[78] Pl. XXV, no. 1, and Pl. XXVII, no. 1.
[79] i.e. away from the interior of the nave. See fig. 24.
[80] On the manual side.

instrument from dust. This rope is conveniently wound round a pulley situated above the ceiling. While the organ is playing, the rope is pulled, and the little tent rises; and when the music stops, the tent is replaced over the

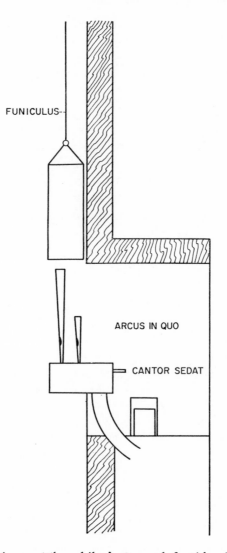

FUNICULUS

ARCUS IN QUO

CANTOR SEDAT

Fig. 24. Theophilus's Organ loft. Side view

instrument. It has a kind of spire made of the same material, held out by four rods radiating like the ribs of a pyramid. At the apex is a small wooden ball, to which the rope is secured.

As for the bellows and their supporting apparatus, arrange them as you please and as the space permits.

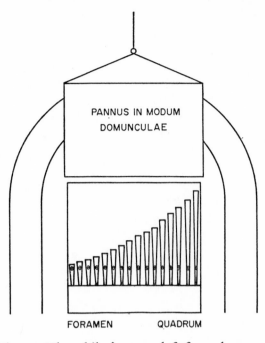

PANNUS IN MODUM
DOMUNCULAE

FORAMEN   QUADRUM

Fig. 25. Theophilus's organ loft from the nave

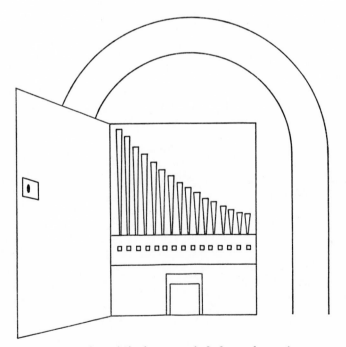

Fig. 26. Theophilus's organ loft from the staircase

In Theophilus's day, then, there was no proper organ loft, and only the wind-chest and pipes were open to view, framed in a rectangular opening knocked in the middle of an arcade. The faithful saw neither the organist nor the blowers, contrary to the evidence of the iconography of that time, though this nearly always illustrates Biblical and symbolic scenes. The organist was, in fact, seated on a bench on the other side of the wall, with the main air duct passing in front of his feet, while the collector was sealed under the floor. Presumably the bellows, whose location is not specified, was housed in the lower storey. This situation, where both organist and blowers are out of sight, is thus directly opposed to that of the Graeco-Roman hydraulic organ, but exactly anticipates the custom adopted by the Catholic Church from the Middle Ages to the present time.

A picturesque detail is added by the description of the small tent designed to protect the organ when not in use. Organ-makers must have learned at a very early stage, to their cost, that dust is a formidable enemy of the mechanism and the pipes.[81] The clergy's practical approach is further evidenced by the fact that the 'loft' is closed off by a locked door which conceals the instrument—perhaps even in those days the visits of undesirable amateurs was something to be avoided.

The placing of the organ in one of the arcades in the nave implies that the instrument produced a fair volume of sound, since, if it were to be clearly audible from below, it must have possessed several ranks of pipes fed by an adequate wind mechanism. However, Theophilus does not enlarge on this point.

MEASURING AND TUNING THE PIPES

After the organ-builder had constructed his wooden or metal wind-chest, completed his bellows, collector and air duct, soldered and tuned his pipes, he had still to create a well-defined sound scale for the instrument, whether it was used to accompany divine worship or to teach music. As early as the tenth, or even the ninth, centuries several authors took the trouble to draw up treatises on pipe measurement which enabled the maker unfamiliar with the rules of acoustics to cut his pipes exactly the right length for the required sound, with the aid of very simple arithmetical formulae. These formulae are valuable, since they indicate fairly precisely the intervals used on the organ manual, and we have already seen the regrettable lack of such information in the case of the ancient hydraulis.

It is virtually impossible to determine with any certainty the original source of these numerous treatises. Presumably the principle underlying the measurements had been passed on to the Carolingian organ-builders by the

---

[81] Protective curtains of this type were still used on the organs of St. Quentin in 1329, of Troyes in 1381 and of Rouen in 1387 (Dufourcq, op. cit., p. 111).

Byzantines and the Arabs, who in turn had them from the Greeks and Romans, nurtured in the Pythagorean tradition. In a famous passage from the *Timaeus*, Plato, as we saw, had referred to the whole and fractional numbers which characterized the intervals in the natural scale. It is this type of scale that the monks of the Middle Ages use on their instruments: but their treatises reveal quite remarkable powers of observation. The musical pipes do not quite correspond to the Pythagorean measurements laid down for vibrating strings. A coefficient of correction must be added if the pipe is to be exactly in tune: and the builders of the time must be given credit for having worked out a series of practical and exact measurements.

We know that if a vibrating string under a constant tension gives a fixed sound, half of that string will give the octave above, two-thirds the fifth, and three-quarters the fourth. These principles, well codified by the Pythagorean school, could also be applied to the pipes of the syrinx, which, having no lip, behaved like strings. This probably explains why, in the manuscripts dating from the Middle Ages, measurement tables for the monochord are often quoted side by side with those for organ pipes.[82]

The simplest process for obtaining a diatonic scale with lipped pipes was to cut them according to the theoretical divisions of the monochord. This method is advocated by Walter Odington,[83] and is also suggested by Odo, a native of Touraine and Abbot of Cluny from 927 until 942, in his treatise *De Musica*:

The Pipes

In measuring the pipes, here are the notes to take into account: C, D, E, F, G, a, ♮, c. Low C, which is the first pipe, will be as long as you wish (longitudo ponitur ad placitum). This pipe will be divided into four parts: and by removing one, you will obtain the F pipe. The same C pipe, divided in three, will give the G pipe if one third is taken away. Then the G pipe will be divided into three parts; and if a fourth third is added, you will have the D pipe, below (retro). This D pipe, divided into three and deprived of one of its thirds, will give the a pipe. This 'a', divided in three and augmented by a fourth third, will give the E pipe, below. This 'E' will in turn be divided into three; and by eliminating one third, you will have the (b) ♮ pipe. The F pipe, divided into four parts, will give 'b' (b flat) if one part is removed. The observant musician will note that all these measurements are obtained by using the fourth and the fifth.[84]

These 'measurements' are thus nothing more than the strict application to organ pipes of the acoustic principles governing strings. In accordance

---

[82] For example, by Bernelin (*P.L.*, 151, col. 654): 'Mensure fistularum et monochordi.'

[83] 'Ad similitudinem autem monocordi sunt organa construenda . . .', Coussemaker, *Script.*, i, p. 207–8.

[84] Gerbert, *Script.*, op. cit., i, p. 303.

with Pythagorean philosophy, only the first four numbers are used: 1, 2, 3, and 4 $(1, \frac{1}{2}, \frac{2}{3}, \frac{3}{4})$. If we take the sound C (low C) as representing 1, the other notes in the series correspond to the following fractions, characteristic of the 'Pythagorean' scale:

$$C (C) = 1$$
$$D (D) = \frac{4}{3} \times \frac{2}{3} = \frac{8}{9}$$
$$E (E) = \frac{16}{27} \times \frac{4}{3} = \frac{64}{81}$$
$$F (F) = \frac{3}{4}$$
$$G (G) = \frac{2}{3}$$
$$a (A) = \frac{8}{9} \times \frac{2}{3} = \frac{16}{27}$$
$$\natural (B\natural) = \frac{64}{81} \times \frac{2}{3} = \frac{128}{243}$$
$$b (B\flat) = \frac{3}{4} \times \frac{3}{4} = \frac{9}{16}$$

It will be observed that the lowest pipe has no fixed length. That is left to the organ-builder to decide, and clearly depends on the uses to which the organ may be put, as well as on its size. Nor is Odo concerned with the diameter of the pipes.

However, it must have become evident at an early stage that while these measurements give exact intervals on the monochord and on pipes with no lips, they are not quite accurate for lipped pipes, since the lip perceptibly disturbs the vibratory phenomena in the body of the pipe. Experiments show that the sounds obtained by Odo's method are, in fact, slightly too low.

It would seem that as early as the ninth century, and perhaps even in classical times, this acoustic anomaly had been noted, and formulae had been devised in an attempt to remedy it. Early evidence for this is to be found in a Latin manuscript, the work of an anonymous author, now in the Bibliothèque Nationale in Paris (No. 12949, 43 a).

If the pipes have the same diameter, if the greater is twice the length of the smaller, plus the diameter of its concavity, together they will give the interval of an octave.[85]

Likewise if the longer pipe is four times the length of the smaller, plus three times the internal diameter, they will give the interval of the double octave.

Likewise if the greater pipe is the full length of the smaller, plus a third of its length and a third of the internal diameter, together they will sound a fourth.

Likewise if the greater pipe is the full length of the smaller, plus half of its length and half the internal diameter, together they will sound a fifth.

Likewise if the greater pipe is the full length of the smaller plus an eighth of that length, the interval between them will be a tone.

Likewise if the greater pipe is the full length of the smaller, plus one-sixteenth of its length, the interval will be a semitone.

[85] The smallest pipe will produce too low a sound in relation to the largest, since the latter has to be lengthened to give the exact octave.

The treatise attributed to Hucbald (early tenth century) uses similar formulae:

The Measurement of Organ Pipes

The length of the first [pipe should be] eight times its diameter.[86] The second should be [the length] of the first plus one eighth [of it] and the eighth of the diameter. The third [should be the length] of the second plus one eighth [of this] and the eighth of the diameter. The fourth [should be the length] of the first plus one third [of this] and one third of the diameter. The fifth [should be the length] of the first plus half [of this] and half the diameter; or else [the length] of the fourth plus one-eighth [of this] and the eighth of the diameter. The sixth [is the length] of the fifth plus one-eighth [of this] and the eighth of the diameter. The eighth [has a length] double that of the first.[87]

The anonymous Latin manuscript No. 8121 A in the Bibliothèque Nationale, of which the following two passages are excerpts, describes the same process:

You are to make the first pipe as long and wide as you wish; all the pipes will be of this width. Taking this first pipe, you will measure the width of its concavity, which is called the diameter. Divide it in eight parts, and add one-eighth to the length of this first pipe, at the top; and from there to the lip, divide it in nine parts. Cut off one-ninth and carry the remaining eight over to the second pipe, from its top to its lip; and there you have the second pipe made . . .

After this, here is how the second alphabet is made. You take the first (pipe) and add to its top the total length of the diameter; then you divide the rest into two equal parts. Take away one of these, plus the length of a diameter; and what remains will form the first pipe of the second alphabet . . . Take care to verify that your measurements are correct . . .

The following treatise from Aribo (second half of the eleventh century) is worth quoting in its entirety because of its precision and the data it provides:

I shall confine myself to indicating here the measurements for two ranks, that is to say sixteen pipes; and from these it will be possible to add as many other ranks as may be required.

The first pipe may be of any length or width, according to a happy mean and your own desires (quantam mediocritas cum arbitrio doceat). The length of a pipe is measured from the lip to the top; and the width is the extent of the hollow circular opening at the top. As we know, the term diameter applies not to the circumference of the circle, but to the line bisecting it into two semi-circles.[88] With a pair of compasses, measure the length of this diameter at the top of the first pipe as soon as it is made. Let it be represented by two equal

---

[86] The rest of the text indicates that this is the smallest pipe.
[87] Gerbert, i, p. 147. The seventh pipe is omitted.
[88] The text has 'duobus hemispheriis'.

lines and divide one in eight, the other in two, three and four equal parts; after that, the entire process of measuring will be very easy for you.

To calculate the length of the second pipe from that of the first,[89] subtract from the latter's length one-eighth of the diameter. Divide the remaining length to the lip in nine parts, take off one ninth at the top, and you will have the second pipe. To find the third in relation to the second, subtract one-eighth of the diameter and divide the remaining length to the lip in nine parts; leave out one-ninth at the top and you will have the third pipe. If you go in search of the fourth pipe, take a third of the diameter away from the length of the first pipe; subtract one quarter (of the remaining length) and you will have the perfect fourth (cum integro diatessaron). To obtain the fifth pipe, subtract half the diameter from the length of the first pipe and divide the remaining length to the lip in three parts; cut one-third from the top and you have added the fifth pipe, which sounds the fifth. If you would add the sixth pipe, likewise take away half the diameter from the length of the second pipe; divide the remaining space in three, and, by abandoning one third, you have the sixth pipe. To introduce (ostenturus) the Synemmenon,[90] subtract one-third of the diameter from the length of the fourth pipe, divide the remaining length to the lip in four; and by leaving aside one quarter, you have the Synemmenon. You will find the seventh pipe[91] by cutting off half the diameter from the length of the third pipe and dividing the rest into three parts; all that remains is to take one-third from the top, and you have the seventh and last pipe.

Having laid out the pipes in this way, you will easily calculate the eighth from the first, the ninth from the second, the tenth from the third, the eleventh from the fourth, the twelfth from the fifth, the thirteenth from the sixth, the upper Synemmenon from the lower Synemmenon, and the fourteenth from the seventh.[92] For this you will cut the total length of the diameter from each of the longer (pipes), divide the remaining length to the lip in two parts, take off the upper part, and for the octave you will retain the lower part, that is to say the part nearer the lip.[93]

By Aribo's method, then, the length and diameter of the lowest-pitched pipe are left to the maker, and serve as a standard for all the others. They at once give the second ($\frac{8}{9}$), the fourth ($\frac{3}{4}$), and the fifth ($\frac{2}{3}$); $\frac{8}{9}$ and $\frac{2}{3}$ of the second pipe in turn give the major third and major sixth. B flat is obtained by taking $\frac{3}{4}$ of the fourth, and B natural by taking $\frac{2}{3}$ of the third. Each of these Pythagorean divisions is corrected by a certain coefficient, a fraction of the diameter common to all the pipes.

---

[89] Here the first pipe is the longest, hence the lowest-pitched.

[90] The minor seventh, B flat if the first pipe is C.

[91] Here the Synemmenon does not count as a regular note. In the Middle Ages it was another form of the B natural. See Chailley, 'Essai sur les structures mélodiques', *Revue de Musicologie*, lxiv (December 1959), p. 144.

[92] By mistake, the text gives 'a sexta' here.

[93] *Antiqua fistularum mensura quae intenditur* (J. Smits van Waesberghe, *Aribon, De Musica*, Rome, 1951, pp. 40–1).

This corrective coefficient deserves some comment. In a communication to the French Academy of Sciences, dated 23 January 1860[94] the celebrated organ-maker A. Cavaillé-Coll drew up an empirical formula by which the exact length of a pipe in relation to a predetermined note might be obtained. In the case of a cylindrical pipe open at one end and closed at the other, if n is the number of vibrations corresponding to this sound, V the speed of the sound in the air, and D the diameter, the length of the pipe is calculated as follows:

$$L = \frac{V}{n} - \frac{5}{3} D$$

Cavaillé-Coll was convinced in all good faith that he was the first to appreciate the need to add a corrective factor to the Pythagorean measurements, and the first to establish the formula for that factor. But, in fact, nine hundred years before, the organ-building monks of the tenth century had already worked out this coefficient, which enabled them to know in advance what the exact height of each of their pipes should be. As we shall see, they devised a formula very near to that of Cavaillé-Coll, allowing for the fact that in those days all the pipes in the same rank were the same width.

If, for example, we take the anonymous treatise 12949 in the Bibliothèque Nationale, together with those of Aribo and Notker Labeo, we find that for the eighth pipe, an octave from the first, all give the following instructions:

$$\text{length of eighth pipe} = \frac{\text{length of first pipe} - \text{one diameter}}{2}$$

Now, in 1860 as today, measurement tables[95] give the following diameters for the 4 ft. Principal, which is the set nearest in size to the pipes made in the Middle Ages:

1st C (4 ft.) : 69 mm.
2nd C (2 ft.) : 43 mm.

The ratio of the diameters, $\frac{43}{69}$, is very nearly $\frac{3}{5}$. If Cavaillé-Coll's formula is applied to two pipes of the same width, the result is:

length of eighth pipe = theoretical length $- \frac{5}{3} D$.

But D $= \frac{3}{5}$ of the diameter of the first pipe, so that

length of eighth pipe = theoretical length $(\frac{L}{2}) - (\frac{5}{3} \times \frac{3}{5})D = \frac{L}{2} - D$

which is the very formula used by tenth-century writers. The same process could be applied to the other intervals.

94 *Comptes rendus* (1860), p. 176 ff. The text gives no indication that Cavaillé-Coll had any knowledge of the measurements used by medieval organ-builders.
95 For example, A. Rougier, *Initiation à la facture d'orgue* (Lyon, 1940–1), p. 91.

Notker Labeo, a monk of St. Gall who died at a great age in 1022, wrote a treatise on measurements, not in Latin like all the others, but in Old High German. His calculations differ slightly from those in the other treatises relating to the A and B natural. For these two notes, instead of taking $\frac{2}{3}$ of the second and third, he uses $\frac{8}{9}$ of the fifth and sixth. However, the main interest of his text lies not in these details but in the information he gives regarding the length of the first pipe:

Whoever is measuring this pipe must take care to avoid what should be avoided on the lyre, namely: if the first (pipes) grow too long, they are not musical and give a coarse sound. If they become too short, then the upper pipes seem thin, though the first sound well enough. For this reason a pipe an ell long from the bevel to the top, for the first note, is too short, and one measuring two ells is too long. But a pipe measuring one and a half ells is well enough.[96]

Unfortunately the ell has altered in value according to place and usage. J. Schmidt-Görg, who has made a study of this problem, says that in this instance it would be equivalent to about 60 cm. For Notker Labeo, therefore, the first pipe should measure approximately 90 cm., the eighth slightly less than 45 cm., and the fifteenth just under 22 cm. Since the measurement is taken from the upper lip of the mouthpiece and thus represents the height of the vibrating column, we may deduce that if the pipe were open the low

pipe would produce a sound somewhere near

Several authors, Hucbald among them, specify that the height of the eighth pipe should be eight times its diameter, so that if the latter measured 3 cm.[97] Hucbald's first pipe measured not more than 50 cm. from lip to top. However, it would seem somewhat dangerous to set about calculating the height of the pipes on a medieval organ from such scanty indications.[98] The iconography offers much more accurate information on this score.

It would be both tedious and pointless to quote every treatise dealing with this question of measurements; there are a great many, and not all have yet been checked.[99] They are very similar in many ways, and seldom containing

---

[96] Joseph Schmidt-Görg, 'Ein althochdeutscher Traktat über die Mensur der Orgel-pfeifen', *Kirchenmusikalisches Jahrbuch* (1932), pp. 58 ff.

[97] See p. 236, note 29.

[98] It has been attempted by K. G. Fellerer, 'Die Mensura Fistularum, Ein Beitrag zur Geschichte des Mittelalterlichen Orgelbaus', *Kirchenmusikalisches Jahrbuch* (1935), pp. 36–50.

[99] Apart from those transcribed in Gerbert and Coussemaker, there are the following manuscripts: Paris, Bibl. Nat., Lat. MSS. 8121 A, fol. 33, and 12949, fol. 43 (pre-viously discussed); 10509, fol. 66; 7377 C, fol. 44; Sélestat Library, 17, fol. 36; Avranches Library, 235, fol. 47; Vienna, Nationalbib., cpv 51; Zurich, Zentralbibl., Car. C. 176; Einsiedeln, Klosterbibl., 319; Leyden, 194. Klaus Weiler has recently published a treatise dating from 1037 (*Kirchenmusikalisches Jahrbuch*, 1956, pp. 16 ff.), but it adds nothing new to the subject.

anything original. The Anonymous of Berne is the only author worth analysing in any detail, simply because he is so circumstantial. Like Odo, he is not concerned with the corrective factor, and, instead of taking the lowest-pitched pipe as the standard length, he uses the smallest, as does Hucbald:

. . . Then, from that part where the bevel is located, the length of the whole pipe is measured, with the compasses, to that place where, as we have said, the upper opening is situated, to ascertain by how much each pipe is greater or smaller than another.

Since in fact it is the diatonic genus that is used in present-day chants, the pipes will be measured in the following way. The length of the first, which is the smallest of all and hence the highest in pitch, is divided in eight; the second will be taller than the first by one-eighth, and between them the interval will be one tone. Likewise the third pipe will be taller than the second by an eighth, and a tone will separate them. Continue thus, so that the fourth is a third taller than the first and will be a fourth apart from the first, and half a tone from the third. Moreover, the fifth pipe will be half as high again as the first, sounding a fifth with it, and a tone below the fourth. The sixth pipe will exceed the fifth by an eighth, and a tone will separate the two. The seventh pipe will be one-third again as long as the fourth, so as to form with it an inverted fourth (rursus diatessaron); and there is a semitone between the seventh and sixth pipes. The eighth pipe will be twice the length of the first and together they will sound an octave, which is invariably composed of a fourth and a fifth.

Another rank should be made in the same way. And just as the measurement of the second pipe (of the second octave) is calculated from the eighth, so they correspond according to their rank, as we have said (?). For the eighth pipe is double the first and the fifteenth is double the eighth. Going up and down the seven notes of the aforesaid scale, you will be able to play any melody whatsoever (unamquamlibet cantilenam). By constant practice, you will learn to recognize the intervals between the notes (distantie vocum), so that some notes are not left out. I mean those which you transpose down because the melody rises too high (acuminis), and transpose up again as the music proceeds. The second rank of pipes will correspond to the first rank . . .

If we reconstruct the series of notes obtained by following the instructions given in the text (disregarding the absence of the corrective coefficient), taking the basic pipe, which is the highest in the scale, as C, the result is:

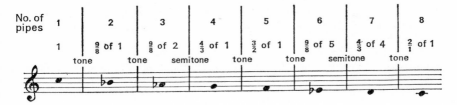

This is not the 'doh scale' but the 'lah scale', the second Gregorian mode (protus plagal). Thus the method of measuring used here, though in principle it resembles the others, deviates considerably from them in its effect. The choice of the highest pipe as the standard length is perhaps explained by a reluctance to cut pipes already made, and a desire to build them up instead from a sheet of copper cut according to specifications worked out by reference to the smallest among them.

The second part of the text is most interesting. Here the author states clearly that the new rank of pipes following on from the first (denuo idem ordo repetatur) sounds an octave higher (ut prime octava dupla est ita quinta decima octave). However, the manual has only seven keys (septem . . . vocibus); so that each must control two pipes, one sounding an octave above the other. Nowadays this would be described as 'diapason and principal'. The limitations inherent in the tessitura of such a manual would therefore not allow for the note-against-note accompaniment of melodies ranging beyond the octave[100]—hence the exhortation to practise transposing down those notes which are too high.

SCALES AND TESSITURA

It will be apparent that the measuring techniques defined by the treatises all correspond to diatonic scales, and certainly the music of the day used this genus almost exclusively: '. . . diatonicum genus quo maxime decurrunt moderne cantilene,' says Anonymous of Berne. The Synemmenon (B flat) nearly always completes the scale: 'The eight sounds thus set out are made up of the seven notes of the scale and an eighth, known as the Synemmenon, [added] for charm and decoration.'[101]

Even on more extensive manuals, corresponding to series of fourteen or twenty-one pipes of various lengths, provision is made for a B flat in each octave.[102] Wilhelm von Hirsau—if it is indeed he whom Aribo quotes—appears to have been the first to add systematically to two-octave organs, three supplementary pipes which probably sounded the two B flats and the final C: 'To the two series, that is to say fourteen pipes, he added three further pipes to establish the tetrachord (Synemmenon) so that the high notes should give the right sound in the smallest pipes, and the low notes reply correctly in the largest pipes.'[103]

[100] Melodies extending beyond the octave seem to have been rare in the eleventh century: the author is probably referring to those which lay in the top register of the manual.
[101] Eberhard of Freising, Gerbert, *Script.*, ii, p. 279.
[102] Eberhard of Freising, op. cit. It should be noted that in his vocal works Pérotin uses C sharp and F sharp in addition to B flat.
[103] Gerbert, *Script.*, ii, p. 224.

Moreover, the system of hexachords devised by Guido d'Arezzo and his disciples made provision, in the high and very high registers (corresponding to the 'acutae et superacutae' pipes referred to by the monk Theophilus), for the B naturals for 'hard' hexachords and B flats for 'soft' hexachords.[104] It is not always easy to discover whether the series of octaves thus obtained were designed to augment the tessitura of the manual or were simply to be superimposed on a single octave. A number of texts do indicate, however, that sometimes manuals with three or four octaves were in use as early as the beginning of the thirteenth century.

If, however, the organ-builder (organicus) desired to make more than three octaves (amplius tria alphabeta) he would in the first place be obliged to take measurements, and likewise measure the second octave from the first, and the others in turn, according to their various ranks, so as to proceed in an orderly and unfaltering manner. But if you would not fall into error, remind yourself frequently that a rank [of pipes] behaves well in the middle register, in proportion to its ability to obtain extreme notes without the distorting effect of dissonances.[105]

But this three-octave tessitura did not meet with unqualified approval even at the end of the thirteenth century:

The human voice cannot extend the number of its notes to encompass three octaves . . . And in organs, the pipes are likewise unequal to this . . . it is impossible to shorten pipes to produce such thin, overshrill sounds.[106]

Nevertheless, three octaves would seem to have been the usual span of the manual on most thirteenth-century organs, if Coussemaker's Anonymous IV is to be believed:

In accordance with more recent usage, though it is in truth somewhat rare, the pure (vocal) organa have a compass extending to the triple octave, although this currently exists in organs and other instruments besides (in instrumento organorum et ulterius aliorum instrumentorum) by the number of strings or pipes, or an even greater range—such as the 'well-tuned cymbals' in the hands of good musicians.[107]

There is, however, a great lack of information regarding the number and

---

104 Th. Gérold, *Histoire de la Musique, des origines à la fin du XIVe siècle* (Paris, 1936), p. 229.
105 Paris, Bibl. Nat., Lat. MS 8121 A.
106 Engelbert d'Amont (Gerbert, *Script.*, ii, p. 138).
107 J. Chailley, 'Un clavier d'orgue', op. cit., pp. 5 ff. This passage probably refers to the pipe organ, judging by the words 'hoc numero . . . fistularum'. The 'well-tuned cymbals', a well-known Biblical formula, are here used purely as a stylistic device. Eberhard of Freising also refers to these extensive tessituras: 'It is enough to give the measurements for two ranks, that is to say sixteen pipes: and from these you may add as many more as you wish' (Gerbert, *Script.*, ii, p. 279).

disposition of the stops. The monk Wulstan specifically says in his poem
that the four hundred pipes on his organ are arranged in ten ranks of forty.
But then this was an exceptional instrument. Theophilus provides for several
pipes to each manual slider, and Anonymous of Berne describes two, one for
the note and the other for the same note an octave lower. Only the Sélestat
manuscript (eleventh century) and that of Anonymous of Berne outline in
any detail the construction of a wind-chest with three sets of pipes and a
seven-key manual. The first and third ranks of pipes, sounding in unison
with one another, flank the second rank, sounding an octave higher. In
describing how these ranks should be installed, the builder advocates that the
low-sounding ranks should be put in position first, and the upper rank last
of all:

When the measuring has been done (the pipes) should be positioned thus.
Between two large pipes a smaller one is set,[108] bearing the number 8; so that
the three together sound the consonance known as the octave. In other words,
there are two low-sounding pipes and a third sounding higher; the measurements have already been given.

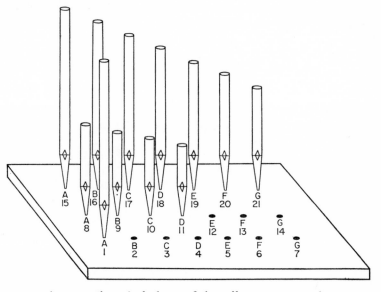

Fig. 27. The wind-chest of the Sélestat manuscript

Thus when it comes to fitting the small pipes,[109] as for instance that which
stands in the 10th hole in the wind-chest, marked 'C', the measurements of the
previous 'C' pipe should be referred to, and, proceeding from the measurements of this large (pipe) you find the pipe appropriate to the empty space.

[108] Going from the front to the back of the wind-chest.
[109] Those that make up the treble set. See fig. 27.

The same procedure obtains for the remaining empty sockets, all that is necessary is to look for the letter marked there, and by repeating the process described for the 'C', every space will be filled.[110]

According to Eberhard of Freising, it was not uncommon for the note to be accompanied by its double octave as well as its octave;[111] and in this way the sound of the organ gained in luminosity and range. It will be recalled that Baldric of Dol described the instrument in the Abbey at Fécamp as producing music composed of a union of low, medium, and high voices. But it should also be borne in mind that at that time there were no wind-chests with draw-stops which would allow the organist to separate these various timbres if the occasion demanded it.

Gastoué believed[112] that as early as the twelfth century the idea of further adding the fifth, a major consonance, occurred to organ-builders. This is not impossible, though Gastoué's line of argument has been refuted by Norbert Dufourcq[113]—Henri Arnaut's text actually relates to an instrument not earlier than the fifteenth century. However, a recently published text[114] throws fresh light on the fascinating problem of mixtures, which, though they do not feature in the measurement tables known to us at present, may have been used even in the time of Notker Labeo. The document in question is a Hebrew manuscript preserved in the Bibliothèque Nationale and containing among other writings the translation of a Latin treatise giving original instructions for measuring the monochord, organ pipes, and the cymbalum. Basing his calculations essentially on philological arguments, H. Avenary places this text in the first half of the eleventh century.

Having set out two methods for measuring pipes, the treatise continues:[115]

Behind each of the pipes [thus obtained], place a [further] pipe, equal in height to the fifth after it.[116] He who has no fifth will place behind it a pipe of smaller dimensions, and smaller than all the others.[117] Behind [the first rank] there will in fact be placed other pipes, each half the size of its fundamental in cut, length, and width. And according to the size of the instrument, place beside each pipe fourths, fifths, and octaves.

The author thus recommends that each note on the manual should be doubled at the fifth or octave, and on large instruments there should be

---

[110] Sélestat Library, Lat. MS. 17, fol. 37.
[111] Op. cit., p. 281.
[112] *L'orgue en France*, p. 39.
[113] Op. cit., pp. 74 ff.
[114] H. Avenary, 'The mixture principle in the medieval organ', *Musica Disciplina*, iv (1950), p. 51–7.
[115] I translate Avenary.
[116] That is to say its fifth.
[117] Higher than the highest pipe of the first rank.

fourths, fifths, and octaves, forming a full organ, which includes an interval foreign to the first harmonics. We shall see later that vocal organum frequently used consecutive fourths;[118] these two facts are not unrelated.

[118] 'There are three simple consonances, one called the fourth, the second the fifth, and the third the octave' (Hucbald, *Mus. Enchir.*, x); Antiquity, as we have seen, was particularly fond of these three intervals: see p. 130.

CHAPTER FOURTEEN

༧ⱲⱭ

The Organ in Western Europe from the Eleventh to the Thirteenth Century

THE ORGAN IN THE ELEVENTH AND TWELFTH CENTURIES

In the eleventh century, besides the two important treatises on organ manufacture and the handbooks of pipe measurements already discussed, various authors give an account of how instruments were installed in their respective churches. In 1060, for instance, Abbot Adalbert put an organ in the monastery of St. Ulrich, in Augsburg, where previously there had been none.[1] Thirty-two years later a similar instrument is described as playing near Salerno, at the consecration of the church in the monastery of Cava. 'The ceremonial for the consecration was magnificent; the most subtle perfumes were burning throughout, and the sweetest music was heard, with the harmony of the organs and oboes sounding in the most delightful cadences.'[2]

In 1077 the monastery of Weltenburg also had its organ, a gift of the priest Didier;[3] and about this time, too, the Abbey of Fleury acquired an instrument.[4] During the next century the organ continued to spread throughout Europe. The monk Gervase records that Canterbury Cathedral had one at the time of the fire in 1114: it stood in the north aisle of the nave.[5] In 1120 the Cathedral of St. Nicholas in Utrecht likewise had an organ;[6] but in 1134, the Abbey of Lobbes, proud of its instrument, lost it, as we have seen, by order of a music-loving bishop. In 1158 the church at Freising was destroyed by fire, and with it its bells and its organ. 'The wind which then

---

[1] Buhle, p. 66.

[2] *Acta SS. Boll. Martii*, i, p. 334.

[3] *M.G.H., Necrologia*, iii, *Necrol. Weltenburgense*, p. 376.

[4] According to Fr. Médard-Louillet, op. cit.

[5] W. Woolnoth, *A Graphical Illustration of the Metropolitan Cathedral Church of Canterbury* (London, 1816). See also E. J. Hopkins and E. F. Rimbault, *The Organ, its History and Construction* (London, 1855), p. 43.

[6] Buhle, op. cit., p. 66, note 6.

sprang up, confounded all; it was a deplorable disaster . . . The entire organ collapsed with its loft, as did the royal tower with its sweet-sounding bells.'[7]

During this period, the monastery of Petershausen is mentioned as having an organ, together with the Cathedral at Constance:

Thereafter Abbot Conrad engaged a certain monk named Aaron, a priest of Chamberch, well versed in the art of music, who built him an organ of wonderful tone (elegantissimae modulationis), and placed it in the south aisle of the basilica. This same monk had previously fabricated an instrument of the same type for the church at Constance.[8]

In 1199 the organ in the monastery church at Merseburg was destroyed by fire, but was rebuilt eight years later: 'Tideric the steward caused a new organ to be made, the previous one having perished when the church was burnt.'[9]

Also from the twelfth century we have a strange poem commemorating the organ in the church of the Benedictine Abbey of Engelberg, in the Swiss canton of Unterwalden. In the first seven lines of the poem each syllable is surmounted by a letter corresponding to a particular key on the manual. Schubiger, who published this piece of verse, believes this notation to be exclusive to the organists, while the singers used neumes.[10] As we have seen, it was customary to set out this kind of 'alphabet' above the manual to help the player's memory.

> Hear now the organ chorus,
> It is the musical instrument
> Of present-day artists,
> A honey-sweet witness.
> You play it and it sings
> In a praiseworthy manner,
> And teaches you to play
> Delightfully,
> In little time,
> With delicacy, sweetness, and ease.
> I know, I tell you; understand me;
> I order and advise you to take heed
> And fix this in your memory.
> Serve Music, so that you may know it well,
> Practise assiduously, and apply yourself to the Art.

[7] *M.G.H., Script.*, 24, p. 322.
[8] ibid., 22, p. 669.
[9] ibid., 23, p. 174.
[10] Schubiger, op. cit., pp. 79–95.

Show a receptive spirit
And an active body.
Take bellows
And fill them full of air.
Do not forget that.
And, thus equipped,
Make melody with cunning fingers,
The sound of music with pleasant tones.
Let the sound sing in the bass,
Let it shout forth its brassy sound,
And let choir sing with choir
In diaphony
And in organum.
Then move to the trebles,
Returning to the bass
With a lyric fall.
Then to the middle notes,
With a swift run
And a noble spring,
With supple, seductive hand
Deserving praise.
In such joyous music,
Honey-sweet,
The crowd will delight,
And will wonder and rejoice
During the music
And their faithful worship of God,
Who reigns in eternity.

As an example, here are the letters superimposed on the first two lines:

```
f e       d · c     f  g  h   f
A u d i   c h o r u  m   o r g a n i c u m

f         e   d    c      d  f  f
I n s t r u m e n t u m   m u s i c u m
```

It seems reasonable to assume that this is, in fact, a sequence of mnemonic tags designed for student organists.

No mention has yet been made of the references to the organ in the Chansons de Geste written prior to the twelfth century. The popular poets are naturally more concerned with the code of chivalry and with amazing adventures than with detailed descriptions. The Norman trouvère Wace appears to have been the first to speak of the organ in a church setting:

Quant li messe fu commensie
Qui durement fu essaucie
Mout oissiés orgues sonner
Et clercs chanter et orguener
Voiz abaissier et voiz lever
Chant avaler et chant monter.[11]

(When mass had begun, which was sung exultantly, one could hear organs playing loudly and clerics singing in unison and in harmony, raising and lowering their voices, the song rising and falling.)

The *Roman de Brut*, from which these lines are taken, dates from 1155; and less than twenty years later, another romance from the Breton cycle, *Lancelot*, by Chrétien de Troyes, contains a similar reference:

Qu'aussi por oir les ogres
Vont au mostier a feste anuel
A Pentecoste ou a Noel
Les janz acostumeement.[12]

(Just as people are accustomed to go to church to hear the organ on the annual feast-days of Pentecost or Christmas.)

In a Middle High German poem also written at this time the instrument is shown taking part in a secular celebration:

Si begunde wol singen
Snaellichen springen,
Mit herphin unde gigen
Mit orgenen unde lyren.[13]

(They began to sing sweetly, and dance with swift steps, to the tune of harps and fiddles, organs and lyres.)

Another German poet mentions it in connection with a public festival held at Mainz in 1184:

Dâ was spil end gesanc
End behurt ende dranc,
Pîpen ende singen
Vedelen ende springen,
Orgeln ende seitspelen,
Meneger slachten frouden vele.[14]

(There was playing and singing, pushing and shoving, piping and singing, fiddling and dancing, music on the organ and stringed instruments, and many other joyful things.)

[11] J. Chailley, 'Un clavier d'orgue à la fin du XIe siècle', *Revue de musicologie*, no. 61, February 1937, p. 8.
[12] Th. Gérold, *La Musique au Moyen Age*, op. cit., p. 419.
[13] E. Buhle, op. cit., p. 62, note 4.
[14] Gérold, p. 419.

The organs which play with other instruments at public gatherings were presumably small portatives, for this type of organ, carried around by the player himself, and probably known among the Byzantines if not by the Romans of the late Empire, had by now made its appearance in Europe. Although they are never specifically described in any of the texts, the iconography shows them as early as the tenth century (Stuttgart Psalter), and a twelfth-century manuscript in the British Museum contains an illustration of just such a small portative organ held on someone's knees. The instrument, similar in every respect to those produced in such abundance in the fourteenth century, has two ranks of seven pipes set between carved lateral pillars, one representing a crenellated tower, the other an animal's head (Plate XXVIII, no. 1).[15]

Pérotin le Grand, the famous 'organista' of Notre-Dame, in Paris, lived during the twelfth century. Little is known about his life; but if this Pérotin may, as seems possible, be identified with the Deacon Pierre, who died around 1197,[16] then it is not at all certain that he was, in fact, an organist, or that the cathedral even possessed an organ at this time. The term 'organista' may be applied to whoever composes the organa, or to whoever sings them, plays them, or accompanies them on the organ. However, Adam of Fulda assures us that instrumentalists were given a title based not on their theoretical knowledge but on the instrument they played: 'a citharist takes his name from the cithara, the tibicen from the tibia, and the organist (organista) from the organ'.[17]

THE ORGAN IN THE THIRTEENTH CENTURY

In the thirteenth century the organ was still essentially the instrument of religious worship. Though, as the iconography proves, the small 'portatives' designed for secular use tended to become more widespread, the 'great organ' was firmly entrenched in the church, from which it gradually ousted all other instruments. The Spanish Franciscan Giles of Zamora (in the province of Léon) makes this clear: 'The Church uses only this musical instrument for its various chants and sequences and hymns; all other instruments have been abolished because they were abused by play-actors.'[18]

According to the *Livre des Propriétés et des Choses*, a French translation of Latin text dating from the first half of the thirteenth century, 'de cest instrument use l'en en Saincte église et non des autres communement.'[19]

---

[15] H. Hickmann, *Das Portativ, ein Beitrag zur Geschichte der Kleinorgel* (Cassel, 1936), Pl. 2, No. 1.

[16] J. Chailley, *Histoire Musicale du Moyen Age*, pp. 157 ff.

[17] Gerbert, *Script.*, iii, p. 347.

[18] Gerbert, *Script.*, ii, p. 388.

[19] N. Dufourcq, *Esquisse d'une histoire de l'orgue en France du XIIIᵉ au XVIIIᵉ siècle* (Paris, 1935), p. 53.

(This instrument, and no others, is commonly used in the Holy Church.) However, Honorius of Autun (early twelfth century), basing himself on the authority of David and Solomon, allows other instruments to join with the organ in praising God:

David and Solomon . . . introduced the custom of having hymns played during the divine sacrifice, by organs and other musical instruments, and of having the people shout out their praises. From this comes the established practice of playing the organs during the serving of the mass, of having the clergy intone, and the people making their responses in chorus.[20]

Guillaume Durand, Bishop of Mende, who died in 1296, shares this view, and finds it reasonable that the organ should sound five times during the Sanctus.[21] At this time, too, St. Thomas Aquinas himself writes that the instrument is such as to 'lift him up to the heights'.[22] It is hardly surprising, therefore, that church organs began to multiply. At Erfurt, two instruments were built one after the other:

Anno 1225. In that year, new organs were built for the church of the Blessed Virgin at Erfurt . . .
Anno 1226. Organs were built for St. Peter's church at Erfurt . . . A remarkable piece of work is being carried out in St. Peter's church: I refer to the organs, which were heard for the first time on Holy Saturday.[23]

But this fine instrument was fated to be damaged by lightning in 1291:

Even the great organ opposite was damaged by the same lightning flash or thunderbolt; and will have to be repaired in a great many places . . .[24]

By 1259, Barcelona Cathedral had an organ, given by one William of Lacera, who specified in his will that the organ should be overhauled at regular intervals.[25] In 1294 the Benedictine Priory at Politz in Austria had its organ,[26] while in Paris an organ was installed in the Sainte-Chapelle before 1299.[27] It has even been suggested that St. Louis carried a small portable organ with him on the ship bearing him off to the Crusades; but the text of Guillaume de Nangis, which records this, is ambiguous, and possibly refers to singing in organum.[28]

This portable instrument, or 'positive', falls half-way between the 'great'

---

[20] *P.L.* clxxii: Liturgica, xlii, 556. Sicard, Bishop of Cremona, expresses himself in similar vein: *P.L.* ccxiii: *Mitrale*, 123.
[21] *Rationale*, iv, 78.
[22] *Psalmus XXXII*, 2, ed. E. Fretté (Paris 1876), xviii, p. 409.
[23] *M.G.H., Cronica S. Petri Erfordensis moderna*, p. 390.
[24] ibid.
[25] Higini Anglès, op. cit., p. 81.
[26] R. Quoika, *Die Altösterreichische Orgel* (Cassel, 1953), p. 9.
[27] Y. Rokseth, *La musique d'orgue au XVe siècle et au début du XVIe* (Paris, 1930), p. 12.
[28] The king hears mass 'a ogre, chant et dechant' (ibid., p. 10).

church organ and the small portative which could be held on the player's knees. It was moved about on a wagon and stood on its own four feet, producing a sufficient volume of sound for it to be used in certain religious ceremonies. The portal of the cathedral at Léon, in Spain, illustrates a 'positive' of this type. It shows an instrument whose over-all height is about 1·20 m., if one measures by the human figures also represented. The wind-chest, decorated with geometric patterns, is of corresponding length, and supports about twenty pipes, whose lips are plainly visible. The high pipes are to the right of the organist, who is seated very low. The perspective prevents us from discovering how many ranks of pipes the instrument has, but they are held in place in the ancient style by a slanting crossbar running between two lateral uprights. On the same side as the bass pipes, air is pumped into the wind-chest by a single pair of bellows operated by a child. Such a modest wind mechanism is hardly adequate for the size of the instrument, and the wind-chest's lack of depth rules out any suggestion that it might contain a stabilizing bellows. This source of air must consequently be regarded as symbolic rather than real.

The thirteenth-century portative organ is in no way different from its predecessors. Light enough to be carried at arm's length, it frequently appears in manuscript illuminations, on capitals and stained glass windows.[29] There are almost invariably two ranks of seven or eight pipes. The organist's right hand operates the manual, while his left pumps the bellows—neither of these manoeuvres an easy task. With a single bellows the sound of the instrument could not possibly be continuous, and players had therefore to pay particular attention to their bellows:

> Quidam organna [sic] exsufflabant
> Dulciter ventus flatum temperantes[30]

Often the portative accompanies the musician's singing, as in the following lines from the *Roman de la Rose* (thirteenth century):

> Orgues i r'a bien maniables,
> A une sole main portables,
> Ou il-meismes soufle et touche
> Et chante avec a plaine bouche
> Motes, ou treble ou teneure . . .[31]

(There are easily manageable organs that can be carried in the hand, the same

---

[29] N. Dufourcq, op. cit., p. 26.

[30] Ed. Francisque-Michel (Paris, 1864), ii, p. 327. The 'treble' or triple is usually the third vocal part of an organum. See Coussemaker, *L'Art harmonique aux XIIe et XIIIe siècles* (Paris, 1865), p. 47.

[31] Aymeric de Peyrac, *Vie de Charlemagne*, quoted by Bottée de Toulmon, *Dissertation sur les instruments de musique employés au Moyen Age*, p. 102.

person simultaneously pumping [the bellows], playing [the instrument], and singing aloud motets, either soprano or tenor. . . .)

In nearly every illustration the two bass pipes of the portative are much longer than their nearest neighbour, as, for instance, in the miniature from MS. 302 in the Bibliothèque Municipale in Arras, where the last pipe is more than twice as long as the penultimate one (Plate XXVIII, no. 3). Frequently, too, these large pipes are enclosed in a tower. For lack of documentation, we cannot be sure of the significance of these pipes, which are clearly outside the normal tessitura. It seems quite possible, however, that they functioned as bourdons. Indeed, the constant drone of a low, unvarying sound in instrumental music was at that time apparently very desirable, and widely appreciated—witness the drone-strings on the fiddles and the drones on a set of bagpipes. The bourdon pipes of the portative organ probably opened directly into the wind-chest, and had no corresponding key on the manual. A pipe of this type is shown at the upper extremity of a (standing) positive, in a fourteenth-century manuscript.[32]

During the Middle Ages the portative organ enjoyed tremendous popularity, and was a feature of every civic occasion. Many a troubadour must have sung his songs to that frail accompaniment, to which reference is made in Gottfried von Strasbourg's *Tristan* and Heinrich von Türlin's *Krone*.[33] The following lines, from a thirteenth-century text, probably refer to portatives:

The people of Bohemia delight in the performance of a dance troupe; everyone rejoices, singing and happiness resound. There is a beating of drums, and a scraping of citharas, and all the while the loud blasts of the trumpet ring out; the lyre twangs, and now the dancers pirouette, the chorus proclaims its joy, the organs peal, and the king arrives, laughing with all those gathered there.[34]

The instrument also appears at private entertainments given by the famous: the German poet Jansen Enikel describes its presence at a concert given during a feast at which Pharaoh, his wife, and Moses are brought together in an allegory.[35]

By the end of the thirteenth century most of the European churches were vying with each other to acquire or enlarge their organs. The large towns in southern Germany, Czechoslovakia, Switzerland, and England were already endowed with instruments—to those already listed must be added Bonn (1230), Prague (1255),[36] Exeter (1256), Strasbourg (1292), Bruges

---

[32] Bibliothèque Nationale, French MS. 13096, fol. 46: Dufourcq, op. cit., Pl. III, No. 4.

[33] L. Söhner, 'Die Orgelbegleitung zum Gregorianischen Gesang', *Kirchenmusikalische Reihe* (1936), p. 20.

[34] V. Nemec, *Pražské Varhany* (Prague, 1944), p. 316, note 20.

[35] *M.G.H., Enikel*, p. 129.

[36] V. Nemec, op. cit., pp. 315–16, note 18.

(1299),[37] together with Zürich, Berne, and Basle,[38] and probably Florence, Lübeck, Salzburg, Worms, and Westminster.[39] The great church organ did not appear in France until later, and while the Sainte-Chapelle and the Cathedrals of Meaux, Senlis, Orleans, and Rheims already had organs,[40] the instrument only became widespread in the following century. Notre-Dame de Paris,[41] St.-Séverin, St.-Gervais, Lille, St.-Quentin, St.-Omer, Douai, Chartres, Laon, Caen, Amiens, Rouen, Nevers, Angers, Langres, Dijon, Avignon—the once pagan organ from Alexandria finally conquered the Church, to become its liturgical instrument *par excellence*.[42]

It is likely that the development of the instrument was not unrelated to the architectural transformation of Western churches. Towards the middle of the twelfth century the style today improperly called 'Gothic' was beginning to replace the Romanesque style of building, solid and heavy, with a new concept of balance which enabled men to build high naves and huge windows of stained glass. In the new cathedrals the limited power of the small positive organ was no longer adequate to accompany the growing congregations of worshippers or to alternate with the choirs. Organ-builders were therefore forced to devise instruments that were more complex, more sonorous, and consequently larger. This evolution was to lead gradually to a decisive transformation in the transmission mechanisms, and from the fourteenth century we find the ingenious 'coupling' device. This meant that the wind-chest could be vastly enlarged to take a very great number of pipes, while the manual was kept to a compact size, so that from then on the instrument was played by only one organist.

However, the free-standing positive by no means disappeared from the sanctuary. Here it continued to play a special role, accompanying the choir-master and giving the note. Presumably it became standard practice to position it face to face with the great organ, so that the organist, at the manual of the larger instrument, had only to turn round in order to play on

---

[37] N. Dufourcq, op. cit., p. 42, note 1. On Strasbourg see F. Raugel, *Les orgues et les organistes de la Cathédrale de Strasbourg* (Colmar, 1948).

[38] Schubiger, op. cit., p. 80.

[39] Hanz Klotz, *Die Musik in Geschichte und Gegenwart*, nos. 90–1, 266.

[40] Gastoué, *L'orgue en France*, p. 44.

[41] The presence of an organ in Notre-Dame, in Paris, as early as 1198, accepted on the strength of a text by Eudes de Sully (A.-P.-M. Gilbert, *Description de la basilique métropolitaine de Paris*, 1911, p. 34), should be viewed with caution, for the report may be referring to vocal organum.

[42] The Council of Milan in 1287 is supposed to have decreed that only the organ should play in church (E. A. Bowles, 'Were Musical Instruments used in the Liturgical Service during the Middle Ages?' *The Galpin Society Journal*, x, May 1957, pp. 48 ff.). Custom varied from place to place; for instance, the general chapter at Ferrara forbade the organist to play during services for reasons of humility. But some towns in the diocese refused to apply the decree (P. Masetti, *Monumenta et Antiquitates veteris disciplinae Ordinis Praedicatorum*, Rome, 1864, i, 13, p. 73).

the smaller, if the need arose. Later, with the invention of the coupling action, the manual of this positive was transferred from its normal position and installed immediately underneath that of the great organ, to save the organist the trouble of turning from one to the other. The tradition of these two organs survived up to the end of the eighteenth century, when each was still separate and enclosed in its own organ case. Even today one of the manuals on the instrument is known as the 'positive'.

ASPECTS OF PERFORMANCE

A certain virtuosity must have been possible where the instrument had a manual with springs. The poem in praise of the instrument at the Abbey of Engelberg refers to 'cunning fingers' performing 'quick runs'. Organs with non-retracting sliders obviously lacked this advantage, for where playing necessitated grasping each key with the whole hand to pull it out and push it back, the process was slow and clumsy. Presumably such instruments confined their activities to marking the long 'tenors', which were often remarkably protracted, especially in the music of Pérotin. (Though this hypothesis, formerly proposed by J. Chailley,[43] is certainly very tempting, it is by no means sure that the organ with sliders was still in use when Pérotin was alive.) The time involved in manipulating such manuals was partly cancelled out by the use of two organists playing simultaneously, one on the low notes, the other at the top end of the scale. This is borne out by the description given by Wulstan and by the miniatures in the Utrecht and Munich Psalters.

The organist of the positive always plays sitting down; he is often a monk, recognizable by his tonsure.[44] The portative is almost invariably played by a layman, usually in a standing position, though occasionally he, too, is seated. In the texts, the organist is sometimes described as *artifex* (Letter of John VIII), sometimes *organarius*,[45] *cantor* (Theophilus), or *organista* (Adam of Fulda). On the miniature in the Munich Staatsbibliothek the word *organista* is inscribed above David's head as he sits at the organ. At the end of the thirteenth century the organist of the St.-Chapelle bears the title *moderator organorum*,[46] while the organist of Notre-Dame is known as the *organator*.[47]

When the church organ was not playing solo it accompanied the voices of the singers, as the portative accompanied the troubadour. It would appear

---

[43] 'Un clavier d'orgue à la fin du XIe siècle', op. cit., p. 9.
[44] These clerk-organists ranked high among church musicians: E. A. Bowles, op. cit., p. 48.
[45] From the time of the Venerable Bede (early eighth century).
[46] M. Brénet, *Les musiciens de la Sainte-Chapelle* (Paris, 1910), p. 12.
[47] J. Handschin, 'Zur Geschichte von Notre-Dame', *Acta Musicologica*, iv (1932), p. 13. Possibly this word is also applied to the organ-builder.

that the first songs in the church to be accompanied were the Sequences, and later the Tropes and Hymns.[48] At other times the instrument alternated with the congregation during the mass, as Honorius of Autun and later (*c.* 1350) Johannes of Florence testify: 'partim organo partim modulatis per concentum vocibus'.[49]

THE CYMBALUM

Frequently, however, the organ played in an ensemble with other instruments—the viol, flute, syrinx, hurdy-gurdy, monochord, cymbalum. The texts and the iconography reveal that the combination of organ and cymbalum was particularly popular. At this period the cymbalum was an instrument consisting of what looked like a gantry, to which were hooked seven or eight small bells graded in size and played with one or two hammers. It features in many illustrations from the tenth century onwards, both in cathedral sculptures and in manuscripts. In an eleventh-century psalter now in the Bibliothèque Municipale at Amiens, the word 'cymbalis' from the psalm is written above an instrument of this type.[50] The cymbalum is, in fact, seldom absent from musical scenes, and has its place in the church on the same basis as the organ.[51] Aelred of Riévaulx finds both deplorable (tot organa, tot cymbala . . .); but the Bishop of Arras thinks nothing of appropriating the organ and cymbalum of the monastery at Lobbes and transferring them to his own church (organum . . . ab ecclesia abstulit . . . in suam fecit transportari ecclesiam; sic et de cymbalis factum est).

Guillaume Durand ranks the cymbalum among the various types of bell,[52] and the monk Theophilus devotes a brief chapter to its fabrication.[53] He reveals that measurement tables existed which gave the different sizes necessary to form a diatonic scale, and the author adds that, after the bells were cast, the pitch of each separate bell was adjusted with a file. Hucbald gives the respective weights of the seven bells,[54] and Aribo relates their tuning to that of the monochord.[55] An anonymous St. Blasien manuscript describes a cymbalum equipped with the Synemmenon.[56]

---

[48] L. Söhner, *Die Orgelbegleitung zum Gregorianischen Gesang*, pp. 22 ff.

[49] L. Söhner, *Die Geschichte der Begleitung des gregorianischen Chorals* (Augsburg, 1931), p. 23.

[50] V. Leroquais, op. cit., vol. i, Pl. XXVI.

[51] Honorius of Autun (twelfth century): '. . . instrumentis huius artis, ut organis, cymbalis et campanis Deo serviamus' (Gerbert, *De Cantu*, ii, p. 100).

[52] R. Brancour, *Histoire des Instruments de Musique* (Paris, 1921), p. 228, note I.

[53] Ch. LXXXVI, 'De cymbalis musicis'.

[54] 'De cymbalorum ponderibus' (Gerbert, *Script.*, i, p. 149).

[55] 'De simplici cymbalorum mensura . . . et cur similis sit monochordi cymbalorumque mensura' (Gerbert, *Script.*, ii, p. 221).

[56] ibid., ii, p. 285. The instrument was also used to teach intervals: J. Smits van Waesberghe, *Cymbala, bells in the Middle Ages* (Rome, 1951), p. 18.

The crystalline sound of the little bells, no doubt similar to that of the modern celeste, probably combined with the sound of the organ to produce music that was both picturesque and sparkling.[57] The cymbalum, which in the sixteenth century was fitted with a keyboard and thus became the carillon, has bequeathed its name to one of the most distinctive of all organ-stops, the 'cymbale', a high-pitched mixture of fifths and octaves. Its use adds an element of sparkling brilliance to the polyphony, which still evokes the memory of the pretty little bells seen so frequently in manuscript illuminations.

[57] In 1474 the organ in the church of Saint-Sulpice de Fougères still had eight little bells (Dufourcq, op. cit., p. 110).

CHAPTER FIFTEEN

༄ཝ༅

Some Illustrations of the Medieval Organ

Up to the end of the thirteenth century, the limit of this study, the appearance of the medieval organ is preserved only in rare and as a rule somewhat primitive illustrations, usually the work not of trained artists but of anonymous monks who wished to illustrate the sacred texts they were copying. Manuscript illustrations of this type are nearly always found on the initial letter of a chapter, usually relating to Psalms 150 (*Laudate Dominum in chordis et organo*), 149 (*Cantate Domino canticum novum*), and 137 (*In salicibus in medio eius, suspendimus organa nostra*), though sometimes to others (the Psalm *Beatus Vir*, for instance).

Despite their crude or clumsy execution, these pictures of the organ illustrations serve to give us a rough idea of the external appearance and the size of the instrument. Organs shown in such manuscripts are always of modest proportions, and fall into three categories. First we have the light, portable instrument, slung round the player's neck or set on his knees; he pumps and plays simultaneously. Then there is a much larger type, which may be carried, but is really designed to be placed on a table or on the ground. This is the 'positive', which requires both a player and a blower. Much more rarely, the iconography shows an organ permanently installed, rather like the instrument Theophilus suggested might be set up in one of the walls of the sanctuary nave. Of these three types, it is, as we shall see, the portative which is most frequently represented.

The organ seldom appears on its own in these illustrations. Usually it is surrounded by other instruments, with which it apparently forms an ensemble. It is possible that sometimes the copyist was concerned to include in his drawing all the musical instruments in use at the time—some documents at least give this impression. But it seems quite certain that the organ was frequently accompanied by the cymbalum, a set of graded bells that was played with one or more hammers. Of the other instruments featured with the organ, the most common are the viol, the transverse flute, the cornett, and the hurdy-gurdy. The cithara and psaltery are the exclusive property of King David, who invariably occupies the central place in the miniature.

It is obviously impossible to give an exhaustive list of these organ illustrations, and probably not all have yet been identified. I shall therefore examine only the most typical of them—those which reveal specially important characteristics in either the structure or the use of the instrument.

1. *The Utrecht Psalter*. Chronology compels me to include this curious illustration,[1] which shows an instrument having nothing whatever in common with the organs usually represented in the tenth to thirteenth centuries. Most writers date the Psalter to the Carolingian era,[2] and certain aspects of it suggest that it was executed in France in the vicinity of Rheims.[3] Under the text of Psalm 149, *Laudate nomen eius in choro, in tympano et psalterio*, the artist has drawn a great concert scene. In the heavens Christ, surrounded by six angels, is apparently blessing the mortals shown in the foreground, among them horn-players, cymbalists, singers, a lutenist, a man playing the psaltery, and another with a bagpipe. In the centre of the miniature is an organ.[4]

In appearance this instrument is quite unusual, for it is a double hydraulic organ. On a strong base are set two cisterns, reinforced with hoops, from the top of which protrude the necks of the funnels leading into the base of the wind-chest. On either side of the instrument stand two cylindrical pumps, each fitted with a handle. The wind-chest, which is very shallow, supports two identical sets of five pipes forming a single line. The treble pipes are to the organist's right. A double framework, presumably designed, in Graeco-Roman fashion, to support these pipes, actually rises well above the tops of even the highest of them. Two organists are depicted in the act of playing, each controlling one set of pipes. One of them is playing with his left hand, while with his right he spurs the blowers on to further efforts; the other organist uses both hands, and darts encouraging looks towards the blowers on his side. There is no manual and the players' fingers are placed between the pipes in a playing attitude. Four blowers, who look like caricature drawings, are working the pump handles.

This piece of evidence is difficult to interpret, for clearly it combines some valuable information with a number of blatant errors. The instrument is double, and really consists of two complete hydraules. The wind-chest, however, appears to be common to both, and feeds two absolutely identical ranks of five pipes, each requiring its own individual organist. This im-

---

[1] E. T. Dewald has published the entire psalter in photograph in *The Illustrations of the Utrecht Psalter* (Princeton, 1930). This scene is in folio 83, on the right-hand side.
[2] P. Durrieu, *L'origine du manuscrit célèbre dit 'le psautier d'Utrecht'* (Paris, 1895).
[3] O. M. Dalton, *Byzantine Art and Archaeology* (Oxford, 1911), p. 468.
[4] Pl. XXIV, no. 1.

mediately brings to mind Wulstan's description, quoted earlier, in which he says that the Winchester bellows-organ demanded the simultaneous presence of two organists. But why so few pipes here, why two identical ranks, and why the useless framework? Clearly whoever drew the scene was not working directly from a model, but simply relying on his imagination, drawing on his own ideas and on his reading. Indeed, this is even more likely to be a badly interpreted copy of an illustration from some older source.

This miniature should, I feel, be regarded as the creation of an educated monk who had heard stories of great organs for two organists, but who also remembered having read Vitruvius—we saw earlier that the study of the *De Architectura* had been brought back into fashion by Eginhard. And if there is some trace of Byzantine[5] or Syrian[6] influences in the actual technique of the illustration, there is no proof that they counted for anything in the concept of the instrument itself.

The Eadwin Psalter (twelfth century), preserved at Trinity College, Cambridge, contains a very mediocre copy of the Utrecht miniature. The two cisterns with their funnels are still there, but the pumps are tiny, there are no blowers, and only one organist is shown.[7]

2. *The Stuttgart Psalter.* This has pictures of four organs, poorly executed. The main interest of this document is its age, for it dates from the beginning of the tenth century.[8] The first illumination shows two small portatives, each with about seven pipes, held in place by a slanting bar, hanging by a strap from the branches of a willow tree. The text reproduces the words of Psalm 137, where the word 'organa' is interpreted by the ill-informed copyist as meaning 'organs'. The instruments themselves appear to be not more than 60 cm. high, judging by the human figures beside them. The manual sliders are plainly visible, but there is no sign of any bellows.

The two remaining organs are of quite different type. They are built on a much larger scale, and are of a type later known as 'standing positives', which could be moved if necessary, but were designed for a static role. Each has a dozen or so pipes, held in place by an oblique bar. On one pipe the lips are clearly visible. The wind-chests are shallow, and the keys on the manual can be seen. Their general appearance recalls the upper part of the Graeco-Roman hydraulis.

The interesting feature of these two instruments is their wind mechanism, consisting of rather primitive bellows shaped like skin bags. In one drawing

---

[5] N. Kondakoff, *Histoire de l'art byzantin* (Paris, 1886), i, p. 22.

[6] Farmer, *The Organ of the Ancients*, p. 53.

[7] Pl. XXIV, no. 2. Another copy, in the Canterbury Psalter, shows four pumps and three cisterns (M. R. James, *The Canterbury Psalter*, London, 1935, fol. 261 b).

[8] There are excellent reproductions of these miniatures in N. Dufourcq, op. cit., Pl. I, nos. 1, 2 and 3.

it looks very much as though two figures are perched on the bellows, in exactly the same attitude shown in the scene sculpted on the Obelisk of Theodosius. Generally, there are unmistakable traces of Byzantine influence.

3. *The Pommersfelden Psalter*. The Pommersfelden manuscript, dating from the eleventh century, shows an instrument answering the first description given by Theophilus (de domo organaria . . . lignea). This sketchy illustration represents a small pedestal organ with thirteen pipes, the trebles lying to the right of the organist. These pipes have clearly visible lips, and are set in a primitive type of wind-chest. The manual consists of only six sliders, nonchalantly operated by a seated figure. The position of his hands clearly indicates that to play, he must pull them out and push them back. Neither bellows nor organ-blower is shown.[9]

4. *The Harding Bible*. This type of organ with sliders is much better illustrated in the Bible of Stephen Harding, third Abbot of Cîteaux. It dates from the end of the eleventh or the beginning of the twelfth century. The drawing, which is well done, shows King David seated on his throne, holding his harp in his left hand and his sceptre in his right. Below him are a musician playing the cymbalum, another with a shawm, a fiddler, and an organist. This last figure, shown in profile, is seated on a chair with a back to it. In appearance he is coarse-featured, with his hair growing down over the lobes of his ears, and he is dressed in a tunic belted at the waist. The instrument he plays is very curious. The wind-chest, which is relatively deep, is mounted on two enormous slanting air ducts, acting as feet. All of the right-hand duct is not shown, but on the left-hand one it is easy to see the junction with the conflatorium described by Theophilus. Into the conflatorium are inserted the nozzles of three pairs of bellows—the blowers are not shown. The fact that the two air ducts are symmetrical and resemble each other suggests that in all the organ was fed by the air from twelve bellows.[10]

The wind-chest supports two ranks of eight pipes, distinctly conical in shape, the highest-pitched being in this instance on the organist's left. The usual oblique bar is not shown; and each pipe has a small square aperture half-way up, whose precise function is not clear. They may be mouthpieces, which the copyist, unfamiliar with the niceties of organ-building, has positioned too high: or else they are correctly placed and have a similar effect to those made nowadays in harmonic flue pipes. This second hypothesis is the more likely, and it will be recalled that the pipes on the instrument in Naples Museum have slits of this type.

The manual, which is well drawn, consists of eight slider keys with sword-hilt handles. Each pulls out quite a distance—further than the

[9] Pl. XXV, no. 2.   [10] Pl. XXV, no. 1.

organist's head is long—and the movement appears to be vertical. However, the perspective of the drawing is certainly at fault, for, since the air comes from below up towards the pipes, it is technically inconceivable that the sliders could move on any but the horizontal plane. Moreover, there is no reason why the sliders should have such free play: so that these details should be regarded as nothing more than an error on the part of the artist, working from memory.

One valuable detail, however, is that each key is marked with a letter, a practice recommended by Anonymous of Berne to ease the organist's task. The sounds marked are as follows: C, D, E, F, G, a, b, ♮—the diatonic scale with the added Synemmenon. The organist is playing the D and preparing to pull out the F. Note that the order of the letters contradicts that of the pipes.

5. *The Cambridge Manuscript*. Another musical scene is illustrated in the manuscript of St. John's College, Cambridge, dating from the twelfth century. The central figure is King David, seated on a magnificent chair, decorated with the heads of animals. He is wearing his royal crown, and is touching the strings of his harp, which a kneeling servant has just brought. On David's left are three musicians: one plays the horn, another the syrinx, and the third is a singer. On his right we see a cymbalist holding his hammer in one hand and plucking with the other at an instrument lying across his knees, which looks like a monochord. Between David and the cymbalist is an organ and its wind mechanism.[11]

In the foreground the artist has drawn the two organ-blowers hard at work; but their method is rather out of the ordinary. Grasping a horizontal bar fixed head-high, while his feet rest on the bellows, each man bears down with his full weight on its upper board. When the bellows is empty, the blower hoists himself up by his arms, and a spring, not shown, raises the mobile table. Contrary to what we see here, there can be no doubt that the two men pumped alternately, one emptying his bellows while the other filled his up. The figures crouched on the bellows of the instrument in the Stuttgart Psalter are probably engaged in an identical operation.

The two bellows converge on a bicorn conflatorium attached to a long air duct which describes a double curve before reaching the wind-chest of the organ. This is of modest proportions, with two ranks of seven pipes arranged in zigzag formation. The pipes in each rank appear to have the same diapason. The treble pipes are to the right of the manual, which has seven round-ended keys. The wind-chest stands on four short legs.

Probably this organ is permanently installed, almost certainly in a church. The wind mechanism suggests this. Its complexity is out of all proportion to

[11] Pl. XXV, no. 3.

the organ it feeds, but it is not clear whether this is a deliberate or accidental error of scale. However, the instrument is certainly of some importance, reminiscent of the organ installed by Theophilus under one of the arcades in his monastery, and which Bishop Durand loved to hear during the Sanctus.

6. *The Cividale del Friuli Manuscript.* This document, generally thought to be from the first third of the thirteenth century, once again shows King David surrounded by a mixed ensemble of instrumentalists—a horn player and a fiddler, a cymbalist who plays in a sitting position, a hammer in each hand, and an organist,[12] dressed in a long robe and seated on an ornate chair, with his head bent over his instrument. He grasps a key in each hand, his attitude indicating clearly that he is pulling and pushing them. Because of an error in the perspective of the drawing, the two sliders seem to jut out from one of the side panels of the wind-chest, while two other keys are visible on the opposite side. The instrument has eleven pipes, held in place by a horizontal bar; but the faulty perspective leaves us in some doubt as to whether the high notes are to the right or left of the organist. The largest pipe is more than twice the height of the smallest, and no lips are visible. The wind-chest, which apparently consists of two slabs of wood superimposed one on another (this, again, is the technique advocated by Theophilus) is supported on two tall, strong-looking columns, between which curves the air duct, ending in a conflatorium. Into this are fixed the nozzles of two large bellows, surprisingly modern in appearance, with their wide inlet valve and their leather gussets. A solitary blower operates both bellows, one with each hand; but his cheerful demeanour suggests that he does not find the task too arduous. Judging by the height of the musicians, the bellows are at least a metre in length.

An interesting feature of this illustration is that the organist appears to be outside the room in which the concert is taking place.

7. *The Belvoir Castle Psalter.* In this manuscript, dating from the thirteenth century, it is King David himself who takes his turn at the organ manual. Richly garbed and wearing his crown, he is seen in three-quarter profile, from behind, seated at a most beautifully made standing positive.[13] The instrument has two ranks of approximately fifteen pipes, the trebles to the right of the organist. The pipes in the second rank are appreciably taller than those in the first, but all are conical in shape, and on some the lips can be distinguished. On the extreme right, at the treble end of the rank, stands a large pipe equally as tall as the lowest bass pipe. It is not clear what its exact function may be. Possibly it produced a uniform sound while the organ was being played, like a bagpipe drone.

[12] Pl. XXVII, no. 1.   [13] Pl. XXVII, no. 2.

The manual is composed of broad keys lying directly underneath the pipes, and the organist, playing with both hands, even appears to be using his fingers separately. The decorated wind-chest appears to be more than a metre across, and into its right side fits the nozzle of a large double bellows, operated by a man wearing a tunic that stops short at mid-thigh. With one foot on each upper board, he supports himself with his hands on a chest-high bar. An apparatus with a balancing pole allows one bellows to fill while the other is emptying.

This organ, accompanied by a child playing a hurdy-gurdy, is quite modern in appearance. Hanging above it is a chime of thirteen small bells, but the cymbalist is not represented.

8. *The Munich Manuscript.* The Library of the University of Munich has in its possession a thirteenth-century manuscript illustrated by an interesting concert scene. The letter B, initial letter of the psalm *Beatus vir*, is decorated with human figures, most of whom are playing a musical instrument—a viol, hurdy-gurdy, transverse flute, and cornett. But most of the space is taken up by the cymbalum and the organ, as though to emphasize their importance; whereas King David, playing his harp, is relegated to a small corner on the left-hand side of the miniature. The cymbalum, a chime of seven small bells, is played by a long-haired youth using two hammers. The organ has a blower and two organists, and its peculiarities warrant a detailed description.[14]

The rectangular wind-chest is fed by three air ducts leading to the right, centre and left sections respectively. This arrangement, probably not a figment of the artist's imagination, constitutes a real step forward in organ-building, and one which is not recorded in any of the treatises. It must have meant that the supply of air to the wind-chest was more balanced, and that the high, middle, and low pipes received an equal share. Supported by the three air ducts, which serve as feet, the wind-chest feeds thirteen cylindrical pipes, though faulty perspective prevents us from forming any precise idea as to their distribution. However, there appear to be three ranks.

At the front of the wind-chest we see four keys, rounded at one end. One of these is actually being depressed by a monk, recognizable by his tonsure. The movement of his hand indicates that these keys are fitted with return springs, similar to those described by Anonymous of Berne. Curiously enough, two more keys are shown on the left side of the wind-chest, both operated by a second organist, also tonsured. These keys are absolutely identical in appearance with those at the front, and are not draw-stops, as has been suggested, but an integral part of the manual, since in any case the wind-chest with registers did not exist in the thirteenth century. This

[14] Pl. XXVI.

anomaly must be ascribed either to the artist's imagination or to his lack of knowledge. The fact remains that the instrument is played by two organists, like the Winchester organ described earlier.

There is no trace of a conflatorium. All three air ducts lead out of the same conduit into which the air flows from a kind of box on trestles. The air is supplied by a single bellows operated by a curly-haired youth.

9. *The Solomon Glossary.* The *Glossarium Salomonis* in the Munich Staatsbibliothek also dates from the thirteenth century. It shows a small organ played by King David himself. Wearing his crown and sumptuously robed, he is seated at his instrument, which looks rather like a small square piece of furniture set on four legs. The wind-chest supports six conical pipes, and the manual is represented by only two keys, long rods hooked at the ends. One of these is held in a depressed position by the organist's right hand, while with the left he seems to stress the words of the psalm inscribed immediately above: 'Laudate Dominum in organis'. A two-handled bellows, whose nozzle is inserted into the base of the wind-chest, is operated by a standing figure.

Above David's head the artist has written the word 'organista'.[15]

10. *Manuscript No. 1076 in the Bibliothèque Nationale.* This Franciscan psalter, dating from the second half of the thirteenth century,[16] has, in the initial letter of the *Beatus vir*, an illustration showing yet another concert scene, in which King David reverts to his traditional role of harpist, surrounded by angelic musicians. To the left of the letter the artist has drawn a youthful figure holding in his arms a very fine portable organ.

The instrument has two ranks of seven pipes held in position by a slanting bar. The largest pipe, more than twice as long as its immediate neighbour, is encased in a wooden sheath carved in the shape of a tower. The smallest is likewise camouflaged in a kind of tapering box, resembling a church spire. The manual is visible, and appears to have seven keys, which the organist plays with his right hand. The wind-chest is very shallow, and under it we glimpse the bellows, clearly worked with the left hand. The overall height of the instrument, judging by the stature of the young man carrying it, is approximately 80 cm. and the width not more than 30 cm.

11. *Manuscript No. 11560 in the Bibliothèque Nationale.* This is a large psalter, again dating from the thirteenth century. Among its rich illuminations, where blues and golds predominate, is one showing a small positive organ of particular interest. The rather bulky wind-chest supports two ranks of ten

[15] Pl. XXVIII, no. 2.
[16] Paris, Bibl. Nat., Latin section, no. 1076, fol. 7. Reproduced by V. Leroquais in *Les psautiers manuscrits latins des bibliothèques publiques de France* (Mâcon, 1940–1), ii, p. 64.

conical pipes. The first rank, on which the lips are clearly visible, is not as tall as the second. One noticeable fact is that the extreme pipes are more or less equal in height, and tower over their neighbours: but there is no method of support. The manual is composed of eight keys with rounded ends, and there is no sign of a bellows. The instrument, which is apparently not very heavy, is borne aloft by a richly dressed man. His stance might be surprising were it not that the miniature illustrates the words of the psalm '. . . in salicibus . . . suspendimus organa nostra'; he is, in fact, attempting to hang his organ on one of the branches of what is supposed to be a willow tree.

The wind-chest would seem to measure approximately 1 m. across, and the over-all height is 48 to 50 cm. in relation to the people present. The pipes are coloured blue, and the wind-chest gold with a red border.[17]

Though it seemed best to devote more space to illustrations of the positive organ, whether free-standing or permanently installed, than to those of the small portative organ, it is nevertheless true that representations of the latter are much more numerous. And while much work remains to be done on the iconography of the medieval organ, it does seem that from the twelfth century onwards the image of the small organ held in the arms, played with the right hand and pumped with the left, tends to occur more frequently both in manuscripts and on capitals and stained-glass windows. To give some idea of the porportional representations of each of the three types of organ, here is a list of known illustrations of the tenth to thirteenth centuries.

1. *Instruments apparently permanently installed*
   Dijon, Harding Bible (end of tenth century).
   Cambridge, St. John's College (twelfth century).
   Belvoir Castle (thirteenth century).
   Munich, University Library (thirteenth century).

2. *Positives*
   Lyon, Bibliothèque Municipale, 35 (twelfth century).
   Laon, Bibliothèque Municipale, 105 (thirteenth century).
   Paris, Bibliothèque Nationale, 11560 (thirteenth century).
   Stuttgart Psalter (thirteenth century).
   Munich, Staatsbibliothek (thirteenth century).
   Léon, central door of the Cathedral (thirteenth century).
   Bratislava Psalter (thirteenth century).

3. *Portatives*
   Stuttgart Psalter (tenth century).
   London, British Museum, 17333 (twelfth century).
   Laon, window in the Cathedral (twelfth to thirteenth centuries).

[17] Paris, Bibl. Nat., Latin section, no. 11560, Réserve, fol. 36. Pl. XXVIII, no. 4.

Paris, Bibliothèque Nationale, 8846, fol. 114 (thirteenth century).
Paris, Bibliothèque Nationale, 8846, fol. 173 (thirteenth century).
Paris, Bibliothèque Nationale, 1076, fol. 7 (thirteenth century).
Paris, Bibliothèque Nationale, Apocalypse (thirteenth century).
Paris, Bibliothèque Nationale, 1328 (thirteenth century).
Brussels, Bibliothèque Royale (thirteenth century).
Arras, Bibliothèque Municipale, 302, fol. 77 (thirteenth century).
Vatican Museum, 1490, fol. 94 (thirteenth century).
Bourges Cathedral, window (thirteenth century).
Bonport Abbey, window (thirteenth century).
Sens Cathedral, window (thirteenth century).
Church of St.-Georges de Boscherville, capital (thirteenth century).

These lists confirm the view, already stated, that apart from the Winchester organ, which was in any case an exceptional instrument for its time, the average organ in the tenth to thirteenth centuries was modest in size.

CHAPTER SIXTEEN

The Organ and Organum

We have seen how the cymbalum was commemorated by an organ stop; the organ itself was destined to lend its name to a particular style of vocal writing. This fact, seemingly of secondary importance, is actually of vital interest to any student of early polyphony because of the obvious analogy between the new technique of vocal writing and the music played on the organ. This being so, the following brief considerations are perhaps not out of place in any history of the medieval organ.

Vocal music had remained essentially monodic since ancient times, despite the differences in vocal registers: 'inter se acutae et graves consonent', writes Seneca.[1] In the wake of the great invasions came the spread of Gregorian melody, a supple vocal line with subtle arabesques, but entirely self-sufficient. However, from the seventh century onwards 'diaphony' began to present a challenge to 'symphony':

Symphony is the combination of a low and high register by means of concordant sounds, between either voices, wind instruments, or strings. In this way the high and low sounds blend, and any dissonant sound would jar on the listener's ear. The opposite of symphony is diaphony, where the voices are different and dissonant (voces discrepantes vel dissonae).[2]

But it was not until the ninth century that the first real attempts at polyphony appeared, at a time when there was a manifest need for a renewal of music. Ever since St. Gregory had formulated his strict rules, sacred music, kept prisoner within narrow and unchanging bounds, 'realized that it had no desire to die, and sent out-adjacent branches, like the trunk of a lopped tree, on whose bark new limbs grow one by one.'[3]

One of these innovations was the trope, originally intended as a mnemonic composition, which introduced an entirely new and more secular style into religious music. The other was organum, which has exercised a decisive influence on Western music since medieval times.

The terms 'organum' or 'descant' (discantus), or even 'diaphony', are

[1] *Ad Lucil.*, xi, 88, 9.
[2] Isidore of Seville, *P.L.*, lxxxii, 164–5.
[3] J. Chailley, *Histoire Musicale du Moyen Age*, p. 63.

applied to a vocal polyphony of two or more strands, where the melodic line is accompanied from beginning to end by another independent melodic line. The word 'organum' in this sense appears for the first time at the beginning of the tenth century.[4] Hucbald, writing at the same period, christened the principal melody 'vox principalis', and the accompanying melody 'vox organalis'.[5] The two strands are in consonance at the octave, the fifth, or the fourth, with passing notes on the second and third. The art involved is not purely intuitive, but demands some skill, for it is not enough simply to sing any interval under the melodic line, any more, says Hucbald, than it is possible to make words with letters put together at random.[6] The ensemble of the voices must charm the ear:

Let him who sings in a pleasant fashion descant with one or more other singers, so that a single song emerges from divers sounds, not in the solitude of uniformity, but by uniting in a sweet and harmonious blend (dulcis concordisque mixtionis).[7]

As early as the eleventh century, what Duns Scotus already refers to as the 'melos organicum', and which seems no different from organum, was obliged to conform 'to the fixed and logical rules of the musical art' (secundum certas rationabilesque artis musicae regulas).[8] The new technique of composition also demanded special study, and the Monk of Angoulême tells us that Charlemagne sent to Rome for two former singers, Theodore and Benedict, who were well versed in this art (in arte organandi)[9] to instruct his own musicians. Organum could presumably be played on the organ, and indeed it was perhaps an attempt to imitate the sound of that instrument. A text by John Cotton (eleventh to twelfth centuries) seems to strengthen this hypothesis:

Diaphony, or organum (de diaphonia, id est organo) is a seemly dissonance between the vocal parts, at least two in number. One of these voices sings the melody as it is written (rectam modulationem), while the other, observing the rules, wanders among alien sounds (per alienos sonos); at each pause, the voices come together on the same note or at the octave. This style of singing is commonly known as 'organum', inasmuch as the human voices, by well-chosen dissonances, imitate the sound of the instrument called the organ (similitudinem exprimat instrumenti quod organum vocatur).[10]

---

[4] Gérold, *La musique au Moyen Age*, p. 237.

[5] Gerbert, *Script.*, i, p. 170. The organal voice is also called *teneure*.

[6] ibid., i, pp. 159–60.

[7] Jean de Muris (thirteenth century): Gerbert, *De Cantu*, ii, p. 110.

[8] *P.L.*, cxxii, 638.   [9] See p. 223.

[10] Gerbert, *Script.*, ii, p. 263. The following lines by J. de Murris are ambiguous and may refer to the vocal organ: 'Dicitur autem organica (diaphonia) ab organo, quod est instrumentum canendi, quia in tali specie cantus multum laborat' (Gerbert, iii, p. 239–40).

Such an origin for the term 'organum' is plausible if we admit that it had been customary for a very long time to play a different part with each hand on the organ, in emulation of the auletus, whose two pipes sounded simultaneously. This independence of each hand, impossible on the manual with the sliders described by the monk Theophilus, could be achieved on Anonymous of Berne's manual with springs, which allowed the organist to produce two distinct melodies as on the ancient hydraulis. At all events, it became customary on the organ to double the vocal line by adding another parallel melodic line at the octave, fifth, or fourth. These intervals, considered by Greek theorists to be elementary consonances, still enjoyed the same status at the time of Hucbald.[11] We have already seen that the Anonymous of Berne treatise allows for two pipes to each key, sounding respectively the fundamental note and its octave. This may well be a primitive type of organum, for attempts were made to recreate the same effect in vocal music—Hucbald records that where two men sang together in unison the high voice of a child was frequently added.[12] The origin of organum at the fourth and fifth is still controversial. The hypothesis linking this practice with the chance effect produced by a badly trained choir does not really stand up; nor does that which is based on the theory relating to different pentatonic scales.[13] But it should be borne in mind that the fifth and fourth are classified as consonances by Boethius, a faithful interpreter of the Greek theorists; so that it is not illogical to suppose that the first medieval composers hit on the idea of breaking the monotony of monodic singing by accompanying each note with one of these consonances—always the same one. Certainly something of this has survived, at least as far as the fifth is concerned, in a number of organ stops still in frequent use today. A mixture or a full organ are nothing but doubled fifths and octaves. The series of these 'direct' fifths and octaves is not heard; but the effect is to add lightness and and brightness to the melodic line. Perhaps vocal ensembles arranged according to this technique sounded pleasantly or splendidly to the ears of the contemporaries of Louis the Fat.

However, organum tended at an early date to liberate the organal from the principal voice, by giving the first a different melodic pattern from that of the second. A two-part composition of this type is sometimes called 'duplum' or 'purum'; when three parts are involved, it is known as 'triplum organum', and in four parts it becomes 'quadruplum organum'.[14] It is quite likely that one of these parts, in particular the tenor, was often played on the organ, and the instrument may even have been used to play the two or three

[11] Gerbert, i, p. 184.
[12] ibid., i, p. 162.
[13] Reese, op. cit., pp. 249 ff.
[14] Coussemaker, *L'art harmonique aux XIIe et XIIIe siècles*, pp. 47 ff.

strands of a piece originally written for voices.[15] We know that in the fourteenth century it was still common practice to transcribe motets for the organ.[16] Another significant point is that, in addition to Chartres and St.-Martial de Limoges, the Abbey of Fleury was one of the centres where the new style of vocal writing is thought to have originated, and, as we have seen, it is possible that organ-building flourished there in the time of Pope Sylvester II (early eleventh century). The coincidence can hardly be accidental.

The strong protests of the Abbot of Riévaulx in 1166 did not prevent organum from reaching the peak of its glory at the end of the twelfth century and during the thirteenth, when the School of Notre-Dame in Paris was made famous by three of the greatest exponents of the genre: Albert, Léonin, and Pérotin. The first is thought to be the composer of a 'conductus' for three voices. The second, described as 'optimus organista', wrote a collection of organa for the Gradual and the Antiphonary. But it was the third, 'optimus discantor', who, more than the others, acquired even in his lifetime a reputation, still undiminished, for his vocal compositions in three or four parts,[17] technically brilliant and impressive in their effect. Other nearly related musical forms stem directly from organum—the rondeau, the motet, and the conductus, which were together later known as *Ars Antiqua*. The influence of these new styles of writing was destined to be profound and enduring, particularly on organ music. Even in the seventeenth and eighteenth centuries the pattern of rich, many-rhythmed polyphonies written round the chorale theme given out in long notes stems recognizably from the contrapuntal style invented five hundred years earlier by composers of organa.

This brief glance at the origins of vocal organum raises a difficult but fascinating problem which is obviously of crucial importance in the history of the medieval organ. The new style of writing, whose name was derived from the organ, is, in fact, closely involved with it. There would seem to be little doubt that the arabesques of the melodic curves in early two-part organum correspond to what the monk-organist could and did improvise in the course of the church service. A different explanation has been suggested, which, though more materialistic, is worth discussing.[18] According to this,

---

[15] Gastoué, op. cit., p. 54. Could it be that the simultaneous playing of the principal voice and the organal voice accounts for the presence of the two organists in the Munich miniature and Wulstan's poem?

[16] Y. Rokseth, op. cit., p. 173.

[17] Coussemaker, p. 39, note 3. Although it is true that the word 'organista' is sometimes used to refer to the organist, it must in this context mean 'the composer of organa', though this would not exempt them from taking their turn at the organ as part of their official functions if the occasion arose.

[18] W. Krüger, *Die authentische Klangform des primitiven Organum* (Cassel, 1958), pp. 15–16.

the cumbersome mechanism of the slider organ may have slowed down the elegant rhythmic formulae of ecclesiastical chants, and thus led to the creation of organum. But although this hypothesis takes into account the style of writing peculiar to Pérotin, it fails to explain early diaphony in two or three parts with organ accompaniment, as it existed in the time of Walahfrid Strabo. True, John Cotton's text is relatively late; but what he says could well correspond to historical reality.

CHAPTER SEVENTEEN

Conclusion

Unlike the majority of other inventions, the historical evidence suggests that the pipe organ, though a complicated and highly original machine, was conceived and constructed by one man. This man, an Alexandrian Greek living at the time of Ptolemy Philadelphus, seems, moreover, to have had no connection whatsoever with music. He was essentially an engineer and an inventor, who had the simple but inspired idea of replacing the short breath of the pipe player with an artifical and abundant supply of air, drawn from a cylinder pump and compressed in an original device in which water played a key role. But Ktesibios's vision did not stop there. Inspired by the panpipe, he attached a graded set of auloi to the air reservoir, and, to make each pipe sound independently, he invented a distributory system with drawers operated by a manual keyboard.

The prototype, described in detail in Hero of Alexandria's book, contains the essential components of the modern organ. All that is missing is the wind-chest with separate stops, and this was familiar to Vitruvius and in common use by the time of Augustus. The numerous improvements since added to the instrument by many generations of clever organ-builders in the last analysis affect only secondary features: the replacement of the pumps by bellows, and of the water by weights; the enlargement of the wind-chest by means of the coupling mechanism; the multiplication of notes and timbres; and the electrification of the wind mechanism and the controls. The great organ we know today, despite the complexity of its mechanical, pneumatic, acoustic, and electrical components, is not essentially different from Ktesibios's original machine.

The organ has travelled far from its birthplace, and by strange paths. Conceived in Egypt, in a Greek milieu, it became established, not there, but in the Roman world. When the great invasions caused it to disappear entirely from western Europe its tradition was happily preserved in Constantinople. In 1453 the tragic fall of that city marked the end of the organ's use in the countries of the East. But meanwhile, by a lucky chance, it had had time to re-establish itself in the Frankish kingdom, where it prospered and remained until our own times.

The most striking feature of the organ's history is its remarkable deterioration in the earlier Middle Ages by comparison with the improved hydraulis used in Roman times. On the one hand we have a complex machine with an abundant and stable supply of compressed air, a manual fitted with springs which enabled quick passages to be played, and several ranks of pipes, which could be used together or separately thanks to a system of register stops. And on the other, we find a very small instrument made from pieces of wood glued together, laboriously fed by a number of bellows, producing one invariable and uniform timbre, and fitted with a primitive manual on which the organist was obliged to pull and then push back each key in order to play his melody. Such a regression in the technique of organ-building can only be explained by the wretched poverty of the later period, the inability of craftsmen to work and solder metal properly, and above all ignorance of the treatises of Hero and Vitruvius. Indeed, it seems likely that the Carolingian organ was only a poor copy of the Byzantine instrument, and had no direct relationship to Antiquity.

One factor, however, remains constant from the Hellenistic era to the reign of St. Louis, and that is the warm admiration of the multitude for the rich, rhythmic music of the pipe organ. The enthusiasm of the Delphic audiences and of Athenaeus's revellers, the passionate connoisseurship of Nero, the arrogant pride of the Byzantine court, recur again and again in the writings of Arab chroniclers, of St. Aldhelm, St. Dunstan, Honorius of Autun, or St. Thomas Aquinas. The musical character of the organ may vary from place to place, but its seductive charm never changes—a miracle continued in our own times.

The creation of a manual keyboard, placed crosswise in front of the instrument, demanded a special fingering technique of the organist. To play cleanly and rhythmically, without smudging, it was absolutely essential that the finger should strike the key with a quick, precise movement, with an immaculate attack and split-second release. The need for this is inherent in the nature of the organ, and still obtains for the would-be organist. It is also worth remarking that the order of the pipes on the wind-chest, bass pipes to the left and trebles to the right, has remained the same since the first documents from Hellenistic times.

There is one further matter which in my view is an integral part of the history of the organ—the development of organum and polyphony. Some twelve hundred years after its invention the instrument helped to stimulate, I believe, the creation of a new and extremely fertile form of vocal writing, organum, which rapidly became true polyphony.

The question whether true polyphonic music was played on the early organ is more difficult. The lack of documentary evidence means that we can only argue by inference. There are two important considerations which suggest an affirmative answer. Firstly, the classical aulos almost certainly doubled its melody with an independent accompaniment, and the organ, based directly on this instrument, must surely have sought at an early stage to emulate this. Secondly, the organist had both hands on the manual, and it is hard to imagine that he would be content to repeat with the left hand the melodic line played by the right. If I am correct in these suggestions, the organ has been largely responsible for the development of polyphonic writing, which is the prime distinguishing feature of Western music.

Appendix

ORIGINAL TEXTS CONCERNING THE HYDRAULIS AND THE MEDIEVAL ORGAN

(*a*) Hero of Alexandria, *Pneumatica*, i, 42

Ὑδραυλικοῦ ὀργάνου κατασκευή.

Ἔστω τις βωμίσκος χάλκεος ὁ ΑΒΓΔ, ἐν ᾧ ὕδωρ ἔστω· ἐν δὲ τῷ ὕδατι κοῖλον ἡμισφαίριον κατεστραμμένον ἔστω, ὃ καλεῖται πνιγεὺς ὁ ΕΖΗΘ ἔχων ἐν τῷ ὑγρῷ διάρρυσιν εἰς τὰ πρὸς τῷ πυθμένι μέρη· ἀπὸ δὲ τῆς κορυφῆς αὐτοῦ δύο ἀνατεινέτωσαν σωλῆνες συντετρημένοι αὐτῷ ὑπὲρ τὸν βωμίσκον, εἷς μὲν ὁ ΗΚΛΜ κατακεκαμμένος εἰς τὸ ἐκτὸς τοῦ βωμίσκου μέρος καὶ συντετρημένος πυξίδι τῇ ΝΞΟΠ κάτω τὸ στόμα ἐχούσῃ καὶ τὴν ἐντὸς ἐπιφάνειαν ὀρθὴν πρὸς ἐμβολέα ἀπειργασμένην. ταύτῃ δὲ ἐμβολεὺς ἁρμοστὸς ἔστω ὁ ΡΣ, ὥστε ἀέρα μὴ παραπνεῖν· τῷ δὲ ἐμβολεῖ συμφυὴς ἔστω κανὼν ὁΤΥ ἰσχυρὸς σφόδρα. πρὸς δὲ τὸν ἁρμόζοντα ἕτερος κανὼν ὁ ΥΦ περὶ περόνην κινούμενος τὴν πρὸς τῷ Υ· ὁ αὐτὸς δὲ κηλωνευέσθω πρὸς ὄρθιον κανόνα τὸν ΨΧ βεβηκότα ἀσφαλῶς. τῇ δὲ ΝΞΟΠ πυξίδι ἐπικείσθω κατὰ τὸν πυθμένα ἕτερον πυξίδιον τὸ Ω συντετρημένον αὐτῇ καὶ ἐπιπεπωμασμένον ἐκ τῶν ἄνω μερῶν καὶ ἔχον τρύπημα, δι' οὗ ὁ ἀὴρ εἰσελεύσεται εἰς τὴν πυξίδα. ὑπὸ δὲ τὸ τρύπημα λεπίδιον ἔστω ἐπιφράσσον αὐτὸ καὶ ἀνεχόμενον διὰ τρηματίων ὑπό τινων περονίων κεφαλὰς ἐχόντων, ὥστε μὴ ἐκπίπτειν τὸ λεπίδιον, ὃ δὲ καλεῖται πλατυσμάτιον. ἀπὸ δὲ τοῦ Ζ ἕτερος ἀνατεινέτω σωλὴν ὁ sΖ συντετρημένος ἑτέρῳ σωλῆνι πλαγίῳ τῷ a⟩, ἐν ᾧ ἐπικείσθωσαν οἱ αὐλοὶ συντετρημένοι αὐτῷ οἱ ͵Α καὶ ἔχοντες ἐκ τῶν κάτω μερῶν καθάπερ γλωσσόκομα συντετρημένα αὐτοῖς, ὧν τὰ στόματα ἀνεῳγότα ἔστω τὰ ͵Β. διὰ δὲ τῶν στομάτων τὰ πώματα διώσθω τρήματα ἔχοντα, ὥστε εἰσαγομένων τῶν πωμάτων τὰ ἐν αὐτοῖς τρήματα κατάλληλα γίνεσθαι τοῖς τῶν αὐλῶν τρήμασιν, ἐξαγομένων δὲ παραλλάσσειν καὶ ἀποφράσσειν τοὺς αὐλούς. ἐὰν οὖν ὁ πλάγιος κανὼν κηλωνεύηται διὰ τοῦ Φ εἰς τὸ κάτω μέρος, ὁ ΡΣ ἐμβολεὺς ἐκθλίψει μετεωριζόμενος τὸν ἐν τῇ ΝΞΟΠ πυξίδι ἀέρα, ὃς ἀποκλείσει μὲν τὸ ἐν τῷ Ω πυξιδίῳ τρύπημα διὰ τοῦ προειρημένου πλατυσματίου· χωρήσει δὲ διὰ τοῦ ΜΛΚΗ σωλῆνος εἰς τὸν πνιγέα· ἐκ δὲ τοῦ πνιγέως χωρήσει εἰς τὸν πλάγιον σωλῆνα τὸν G⟩ διὰ τοῦ sΖ σωλῆνος· ἐκ δὲ τοῦ πλαγίου σωλῆνος εἰς τοὺς αὐλοὺς χωρήσει, ὅταν κατάλληλα ᾖ κείμενα ἐν τοῖς αὐλοῖς τά ἐν τοῖς πώμασι τρήματα, τουτέστιν ὅταν εἰσηγμένα ᾖ τὰ πώματα ἤτοι πάντα ἢ τινα αὐτῶν. ἵνα οὖν, ὅταν προαιρώμεθα τῶν αὐλῶν τινα φθέγγεσθαι, ἀνοίγηται τὰ κατ' ἐκείνους τρήματα, ὅταν δὲ βουλώμεθα παύεσθαι, ἀποκλείηται, κατασκευάσωμεν τάδε.

Νοείσθω ἓν τῶν γλωσσοκόμων ἐγκείμενον χωρὶς τὸ ͵Γ ͵Δ, οὗ τὸ στόμα ἔστω τὸ ͵Δ, ὁ δὲ συντετρημένος τούτῳ αὐλὸς ὁ ͵Ε, πῶμα δὲ ἔστω ἁρμοστὸν αὐτῷ τὸ ͵s ͵Ζ τρῆμα ἔχον τὸ ‚Η παρηλλαγμένον ἀπὸ τοῦ ‚Ε αὐλοῦ. ἔστω δέ τις καὶ ἀγκωνίσκος τρίκωλος ὁ ‚Ζ ‚Θ M̅B̅, οὗ τὸ ‚Ζ ‚Θ κῶλον συμφυὲς μὲν ἔστω τῷ ‚ς ‚Ζ πώματι· πρὸς δὲ τῷ, Θ M̅ περὶ περόνην κινείσθω μέσην τὴν M̅. ἐὰν οὖν κατάξωμεν τῇ χειρὶ τὸ M̅ ἄκρον τοῦ ἀγκωνίσκου ἐπὶ τὸ ‚Δ στόμιον τοῦ γλωσσοκόμου, παρώσομεν τὸ πῶμα εἰς τὸ ἔσω μέρος, ὥστε ὅταν ἐμπέσῃ εἰς τὸ ἐντὸς μέρος, τότε τὸ ἐν αὐτῷ τρῆμα κατάλληλον τῷ αὐλῷ γίνεται. ἵνα οὖν, ὅταν ἀφέλωμεν τὴν χεῖρα, αὐτόματον τὸ πῶμα ἐξελκυσθῇ καὶ παραλλάξῃ τὸν αὐλόν, ἔσται τάδε. ὑποκείσθω ὑπὸ τὰ γλωσσό-κομα κανὼν ἴσος τῷ G‿λ σωλῆνι καὶ παράλληλος αὐτῷ κείμενος ὁ M̅M̅. ἐν δὲ τούτῳ ἐμπεπηγέτω σπαθία κεράτινα εὔτονα καὶ ἐπικεκαμμένα, ὧν ἓν ἔστω τὸ M̅ κείμενον κατὰ τὸ ‚Δ ‚Γ γλωσσόκομον. ἐκ δὲ τοῦ ἄκρου αὐτοῦ νευρὰ ἀποδεθεῖσα ἀποδεδόσθω περί τὸ ‚Θ ἄκρον, ὥστε ἔξω παρωσθέντος τοῦ πώματος τετάσθαι τὴν νευράν. ἐὰν οὖν κατάξαντες τὸ M̅ ἄκρον τοῦ ἀγκωνίσκου παρώσωμεν τὸ πῶμα εἰς τὸ ἔσω μέρος, ἡ νευρὰ ἐπισπάσεται τὸ σπαθίον, ὥστε ἀνορθῶσαι τὴν καμπὴν αὐτοῦ βίᾳ. ὅταν δὲ ἀφῶμεν, πάλιν τὸ σπαθίον εἰς τὴν ἐξ ἀρχῆς τάξιν καμπτόμενον ἐξελκύσει τὸ πῶμα τοῦ στόματος, ὥστε παραλλάξει τὸ τρῆμα. τούτων οὖν καθ᾽ ἕκαστον γλωσσόκομον γενηθέντων, ὅταν βουλώμεθά τινας τῶν αὐλῶν φθέγγγ-εσθαι, κατάξομεν τοῖς δακτύλοις τὰ κατ᾽ ἐκείνους ἀγκωνίσκια· ὅταν δὲ μηκέτι φθεγγεσθαι βούλωμεθα, ἐπαροῦμεν τοὺς δακτύλους, καὶ τότε παύσονται τῶν πωμάτων ἐξελκυσθέντων. τὸ δὲ ἐν τῷ βωμίσκῳ ὕδωρ ἐμβάλλεται ἕνεκα τοῦ τὸν περισσεύοντα ἀέρα ἐν τῷ πνιγεῖ, λέγω δὴ τὸν ἐκ τῆς πυξίδος ὠθούμενον, ἐπαίροντα τὸ ὕδωρ συνέχεσθαι πρὸς τὸ ἀεὶ ἔχειν τοὺς αὐλοὺς δυναμένους φθέγγεσθαι. ὁ δὲ ΡΣ ἐμβολεὺς ἐπαιρόμενος μὲν ἐπὶ τὸ ἄνω, ὡς εἴρηται, ἐξωθεῖ τὸν ἐν τῇ πυξίδι ἀέρα εις τὸν πνιγέα, καταγόμενος δὲ ἀνοίγει τὸ ἐν τῷ Ω πυξιδίῳ πλατυσμάτιον, δι᾽ οὗ ἡ πυξὶς ἀέρος ἔξωθεν πληροῦται, ὥστε πάλιν τὸν ἐμβολέα ἀνωθούμενον ἐκθλίβειν αὐτὸν εἰς τὸν πνιγέα. βέλτιον δέ ἐστι καὶ τὸν ΤΥ κανόνα περὶ περόνην κινεῖσθαι πρὸς τῷ Τ διτορμίας οὔσης ἐν τῷ πυθμένι τοῦ ἐμβολέως ἁρμοσθήσεται, δι᾽ ἧς δεήσει περόνην διωθεῖσθαι πρὸς τὸ τὸν ἐμβολέα μὴ διαστρέφεσθαι, ἀλλὰ ὀρθὸν ἀνωθεῖσθαί τε καὶ κατάγεσθαι.

(b) Vitruvius, *De Architectura*, x, 83

De hydraulicis autem quas habeant ratiocinationes quam brevissime proxi-meque attingere potero et scriptura consequi, non praetermittam. De materia compacta basi ara in ea ex aere fabricata conlocatur. Supra basim eriguntur regulae dextra ac sinistra scalari forma compactae, quibus inclu-duntur aerei modioli ex torno subtiliter subacti fundis ambulatilibus haben-tibus fixos in medio ferreos ancones et verticulis cum vectibus conjunctos, pellibusque lanatis involutis. Item in summa planitia foramina circiter digi-torum ternum. Quibus foraminibus proxime in verticulis conlocati aerei delphini pendentia habent catenis cymbala ex ore infra foramina modiolorum calata. Intra aram, quo loci aqua sustinetur, inest pnigeus uti infundibulum inversum, quem subter taxilli, alti circiter digitorum ternum suppositi, librant spatium imum intra labra pnigeos et arae fundum. Supra autem cerviculam ejus coagmenta arcula sustinet caput machinae, quae graece κανὼν μουσικός appellatur. In cujus longitudine canales, si tetrachordos est, fiunt quattuor, si hexachordos, sex, si octochordos, octo. Singulis autem canalibus singula epitonia sunt inclusa, manubriis ferreis conligata. Quae manubria, cum torquentur, ex arca patefaciunt nares in canales. Ex canalibus autem canon habet ordinata in transverso foramina respondentia naribus quae sunt in tabula summa, quae tabula graece πίναξ dicitur. Inter tabulam et canona regulae sunt interpositae ad eundem modum foratae et oleo subactae ut faciliter impellantur et rursus introrsus reducantur, quae obturant ea foramina plinthidesque appellantur. Quarum itus et reditus alias obturat alias aperit terebrationes. Haec regulae habent ferrea choragia fixa et juncta cum pinnis, quarum pinnarum tactus motiones efficit regularum continenter. Supra tabulam foramina quae ex canalibus habent egressum spiritus sunt anuli adglutinati, quibus lingulae omnium includuntur organorum. E modiolis autem fistulae sunt continentes conjunctae pnigeos cervicibus pertinentesque ad nares quae sunt in arcula. In quibus asses sunt ex torno subacti et ibi conlocati (ubi fistulae modiolis sunt conjunctae) qui, cum recepit arcula animam, spiritum non patientur obturantes foramina rursus redire. Ita cum vectes extolluntur, ancones deducunt fundos modiolorum ad imum delphinique qui sunt in verticulis inclusi, calantes in eos cymbala, aere implent spatia modiolorum atque ancones extollentes fundos intra modiolos vehementi pulsus crebritate et obturantes foramina cymbalis superiora, aera qui est ibi inclusus pressionibus coactum in fistulas cogunt, per quas in pnigea concurrit et per ejus cervicem in arcam. Motione vero vectium vehementiore spiritus frequens compressus epitoniorum aperturis influit et replet anima canales. Itaque cum pinnae manibus tactae propellunt et reducunt continenter regulas, alternis obturando foramina, alternis aperiundo e musicis artibus multiplicibus modulorum varietatibus sonantes excitant voces.

Quantum potui niti, ut obscura res per scripturam dilucide pronuntiaretur, contendi, sed haec non est facilis ratio. Neque omnibus expedita ad intelligendum praeter eos qui in his generibus habent exercitationem. Quodsi qui parum intellexerit ex scriptis, cum ipsam rem cognoscet, profecto inveniet curiose et subtiliter omnia ordinata.

(c) Theophilus, *Diversum Artium Schedule*, De organis

Facturus organa primum habeat lectionem mensurae, qualiter metiri debeant fistulae graves et acutae et superacutae; deinde faciat sibi ferrum longum et grossum ad mensuram qua vult esse fistulas, quod sit rotundum in circuitu summa diligentia limatum et politum, in una summitate grossius et modice attenuatum, ita ut possit imponi in alterum ferrum curvum, per quod circumducatur, iuxta modum ligni in quo volvitur runcina, et in altera summitate gracile, secundum mensuram inferioris capitis fistulae, quod conflatorio debet imponi.

Deinde attenuatur cuprum purum et sanissimum, ita ut unguis impressus ex altera parte appareat. Quod cum fuerit secundum mensuram ferri limatum et incisum ad longiores fistulas, quae dicuntur graves, fiat secundum praeceptum lectionis foramen, in quo plectrum imponi debet, et circumradatur modice ad mensuram fistulae, atque superlineatur stagnum cum ferro solidatorio, radaturque in una ora longitudinis interius, et in altera ora exterius eadem mensura, et superstagnetur tenue. Quae stagnatura, prius quam fiat, ac sint tractus noviter facti, modice calefacto cupro lineatur cum resina abietis, ut stagnum levius et citius adhaereat. Quo facto complicetur ipsum cuprum circa ferrum et circumligetur filo ferreo mediocriter grosso fortiter, ita ut stagnati tractus conveniant sibi. Quod filum primo induci debet parvulo foramini, quod est in gracili summitate ferri, et in eo bis contorqueri, sicque deduci involvendo usque ad alteram summitatem, ibique similiter obfirmari. Deinde iuncturis sibi invicem convenientibus et diligenter iungentibus, ponatur ipsa ligatura pariter cum ferro ante fornacem super prunas ardentes, et sedente puero ac mediocriter flante teneatur dextera manu lignum gracile, in cuius summitate fissa haereat panniculus cum resina, et sinistra teneatur stagnum longum gracile percussum, ut mox cum fistula incaluerit lineat iuncturam cum paniculo resina infecto, appositumque stagnum liquefiat, ipsamque iuncturam diligenter consolidet.

Quo facto refrigerata fistula, ponatur ferrum in instrumento tornatoris modo parato, impositoque curvo ferro et filo soluto circumvolvat unus ferrum curvum alter vero utrisque manibus chirotectis iam indutis fortiter fistulam teneat, ita ut ferrum circumducatur et fistula quieta maneat, donec omnino oculis gratiosa appareat, quasi tornata sit.

Deinde educto ferro percutiatur ipsa fistula cum malleo mediocri iuxta foramen superius et inferius, ita ut pene usque ad medium descendat ipsa rotunditas spatio duorum digitorum; fiatque plectrum ex cupro aliquantulum spissiori, quasi dimidia rotula, et superstagnetur circa rotunditatem sicut fistula superius, sicque imponatur in inferiori parte foraminis ita ut sub ipsius ora aequaliter stet, nec procedat inferius aut superius. Habeat quoque ferrum solidatorium eiusdem latitudinis et rotunditatis, qua plectrum est. Quo calefacto, ponat modicas particulas stagni super plectrum, parum resinae, et diligenter circumducat ferrum calidum ne plectrum moveatur, sed liquefacto stagno sic adhaereat ut in circuitu eius nihil spiraminis exeat, nisi tantum superiori foramine.

Quo facto apponat fistulam ori et sufflet primum, modice, deinde amplius, sicque fortiter, et secundum quod auditu discernit, disponat vocem, ut si eam vult esse grossam, foramen fiat latius; si vero graciliorem, fiat strictius.

Hoc ordine omnes fistulae fiant; mensuram vero singularum, a plectro superius, secundum magisterium lectionis faciat, a plectro autem inferius, omnes unius mensurae et eiusdem grossitudinis erunt.

★   ★   ★   ★

Domum vero facturus, super quam statuendae sint fistulae, vide utrum volueris eam ligneam habere aut cupream. Si ligneam, acquire tibi duo ligna de platano valde sicca, longitudine duorum pedum et dimidii, et latitudine modice amplius quam unius, unum quatuor alterum duobus digitis spissum, quae non sint nodosa sed pura. Quibus diligentissime sibi coniunctis, in inferiori parte spissioris ligni fiat in medio foramen quadrangulum, amplitudine quatuor digitorum et circa quod reliquatur de eodem ligno limbus, unius digiti latitudinis et altitudinis, in quo conflatorium imponatur. In superiori parte vero lateris fiant cavaturae, per quas flatus ad fistulas possit pervenire.

Altero vero pars ligni, quae et superior esse debet, metiatur interius aequaliter, ubi disponantur septem vel octo cavaturae, in quibus diligenter iungantur linguae, ita ut habeant facilem cursum educendi et reducendi, sic tamen ut nichil spiraminis inter iuncturas exeat. In superiori autem parte tonde cavaturas, contra inferiores, quae sint aliquantulum latiores, in quibus iungantur totidem ligna, ita ut inter haec et maius, ligni cavatura remaneat vacua per quam ventus ascendat ad fistulas; nam in eisdem lignis foramina fieri debent, in quibus fistulae stabiliendae sunt.

Cavaturae in quibus linguae iunctae sunt in anteriori parte procedere debeant quasi obliquae fenestrae, per quas ipsae linguae introducantur et extrahantur. In posteriori vero parte, sub fine ipsarum linguarum, fiant foramina aequaliter lata et longa, mensura duorum digitorum, per quae ventus possit ascendere ab inferioribus ad superiora, ita ut cum linguae impinguntur, illa foramina ab eis obstruantur, cum vero trahuntur denuo pateant. In his vero lignis, quae super linguas iunguntur, fiant foramina diligenter et ordinate, secundum numerum fistularum unius cuiusque toni, in quibus ipsae fistulae imponantur, ita ut firmiter stent, et ab inferioribus ventum suscipiant. In caudis autem linguarum scribantur litterae secundum ascensum et descensum cantus, quibus possit cognosci quis ille vel ille tonus sit. In singulis autem linguis fiant foramina singula gracilia longitudine demidii digiti minoris, in anteriori parte iuxta caudas in longitudine, in quibus ponantur singuli clavi cuprei capitati, qui pertranseant in medio fenestellas, quibus inducuntur ipsae linguae, a superiori latere domus usque ad inferius, et appareant clavorum capita superius ita ut, cum linguae cantantibus organis educuntur, non penitus extrahantur.

His ita dispositis conglutinentur haec duo ligna, quae domum organorum conficiunt, glutine casei; deinde partes illae, quae super linguas sunt iunctae, in quibus foramina stant, sicque circumcidantur diligenter et radantur.

★   ★   ★   ★

Secundum abundantiam fistularum dispone longitudinem et latitudinem domus, et fac formam in argilla macerata siccatamque diligenter incide quacunque mensura volueris, et cooperi cera diligenter inter duas aequaliter spissas hastulas cum rotundo ligno attenuata. Deinde incide foramina linguarum in ipsa cera, et foramen inferius, per quod ventus introeat; additis spiraculis cum infusorio cooperi eadem argilla semel, et iterum ac tertio. Cumque siccata fuerit forma, eodem modo funde quo supra formam turibuli . . . Cumque domus funderis, coniunges interius altitudine unius digiti a fundo tabulam cupream ductilem sub foraminibus linguarum aequaliter, et supra eam ipsae linguae iaceant, ita ut possint aequaliter produci et induci, illitisque ipsis linguis tenui argilla, reliquum domus perfundes liquefacto plumbo per omnia, super ipsas linguas usque ad summum.

Quo facto, eiicies ipsum plumbum diligenter designabisque foramina fistularum in linguis; deinde in ipso plumbo et cum gracili ferro vel terebro perforabis diligentissime. Deinde sub linguis ventorum aditus facies, induces ipsas linguas singulas in suis locis, atque reponens plumbum et cum malleo in percutiendo coniunges domui, ut nichil spiraminis exeat, nisi per foramina quibus fistulae imponendae sunt . . .

★   ★   ★   ★

Hoc quoque sollertius procurandum est, ut in capite uniuscuiusque follis, ante foramen fistulae suae, cuprum tenue dependeat, quod spiraminis claudat aditum, ita ut cum follis flando deponitur illud cuprum se elevet, et ventus pleniter exeat; cumque follis elevatur, ut per ventilabrum suum flatum resumat, illud cuprum os eius penitus claudat, et ventum, quem emisit redire non permittat.

★   ★   ★   ★

Conflatorium facturus, coniunge tibi duo ligna de platano modo quo supra, longitudine pedis unius, quorum sit unum palma spissum, alterum tribus digitis, sintque in una fronte rotunda in modum scuti, et ibi pede et dimidio lata; in altera fronte obtusa, latitudine unius palmi. Quae cum diligenter coniuncta fuerint, incide in spissori ligno in rotunda fronte foramina, quot volueris, secundum numerum follium, et in obtusa fronte unum, quod sit maius. Deinde incide ab unoquoque foramine fossam unam deductim usque ad maius, per quas viam possit habere ventus flantibus follibus. Sicque conglutinabis ipsa ligna glutine casei, et circumdabis panno lineo novo et forti, quem linies eodem glutine, ut adhaereat.

Facies quoque ligaturas ferreas fortes, interius et exterius circumstagnatas, ne possint ex tignea dissolvi, quas configes clavis longis capitis atque stagnatis, ita ut inter duo foramina ligatura sit, quae comprehendat utrumque lignum a superiori latere usque ad inferius.

★   ★   ★   ★

Deinde aquire tibi lignum curvum de quercu, sanum et forte, quod habeat in una fronte a cavatura longitudinem pedis unius, in altera duorum quod perforabis in utraque fronte terebro magno, quo forantur medioli in rotis arati. Sed quia foramina non possunt sibi obviare propter curvaturam, fac tibi ferrum, quod habeat caput rotundum in modum ovi, et caudam longam gracilem, quae imponatur manubrio, sitque iuxta caput modice curvum, cum quo calefacto, combures foramina interius in curvatura, donec sibi aequaliter conveniant. Quo facto, incide ipsum lignum quadrico statum, ita ut in unoquoque latere uno palmo latum sit, ad mensuram conflatorii in obtusa parte.

Post haec coniunge ipsum lignum in longiori parte ad inferius foramen domus organariae, ita ut eidem ligno cauda incidatur, unius pollicis longa, quae ipsi foramini imponatur vel inferatur, et iunctura tam subtilis sit, ut nichil flatus inter eam exire quaeat. Alteram vero frontem coniuges eodem modo ad conflatorium, et ipsum lignum glutine casei firmabis atque circumvolves panno totum lignum cum iunctura, cui etiam circumfiges cuprum latum quod utriusque ligni oram capiat.

★   ★   ★   ★

Conflatorium quoque formabis in argilla procedentibus undique inferius venti aditibus, similitudinem radicis unius arboris, et in summo in unum foramen convenientibus. Quod cum mensurate dispositum cultello incideris, cooperi cera, et fac sicut supra . . .

★   ★   ★   ★

Cum vero conflatorium fuerit fusum et limatum, atque uniuscuiusque follis fistula suo inductorio coaptata, coniungi et firmiter consolidari debet ad domum organariam inferius, ita ut ventus suos aditus libere inveniat, et per alias iuncturas nullatenus exeat.

★   ★   ★   ★

His ita completis, si volueris organa ultra maceriam muri stabilire, ita ut infra monasterium nichil appareat, nisi sola domus cum fistulis, et ex altera parte muri folles iaceant, ita oportebit te ipsam domum convertere ut linguae versus folles extrahantur, et in ipso muro arcus fiat, in quo cantor sedeat, cuius sedes ita aptetur, ut pedes supra conflatorium teneat.

Est autem foramen quadrum in medio arcus trans maceriam, per quod domus cum fistulis exponitur; et super collum conflatorii quod in muro infra foramen lapidibus obfirmatum est, in sua iunctura sistitur, atque super duos clavos ferreos aequaliter in muro confixos nititur, cui foramini fenestra lignea appendet, quae dum clausa, sera et clave munitur, nemo ignotus superveniens cognoscere valet, quid in ea contineatur.

Exterius quoque super organa pannus spissus lignis interius extensus, in modum domunculae, a laqueari in funiculo ad arcendum pulverem dependeat, qui funiculus super ipsum laquear circa rotulam arte compositus, dum cantandum est organis trahitur, et domunculam elevat, finitoque cantu, denuo super organa deponitur. Habet quoque ipsa domuncula pinnam ex eodem panno, lignis quatuor in speciem trianguli extensam, in cuius summo spherula lignea, stet, cui funiculus inhaeret.

Folles et instrumentum super quod iaceant, secundum situm loci ad libitos tuos dispone.

(*d*) Anonymous of Berne, *De fistulis organicis, quomodo fiant*

Cuprum purissimum tundendo ad summam tenuitam extenditur. et complicatur ferro. ad hanc rem propter equalem latitudinem omnium fistularum aptato. pene quattuor pedibus longo. in modum chilindri bene rotundo. tantum ex una parte plus minus uno palmo. paulatim restringitur acuendo. ut concauitas omnium fistularum in superiori foramine. ouum columbae. in inferiori ouum lodic(i) (vel) alaudae. possit recepire. In eo uero loco ubi incipit equalis grossitudo ex transuerso admorsa et patefacta fistula ex cupro. in modum semicirculi. uua interius solidatur. ad quam hinc inde fistulam oportet comprimi. ut uox possit formari.

★　　　★　　　★　　　★

Capsam cui superponantur fistule. oportet fieri quadratam. aut parte altera longiorem. per quattuor angulos . . . singula receptacula. Reliqua concauitate profundiora. ut uentus diuisus equaliter se infundat omnibus tuer (?) partes recipiat geminos folles. An foraminibus. A cuius capse medio demittitur fistula maxima. que per quattuor partes recipiat geminos folles . . . Tunc tabula tenuis et plana. subtilis et recta. fiat eidem capse superponenda. in qua ordinantur hinc inde rectis lineis foramina. equalibus a se spaciis distantia. et secundum numerum fistularum. sit numerus eorundem foraminum.

Sub qua tabula est alia opposita maxime fistule. non ut ipsam obturet. sed ut uentum diuidat. Per ora etiam capse. ante et retro super ipsam tabulam. ponuntur lingue tenues. plane. subtiles et recte. quarum foramina cum omnibus foraminibus tabule conuenient. tanta concordia ut uideantur una vel equales. Post obturatis ipsis foraminibus ut aperiri possent liquefacto plumbo super tabulam et linguas capsa replebitur. Denuo extracte lingue in suis foraminibus erunt mobiles et cursoriae.

Post hoc ordinantur fistulae. ita ut a dextra modulantis in sinistram paulatim maiores prodeant. Super unamquamque uero linguam numquam nisi simple et duple fistule possunt constitui. quia his est una uox acuta et gravis. et ex his quot placuerit. scilicet aut quinque aut decem aut quotlibet. Nam in his mensuris quas nos facimus. sunt lingue quindecim.

Deinceps instrumenta reliqua fiunt. id est in quodam ligno ante capsam firmo. fiunt secundum numerum linguarum. ex cornu semicirculi et lamine ligneae in summo ferrate ferro. quod hereat medietati uirgule ferreae herenti capitibus semicirculorum et linguarum. ut a tergo depressa lamina. tota lingua usque ad herentem uirgam ferream recondatur laxa lamina lignea usque ad medietatem primi foraminis extrahatur. Summopere tamen cauendum. ne in iuncturis capse aliqua rima remaneat. Per quem uentus exeat.

In lamminis uero ligneis scribantur alphabeti littere dupliciter ita. A. B. C. D. E. F. G. A. B. C. D. E. F. G. H. ut citius modulator possit scire quam linguam debeat tangere.

★ ★ ★ ★

[Instrumentum bicornum] . . . quod in ipso augusto aditu faucium a fistula uno palmo. aperientem et claudentem habeat uuam ex cupro vel ferro . . .

★ ★ ★ ★

. . . A cuius capse medio demittitur fistula maxima. qui per quattuor partes recipiat geminos folles. Antequam tamen folles iungantur predicte fistule. bicorni instrumento perforato recipiuntur . . .

★ ★ ★ ★

. . . Denique ab eo loco ubi ponitur uua, sumitur cum circino totius fistule mensura. ad eam partem ubi diximus esse superius foramen. ut quantum debet esse unaqueque uel maior uel minor quam altera noscatur.

Si quidem que sit diatonicum genus quo maxime decurrunt moderne cantilene. hoc modo metientur fistule. prima que omnibus minor est et idcirco acutior. in octo partibus diuidatur. et octaua parte prime sit maior secunda. quam prima. ut faciant inter se tonum. Secunde similiter. octaua parte. sit maior tertia quam secunda. et inter eas tonus. Deinde fac ut tertia parte prime sit maior quarta quam prima. et ita faciet quarta quidem a prima diatessaron. ad tertiam hemitonium. Quinta quoque sit maior. quam prima medietate. prime. ut faciat ad eam simphoniam diapente. ad quartam uero tonum. Ipsius etiam quinte octava parte. sit maior sexta quam quinta et inter eas tonus. Quarte quoque tertia parte sit maior septima quam quarta. ut faciat ad eam rursus diatessaron. ad sextam uero (h)emitonium. Octaua quoque sit dupla prime. et inter eas simphonia diapason. que semper ex diatessaron et diapente componitur.

Denuo idem ordo repetatur. ut sicut colligitur mensura secunde fistule ex octaua. ita per ordinem ut dictum est intexantur. Nam ut prime octaua dupla est ita quinta decima octaue. In septem quoque uocibus praedicte diapason ascendendo et descendendo. unamquamlibet cantilenam perficies. Frequenti tamen exercitatione. distantie uocum sunt colligende. ne sonos intercipias quos pre summam extensionem acuminis graues facis. et eosdem iterum secundum ceptam melodiam acuis. Et primo fistularum ordini. secundus ordo respondebit . . .

(e) Aribo, *Antiqua fistularum mensura quae intenditur*

Mensuram duorum ordinum, id est XVI fistularum hic dicere sufficiat, secundum quam alios quot libeat ordines quivis adiiciat. Primam fistulam tantae longitudinis ac latitudinis delibera, quantam mediocritas cum arbitrio doceat; longitudo aut fistulae ac plectro sursum habetur, et latitudo est ipsius concavitatis capacitas, qua se in summitate in modum circuli aperit; qui nimirum circulus non secundum ambitum suum, sed per medium duobus hemispheriis divisus diametrum dicitur. Huius diametri longitudinem circino deprehensam statim post primae fistulae informatonem in summitate eiusdem primae fistulae duabus lineis aequalibus depinge, et unam earum in octo, alteram in duas et in tres, et in quatuor aequas partes divide, et post haec tota mensura tibi erit facillimma.

Secundam autem a prima sumpturus octavam diametri eiusdem primae fistulae longitudini aufer, reliquum eius spatium usque ad plectrum in octo partire, et nona in summitate reiecta, habebis secundam. Tertiam inventurus secundae fistulae longitudini octavam diametri tolle, residuum eius spatium usque ad plectrum in novem divide, et nona parte in summitate praetermissa tertiam invenisti. Quartam quaesiturus primae fistulae longitudini tertiam diametri adime, et quartae parte ablata quartam cum integro diatessaron addidisti. Quintam reperturus primae fistulae diametri medietatem disiunge, reliquum eius usque ad plectrum spatium in tria divide, et tertia in summitate separata, quintam cum diapente aggregasti. Sextam appositurus secundae fistulae longitudini item medietatem diametri abscide, reliquum eius spatium in tres partire, et tertia relicta sextam subiunxisti. Synemmenon ostenturus quartae fistulae tertiam diametri reseca, residuum ad plectrum spatium in quatuor divide, et quarta parte omissa synemmenon designasti. Septimam invenies si tertiae medietatem diametri amputabis, et reliquum in tres divides, et tertia in summitate reiecta, septimam finalem constituisti.

His ita dispositis octavam a prima, nonam a secunda, decimam a tertia, undecimam a quarta, duodecimam a quinta, decimam tertiam a sexta, inferius synemmenon a superiori synemmenon, decimam quartam a sexta (*sic*), hoc modo facillime ordinabis, ut unicuique superiorum integrum diametrum excipias, et reliquum eius spatium usque ad plectrum in duas partes dividas, ac superiore declinata, inferiorem, plectro dico contiguam, pro octava suspicias.

*   *   *   *

Sicut fistulae eiusdem sunt grossitudinis, ita laminae, de quibus fiant, eiusdem sunt latitudinis. Prius iuxta domnum Willehelmum grossitudinis depinximus circulum. Qui de qua latitudine possit provenire, caute debemus perpendere. Dicit Macrobius de somno Scipionis: Omne diametrum cuiusque orbis triplicatum cum adiectione septimae partis suae mensuram facit circuli. Haec sunt verba Macrobii. Unde eius auctoritatem sequentes praescripti circuli diametrum triplicemus, septimamque diametri simul adiungamus: et secundum quantitatem lineae, quae inde procedat, omnium laminarum fistulis materialium latitudo fiat. Hae laminae in lateralibus extremitatibus attenuantur; praecipue, quae extremitates cum fabrili manu eas incurvante conveniant, non superponantur sibimet, sed osculo tantum collidantur coniunctissimo. Adcuius osculi commissuram tegendam praeparentur laminellae festucae tenuitatem et latitudinem habentes, quae sibi tenacissimo conglutintentur stagno, seu alio, quod lentius diuturniusque perseveret, lotario. Postquam autem in lamina adhuc patula cuiusque fistulae longitudo determinetur punctis utrimque in lateribus fixis, linea per transversum de puncto tendat in punctum. Illa linea terminalis sit foramini et ori fistulae; quod os super ipsam ita excidatur lineam, ut ad medietatem latitudinis fistulae aperiatur. In ipsam quoque lineam plectrum arctissime conglutinetur. A quo plectro subterius oris labrum mediocris festucae distet latitudine.

*   *   *   *

[Domnus Willehelmus] . . . qui duobus ordinibus, quatuordecim videlicet fistulis tres adjecit, ut tetrachordum praestrueret, ut competens acumen in minimis, et opportuna gravitas responderet in maximis.

Index of Instruments and their Components

Accordion, xx
Aeolipyle, 227
Air-collector, 246, 248, 252
Air ducts, 148–50, 156–7, 229, 231, 242, 245–7, 249, 252, 280–4
Air leaks, 33, 71, 148–9, 151, 156–7, 159, 162, 172, 198
Alphabet (=manual), 230–2, 255, 266
'Altar' (βωμίσκος), 28–30, 36–7
Amurchus, 156
Anuli, 160
Arcula, 148, 150, 153, 157
Aulos, xv, xvi, 23, 26, 33, 45, 50, 53, 55, 67, 69, 80, 117, 126–30, 132, 137–8, 140, 143, 159, 163, 164, 173, 177, 292, 294

Bagpipe, xix, xxi, 49, 52, 131, 162, 272, 278, 282
Barker action, 152
Bellows, x, xi, xvii, xix, xx, 24, 51–4, 60, 64, 68, 80, 93, 115, 153, 162, 165, 172–3, 175, 180, 187–9, 198, 200–2, 209, 216, 220, 230–1, 244–50, 252, 267, 271, 279–85, 293
Blowing mechanism, 39–40
Bourdons, 115, 272
'Bull glue', 157

Canon, 37–8, 148, 150–1, 153, 157
Celeste, 276
Choragia, 112, 151
Cistern, water, xi, 9, 23, 25, 27, 30–1, 39, 41–2, 52, 71, 73–9, 81–7, 89–94, 96, 98, 100–1, 103–5, 115, 143–9, 152–7, 162, 200–1, 203, 216, 278–9
Cithara and citharist, xiv, xvii, 45, 48, 50, 60, 63–7, 129, 137, 164–5, 224–5, 269, 272, 277
Clarinet, 138
Clepsydra, 8–9, 23
Conflatorium, 282, 284

Console, 249
Cornett, 277, 283
Cornu, 74, 88
Coupling device, 273–4, 292
Crankrods and crankshafts, 38, 90
Cylinder, 30–1, 34, 36, 38–40, 46, 59, 149, 155–6, 236
Cymbal, 38–40, 61, 105, 149–50, 153, 163, 261, 278
Cymbalum, 36, 209–10, 220–2, 227, 275–7, 280–3, 287

Diastoles, 123
Dolphins, 36, 39–40, 48, 150, 153, 156
Draw-stops, 27, 33, 41, 243–4, 263

Epitonia, see Stopcocks

Fiddle, 268, 272, 282
Fire pump, 25–6, 31
Fistula, 42
Flute, 61, 64, 65, 68, 129, 186, 195, 201–3, 220, 275, 277, 283
Foramina, 39

Harmonium, 135, 165
Harp, 65, 268, 281
Horn, 65, 73, 163–4, 181, 225, 281–2
Horn players, 278, 282
Horn spatulas, 32, 41, 158, 242
Hurdy-gurdy, 275, 277, 283
Hydra, xvi, 55, 57, 110, 116
Hydraulic compressor, 143–5
Hydraulis, see Organs

Key, 33, 38, 67, 74, 97, 112–13, 158, 165, 196
Keyboard, viii, xix, xx, xxi, 152, 165, 293

Lips, 80, 84, 86, 95, 97, 99, 101–2, 114–15, 140, 236–8, 253–6, 258, 271, 279–80, 282, 285

Lituus, 105
Longitudinal channel, 41, 111
Lute, 186
Lutenist, 278
Lyre, xvii, 48, 62–3, 65, 67, 118, 125, 129, 132, 136, 163, 176, 209, 220, 258, 268, 272

Magrephah, xx–i, 196
Mandrel, 114, 116, 234–5, 237
Manuel, 5, 27, 31, 40–1, 57, 59, 60, 68, 71–6, 79, 86, 90–3, 97, 99, 100, 102–4, 108, 112, 114, 116–17, 131, 133–5, 138, 140, 142, 147–8, 151–2, 158, 163, 165, 180, 188, 196, 208, 216, 229–31, 260–3, 266, 272–4, 278, 280, 282–5, 289, 293
Monochord, 253–4, 275
Mouthpieces, 237–8, 280
Mu-lien wood, 188

Nan wood, 188

Oboe, 33, 126, 220
Octochordos, 37, 159
ORGANS
Bellows organs
  Aquincum, vii, xiii, 52, 54, 55, 57, 68–9, 72, 101–2, 109–16, 135–6, 138, 140–1, 148, 151–4, 157–60
  Arras, Bibliothèque Municipale, 272, 286
  Autun Museum, 95
  Barcelona Cathedral, 270
  Basil I, 171–2
  Basle, 273
  Belvoir Castle Psalter, 282–3, 285
  Berne, 273
  Bonn, 272
  Bonport Abbey, 286
  Bourges Cathedral, 286
  Bratislava Psalter, 286
  Bruges, 272
  Brussels, Bibliothèque Royale, 286
  Cambridge, 281–2, 285
  Canusina, 223
  Cava, monastery of, 265
  Cividale del Friuli MS, 237, 244–5, 249, 282
  Constance Cathedral, 266
  Engelberg, Abbey of, 246, 266, 274
  Erfurt, 228, 270
  Exeter, 272
  Fécamp, Abbey of, 220–1, 263
  Florence, 273

Gentilla, 102–3
Harding Bible, 231–2, 237, 244, 249, 280–1, 285
Laon, Bibliothèque Municipale, 273, 285; Cathedral, 285
Léon Cathedral, 271, 285
Lobbes, Abbey of, 222, 265, 275
London, British Museum, 285
Louis the Pious, 213–14
Lübeck, 273
Lyon, Bibliothèque Municipale, 285
Malmesbury, monastery of, 223–4
Meaux Cathedral, 273
Merseburg, monastery of, 266
Munich, Staatsbibliothek, miniature, 274, 285
Munich University, 231, 283–4, 285
Muristus, 17, 171, 189–202, 232
Naples Museo Nazionale glass vase, 105–6
Obelisk of Theodosius, 60, 80, 162, 164, 175, 180, 280
Orléans, Cathedral of, 273
Oswald, St., 223
Paris, Bibliothèque Nationale MS. 11560, 284, 285; MS. 1076, 284, 286; MS. 1328, 286; MS. 8846, 286
Pepin the Short, 207–8
Petershausen, monastery of, 266
Politz, priory at, 270
Pommersfelden Psalter, 280
Prague, 272
Pseudo-Jerome, 162, 196, 201–2
Rheims, Cathedral of, xi, xii, 273
Rheinzabern terracotta, 105
Rome, Vatican Museum, 286
St. Benedict of Bages, monastery of, 228
St.-Georges de Boscherville, church of, 286
St. Ulrich, Augsburg, monastery of, 265
Ste.-Chapelle, Paris, 270, 273–4
Salzburg, 273
Senlis, Cathedral of, 273
Sens Cathedral, 286
Shih Tsu, 163, 186–9
Solomon Glossary, 284
Strasburg, 272
Stuttgart Psalter, 269, 279–81, 285
Theophilus, Emperor, 178
Westminster, 273
Winchester, 229–32, 279, 284, 286
Worms, 273
Zürich, 273

Hydraulic organs
  Alexandrian terracotta, 77–8, 140, 156, 163, 166
  Aphrodisis, 86–7, 88, 126, 154, 166
  Arles uninscribed sarcophagus, 83–4, 134, 156, 165
  British Museum gem, 84–5, 105, 133, 140–1, 155–6, 165
  Caracalla contorniates, 91–2, 156
  Carthage Museum lamp, 96–8, 134, 140, 147, 149, 156, 159–60, 210
  Copenhagen Museum lamp, 98–9, 155, 157–60
  Copenhagen vase, 82–3, 157, 161, 164
  Julia Tyrrania, 88, 100–1, 126, 134, 140, 141, 156, 166
  Nennig mosaic, 73–5, 76, 105, 134, 155, 157–8, 161, 164–5
  Nero contorniates, 90–1, 140
  Orange medallion, 93–4, 116, 161
  Rheims vase, 81–2, 164–5
  Rheinzabern vase, 85–6, 94, 161, 164, 166
  Roman terracotta, 81, 140, 155, 165
  Rusticus, 88, 101–2, 155
  St.-Germain Museum, 93, 104–5, 155, 157
  St.-Maximin sarcophagus, 94–5, 134, 140–1, 159–60, 166, 238
  Tarsus terracotta, 99–100, 134, 140–1
  Tatarevo, 87–9, 161
  Utrecht Psalter, 95, 180, 218, 231, 274 278–9
  Valentinian III medallion, 89–90, 134, 140–1, 156
  Verona consular diptych, 79, 156, 164–5, 228
  Via Appia graffito, 78
  Winghe manuscript, 103
  Zliten mosaic, 75–7, 78–9, 155, 161, 164–6
Portative organs, 106, 116, 172, 189, 269–74, 277, 279, 285–6
Positive organs, 270–1, 273–4, 277, 279, 284–5
Organum, meanings of, xvii–xviii, 62, 66–7, 206, 287–8; vocal organum, 206, 287–91, 293

Pandora, 62, 67, 201
Pinax, 37, 41
Pinnae, 151
Pipes, flue, 33, 41, 60, 74, 76, 97, 101–2, 108, 113–15, 120, 132, 134–5, 151–2, 159, 172, 182, 197–201, 210, 221; organ, x, xix, 59, 71, 72, 74–87, 90–5, 97–102, 104–11, 113, 120, 131–4, 139–41, 147–8, 150–3, 156, 158–60, 171–3, 186–8, 191–201, 209–10, 213, 215, 217–18, 220, 227, 231, 233–45, 249, 252–63, 269, 271–2, 278–85, 289, 293; reed, 27, 51, 76–7, 159–60, 210, 231
Piston or piston-rods, 28, 30–1, 39, 52, 74, 78, 84–5, 96, 100, 147–9, 153, 156
Platysmation 28–9 39
Plectra, 176
Plectrum, 235
Plinthides, *see* Sliders
Plinthion, auletic, 181
Pnigeus, vii, 24, 28–31, 36, 38, 40, 41, 52, 59, 83, 85, 115, 145–7, 150, 152, 156–7, 200
Polyphony, 130, 287–8, 293–4
Psalterion, 181
Psaltery, 277–8
Pump, air, 27, 30, 79, 90, 152; cylinder, 10, 18, 24–5, 30, 34, 47, 72, 82–3, 85–7, 90, 96, 100, 104–5, 146–7, 162, 292; fire, 25–6, 31, 39; piston, 30–1; suction and thrust, 25
Pump handle, 28–9, 78, 82, 148–9, 156, 278
Pump lever, vii, 82, 84, 96–7, 104

Recorder, 164
Regulator, 41, 80, 188

Sambuca, 67
Shawm, 280
Shêng, xix, 68
Sistrum, 61
Sliders or plinthides, vii, 31–3, 37–8, 41, 54, 59–60, 97, 111–13, 148, 150–1, 153, 158–9, 162, 188, 231–2, 239, 240–2, 244–5, 249, 262, 274, 280–2, 289
Sound box, 193
Stele, 69, 87, 88, 95
Stopcocks, 148, 150–1, 153, 157
Stop handles, 100
Stoppers, 193–5, 199, 201
Stops, number and disposition of, 261–2
Syrinx or panpipe, xix, 5, 18, 24, 50, 53, 57, 62, 73, 79, 80, 93, 95, 100, 105–8, 126, 132, 164, 253, 275, 281, 292

Tabula summa, 60, 81–2, 95, 112–14, 148, 151–2, 160
Tampons, 136, 160

Tetrachordos, 37, 111
Tibia, xvii, 42, 49, 60, 61, 62, 68, 70, 126–7, 129, 140, 159, 163, 166, 217, 269
Tibicen, 60, 127, 131, 269
Timbre, 41, 50, 128, 159, 172, 182, 210, 231, 237, 244, 292–3
Trumpet, 26–7, 50, 60, 62, 69, 72, 75, 78, 125, 127

Valves, 25, 28, 40–1

Viol, 275, 277, 283

Water compressor, 53
Wind-chest, vi, viii, xix, 5, 27, 30–2, 34, 39, 40–1, 52, 54, 57, 59, 60, 71, 74–87, 90–4, 97–105, 108, 110–13, 115–16, 140–1, 143, 146–8, 150–2, 155–7, 159–60, 162, 165, 172–3, 188, 229–31, 234, 238–46, 248, 249, 252, 262–3, 271–3, 278–85, 292–3

General Index

Abbasids, 184, 191
Aboul' Abbas, 184
Abu'l-Faraj al-Isfahani, 181–2
Abu'l-Majd, 186
Abu Zakariyya, 186
Académie des Inscriptions et Belles-Lettres, 96
Adalbert, Abbot, 265
Adam of Fulda, 269, 274
Ademar, 223
Aelia Sabina, 101, 110–11, 126, 163, 166
Aelius Julius, 69
Agesistratus, 16
Aistulf, 207
Aix-la-Chapelle: Palace of, 213; school of music, 205–6
Al-Hakam II, Caliph, 226
Al-Jahiz, 190
Al Ma'mun, Caliph, 184, 203
Al-Mas'udi, 172
Al-Muqtadir, Caliph, 202
Albert, 290
Alcides, 5–6, 8, 11, 55
Alexander, 3
Alexandria, 3–4, 7, 9, 11, 14, 16, 17, 18, 21, 43, 54, 77, 169, 273
Alexis III, Basileus, 172–3
Alföldi, 93
Alypius, Tables of, 124, 130, 137–9
Amaury, Bishop of Meaux, 206
Ameristos, 190
Ammianus Marcellinus, xvi, 61, 90
Anastasius I, Emperor, 79
Annals of Fulda, The, 207
Anno of Friesing, Bishop, 222
Anonymous, Bellermann's, xvi, 136, 137–8, 183
Anonymous II, Bellermann's, 124, 130
Anonymous of Berne, 235, 237, 242, 244–6, 249, 259–60, 262, 281, 283, 289, 302–4
Anonymous IV, Coussemaker's, 261
Anthemios, 17
Antioch, 63, 65, 169
Antipatros, 44, 125, 161, 163, 166
Antonines, viii, 7, 35, 164

Apel, Willi, 231
Apollo, Temple of, 44–5
Apollodorus of Athens, 7, 16, 17
Apollodorus of Damascus, 25
Apollonios of Perga, 4, 12, 15, 169, 177, 203
Apuleius, 129
Arbus, Fr., 95
Arcesilas, 11
Archimedes, 4, 9, 15, 16, 17, 19, 20, 21, 23, 51, 144–5, 190, 202
Archytas of Tarentum, 16, 19, 119
Aribo, 233, 236–8, 255–7, 260, 275, 304
Aristarchus of Samos, 14
Aristides Quintilianus, 136
Aristocles, 6, 7, 8, 9, 11, 39, 117
Ariston, 18, 190
Aristophanes, 30
Aristotle, xv, 4, 30, 123, 125, 128, 130, 143, 157, 166, 185
Aristoxenus, 6, 118–19, 123, 126, 128, 136, 141, 185
Aristyllus, 3
Arnaut, Henri, 263
Arras, Bishop of, 222, 275
Arsinoë II, Queen, 12, 14, 78
Arsinoë-Zephyritis, temple of, 23, 33, 177, 233
Ars Antiqua, 290
Asclepiades, 14
Ascra, 11
Asho bar'Ali, 185
Aspendus, 9
Athenaeus of Naucratis, viii, xvi, xvii, 5, 6, 7–9, 10, 11, 13, 27, 39, 46, 54–5, 84, 117, 163
Athenaeus the Engineer, 11, 16, 17, 21–2
Attiolus, 81
Audax, 82
Augsburg, 228
Augustus, 35, 151, 162, 292
Aurigemma, 76–7
Aurelianus Reomensis, 217
Aurillac, monastery of, 226
Ausonius, 53

Avenary, H., 263
Avicenna (Ibn Sina), 185

Babylonian Talmud, xx, 196
Bacchius, 123
Bacon, Roger, 202
Bagatti, Fr. Bellarmino, 102
Baghdad, 184–5, 202, 204
Balbus, 35
Baldric, Bishop of Dol, 220–1, 263
Baldric, Count of, 211
Banu-Musa automaton, 203–4
Barbaro, ix
Bardi Museum, Tunis, 164
Basil I, Emperor, 171
Basileus, coronation of a, 174
Battista of Mantua, 219
Bedos, Dom, x, xiv
Belisarius, 182
Bellermann, xvi, 51; Anonymous of, xvi,
    136, 137–8, 183; 2nd Anonymous, 124,
    130
Benedict, 223, 288
Bernard, monk, 225
Berne, Anonymous of, *see* Anonymous
Bibliothèque Municipale, Amiens, 275
Bibliothèque Nationale, Paris, xviii, 254–
    5, 257, 263, 285–6
Biton, 16
Boethius, xvii, 65–6, 118, 139, 158, 217
Boniface, Archbishop, 206
Bonport Abbey, 286
Boule, 44
British Museum, 91, 92, 269, 285
Bruno, Archbishop, 227

Cabinet des Médailles, Paris, 90
Caesarea, 35
Caligula, 48, 49
Callimachus, 3, 13
Q. Candidus Benignus, 69
Canon of Samos, 4
Canterbury Cathedral, 265
Capet, Hugh, 226
Caracalla, 56, 89, 91–2
Carinus, 161
Carme, Fr. Sebastian, xiii
Carra de Vaux, 18
Cassiodorus, xvii, 67–8, 158–9
Cassius, Dio, xvi, 49
Castronovo, 25
Cavaillé-Coll, A., 257; formula of, 257
Chailley, J., vii, 135–6, 274
Chansons de Geste, 267

Chappell, W., xiv
Charias, 16
Charlemagne, viii, 205, 208–9, 212, 214,
    223, 228, 288
Charles the Bald, 208, 214, 227
Chartres, 273, 296
Cheïkko, Fr. L., 191
Chêng Hsiu, 187
Chieti Museum, 164
Choniate, Nicetas, 172
Chou-King, xx
Christina of Sweden, Queen, 89
Chung-t'ung, 187
Cicero, 45–6, 70, 125, 161
Claudian, 60–1, 158, 160
Claudius, Emperor, 47, 161
Cleandros, 44
Cleonides, 136
Clermont-Ferrand Cathedral, 206
Cloncarff, church at, 228
Colin, J., 88
Collangettes, Fr., 203
Collegium Centonariorum, 109
Cologne Cathedral, 227
Commandini, Federico, ix
Commodilla, Ostia, 102
Commodus, 5
Confession of St. Paul, altar of, 101
Conrad, Abbot, 266
Constantine, 56, 59, 94, 169
Constantine V Copronymus, Emperor,
    170, 188, 207–8, 225, 244
Constantine VI, Emperor, 177–8
Constantine VII Porphyrogenitus, Em-
    peror, 140, 170, 173, 174, 175, 177, 180
Constantine XI, Emperor, 183
Constantinople, 170, 179, 206–7, 212, 224,
    292
Constantius II, 61, 233
Contorniate medallions, 89, 166
Cornicen, 74–6
Corripus, 176
Cortina, 46
Cotton, John, 288, 291
Coussemaker, 261
Cryton, 44
Cybele, 62, 210

Damascus, 184, 186, 204
Damoxenus, 130
Dar Buk Ammera, 75
Dardanus, Letter to, 201, 202
d'Arezzo, Guido, 261
Datius, 81

David, King, 274, 278, 280–4
Degering, H., xii, 93, 94, 98
Delattre, Fr., 96, 98
Delphi, 43–5, 125, 153, 161, 163, 166
Demetrius of Phalerum, 3, 17
Democles, 16
Democritus, 143
Demosthenes, 10
Deneauve, J., 98
Diadus, 16
Didier, 265
Digenis Akritas, 181
Dinocrates, 4
Dio, 44
Dio Chrysostomos, xix
Diodorus of Halensia, 9, 11
Diogenes Laertius, 7, 11
Dionysos, 210
Dionysius, 17, 56
Diophantus, 4
Diphilus, 16
Dorian mode, 51, 128, 133, 136, 139
Douai, 273
Du Cange, Charles, 228
Dufourcq, Norbert, 263
Duns Scotus, 288
Durand, Guillaume, Bishop of Mende, 270, 275, 282

Eadwin Psalter, 279
Eberhard of Freising, 263
Eginhard, viii, 211, 212, 216, 279
Elagabalus, Emperor, 62, 166
Eleuthernes, 44
Elias bar'Shinaya, 186
Elphege, Bishop, 225, 229
English Mechanic and World of Science, xv
Enikel, Jansen, 272
Ephesus, 169
Epicurus, 45
Epimenides, 11
Epiptas, 88
Erasistratus, 4
Eratosthenes, 4
Ermold le Noir, 213–15
Euclid, 3, 4, 20, 44, 185
Eugenius Vulgaris, 216
Euplous the Pontorean, 56
Eusebius, 22
Eutropius, 35

Farmer, H. G., xii–xiii, 17
Fatimids, 184
Fétis, xii

Fleury (St. Benoît-sur-Loire), Abbey of, 225, 233, 265, 290
Flood, Grattan, 228
Fortunatus, Bishop of Poitiers, 219
Franck, K., 116
Franks, 205, 207, 213
Freising, church at, 265–6
French Academy of Sciences, 257
Fröhner, 77
Frontinus, 35, 39, 70
Fulcium, Abbot, 222

Galen, 20
Gallienus, Emperor, 63
Gallus, Caesar, 61
Galpin, F. W., xiv
Gastoué, A., xii, 137, 227, 263
Georgius, 210–13, 216, 218–19, 222
Gerald, Abbot, 226
Gerbert of Aurillac, *later* Pope Sylvester II, xi, 179, 225–8, 232–3, 290
Gervase, monk, 265
Giles of Zamora, 269
Gorgonios, 63, 166
Gräbner, R., xii
Grassineau, James, xi
Gréau collection, 77, 81
Gregory I, Pope, 205
Grenoble medallion, 92

Hagen, H., 233
Hagia Sofia, Constantinople, Library of, 18
Hagiopolites, 137, 183
Halberstadt, 228
Harding, Stephen, 3rd Abbot of Cîteaux, 280
Haroun ben-Jahja, 171
Haroun al-Rashid, 185, 212
Hedylus, 11–14, 109, 203
Heraclides Ponticus, 123–4
Herculaneum, 109
Hermes, 81
Hero of Alexandria, vi, vii, viii, ix, xii, xv, 9, 16–48 *passim*, 77, 110, 112–13, 144, 146–8, 155–9, 169, 170, 171, 177, 179, 200–2, 226–7, 229, 231, 244–5, 292–3, 295–6; Venice manuscript of, ix, 28
Hero of Byzantium, 11, 15, 17, 21–2
Herodian, 20
Herodotus, 20, 24
Herophilus, 3, 20
Hertz collection, 84
Hesiod, 11

Hildebrandt, 47
Hipparchus, 4
Hippocrates, 20
Hirsau, Wilhelm von, 260
Historiae Musicae Gallus, xiii
Hollendonner, Dr., 115
Homer, 24
Honorius of Autun, 270, 275, 293
Hrabanus Maurus, 201
Hsing lung shêng, 186–7
Hucbald, 217, 255, 258–9, 275, 288–9
Hyagnis, 127, 130
Hypatia, 4

Ibn al-Nadim, 190
Ibn al-Naqqash, 186
Ibn al-Qifti, 190
Ibn Khurdadhbih, 172
Ibn Sina, *see* Avicenna
Illustrated London News, xv
Ingelheim, 212
Isaac of Antioch, 64–5
Isho bar'Bahlul, 185
Isoes, 17

Jerome of Moravia, 218
John, Bishop of Ephesus, 182
John the Grammarian, 178
John VIII, Pope, 222, 274
Johannes of Florence, 275
Joshua (Isho) Bar-Bahlul, 185, 189
Julian the Apostate, 59–60, 84, 158–63, 170
Justin II, Emperor, 182
Juvenal, 62, 70

Kiev Cathedral, 181
Kircher, Father, x, xi, xii, 204
Ktesibios, v, vi, viii, x, xv, xvi, 4–47 *passim*, 54, 77, 78, 115, 117, 126, 128, 143–4, 166, 177, 179, 189–91, 202, 227, 244, 292; cylinder pump, 25–6; automaton, 26–7; hydraulic organ, 28–33
Kusuk-Kolah, 99

Labeo, Notker, 257–8, 263
Lampridus, xvii, 62
Langlois, 99
Langres, 273
Laon Cathedral, 273, 285
Laurentius, 91, 100–1
Lavigerie Museum, Carthage, 96, 98
Lavoisier, 19
Lemerle, Professor, 89

Leo Magister, 176–7
Leo 'the wise', 176
Léonin, 290
Lespiotus, 20
Lezoux, 104
Lille, 273
Linus, 216
Liutprand, Bishop of Cremona, 179
Lombards, 205, 207
Loret, Clément, xii, 97–8
Louis the Fat, 289
Louis the Pious, ix, 210–15, 218
Louvre, The, 99
Lübeck, 273
Lucian, 11
Lucretius, xvii, 46, 157
Ludowisi, 105

Macrobius, 130, 236
Mainz, 213, 268
Mallius Theodorus, 60
Manual Bryennius, 170
Marcellus, M. Claudius, 16
Marcellus, M. Claudius, 35
Marcheti of Padua, 217–18
Marcus Aurelius Cyrus, 56
Marcus Aurelius Heliodorus, 56
Marcus Aurelius Hermes, 56
Marsyas, 125, 130
Martianus Capella, xvi, 67
Matthias, Canon, 131
Mau, 108
Mazaca, 35
Mazoillier, 99
Meister, A. L. F., xii
Melanippos, 69
Meleager, 13, 14
Menedemus, 10
Menelaus of Alexandria, 4, 20, 21
Mersenne, ix, 54, 73
Metz, 70; school of music at, 206
Michael III, Emperor, 179
Milion, Albert, 223
Morfova, Zlaska, 88
Mortet, V., 35
Muhammad ibn Ahmad al-Khwarizmi, 162, 172–3
Munich Glyptothek, 164
Murator, 228
Musée des Antiquités Nationales, St. Germain-en-Laye, vi
Musée Lapidaire, Arles, 83, 100
Museum of the German Cemetery, Vatican, 81

Museo Nazionale, Naples, 54, 108
Musicians' Company's Exhibition, xiv
Mysians, 139

Nagy, Lajos, 109, 116
Nangis, Guillaume de, 270
Naples Museum, 159, 280
Nationalmuseet, Copenhagen, 82-3
Nero, Emperor, xvii, xix, 47-9, 62, 89, 90, 125, 161, 166, 293
Nevers, 273
Newton, William, xii
Nicomachus of Gerasa, xvi, 50, 132, 185
Nicomedia, 26
L. Norbanus Flaccus, 125
Notker Labeo, 257-8, 263
Notker the Stammerer, 208-9
Notre Dame de Paris, 219, 269, 273-4; School of, 290
Nymphodorus, 16

Odington, Walter, 253
Odo, 253-4
Origen, 51
Otho I, Emperor of Germany, 227
Otho II, Emperor of Germany, 226
Ovid, 126, 130
Oxyrhynchus, xvi, 63

Pachymeres, 141, 170
Palladas the Athenian, 17
Pamphilus, 22
Pannonia, 163, 166
Pappus, 4, 14, 17, 20
Parmenion, 14
Patrikios, 178
Patroclus, 14, 17
Patsch, Carl, 86
Pausanias, 127-8
Pepin the Short, 170, 188, 205-7, 209, 218-19, 225
Pérotin, 269, 274, 290-1
Perrault, Claude, xi, xii, xiii, xiv
Petit Palais, Paris, 81
Petronius, xvi, 50, 161, 164
Philaterios, 17
Philo Judaeus, 17
Philo of Athens, 8, 17
Philo of Byzantium, xv, 8, 9, 10, 11, 14, 16, 17-19, 21, 23, 24, 25, 27, 30-1, 39, 43, 143-4, 169, 177, 190, 202
Philo of Tyana, 17
Phrantzes, 183
Platina, 219

Plato, 4, 6, 8, 9, 20, 45, 117, 123-6, 128-9, 253
Pliny the Elder, xvi, 8, 9, 16, 20, 21, 35, 40, 47, 127, 156-7, 159
Pliny the Younger, 25-6
Plutarch, 9, 139, 163
Pollio, Tribellius, 63
Polites, 44
Pollux, Julius, 30, 52-3, 60, 93, 116, 126-7, 160-1
Polyeidus, 16
Polyphemus, 126
Pompeii, 72, 75, 88, 107-8
Porfyrius Optatianus, xvii, 56-9, 62, 84, 158
Porphyry of Tyre, 55, 132
Posidippus, 13, 14
Posidonius, 21
Praetorius, 228
Proclus, 16, 22
Pronomius of Thebes, 127-8
Prudentius, 69, 159
Psellus, Michael, 170
Pseudo-Prosper, 159-60
Pteron, 137
Ptolemy, Claudius, 4, 20, 55, 56, 135, 185
Ptolemy III Euergetes, 14
Ptolemy VIII Euergetes, 11-12, 13-14
Ptolemy Philadelphus, 3, 11, 12, 14, 20, 292
Ptolemy Soter, 3
Pyrrhus, 16
Pythagoras, 118, 132, 185

Raphael, 72
Raymond, Abbot, 226
Reichnau, Monastery of, 227
Reinach, T., 56
Reliquary, The, xiv
Rheims, 278
Rhodes, xvi, 56
Rhyton, 11-13, 33
Riévaulx, Abbot of, 290
Romanus I, 177
Ruelle, Charles, xiii
Ruffel, P., 35

Sabatier, J., 92
Sachs, Curt, 5, 136
St. Aelred, Abbot of Riévaulx, 221, 275
St. Aldhelm, 224, 293
St. Arnulph, Chronicle in monastery of, 208
St. Athanasius, 159

St. Augustine, xvii, xviii, 62, 65, 66, 93, 125, 161, 219
St. Corneille, 208
St. Dunstan, 223–4, 293
S. Sebastian, Rome, graffiti, 78, 141, 156, 164
St. Florent, Saumur, monastery of, 225
St. Gall, school of music at, 205, 208
St. Germanus, 219
St. Georges de Boscherville, church of, 286
St. Gervais, 273
St. Gregory of Nazianzus, 20, 287
St. Honorat, 101
St. Jacques, Church of, 208
St. Jerome, 35, 201
St. John's College, Cambridge, 281, 285
St. Lambert, 220
St. Louis, 270, 293
S. Maria de Navicolla, 103
St. Martial de Limoges, 290
St. Nicholas, Utrecht, Cathedral of, 265
St. Omer, 273
St. Oswald the Younger, 223q., 228
St. Paul-Outside-the Walls, Rome, 101
St. Peter, Winchester, Church of, 225, 229, 232, 245
St. Quentin, 273
St. Sauve, Abbacy of, 212
St. Séverin, 273
St. Stephen, Church of, 174
St. Thomas Aquinas, 270, 293
Salustius Autor, 92
Saridakis, 5, 56
Saroshwai, Bar, 185
Schott, Gaspar, x
Schubiger, 215, 233, 266
Sélestat manuscript, 262
Seneca, 26, 47, 127, 157, 161, 287
Sens Cathedral, 286
Servius, xvi, 35, 65
Severus, Alexander, 62, 110, 166
Severus, Septimius, 51
Sextus Empiricus, 141
Shih Tsu, Emperor, 163, 186–7, 189
Sidonius Apollinaris, Bishop of Auvergne, xvi, 65
Sigon, Abbot, 225
Silchester, 25
Silvagni, A., 101
Simeon Magister, 179
Simplicius of Cilicia, 67, 159
Sixtus IV, 219
Sixtus V, 101

Sogliano, 107
Soranus, 20
Sosigenes, 4
Sostratus, 3, 17
Soubiran, J., 35
Speyer Museum, 85, 105
Stephen II, Pope, 207
Strabo, Walahfrid, 214–16, 227, 291
Strato of Lampsacus, 3, 4, 15, 19, 143
Suetonius, xvi, xvii, xix, 48–9
Suidas Lexicon, 7, 30, 35
Sumegi, L., 116
Symphony, 287

Tabitha, resurrection of, 94–5
Talmud, xx–xxi
Tanney, Paul, 7, 14
Temistius, 202
Terpnos, 48
Tertullian, xvi, 50–1, 60, 132, 139, 159
Thaïs, 43, 78, 165–6
Thallos, 69
Theocritus, 14
Theodore, 223, 288
Theodoric I, King of the Ostrogoths, 66
Theodoric II, King of the Visigoths, 66
Theodoret of Cyrrhus, Bishop, 63–4, 158, 160, 165, 180
Theodosius II, 180
Theodosius the Great, 80
Theon, 4, 20
Theophania, wife of Emperor Otho II, 226
Theophilus, Emperor, 170, 178–9, 202
Theophilus, monk, 232–52, 261, 274–5, 277, 280–2, 289, 297–302
Theophrastus, 3, 4, 24, 30
Theotokos of Pharus, Church of the, 174
Theoxenes, 44
Thorslunde, 82
Tiberius, 35, 125
Timocharis, 3
Timon, 10
Tittel, xiii, 11
Titus, Emperor, 35
Titus Aelius Justus, 68, 166
Tona, church at, 223
Trajan, Emperor, 26, 77, 91
Trichet, Pierre, ix–x
Trier, 73, 75
Trimalchio, 50
Trinity College, Cambridge, 279
Troyes, Chrétien de, 268

Tryphon, 6, 7, 8, 20, 117
Tubicen, 75–6, 78
Tzetzes, 17, 20

Ugelli, 228
Ulpian, 5–6
Umayyad dynasty, 184

Valentinian III, Emperor, 89
Valerius Festus, 77
Varro, 35, 130
Vatican Museum, 286
Viatorinus, Gaius Julius, 110–11
Vienne Museum, 93
Villa Ludovisi, 81
Ville, Georges, 77
Vindex, xvii, 48–9
Virgil, xix, 46, 66, 232
Vitalian, Pope, 219
Vitruvius, vi, vii, viii, ix, x, xi, xii, xiv, xv, xvi, xvii, 8–42 *passim*, 43, 48, 49, 51, 59, 71, 73, 77, 95–6, 110–13, 115, 139–40, 146–51, 155–60, 162, 170–1, 188,

201, 216, 227, 229, 231, 243, 279, 292–3, 296–7
von Strasbourg, Gottfried, 272
von Türlin, Heinrich, 272
Voss, Isaac, xi, xii
Vulgate, xviii

Wace, 267, 268
Warman, J. W., xiv–xv
Weltenburg monastery, 265
Westminster, 273
William of Lacera, 270
William of Malmesbury, 226–7
Willelm, Dom, 236
Winghe, Philippe de, 103
Wulstan, monk, 228–9, 232, 243, 245, 262, 274, 279

Zachary, Pope, 206–7
Zephyrion promontory, 12, 13
Ziegelbauer, 228
Zoë, 69
Zosimus, 202

PRINTED IN GREAT BRITAIN BY
W. & J. MACKAY & CO LTD, CHATHAM